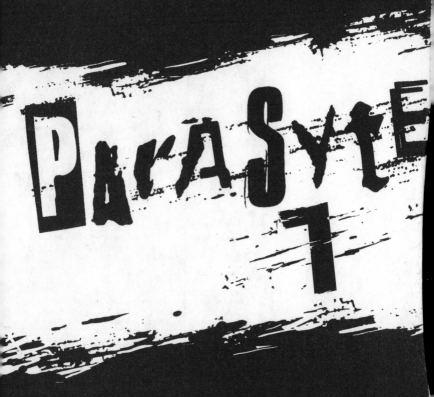

PARASYTE 7

HITOSHI IWAAKI

TRANSLATED AND ADAPTED BY ANDREW CUNNINGHAM
BY FOLTZ DESIGN

KC
KODANSHA
COMICS

Parasyte volume 7 is a work of fiction. Names, characters, places, and incidents are the products of the author's imagination or are used fictitiously. Any resemblance to actual events, locales, or persons, living or dead, is entirely coincidental.

A Kodansha Comics Trade Paperback Original

Published in the United States by Kodansha Comics, an imprint of Kodansha USA Publishing, LLC., New York.

Publication rights for this English edition arranged through Kodansha Ltd., Tokyo.

First published in Japan in 2003 by Kodansha Ltd., Tokyo.

ISBN 978-1-61262-341-2

Printed in Canada.

www.kodansha.us

9 8 7

Translatorl/adapter: Andrew Cunningham
Lettering: Foltz Design

CONTENTS

HONORIFICS EXPLAINED

Throughout the Kodansha Comics books, you will find Japanese honorifics left intact in the translations. For those not familiar with how the Japanese use honorifics and, more important, how they differ from American honorifics, we present this brief overview.

Politeness has always been a critical facet of Japanese culture. Ever since the feudal era, when Japan was a highly stratified society, use of honorifics—which can be defined as polite speech that indicates relationship or status—has played an essential role in the Japanese language. When addressing someone in Japanese, an honorific usually takes the form of a suffix attached to one's name (example: "Asuna-san"), is used as a title at the end of one's name, or appears in place of the name itself (example: "Negi-sensei," or simply "Sensei!").

Honorifics can be expressions of respect or endearment. In the context of manga and anime, honorifics give insight into the nature of the relationship between characters. Many English translations leave out these important honorifics and therefore distort the feel of the original Japanese. Because Japanese honorifics contain nuances that English honorifics lack, it is our policy at Kodansha not to translate them. Here, instead, is a guide to some of the honorifics you may encounter in Kodansha Comics books.

-san: This is the most common honorific and is equivalent to Mr., Miss, Ms., or Mrs. It is the all-purpose honorific and can be used in any situation where politeness is required.

-sama: This is one level higher than "-san" and is used to confer great respect.

-dono: This comes from the word "tono," which means "lord." It is an even higher level than "-sama" and confers utmost respect.

-kun: This suffix is used at the end of boys' names to express familiarity or endearment. It is also sometimes used by men among friends, or when addressing someone younger or of a lower station.

-chan: This is used to express endearment, mostly toward girls. It is also used for little boys, pets, and even among lovers. It gives a sense of childish cuteness.

Bozu: This is an informal way to refer to a boy, similar to the English terms "kid" and "squirt."

Sempai/
Senpai: This title suggests that the addressee is one's senior in a group or organization. It is most often used in a school setting, where underclassmen refer to their upperclassmen as "sempai." It can also be used in the workplace, such as when a newer employee addresses an employee who has seniority in the company.

Kohai: This is the opposite of "sempai" and is used toward underclassmen in school or newcomers in the workplace. It connotes that the addressee is of a lower station.

Sensei: Literally meaning "one who has come before," this title is used for teachers, doctors, or masters of any profession or art.

-[blank]: This is usually forgotten in these lists, but it is perhaps the most significant difference between Japanese and English. The lack of honorific means that the speaker has permission to address the person in a very intimate way. Usually, only family, spouses, or very close friends have this kind of permission. Known as *yobisute*, it can be gratifying when someone who has earned the intimacy starts to call one by one's name without an honorific. But when that intimacy hasn't been earned, it can be very insulting.

PARASYTE 1

HITOSHI IWAAKI

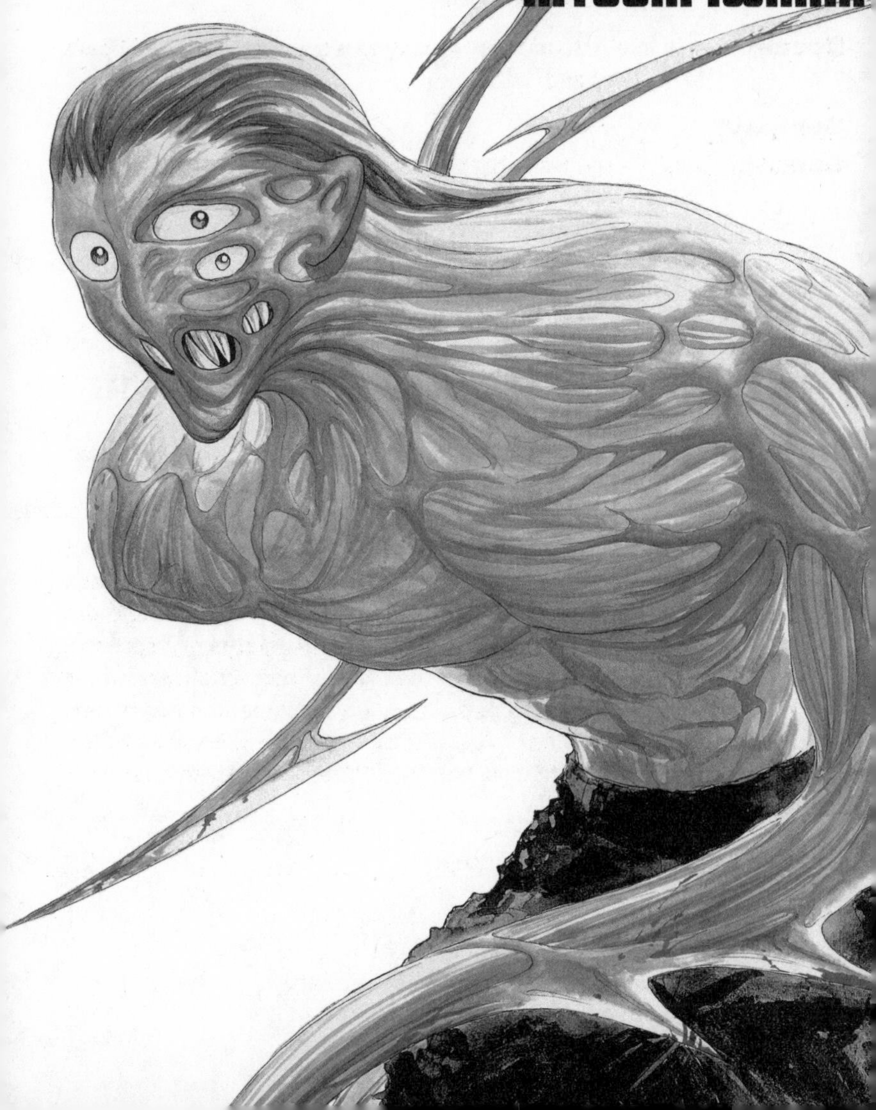

CONTENTS

CHAPTER 50: WEAPON

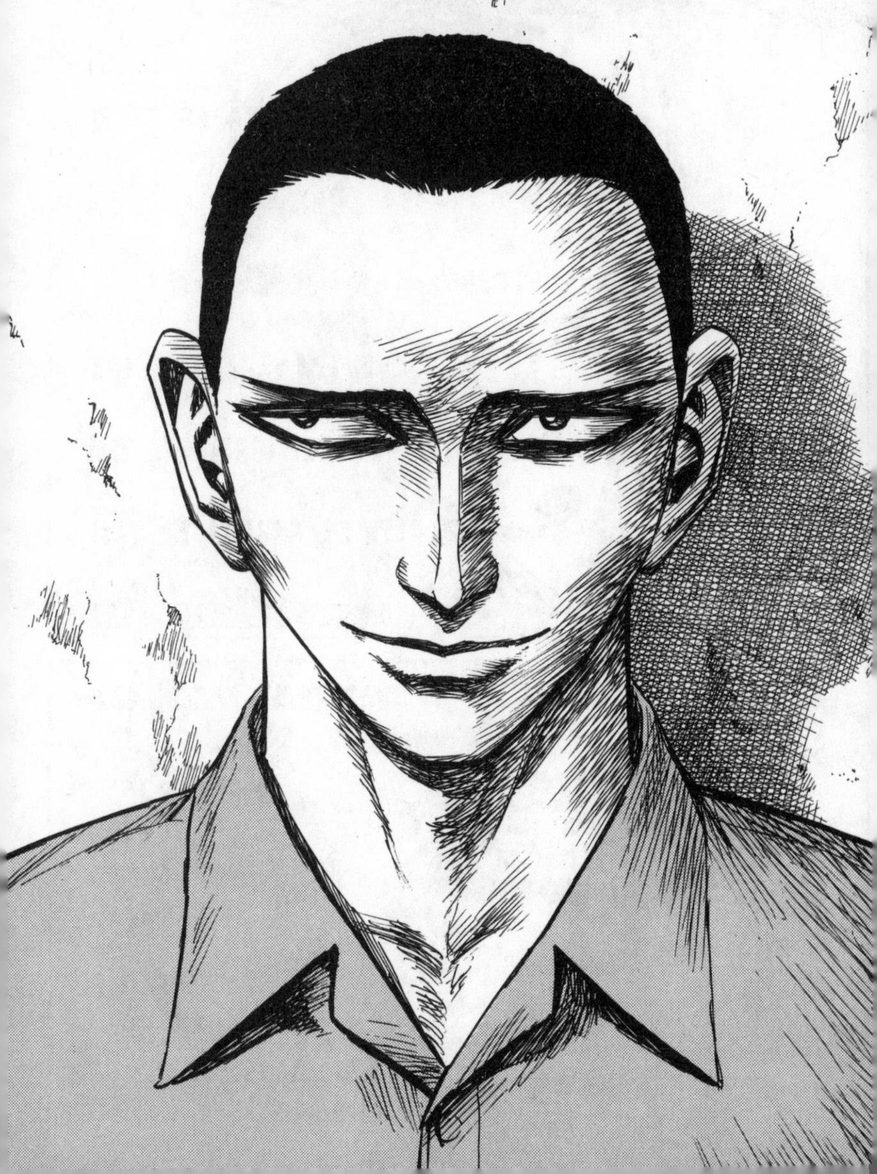

WH-WHO IS THIS GUY?

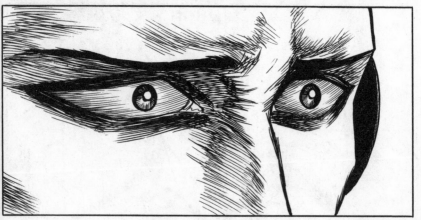

4

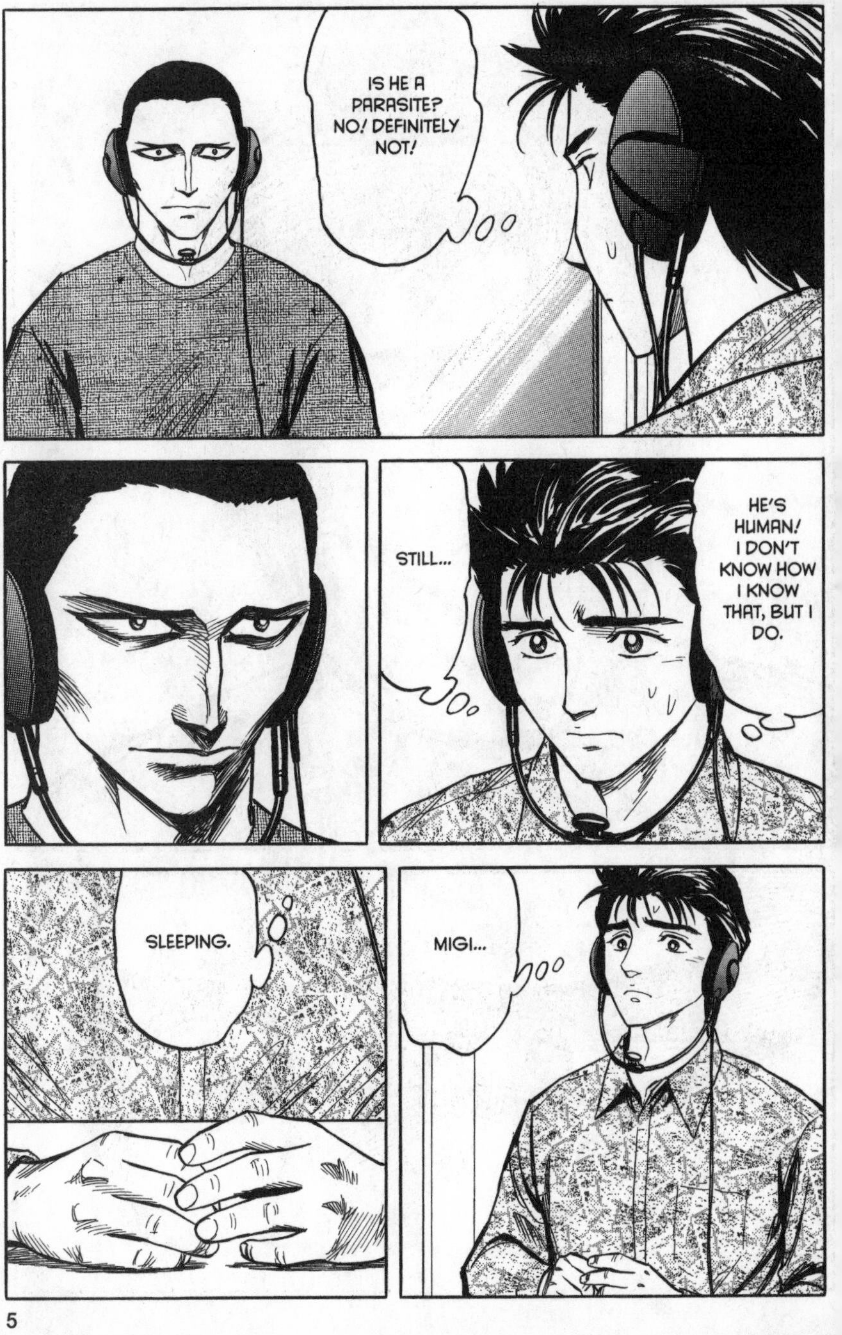
IS HE A PARASITE? NO! DEFINITELY NOT!
HE'S HUMAN! I DON'T KNOW HOW I KNOW THAT, BUT I DO.
STILL...
MIGI...
SLEEPING.

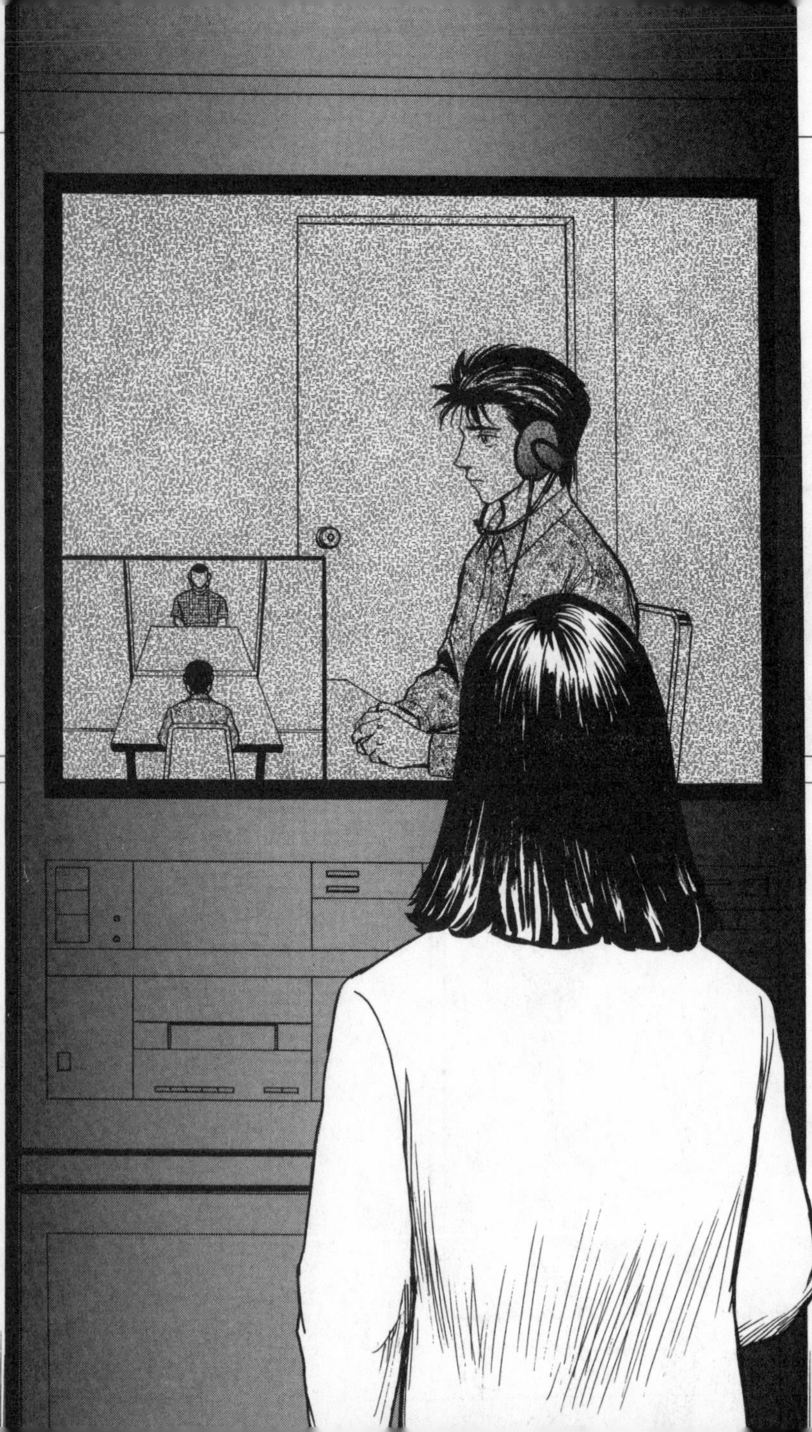

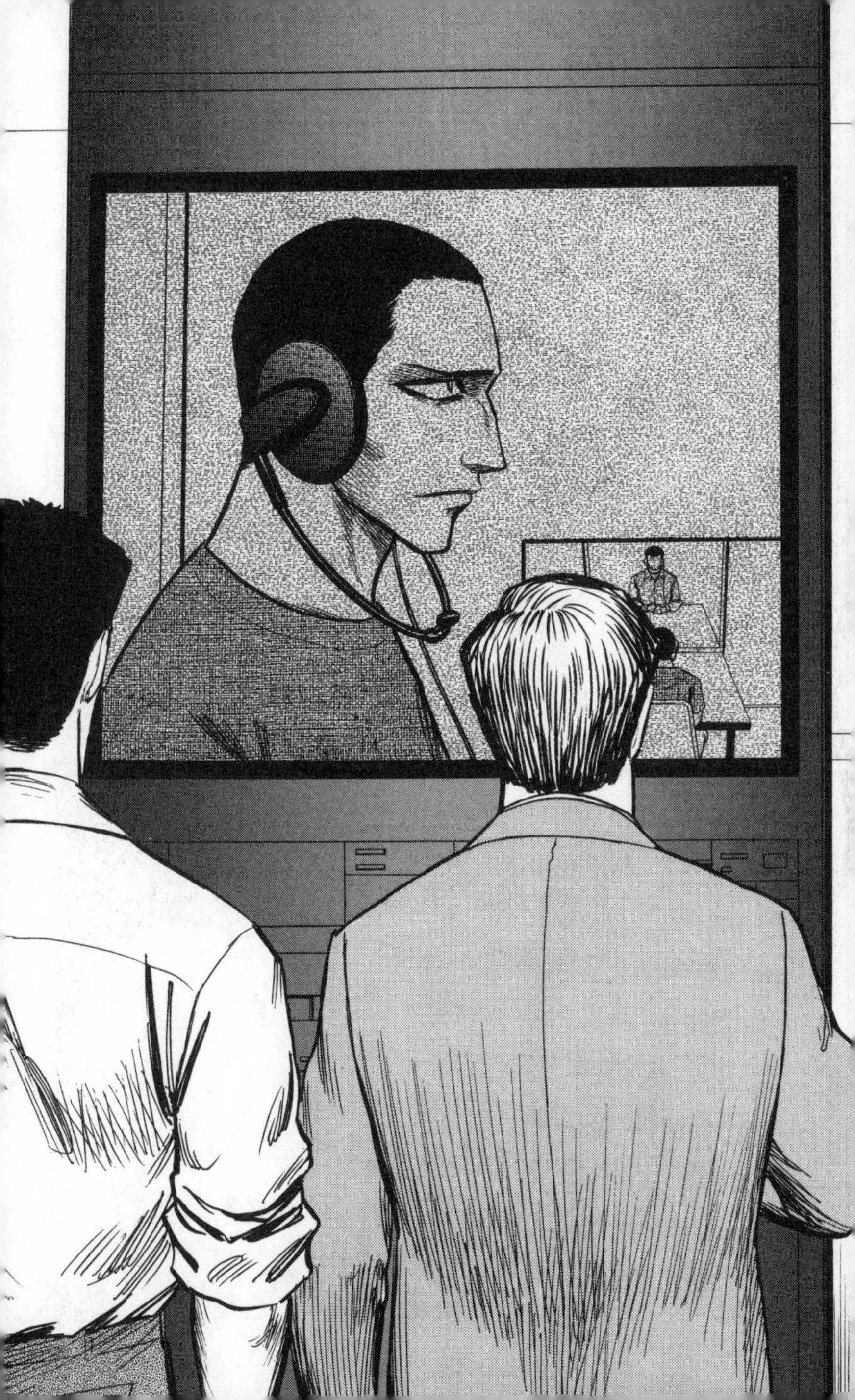

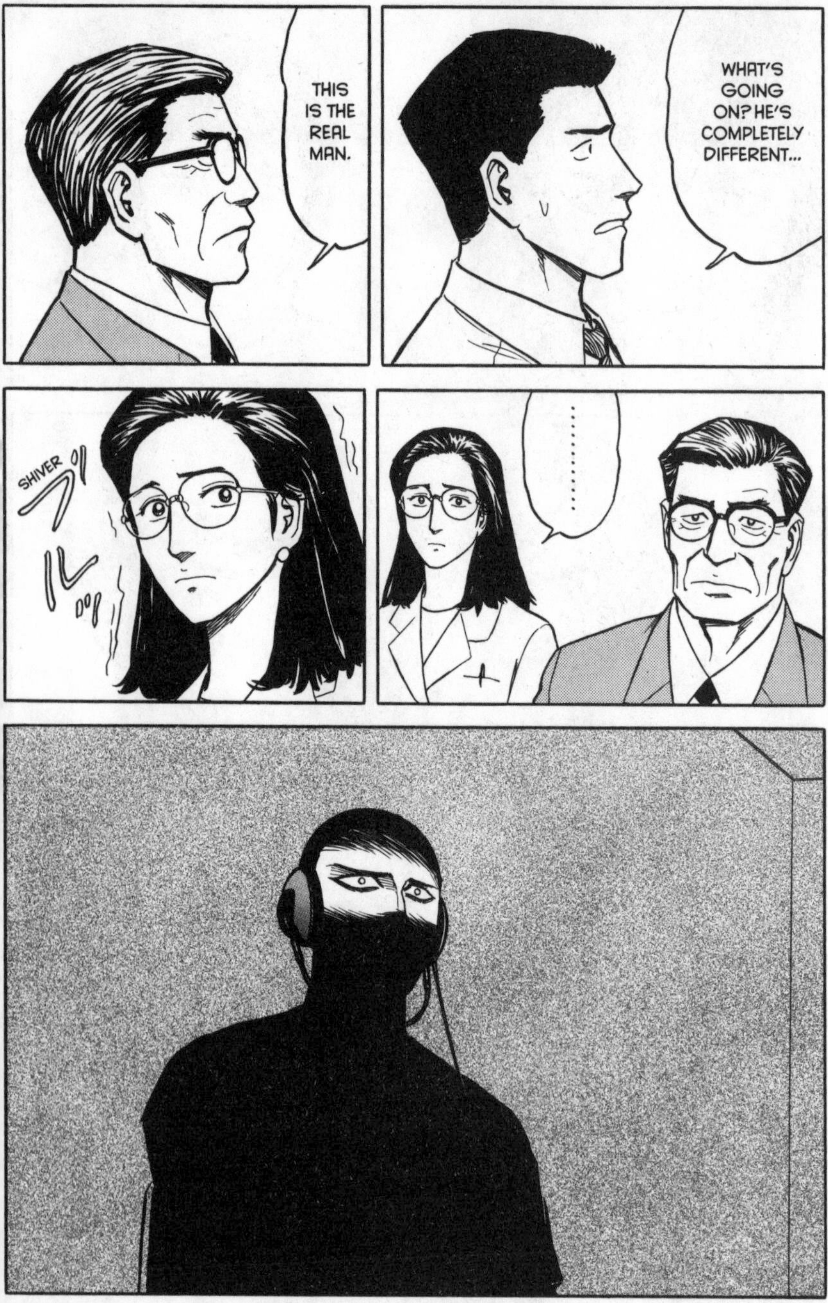
WHAT'S GOING ON? HE'S COMPLETELY DIFFERENT...
THIS IS THE REAL MAN.
......
SHIVER
ブルッ

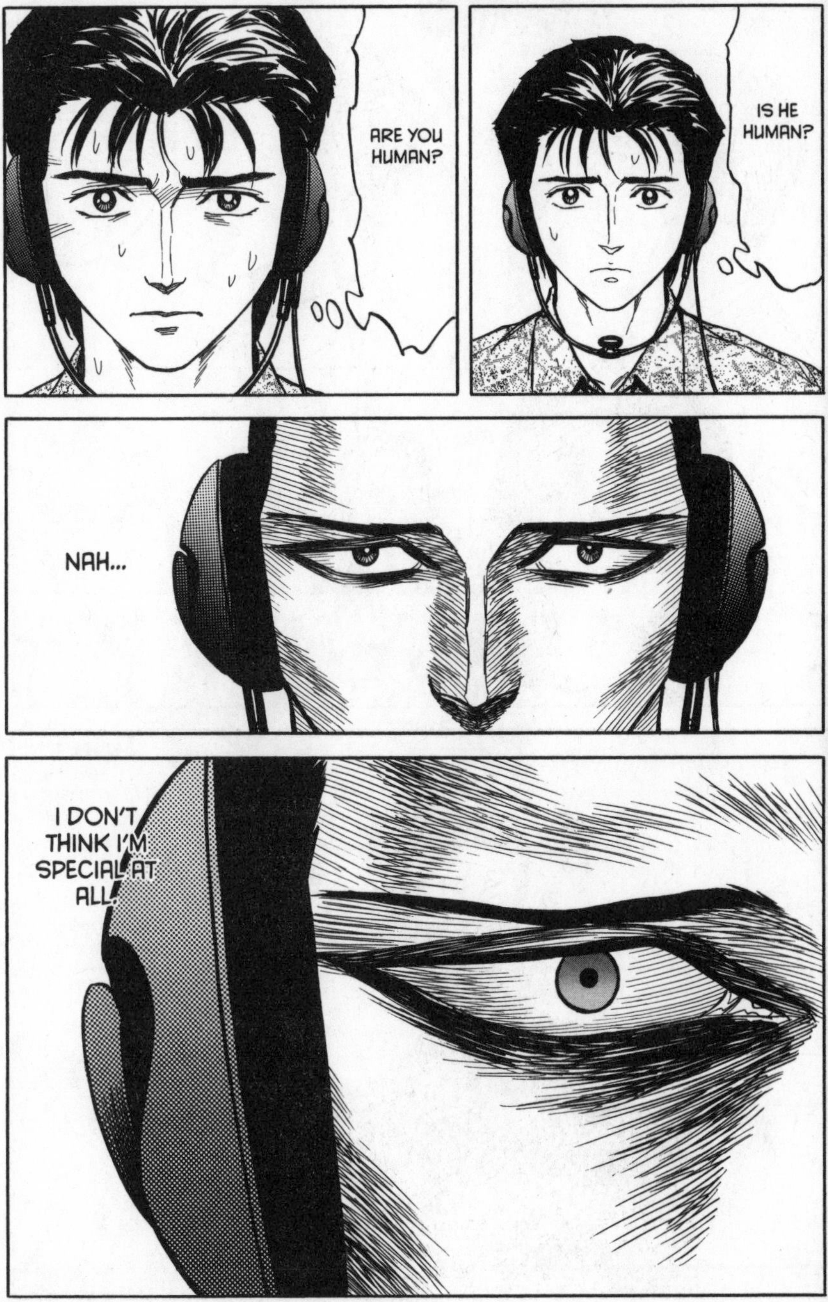
IS HE HUMAN?
ARE YOU HUMAN?
NAH...
I DON'T THINK I'M SPECIAL AT ALL.

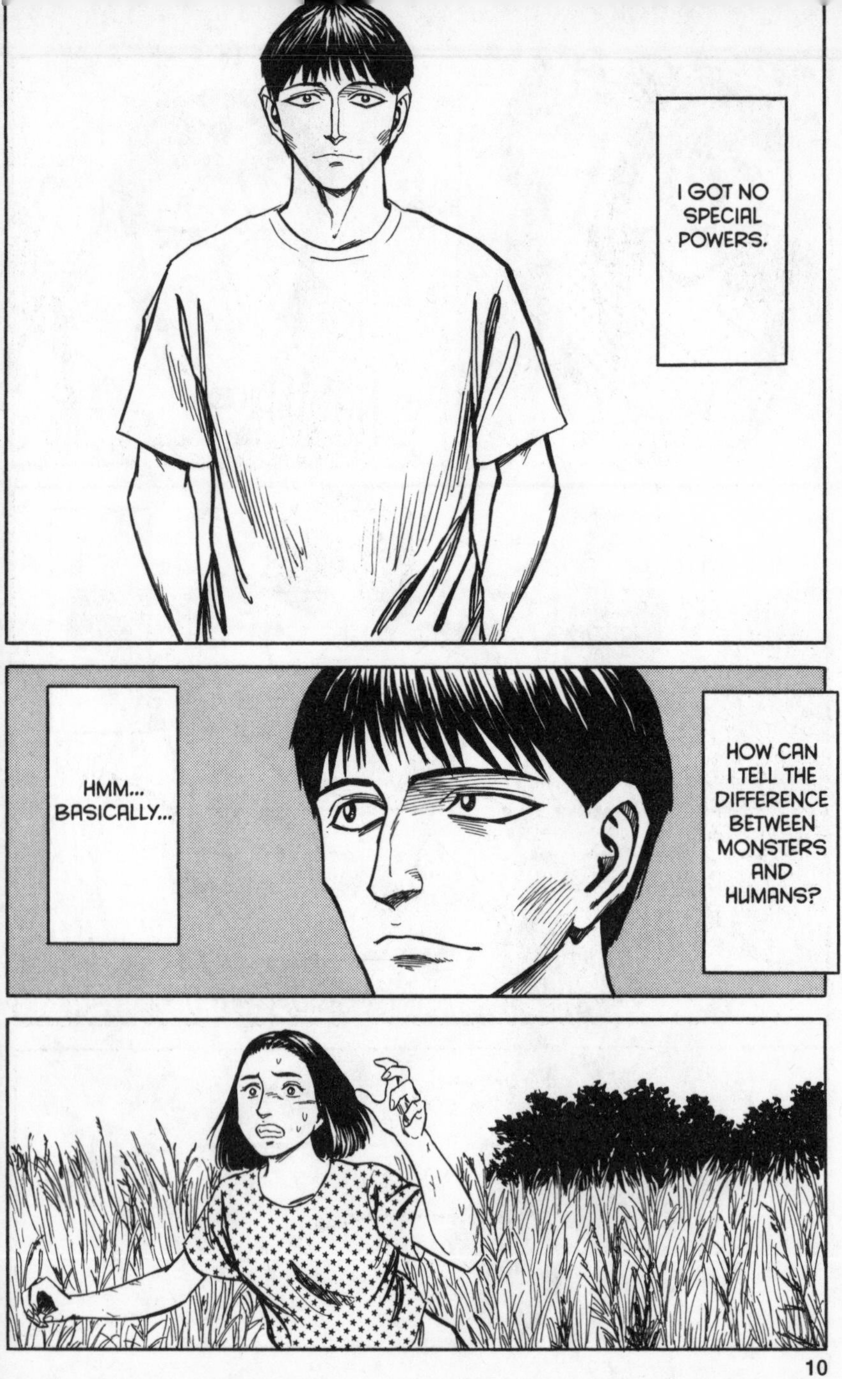
I GOT NO SPECIAL POWERS.
HOW CAN I TELL THE DIFFERENCE BETWEEN MONSTERS AND HUMANS?
HMM... BASICALLY...

...I'VE PLAYED ALL KINDS OF GAMES.

WITH HUMANS...

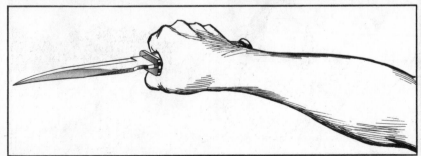

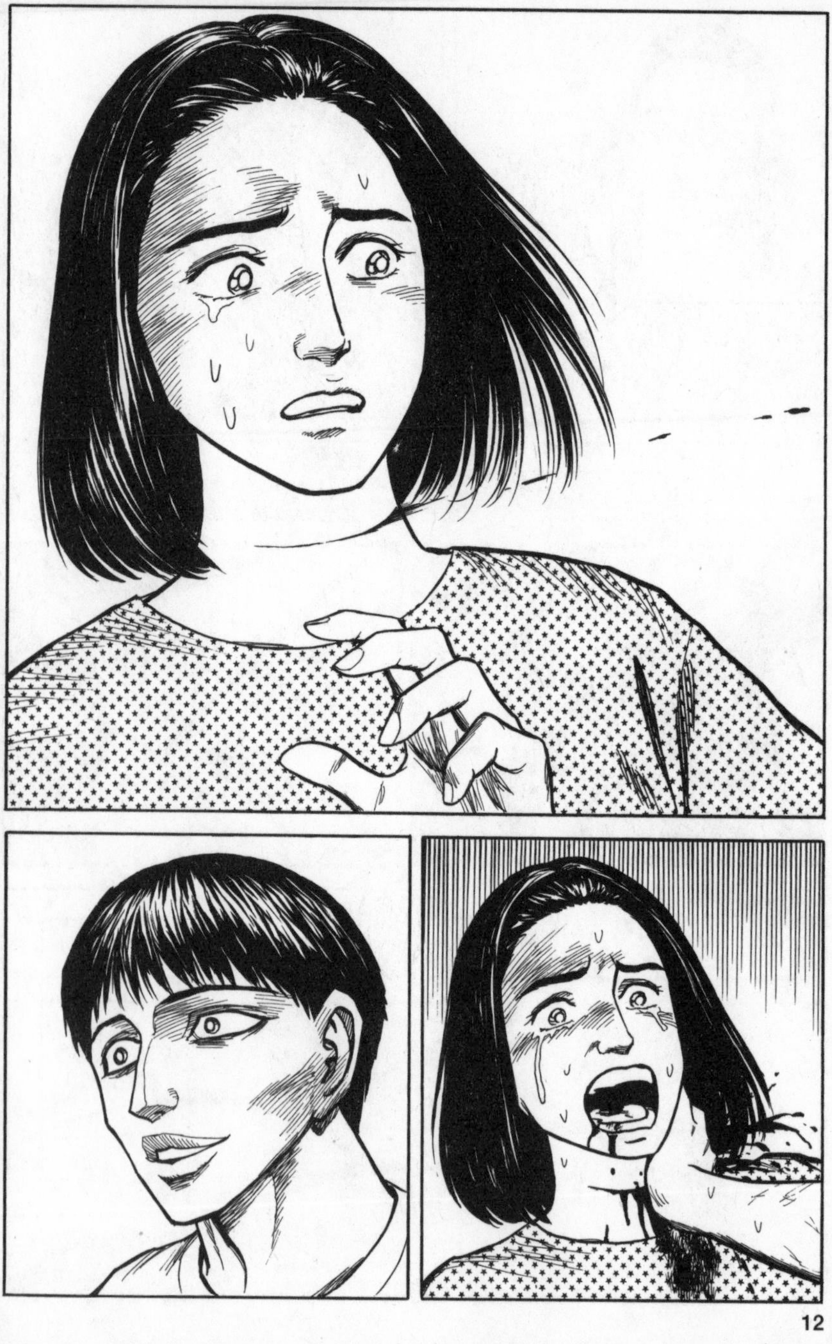

SO I
KNOW A
LOT ABOUT
BASIC
HUMAN
NATURE.

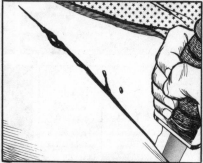

THESE
TOYS JUST
BREAK SO
EASILY...

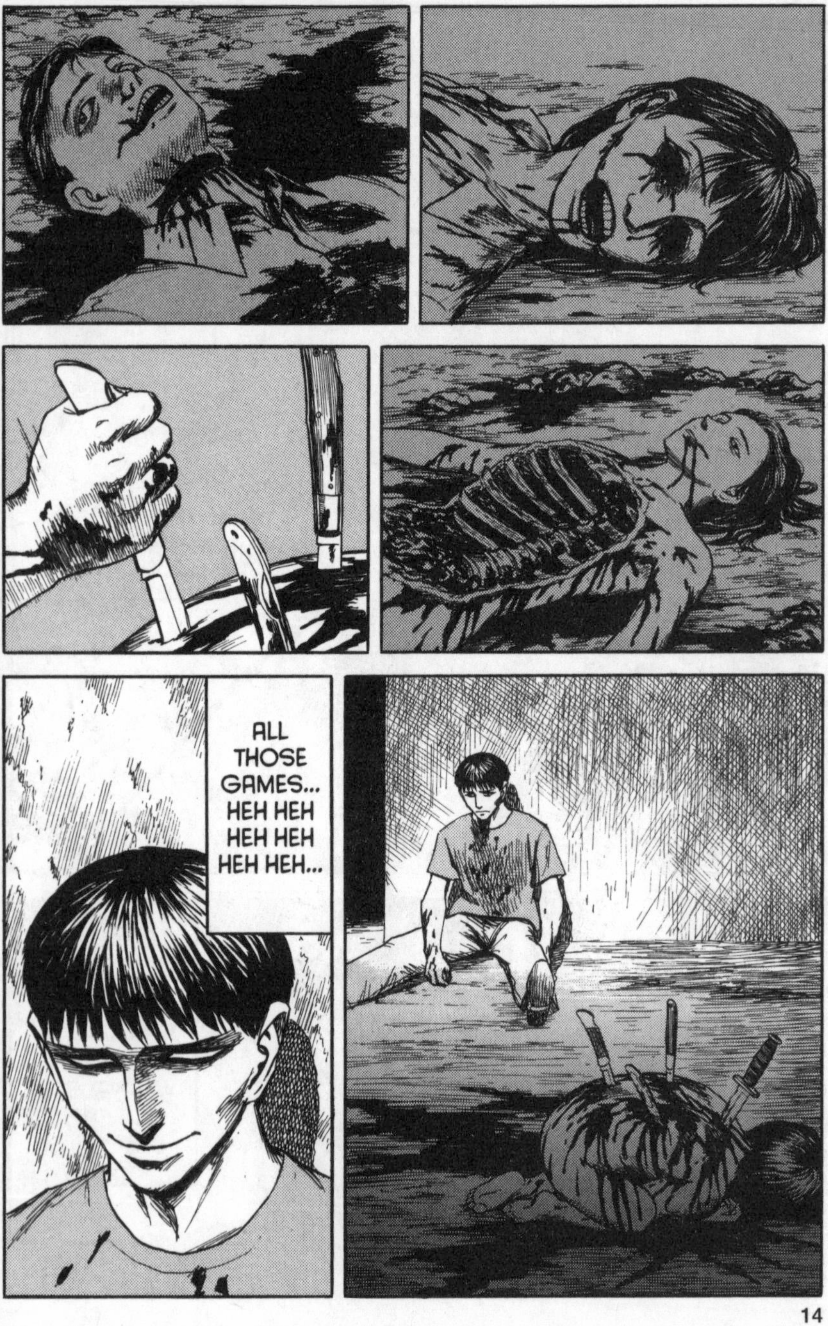
ALL THOSE GAMES... HEH HEH HEH HEH HEH HEH...

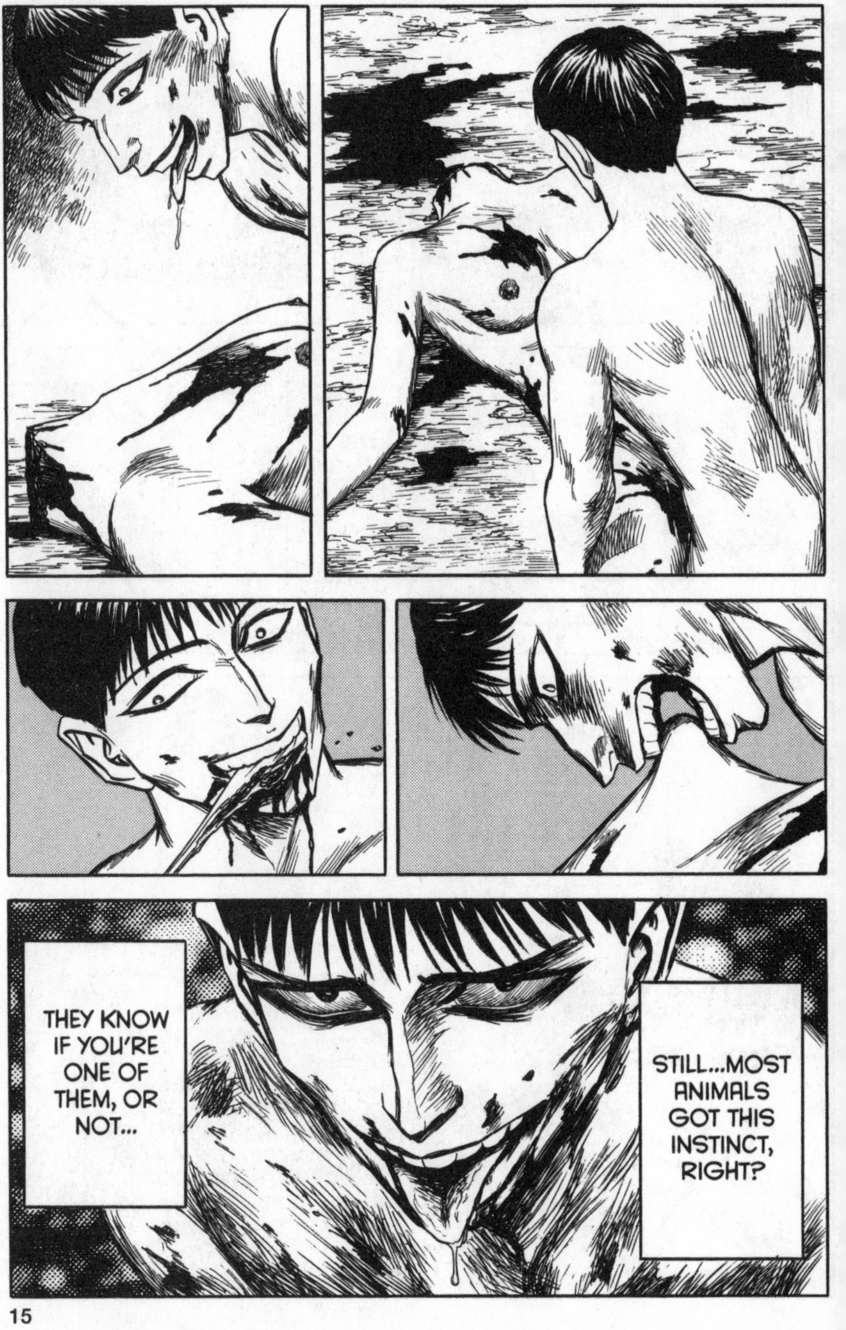
STILL...MOST ANIMALS GOT THIS INSTINCT, RIGHT?
THEY KNOW IF YOU'RE ONE OF THEM, OR NOT...

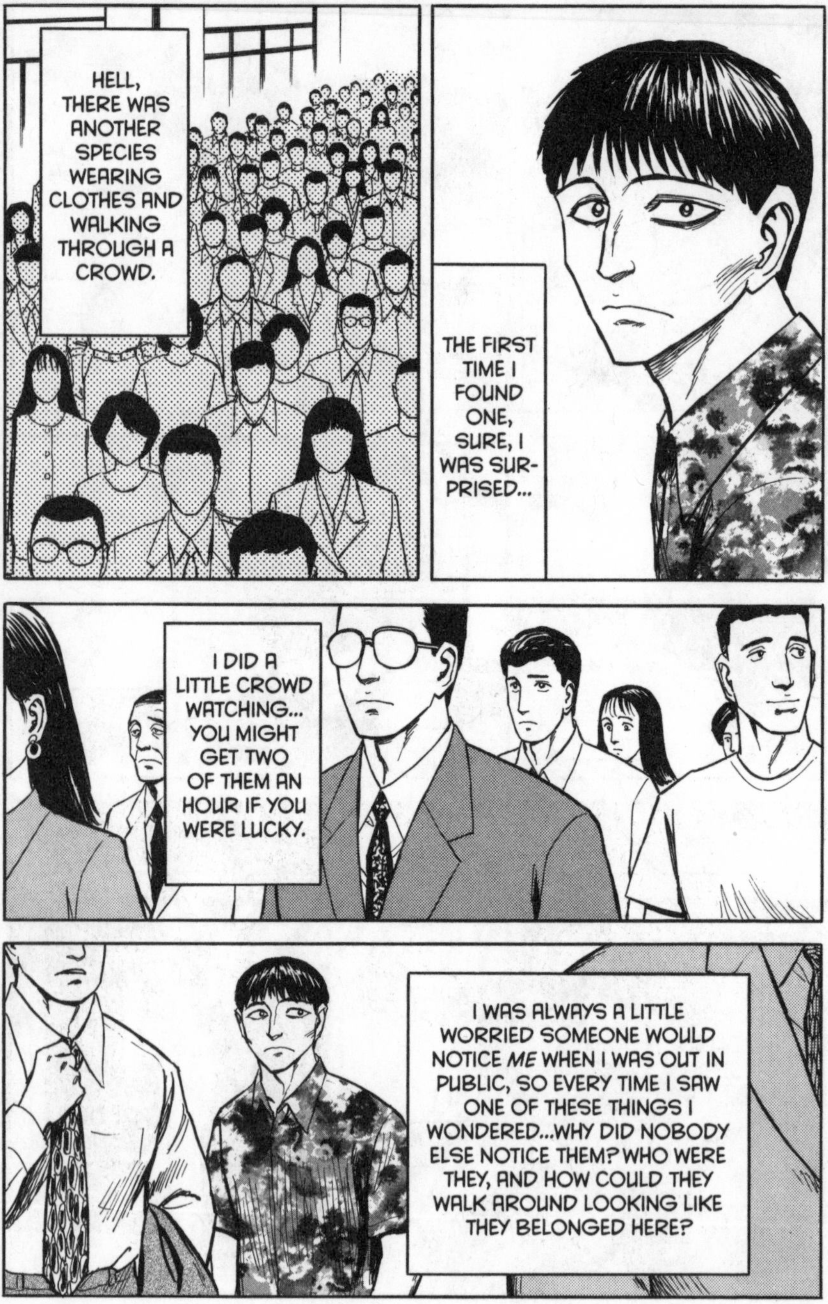
THE FIRST TIME I FOUND ONE, SURE, I WAS SUR-PRISED...
HELL, THERE WAS ANOTHER SPECIES WEARING CLOTHES AND WALKING THROUGH A CROWD.
I DID A LITTLE CROWD WATCHING... YOU MIGHT GET TWO OF THEM AN HOUR IF YOU WERE LUCKY.
I WAS ALWAYS A LITTLE WORRIED SOMEONE WOULD NOTICE *ME* WHEN I WAS OUT IN PUBLIC, SO EVERY TIME I SAW ONE OF THESE THINGS I WONDERED...WHY DID NOBODY ELSE NOTICE THEM? WHO WERE THEY, AND HOW COULD THEY WALK AROUND LOOKING LIKE THEY BELONGED HERE?

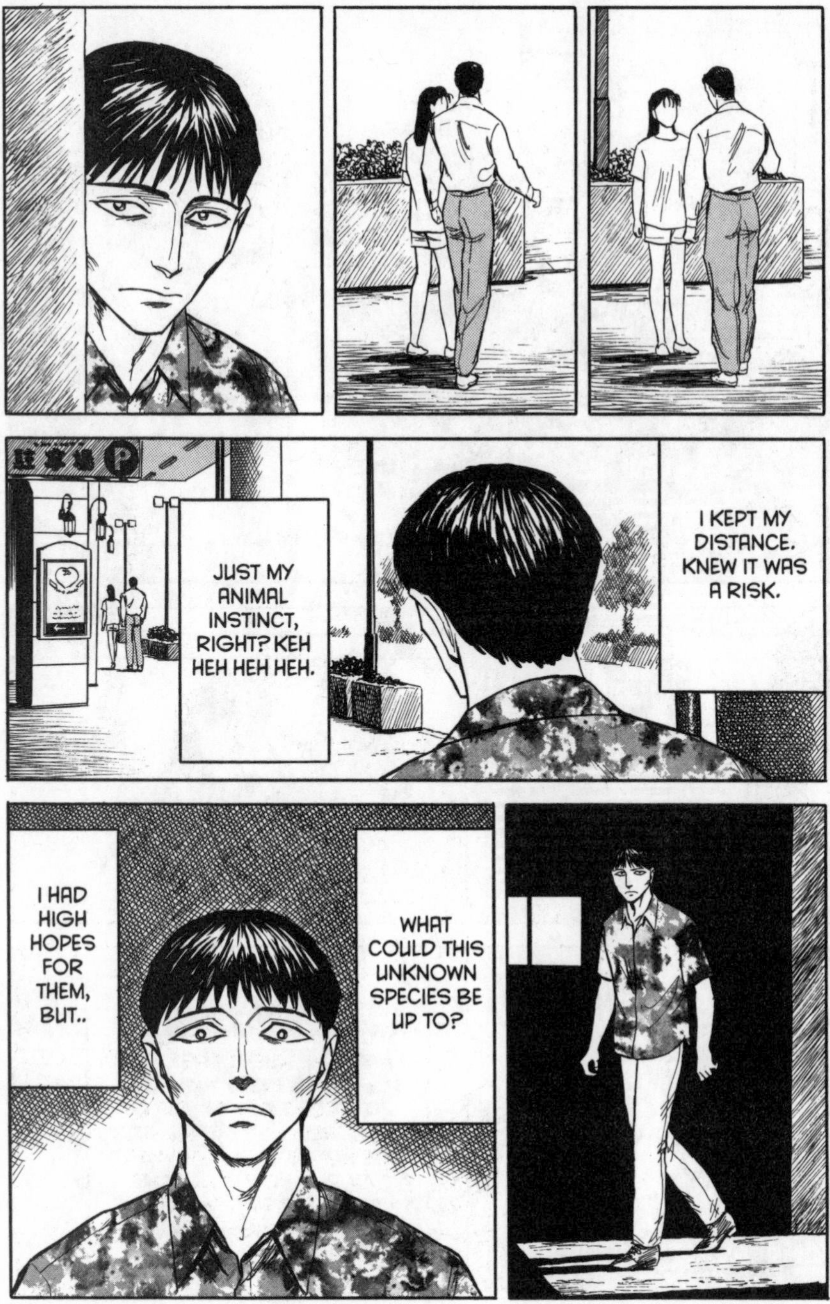
I KEPT MY DISTANCE. KNEW IT WAS A RISK.
JUST MY ANIMAL INSTINCT, RIGHT? KEH HEH HEH HEH.
WHAT COULD THIS UNKNOWN SPECIES BE UP TO?
I HAD HIGH HOPES FOR THEM, BUT..

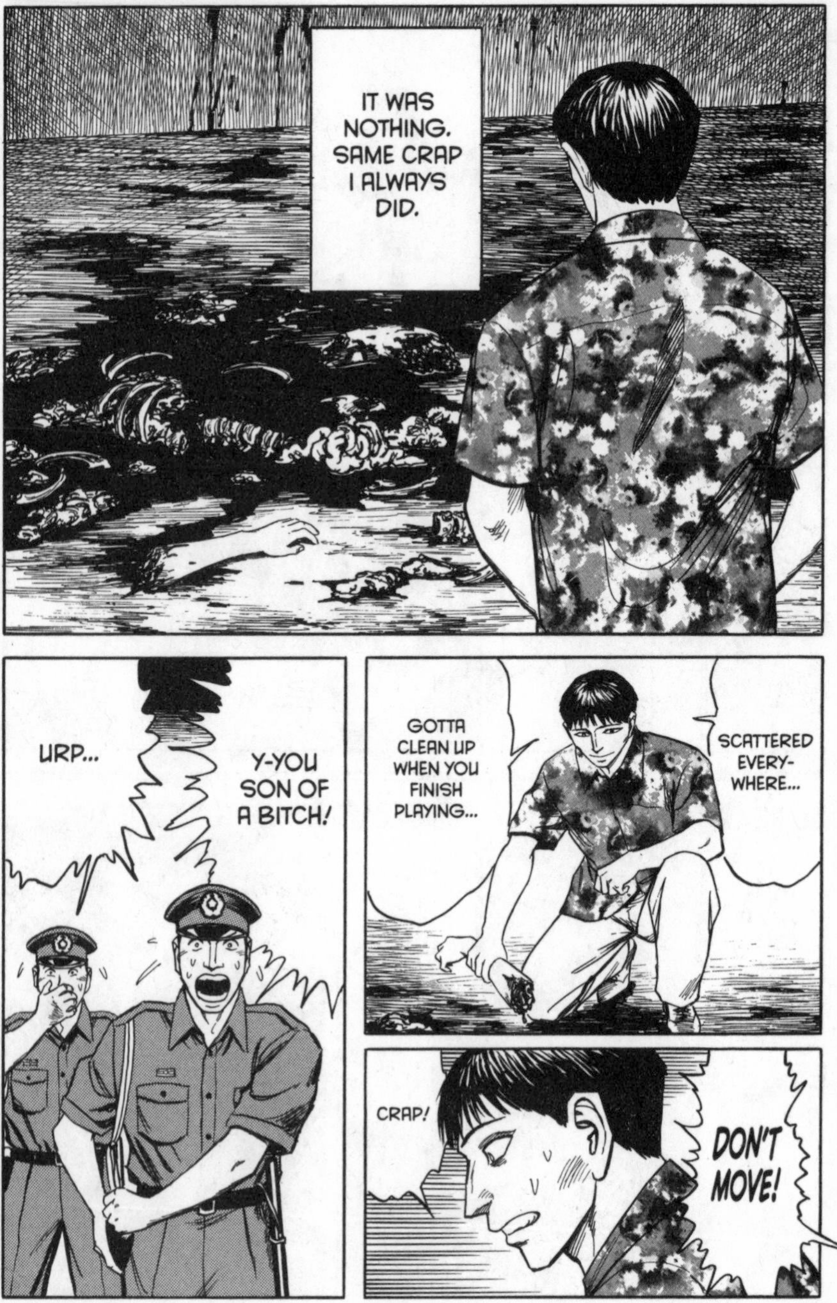
IT WAS NOTHING. SAME CRAP I ALWAYS DID.
SCATTERED EVERY-WHERE...
GOTTA CLEAN UP WHEN YOU FINISH PLAYING...
DON'T MOVE!
CRAP!
Y-YOU SON OF A BITCH!
URP...

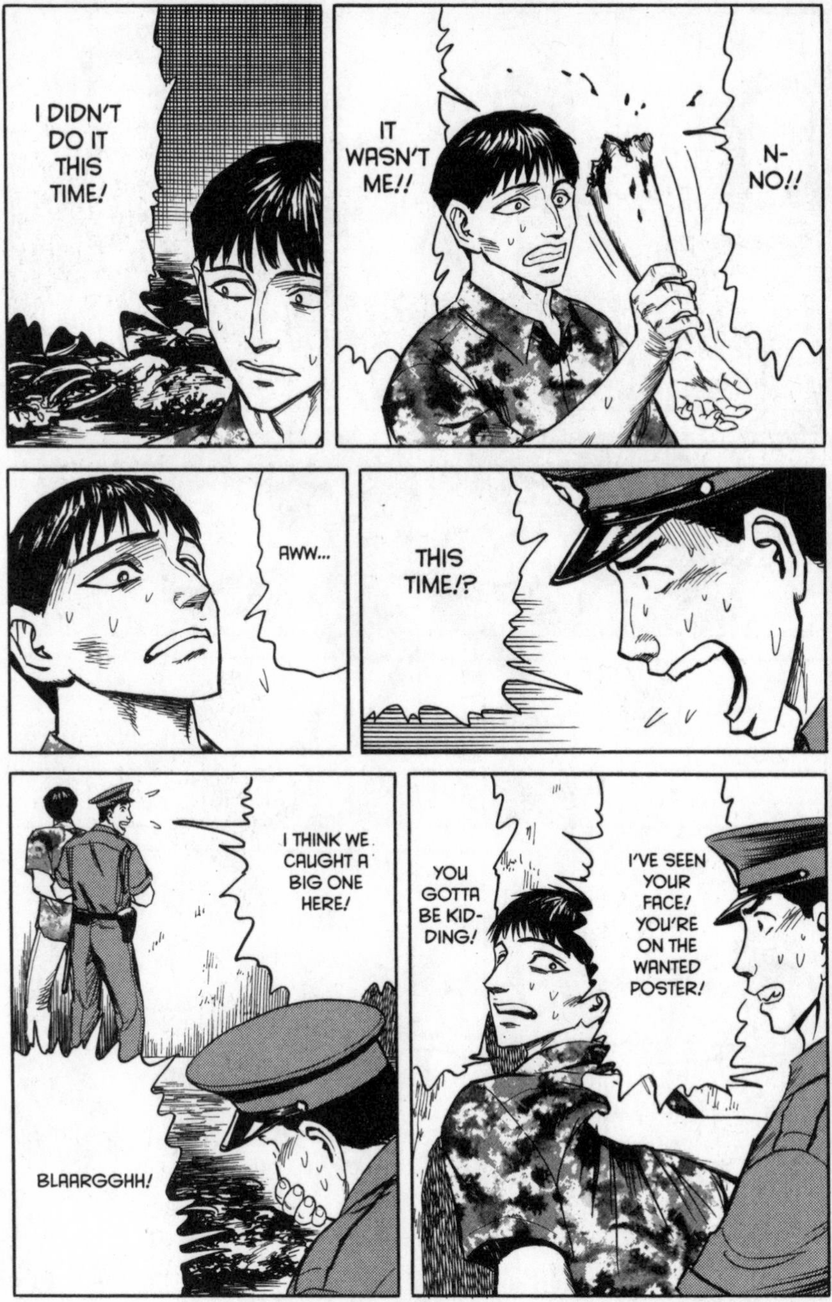
N-NO!!
IT WASN'T ME!!
I DIDN'T DO IT THIS TIME!
THIS TIME!?
AWW...
I'VE SEEN YOUR FACE! YOU'RE ON THE WANTED POSTER!
YOU GOTTA BE KID-DING!
I THINK WE CAUGHT A BIG ONE HERE!
BLAARGGHH!

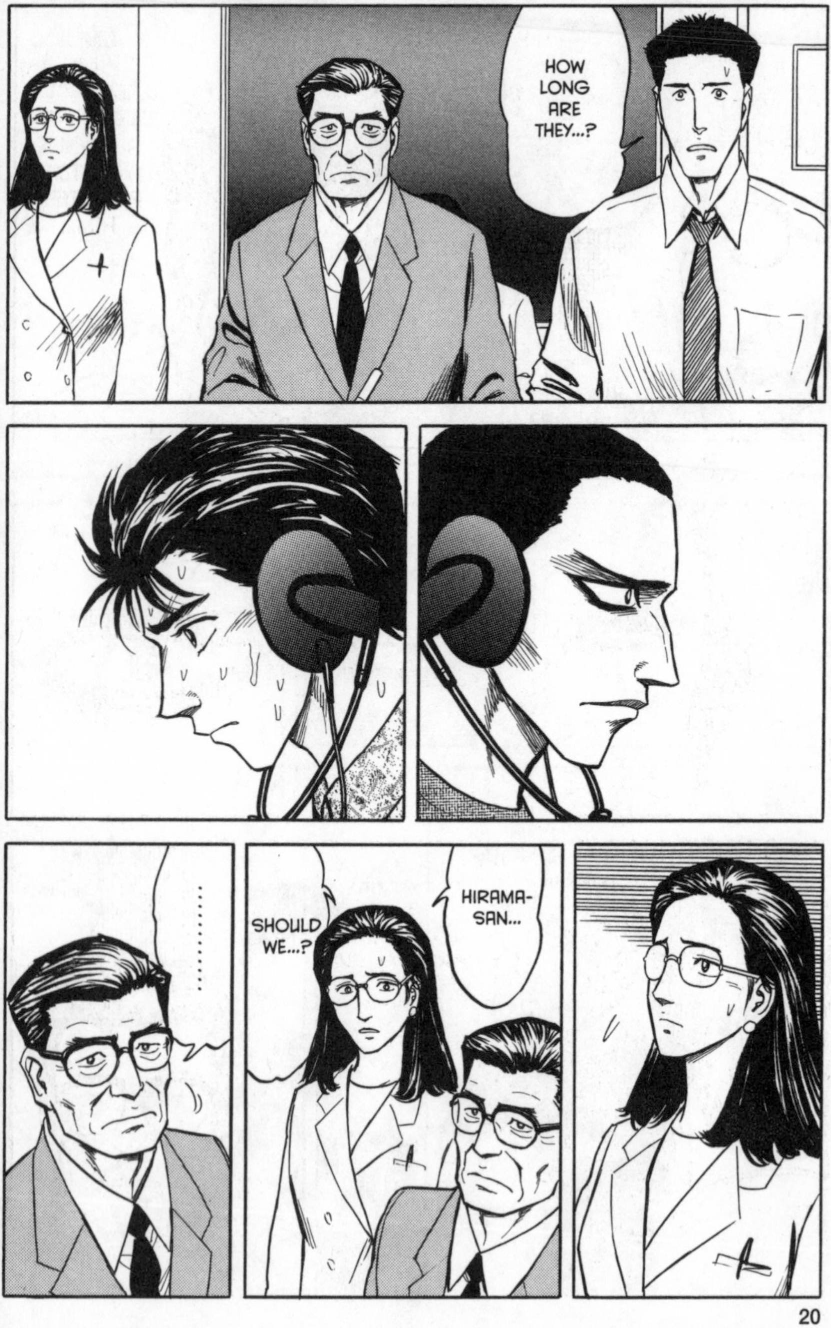
HOW LONG ARE THEY...?
HIRAMA-SAN...
SHOULD WE...?
......

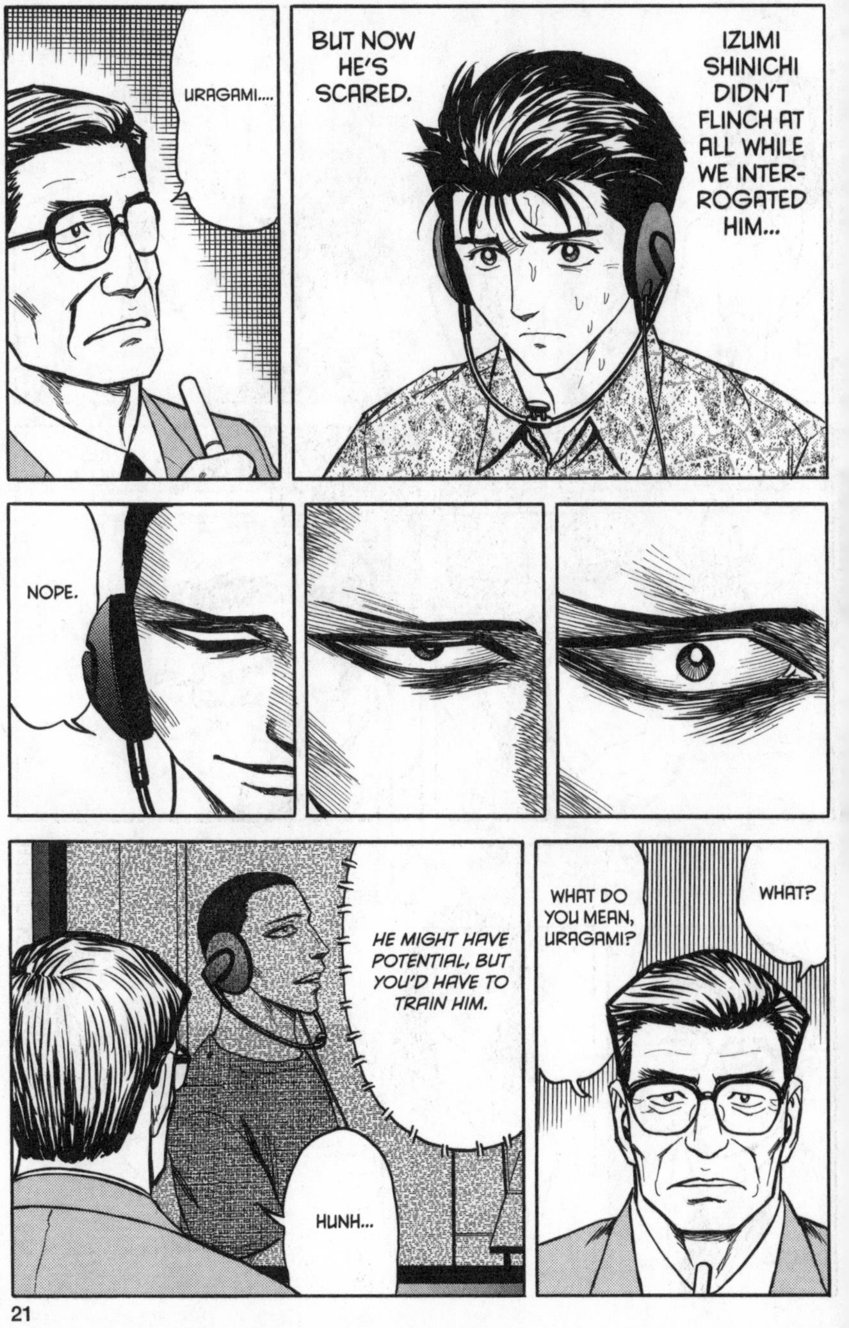
IZUMI SHINICHI DIDN'T FLINCH AT ALL WHILE WE INTER-ROGATED HIM...
BUT NOW HE'S SCARED.
URAGAMI....
NOPE.
WHAT?
WHAT DO YOU MEAN, URAGAMI?
HE MIGHT HAVE POTENTIAL, BUT YOU'D HAVE TO TRAIN HIM.
HUNH...

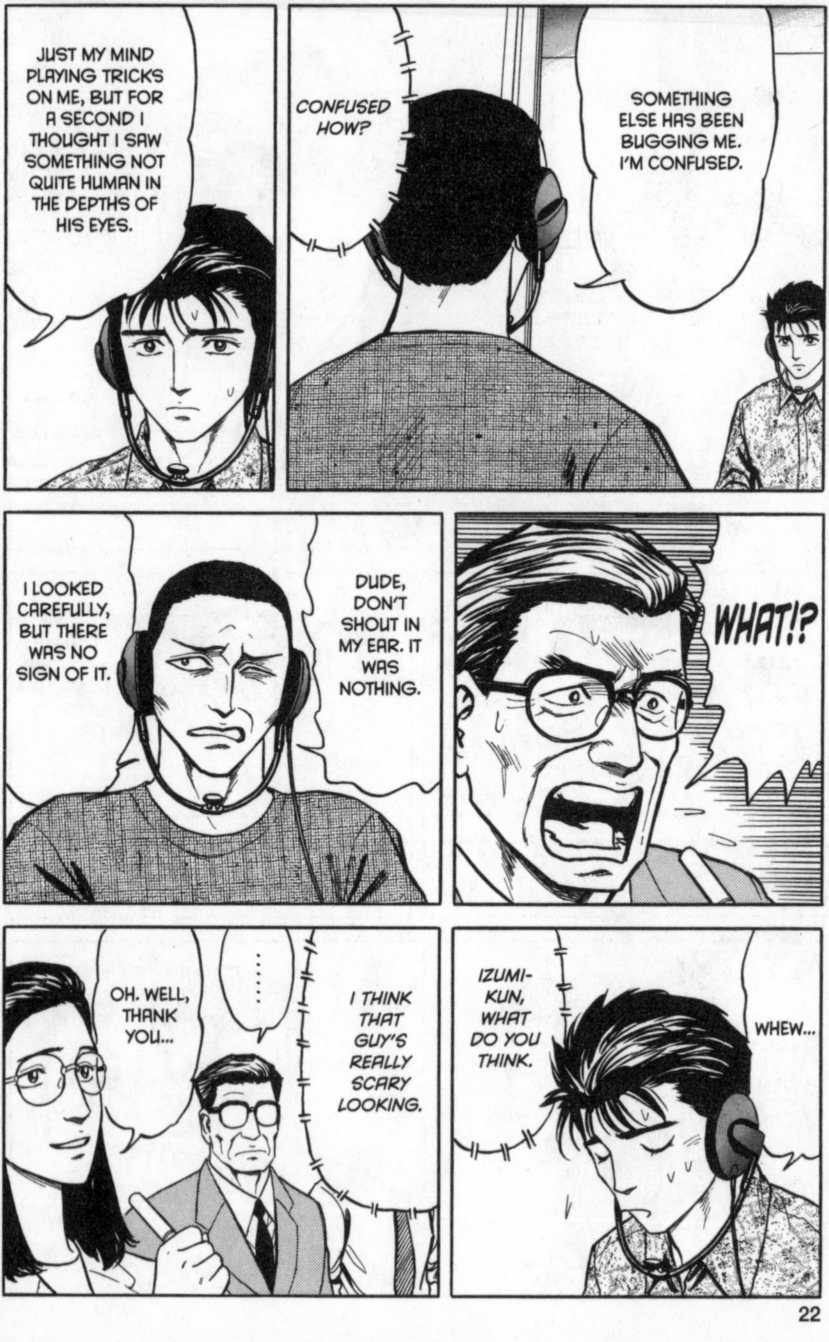
SOMETHING ELSE HAS BEEN BUGGING ME. I'M CONFUSED.
CONFUSED HOW?
JUST MY MIND PLAYING TRICKS ON ME, BUT FOR A SECOND I THOUGHT I SAW SOMETHING NOT QUITE HUMAN IN THE DEPTHS OF HIS EYES.
WHAT!?
DUDE, DON'T SHOUT IN MY EAR. IT WAS NOTHING.
I LOOKED CAREFULLY, BUT THERE WAS NO SIGN OF IT.
WHEW...
IZUMI-KUN, WHAT DO YOU THINK.
I THINK THAT GUY'S REALLY SCARY LOOKING.
......
OH. WELL, THANK YOU...

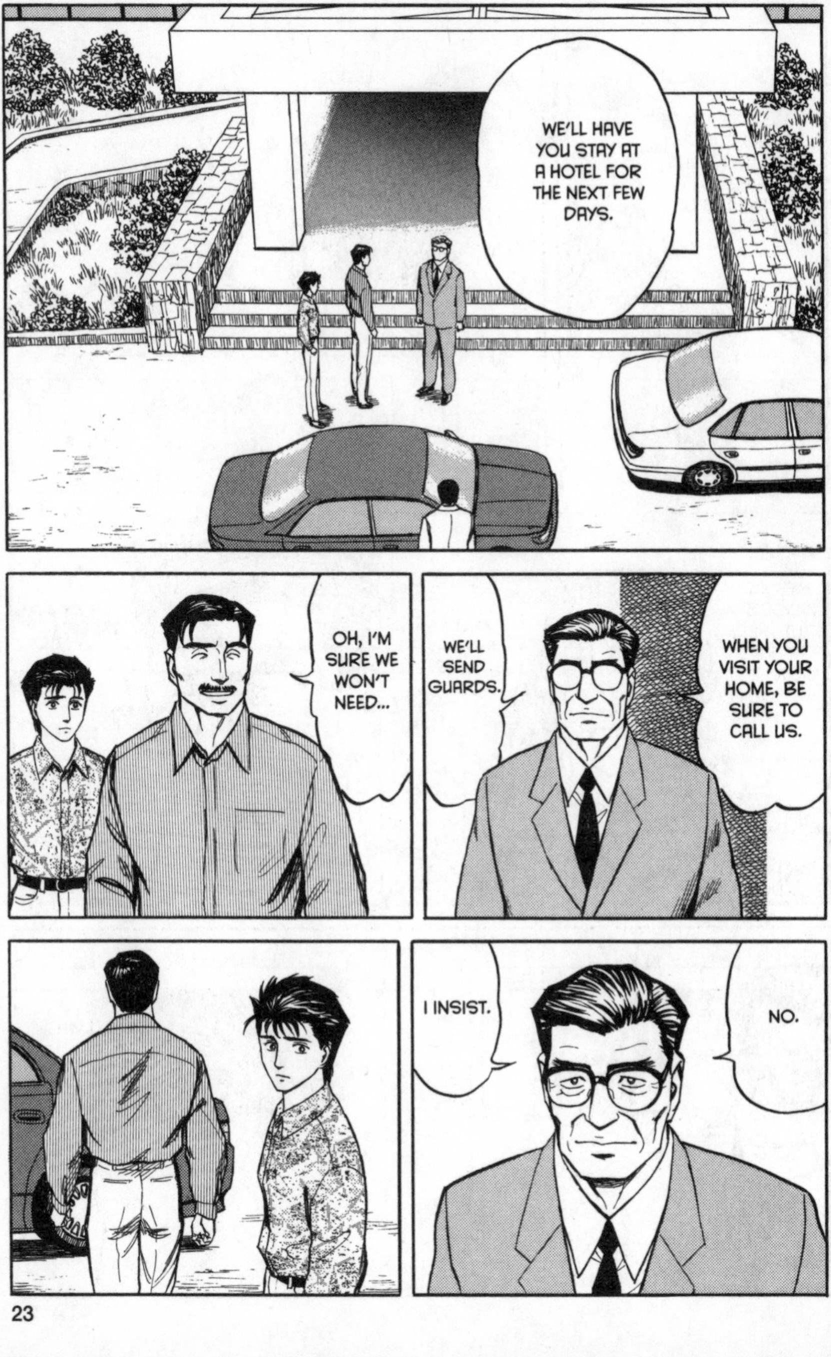
WE'LL HAVE YOU STAY AT A HOTEL FOR THE NEXT FEW DAYS.
WHEN YOU VISIT YOUR HOME, BE SURE TO CALL US.
WE'LL SEND GUARDS.
OH, I'M SURE WE WON'T NEED...
NO.
I INSIST.

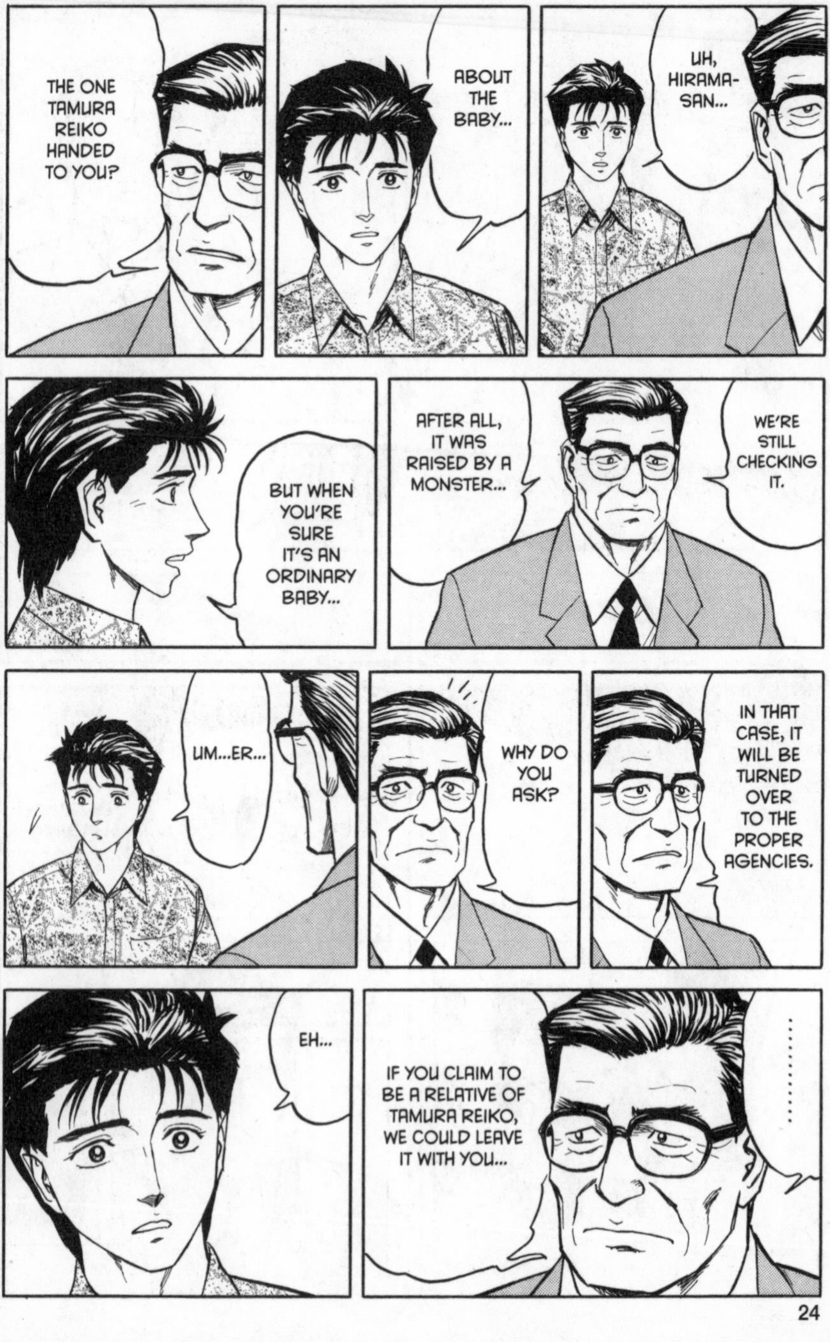
UH, HIRAMA-SAN...
ABOUT THE BABY...
THE ONE TAMURA REIKO HANDED TO YOU?
WE'RE STILL CHECKING IT.
AFTER ALL, IT WAS RAISED BY A MONSTER...
BUT WHEN YOU'RE SURE IT'S AN ORDINARY BABY...
IN THAT CASE, IT WILL BE TURNED OVER TO THE PROPER AGENCIES.
WHY DO YOU ASK?
UM...ER...
....
IF YOU CLAIM TO BE A RELATIVE OF TAMURA REIKO, WE COULD LEAVE IT WITH YOU...
EH...

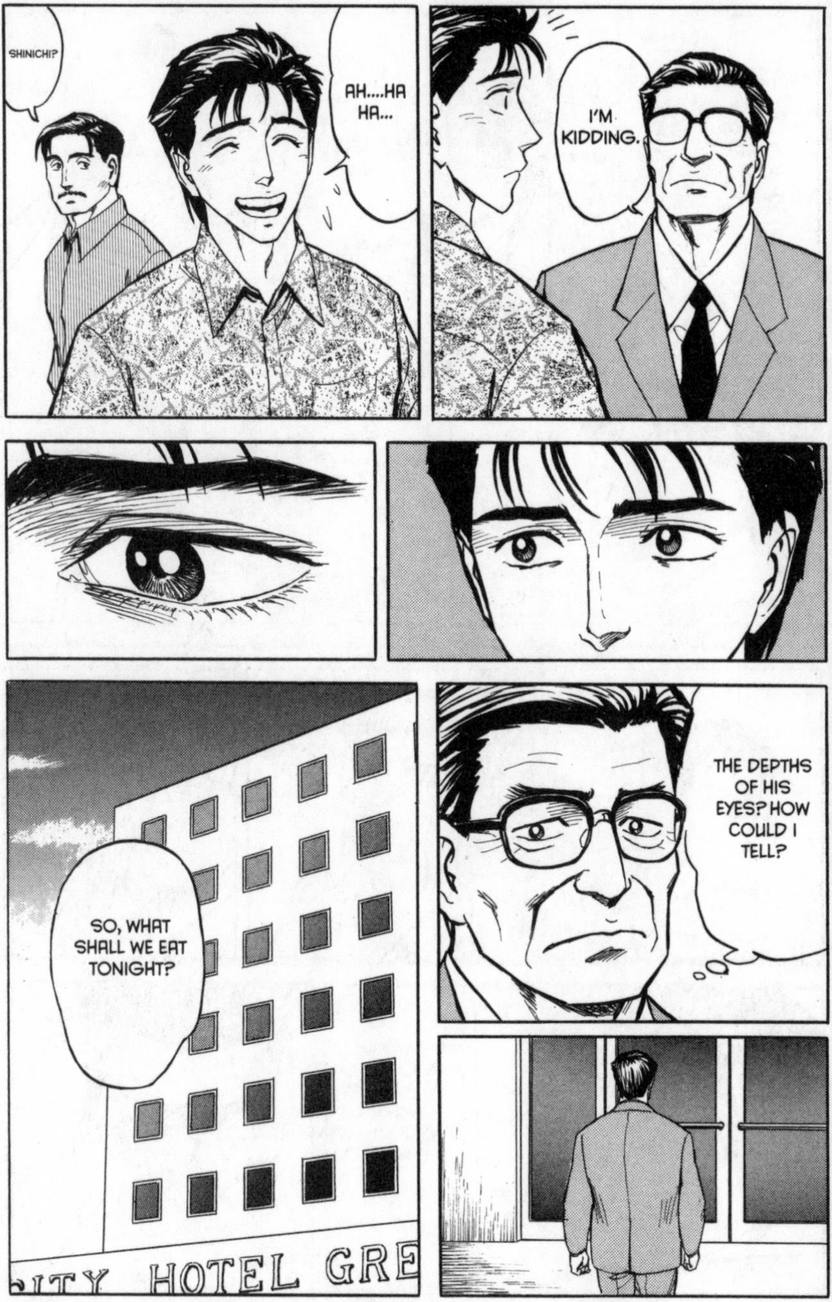
I'M KIDDING.
AH....HA HA...
SHINICHI?
THE DEPTHS OF HIS EYES? HOW COULD I TELL?
SO, WHAT SHALL WE EAT TONIGHT?
ITY HOTEL GRE

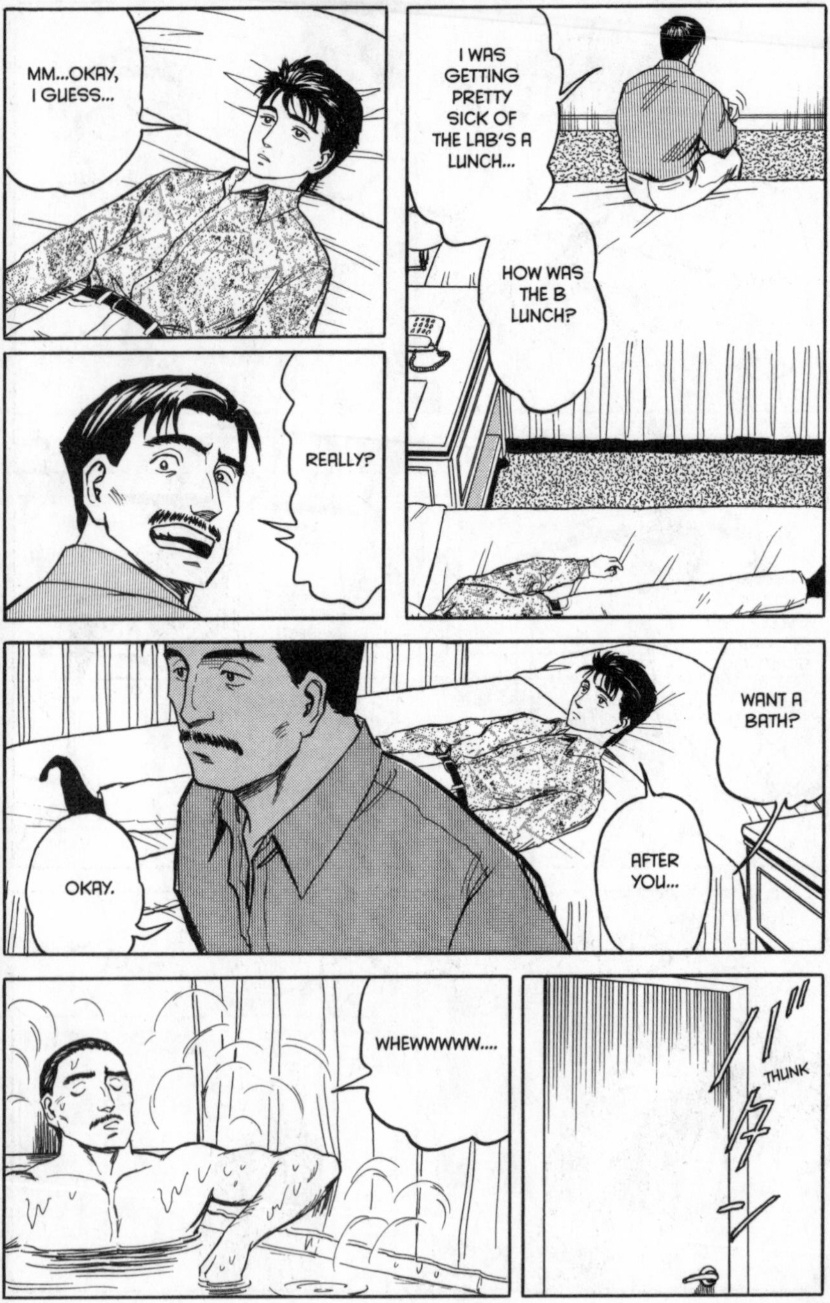
I WAS GETTING PRETTY SICK OF THE LAB'S A LUNCH...
HOW WAS THE B LUNCH?
MM...OKAY, I GUESS...
REALLY?
WANT A BATH?
AFTER YOU...
OKAY.
THUNK
WHEWWWWW....

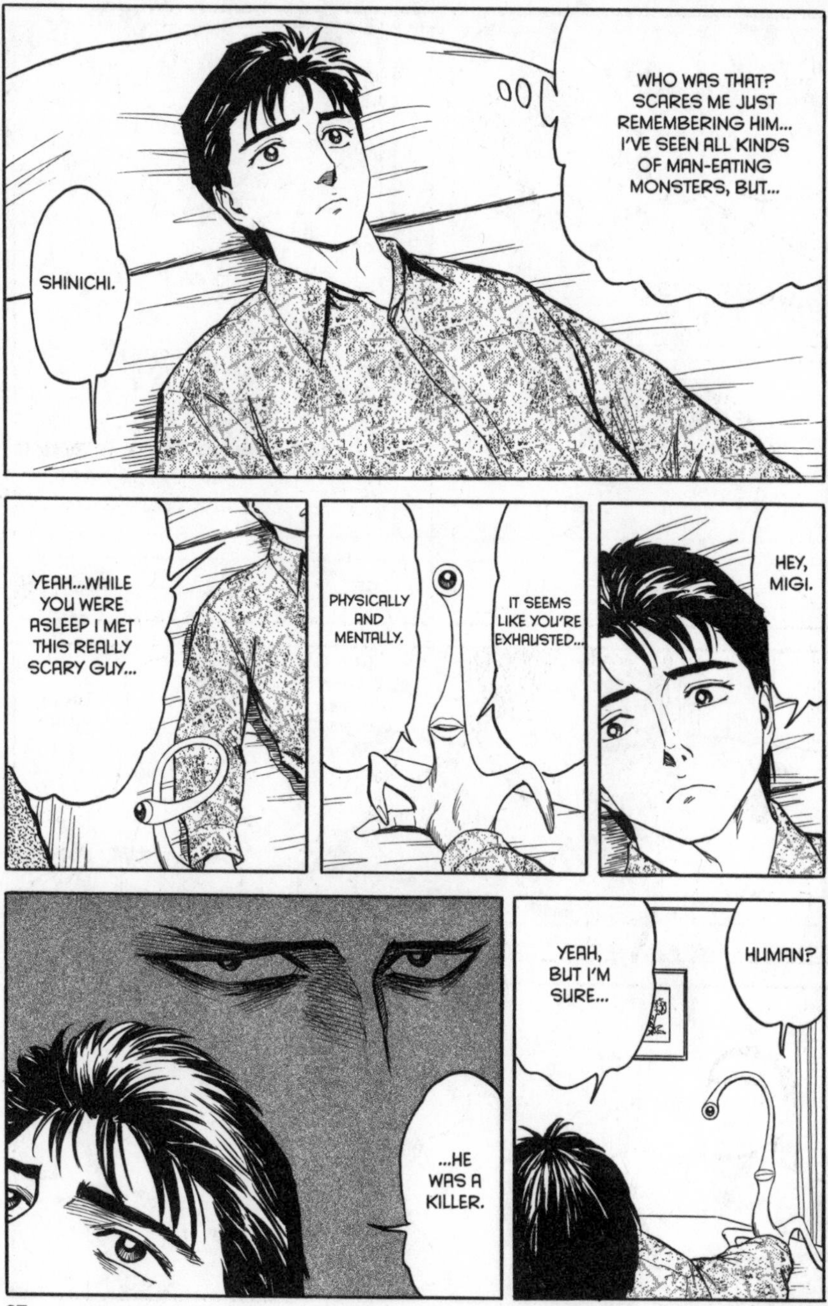
WHO WAS THAT? SCARES ME JUST REMEMBERING HIM... I'VE SEEN ALL KINDS OF MAN-EATING MONSTERS, BUT...
SHINICHI.
HEY, MIGI.
IT SEEMS LIKE YOU'RE EXHAUSTED...
PHYSICALLY AND MENTALLY.
YEAH...WHILE YOU WERE ASLEEP I MET THIS REALLY SCARY GUY...
HUMAN?
YEAH, BUT I'M SURE...
...HE WAS A KILLER.

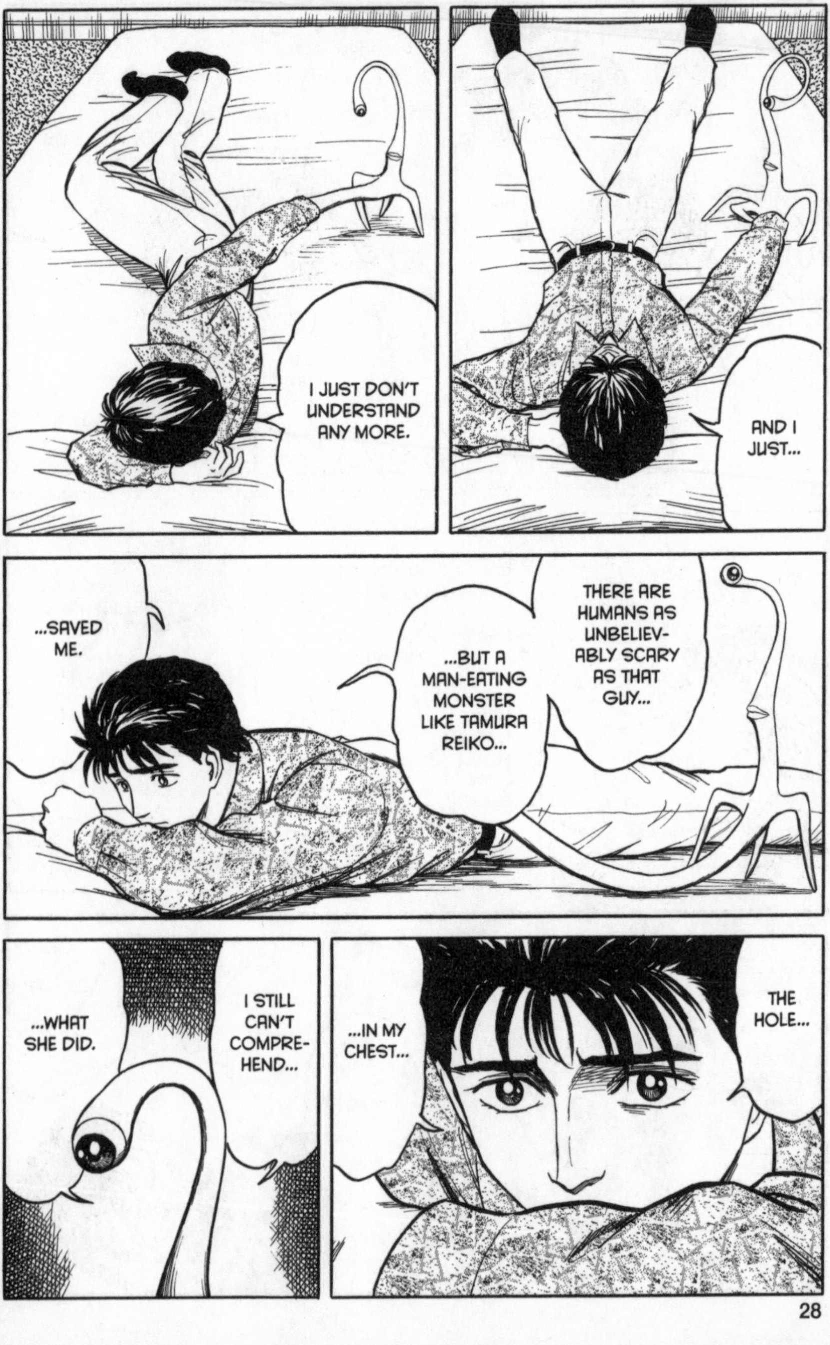
AND I JUST...
I JUST DON'T UNDERSTAND ANY MORE.
THERE ARE HUMANS AS UNBELIEVABLY SCARY AS THAT GUY...
...BUT A MAN-EATING MONSTER LIKE TAMURA REIKO...
...SAVED ME.
THE HOLE...
...IN MY CHEST...
I STILL CAN'T COMPREHEND...
...WHAT SHE DID.

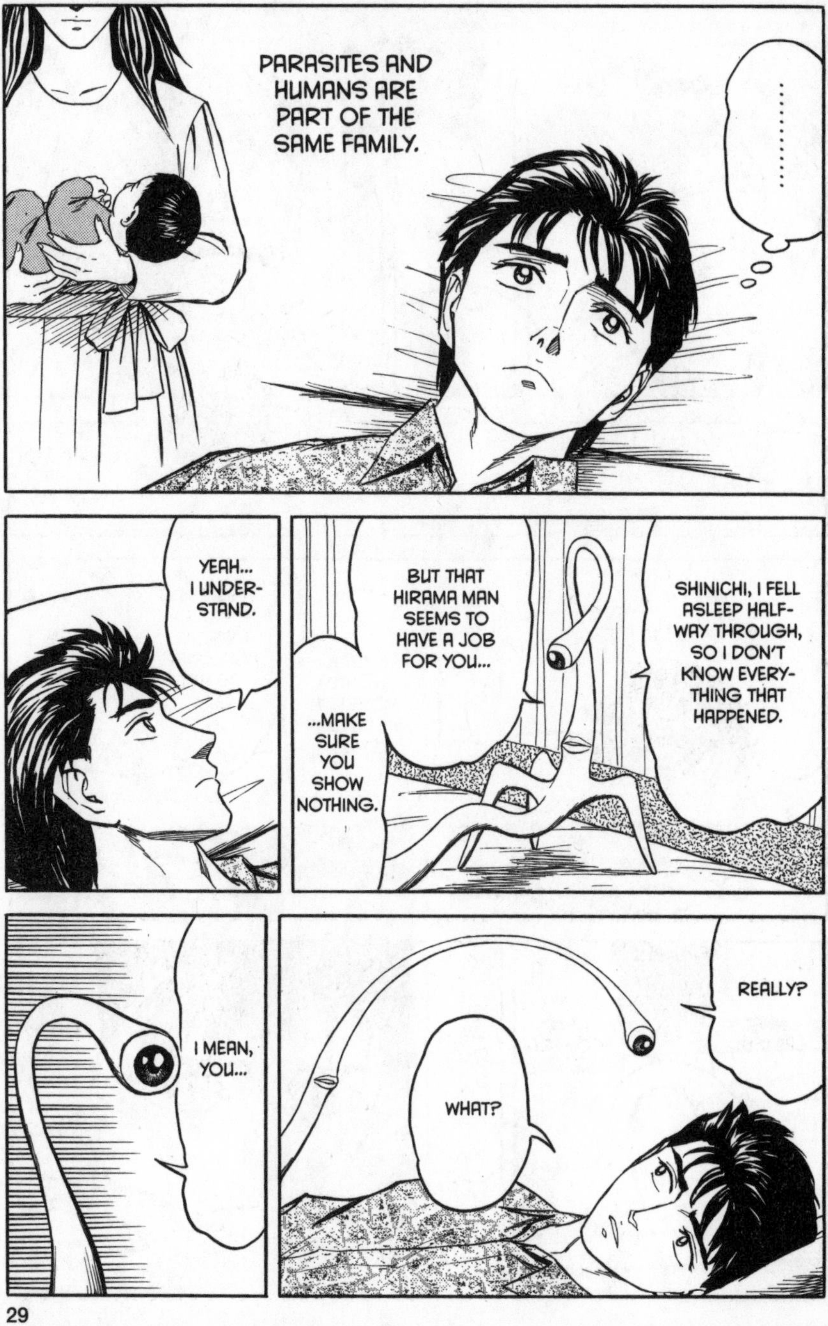
......
PARASITES AND HUMANS ARE PART OF THE SAME FAMILY.
SHINICHI, I FELL ASLEEP HALF-WAY THROUGH, SO I DON'T KNOW EVERY-THING THAT HAPPENED.
BUT THAT HIRAMA MAN SEEMS TO HAVE A JOB FOR YOU...
...MAKE SURE YOU SHOW NOTHING.
YEAH... I UNDER-STAND.
REALLY?
WHAT?
I MEAN, YOU...

DAD'S COMING OUT.

SWISH

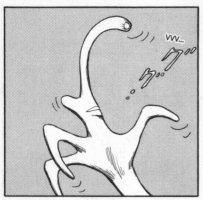

VVV...

ブ゛ー゛゛

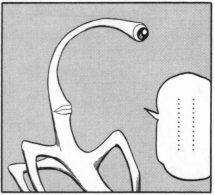

HOTEL GR

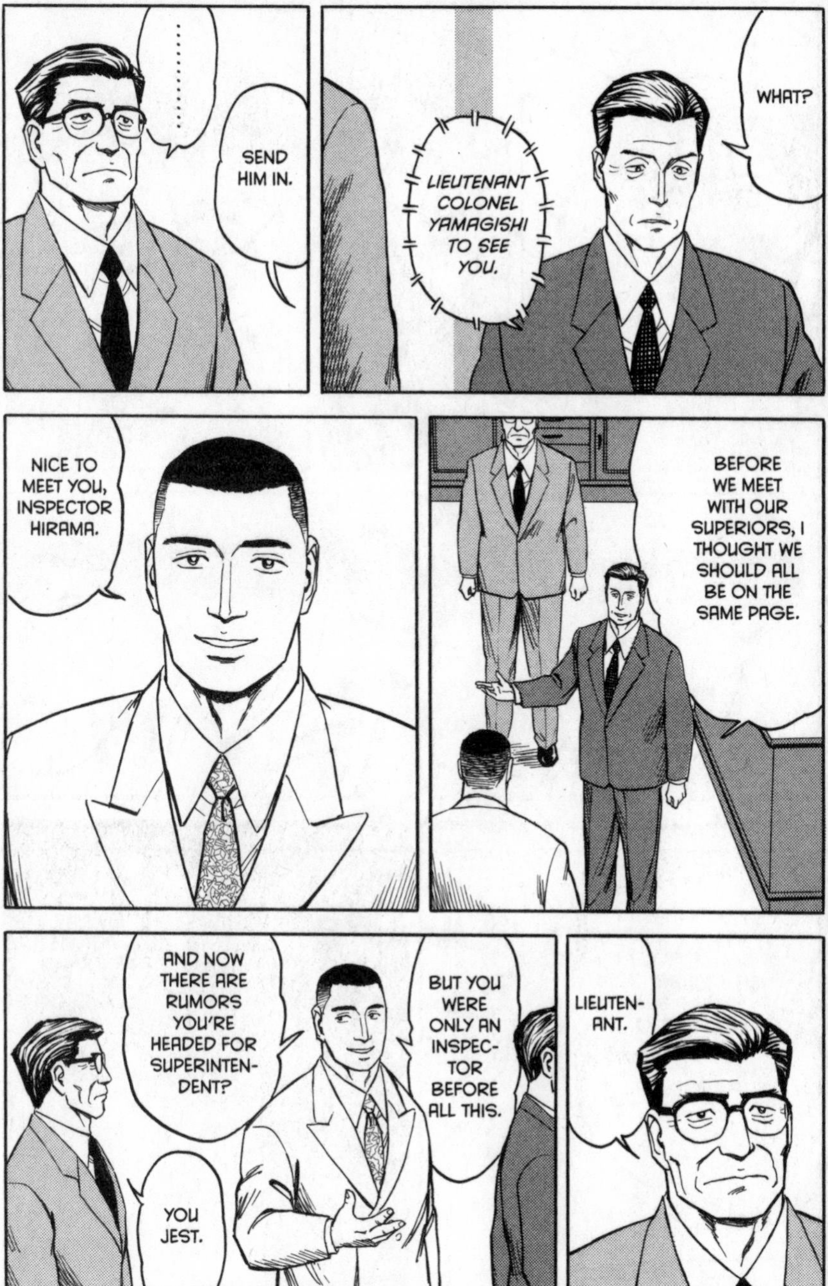
WHAT?
LIEUTENANT COLONEL YAMAGISHI TO SEE YOU.
......
SEND HIM IN.
BEFORE WE MEET WITH OUR SUPERIORS, I THOUGHT WE SHOULD ALL BE ON THE SAME PAGE.
NICE TO MEET YOU, INSPECTOR HIRAMA.
LIEUTEN-ANT.
BUT YOU WERE ONLY AN INSPEC-TOR BEFORE ALL THIS.
AND NOW THERE ARE RUMORS YOU'RE HEADED FOR SUPERINTEN-DENT?
YOU JEST.

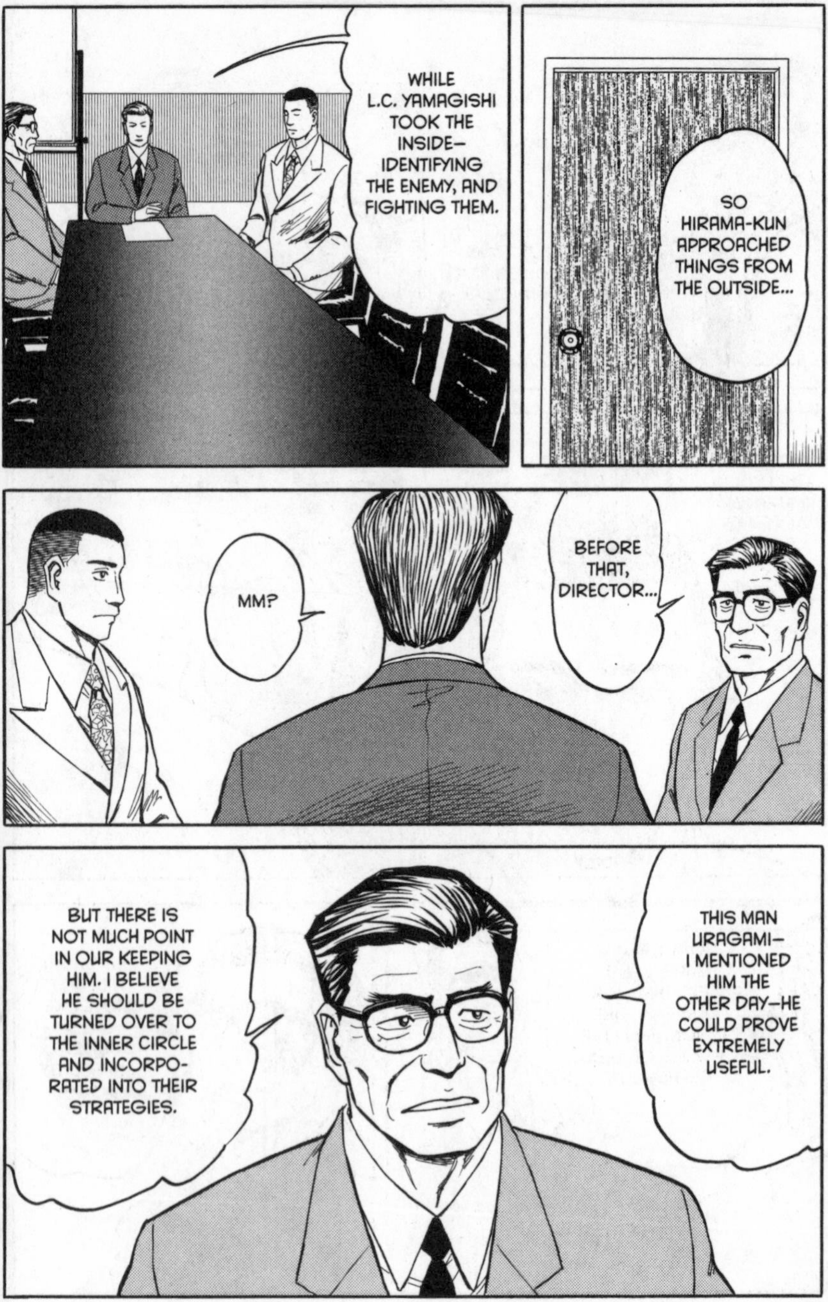
SO HIRAMA-KUN APPROACHED THINGS FROM THE OUTSIDE...
WHILE L.C. YAMAGISHI TOOK THE INSIDE—IDENTIFYING THE ENEMY, AND FIGHTING THEM.
BEFORE THAT, DIRECTOR...
MM?
THIS MAN URAGAMI—I MENTIONED HIM THE OTHER DAY—HE COULD PROVE EXTREMELY USEFUL.
BUT THERE IS NOT MUCH POINT IN OUR KEEPING HIM. I BELIEVE HE SHOULD BE TURNED OVER TO THE INNER CIRCLE AND INCORPO-RATED INTO THEIR STRATEGIES.

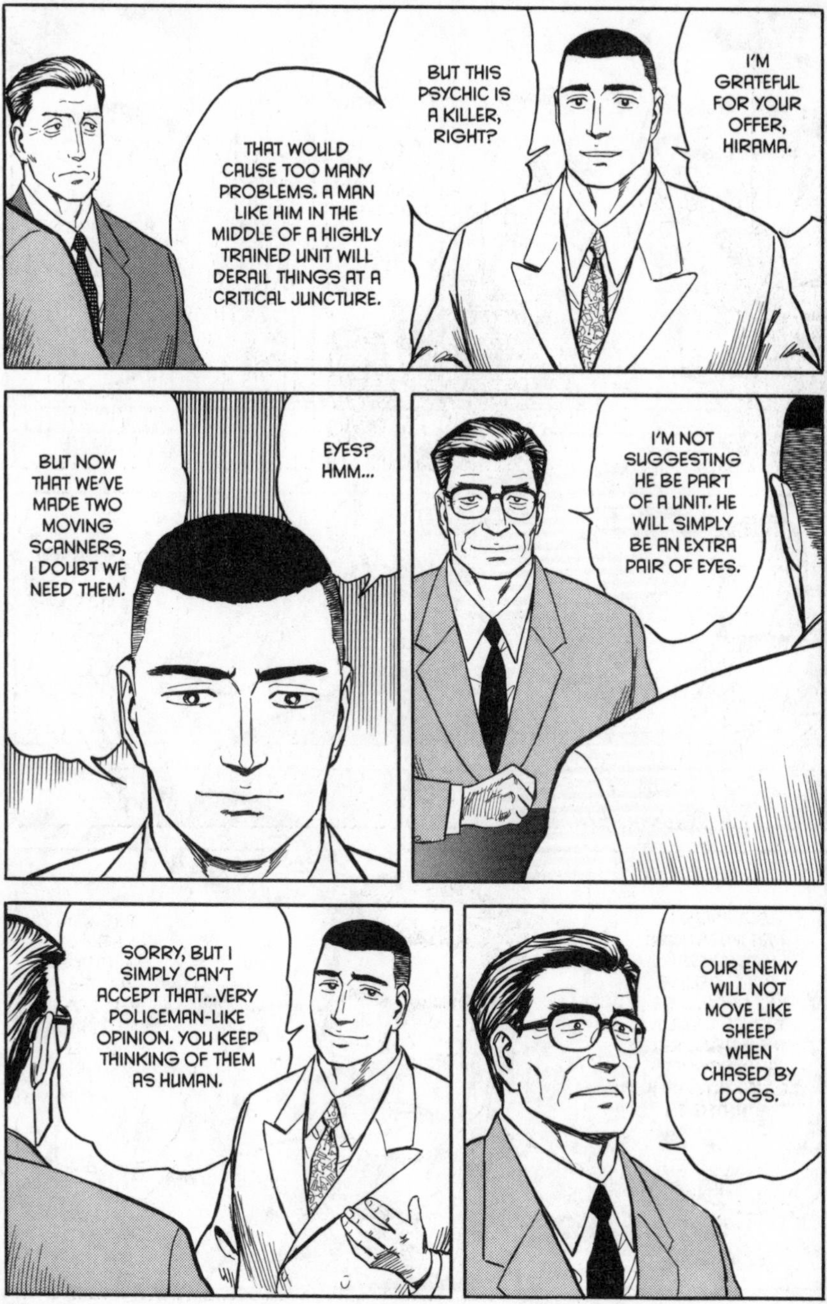
I'M GRATEFUL FOR YOUR OFFER, HIRAMA.
BUT THIS PSYCHIC IS A KILLER, RIGHT?
THAT WOULD CAUSE TOO MANY PROBLEMS. A MAN LIKE HIM IN THE MIDDLE OF A HIGHLY TRAINED UNIT WILL DERAIL THINGS AT A CRITICAL JUNCTURE.
I'M NOT SUGGESTING HE BE PART OF A UNIT. HE WILL SIMPLY BE AN EXTRA PAIR OF EYES.
EYES? HMM...
BUT NOW THAT WE'VE MADE TWO MOVING SCANNERS, I DOUBT WE NEED THEM.
OUR ENEMY WILL NOT MOVE LIKE SHEEP WHEN CHASED BY DOGS.
SORRY, BUT I SIMPLY CAN'T ACCEPT THAT...VERY POLICEMAN-LIKE OPINION. YOU KEEP THINKING OF THEM AS HUMAN.

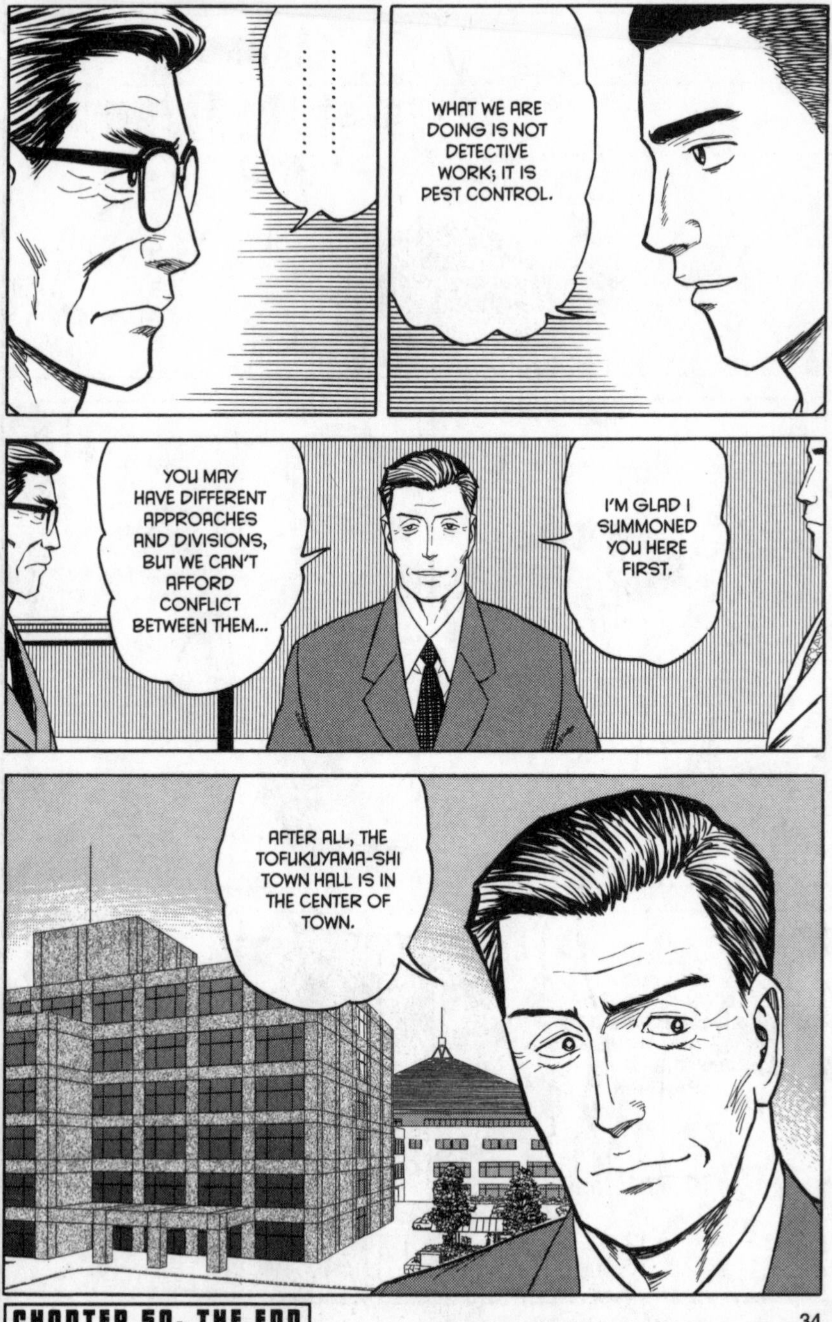
WHAT WE ARE DOING IS NOT DETECTIVE WORK; IT IS PEST CONTROL.
......
I'M GLAD I SUMMONED YOU HERE FIRST.
YOU MAY HAVE DIFFERENT APPROACHES AND DIVISIONS, BUT WE CAN'T AFFORD CONFLICT BETWEEN THEM...
AFTER ALL, THE TOFUKUYAMA-SHI TOWN HALL IS IN THE CENTER OF TOWN.

CHAPTER 51: BEARING

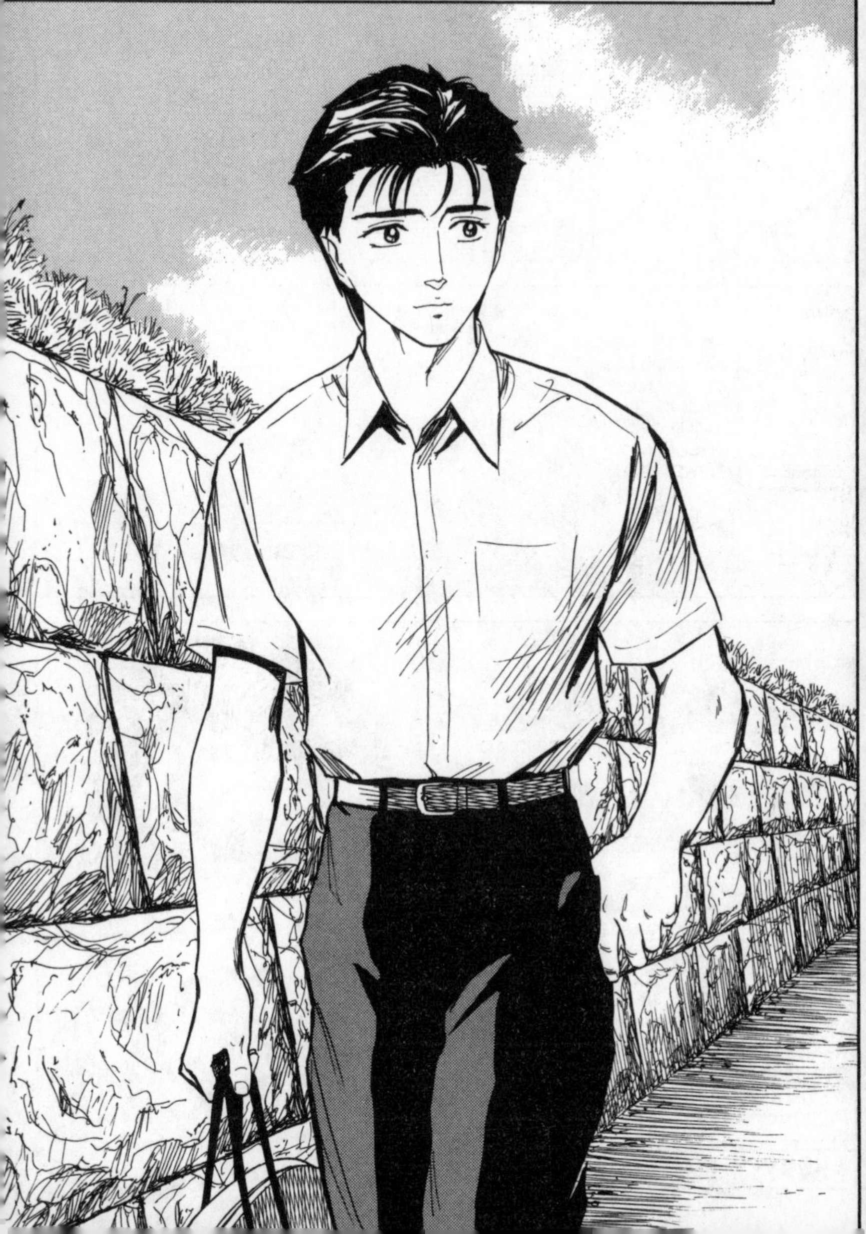

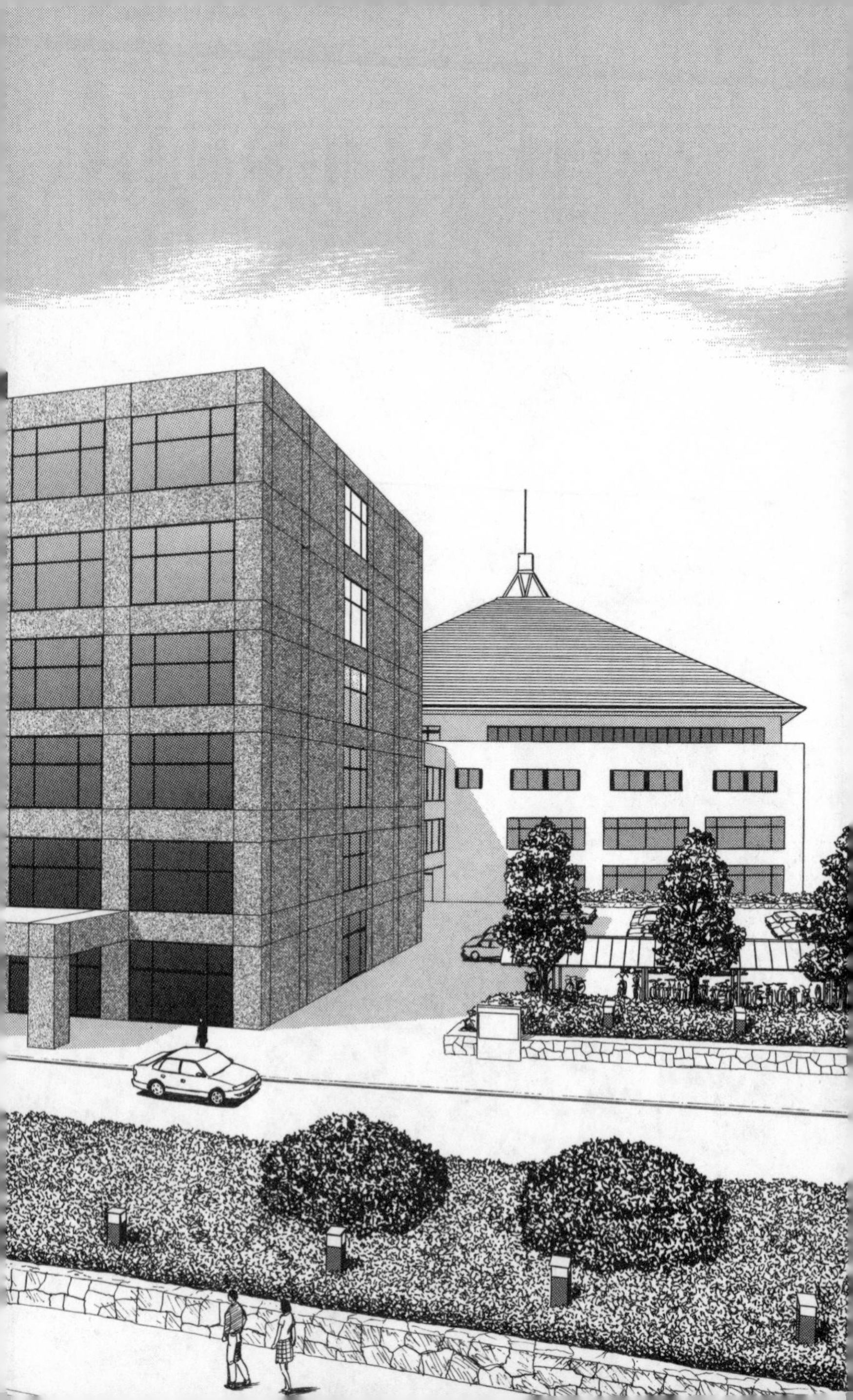

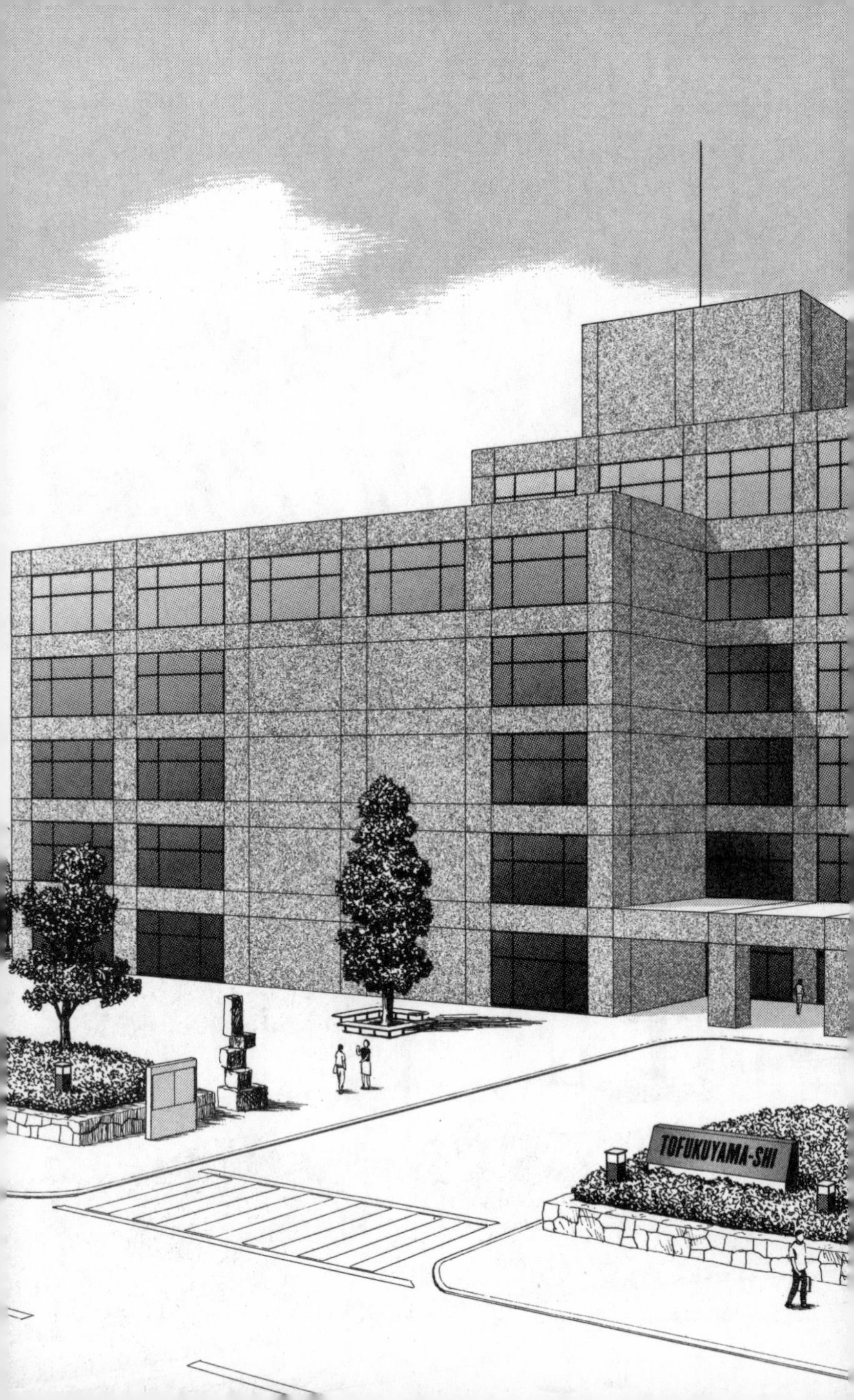
TOFUKUYAMA-SHI

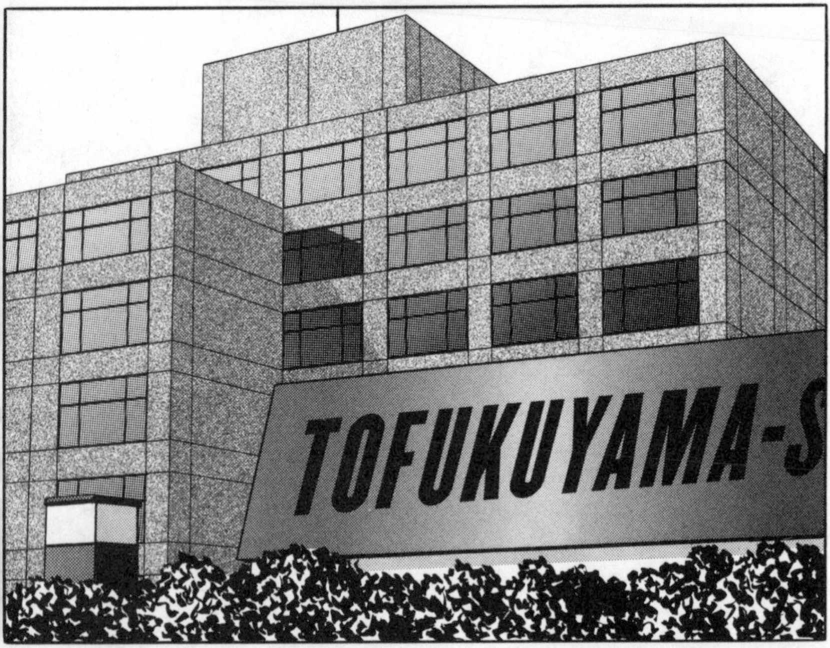
TOFUKUYAMA-S

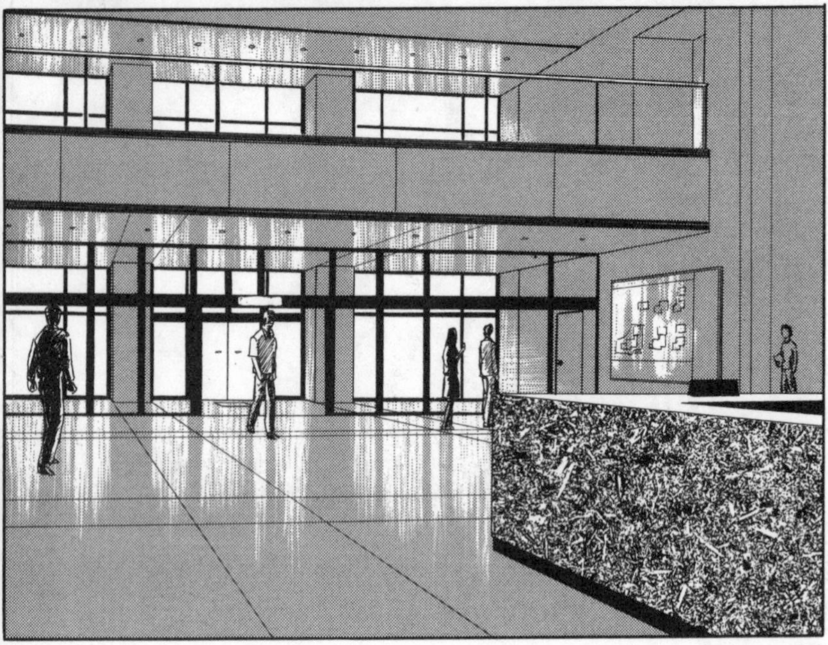

福祉課

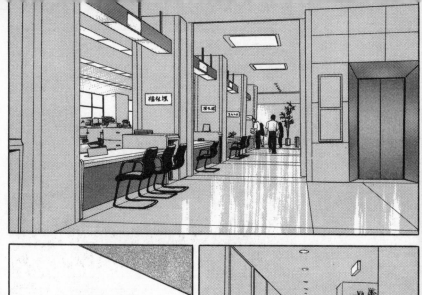

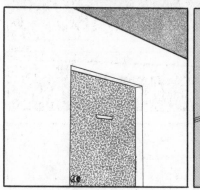

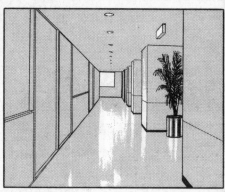

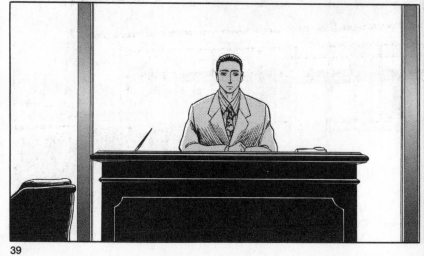

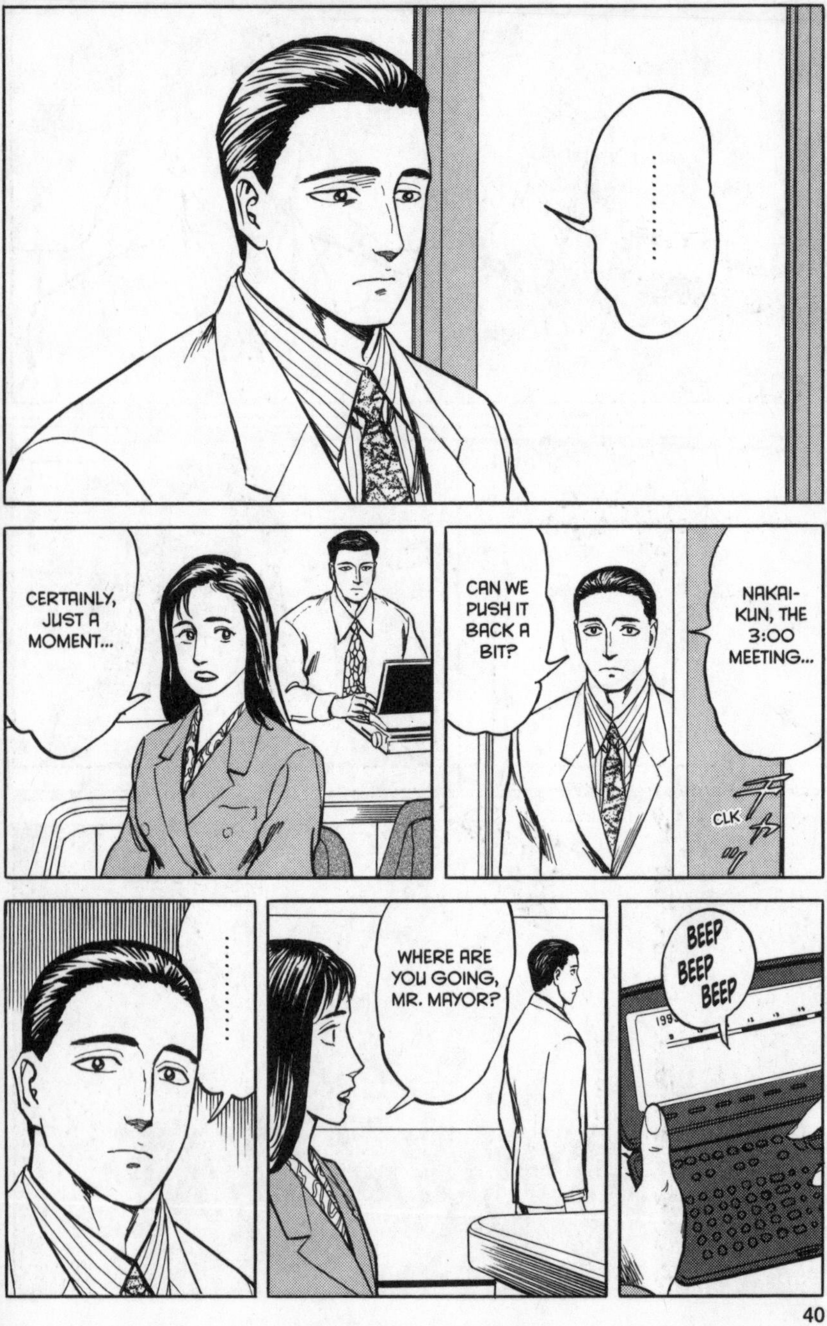
……
NAKAI-KUN, THE 3:00 MEETING...
CLK
CAN WE PUSH IT BACK A BIT?
CERTAINLY, JUST A MOMENT...
BEEP BEEP BEEP
WHERE ARE YOU GOING, MR. MAYOR?
……

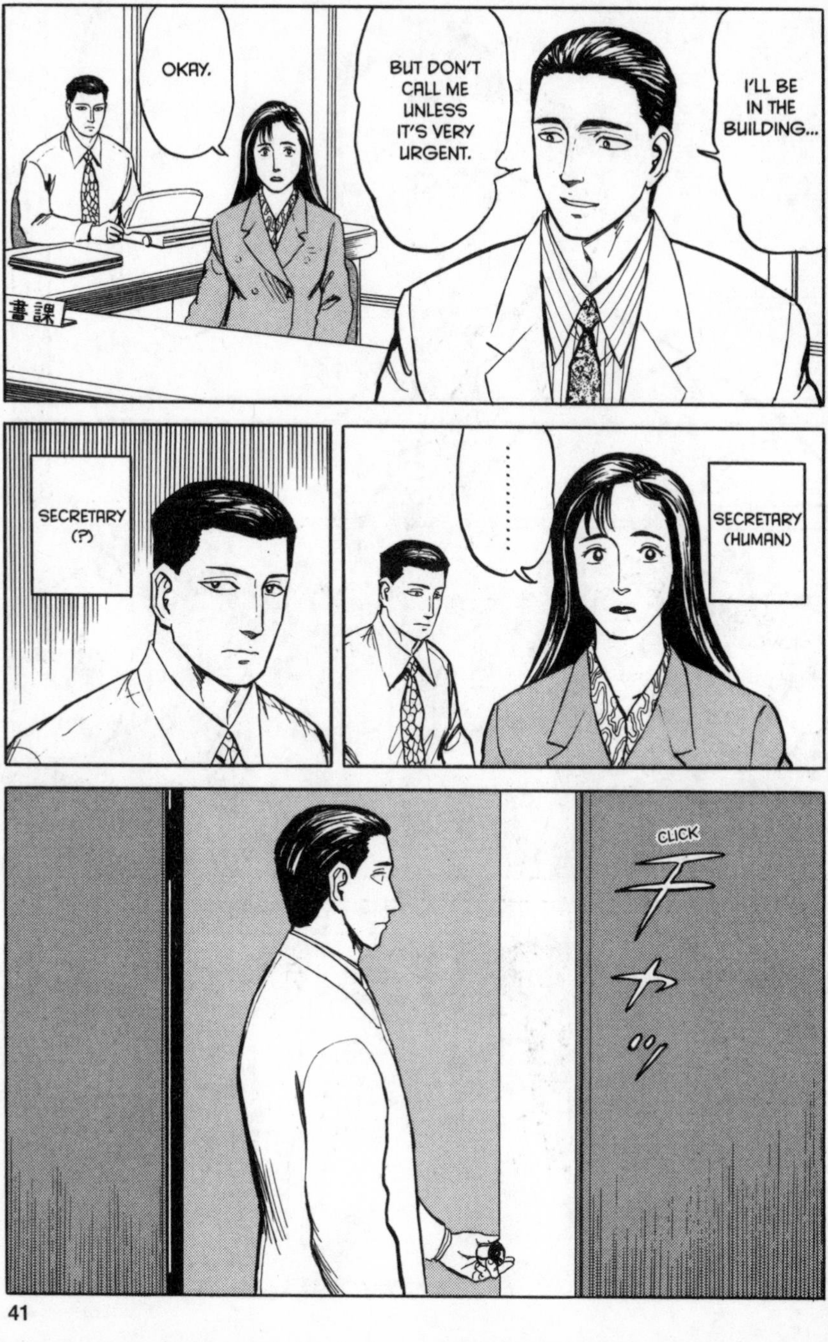
I'LL BE IN THE BUILDING...
BUT DON'T CALL ME UNLESS IT'S VERY URGENT.
OKAY.
......
SECRETARY (HUMAN)
SECRETARY (?)
CLICK
チャッ

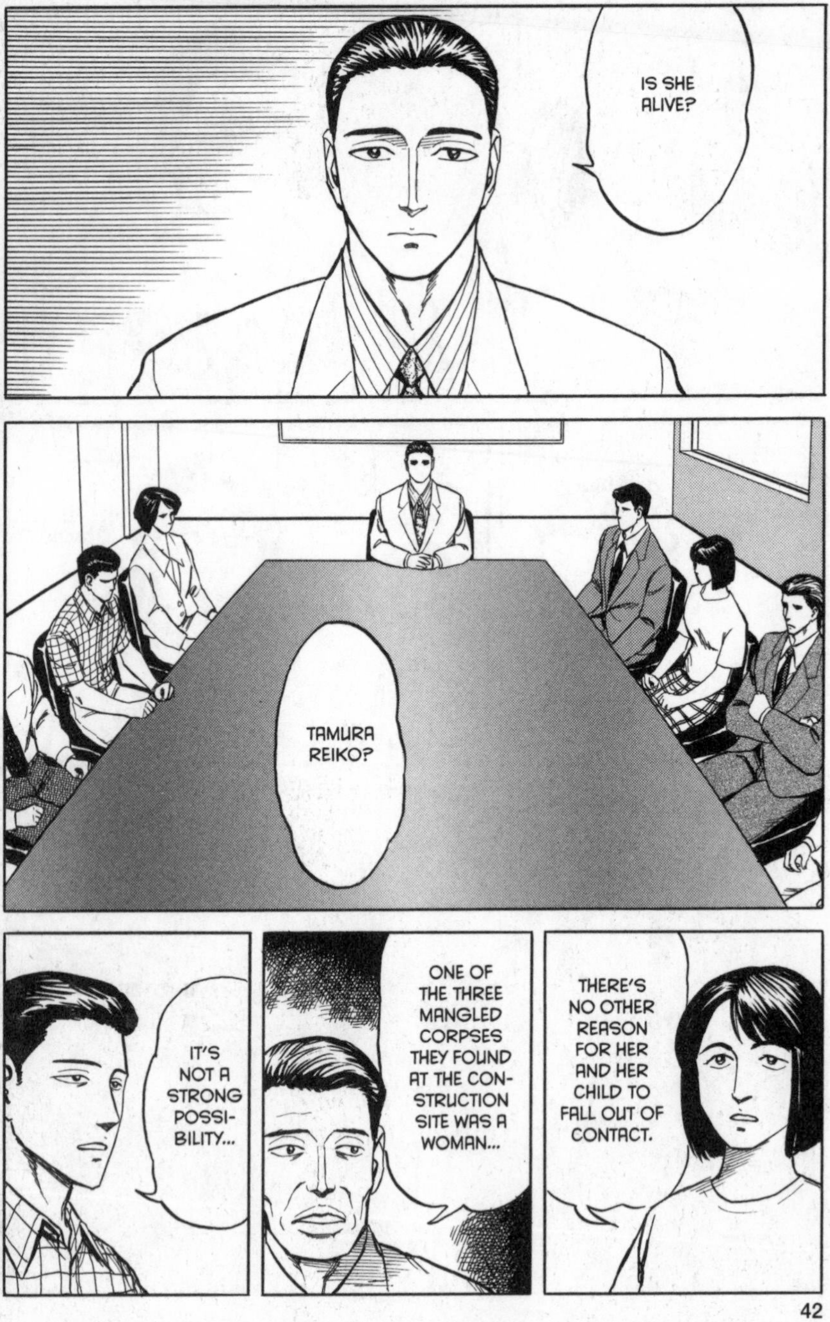
IS SHE ALIVE?
TAMURA REIKO?
THERE'S NO OTHER REASON FOR HER AND HER CHILD TO FALL OUT OF CONTACT.
ONE OF THE THREE MANGLED CORPSES THEY FOUND AT THE CON-STRUCTION SITE WAS A WOMAN...
IT'S NOT A STRONG POSSI-BILITY...

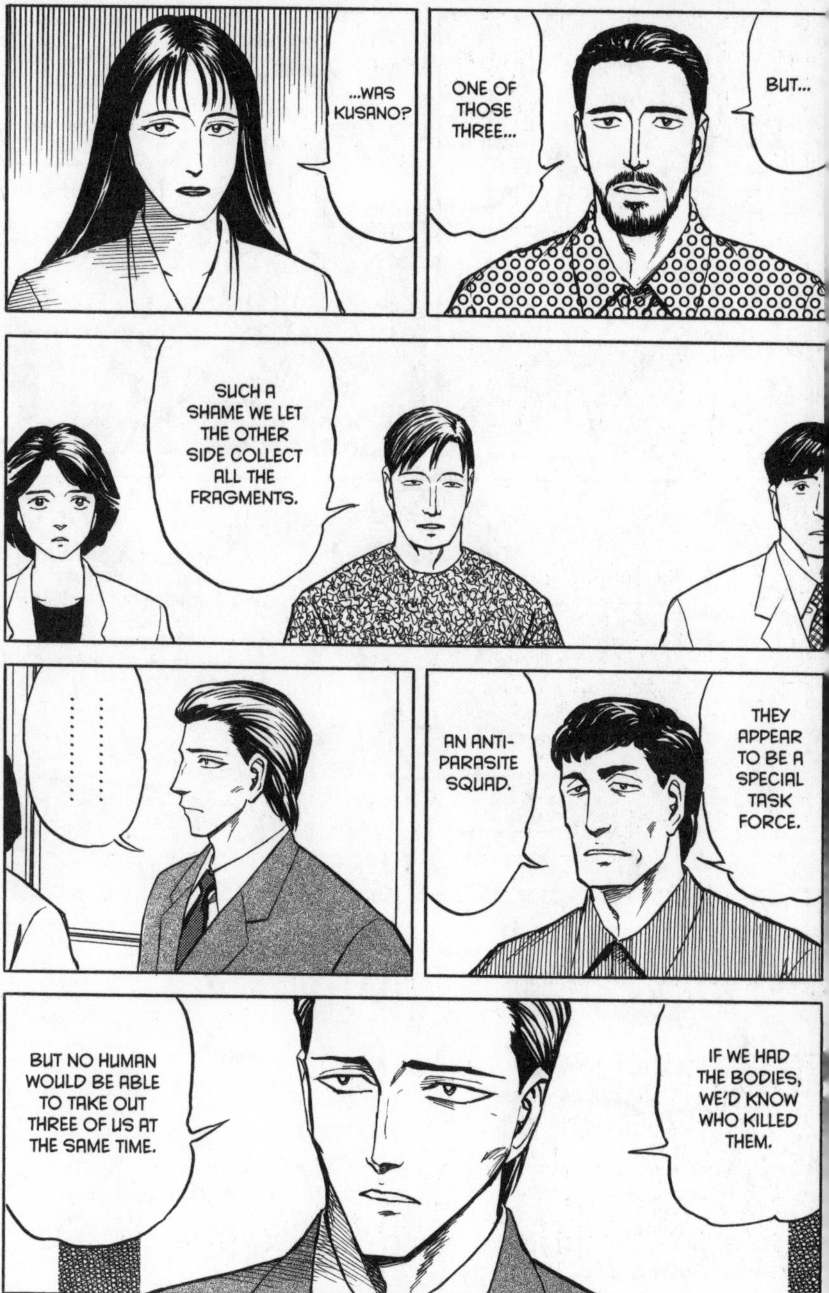
BUT...
ONE OF THOSE THREE...
...WAS KUSANO?
SUCH A SHAME WE LET THE OTHER SIDE COLLECT ALL THE FRAGMENTS.
THEY APPEAR TO BE A SPECIAL TASK FORCE.
AN ANTI-PARASITE SQUAD.
......
IF WE HAD THE BODIES, WE'D KNOW WHO KILLED THEM.
BUT NO HUMAN WOULD BE ABLE TO TAKE OUT THREE OF US AT THE SAME TIME.

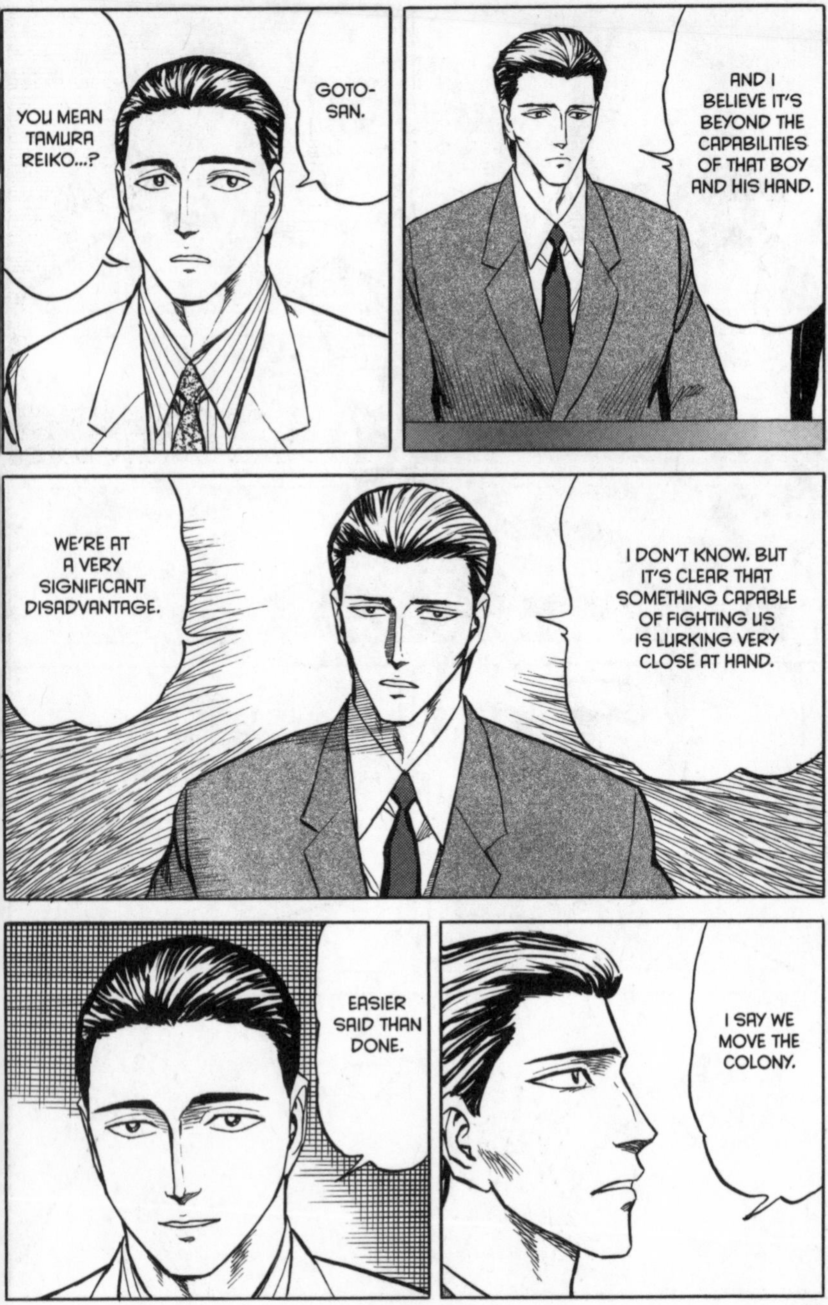
AND I BELIEVE IT'S BEYOND THE CAPABILITIES OF THAT BOY AND HIS HAND.
GOTO-SAN.
YOU MEAN TAMURA REIKO...?
I DON'T KNOW. BUT IT'S CLEAR THAT SOMETHING CAPABLE OF FIGHTING US IS LURKING VERY CLOSE AT HAND.
WE'RE AT A VERY SIGNIFICANT DISADVANTAGE.
I SAY WE MOVE THE COLONY.
EASIER SAID THAN DONE.

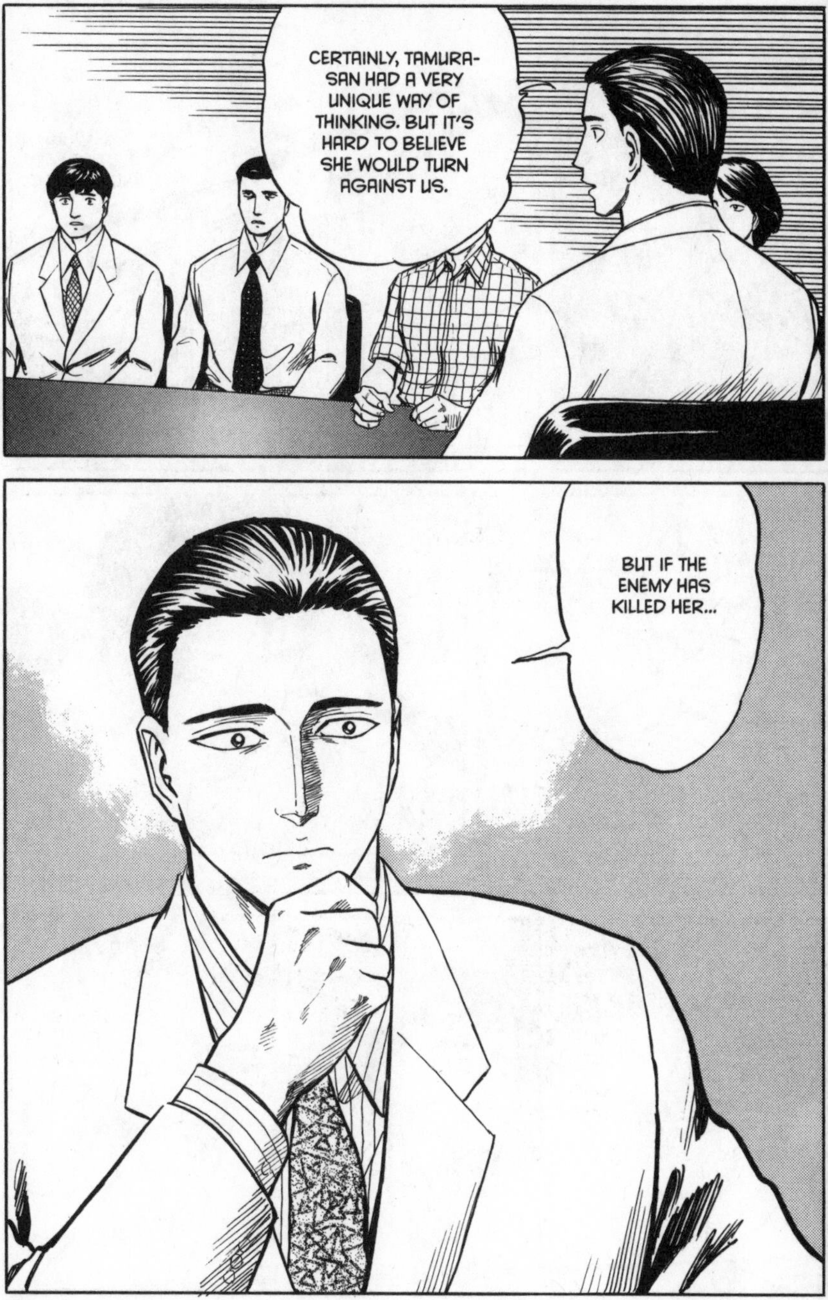
CERTAINLY, TAMURA-SAN HAD A VERY UNIQUE WAY OF THINKING. BUT IT'S HARD TO BELIEVE SHE WOULD TURN AGAINST US.
BUT IF THE ENEMY HAS KILLED HER...

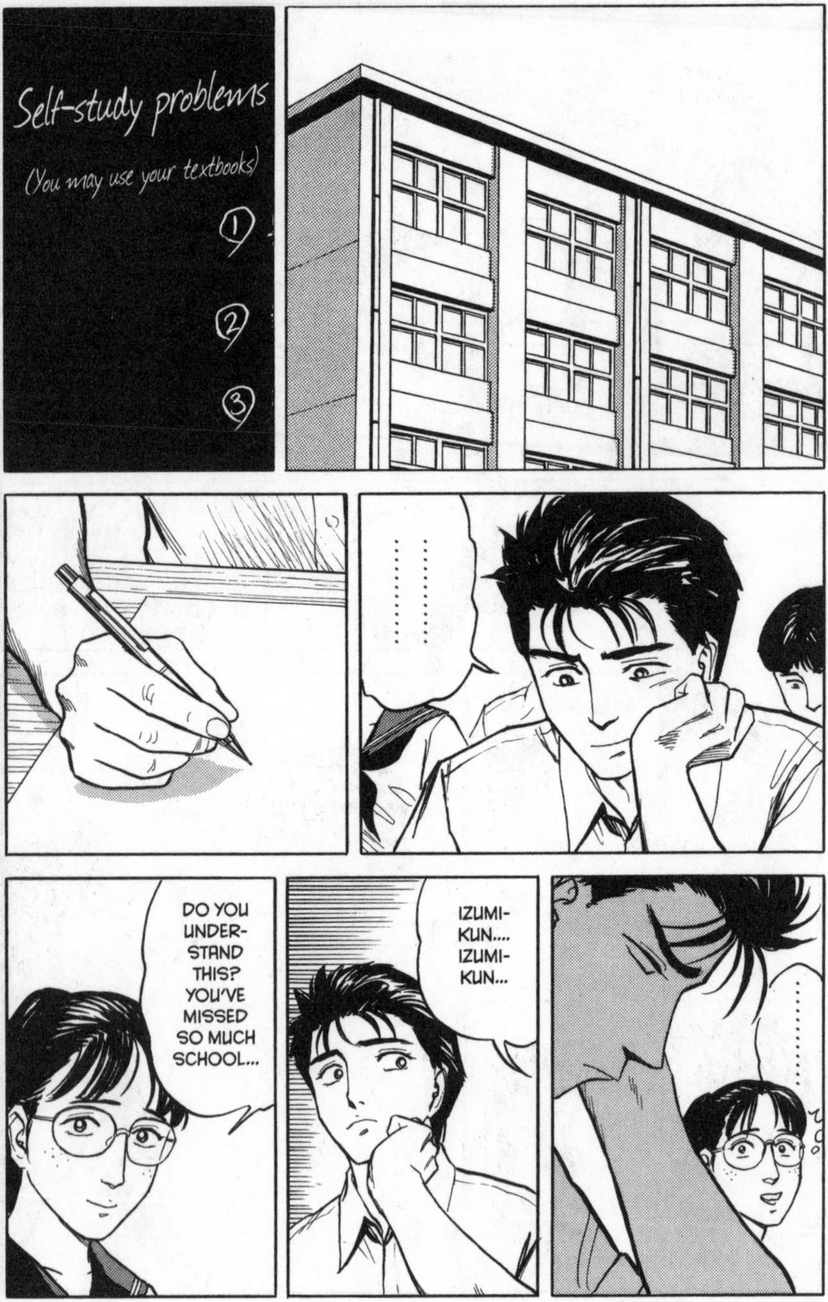
Self-study problems
(You may use your textbooks)
1
2
3
IZUMI-KUN.... IZUMI-KUN...
DO YOU UNDER-STAND THIS? YOU'VE MISSED SO MUCH SCHOOL...

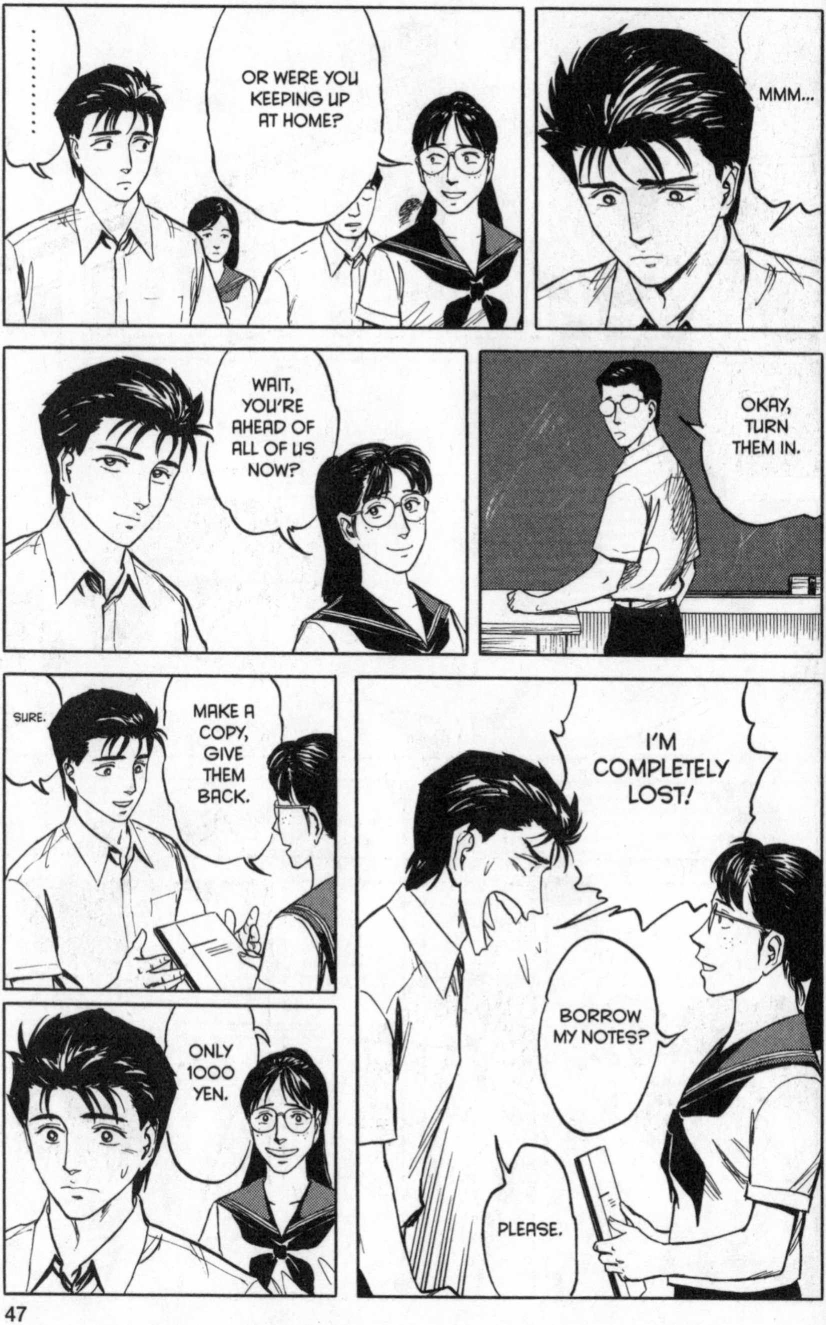
MMM...
OR WERE YOU KEEPING UP AT HOME?
....
OKAY, TURN THEM IN.
WAIT, YOU'RE AHEAD OF ALL OF US NOW?
I'M COMPLETELY LOST!
BORROW MY NOTES?
PLEASE.
MAKE A COPY, GIVE THEM BACK.
SURE.
ONLY 1000 YEN.

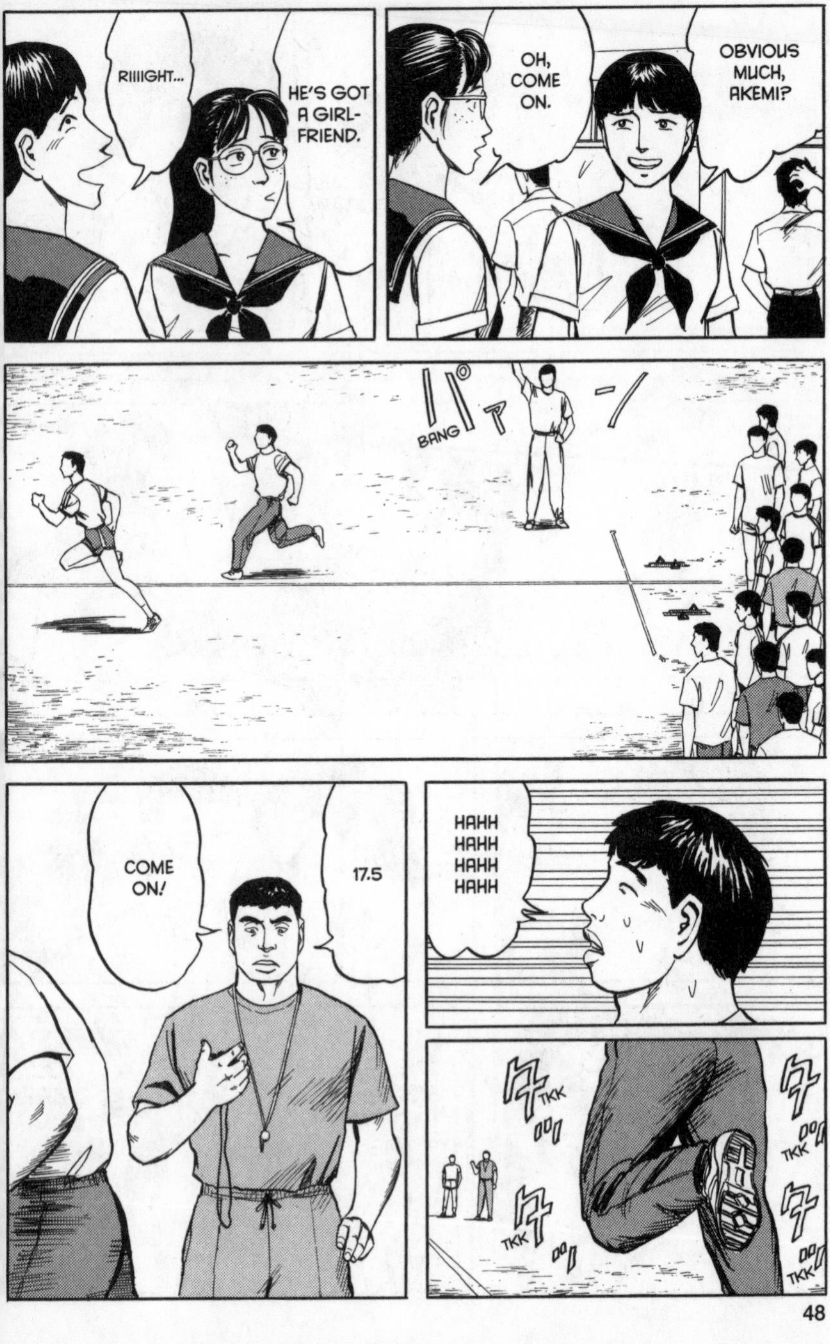
OBVIOUS MUCH, AKEMI?
OH, COME ON.
HE'S GOT A GIRL-FRIEND.
RIIIGHT...
BANG
HAHH HAHH HAHH HAHH
TKK
TKK
TKK
TKK
17.5
COME ON!

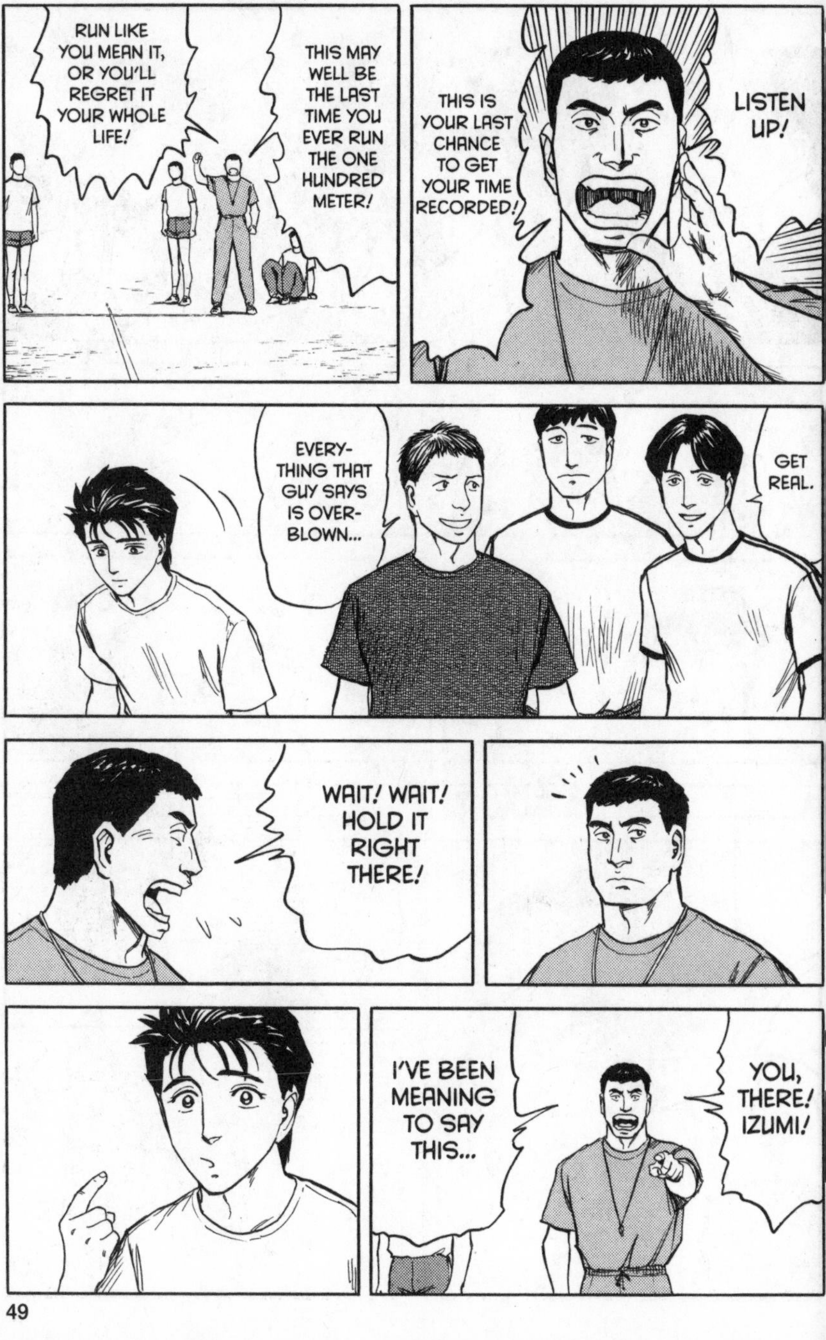
LISTEN UP!
THIS IS YOUR LAST CHANCE TO GET YOUR TIME RECORDED!
THIS MAY WELL BE THE LAST TIME YOU EVER RUN THE ONE HUNDRED METER!
RUN LIKE YOU MEAN IT, OR YOU'LL REGRET IT YOUR WHOLE LIFE!
GET REAL.
EVERYTHING THAT GUY SAYS IS OVERBLOWN...
WAIT! WAIT! HOLD IT RIGHT THERE!
YOU, THERE! IZUMI!
I'VE BEEN MEANING TO SAY THIS...

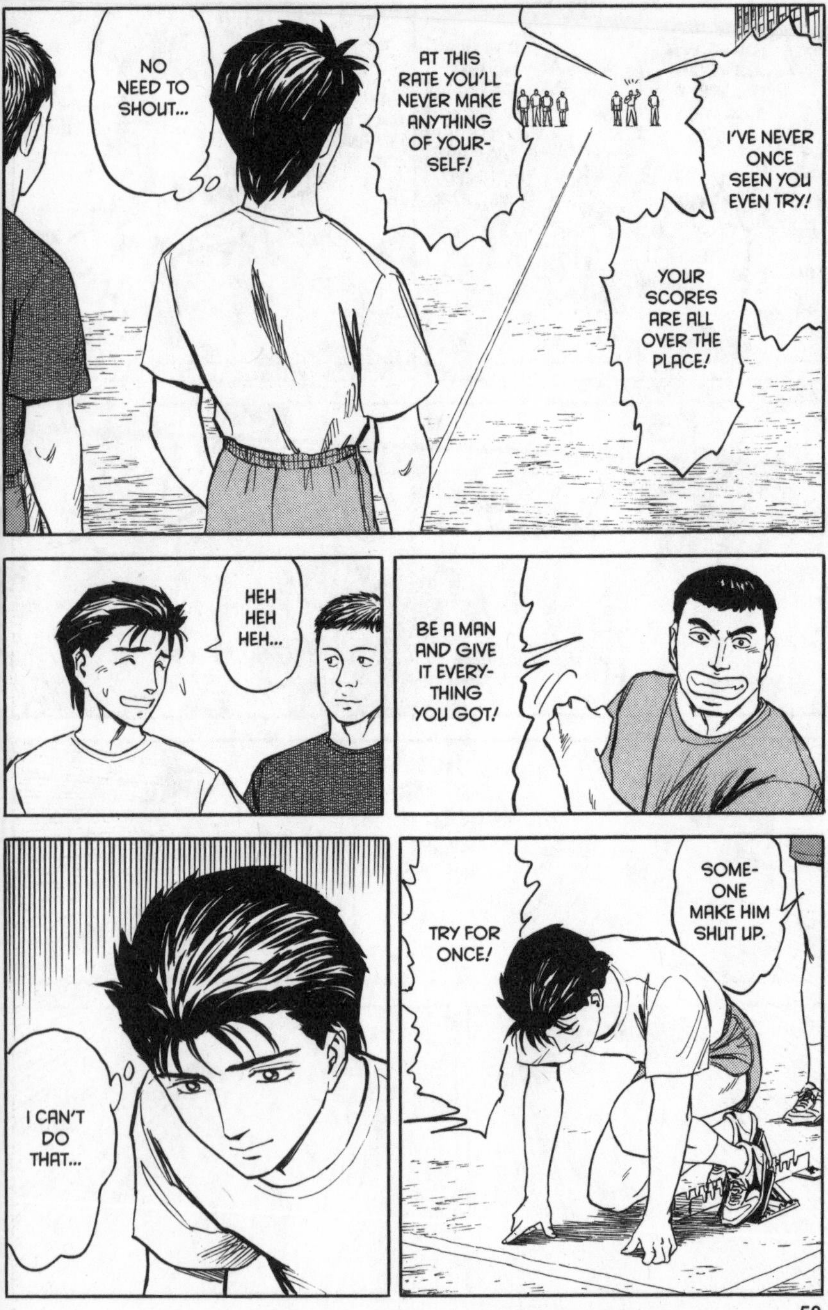
I'VE NEVER ONCE SEEN YOU EVEN TRY!
YOUR SCORES ARE ALL OVER THE PLACE!
AT THIS RATE YOU'LL NEVER MAKE ANYTHING OF YOUR-SELF!
NO NEED TO SHOUT...
BE A MAN AND GIVE IT EVERY-THING YOU GOT!
HEH HEH HEH...
SOME-ONE MAKE HIM SHUT UP.
TRY FOR ONCE!
I CAN'T DO THAT...

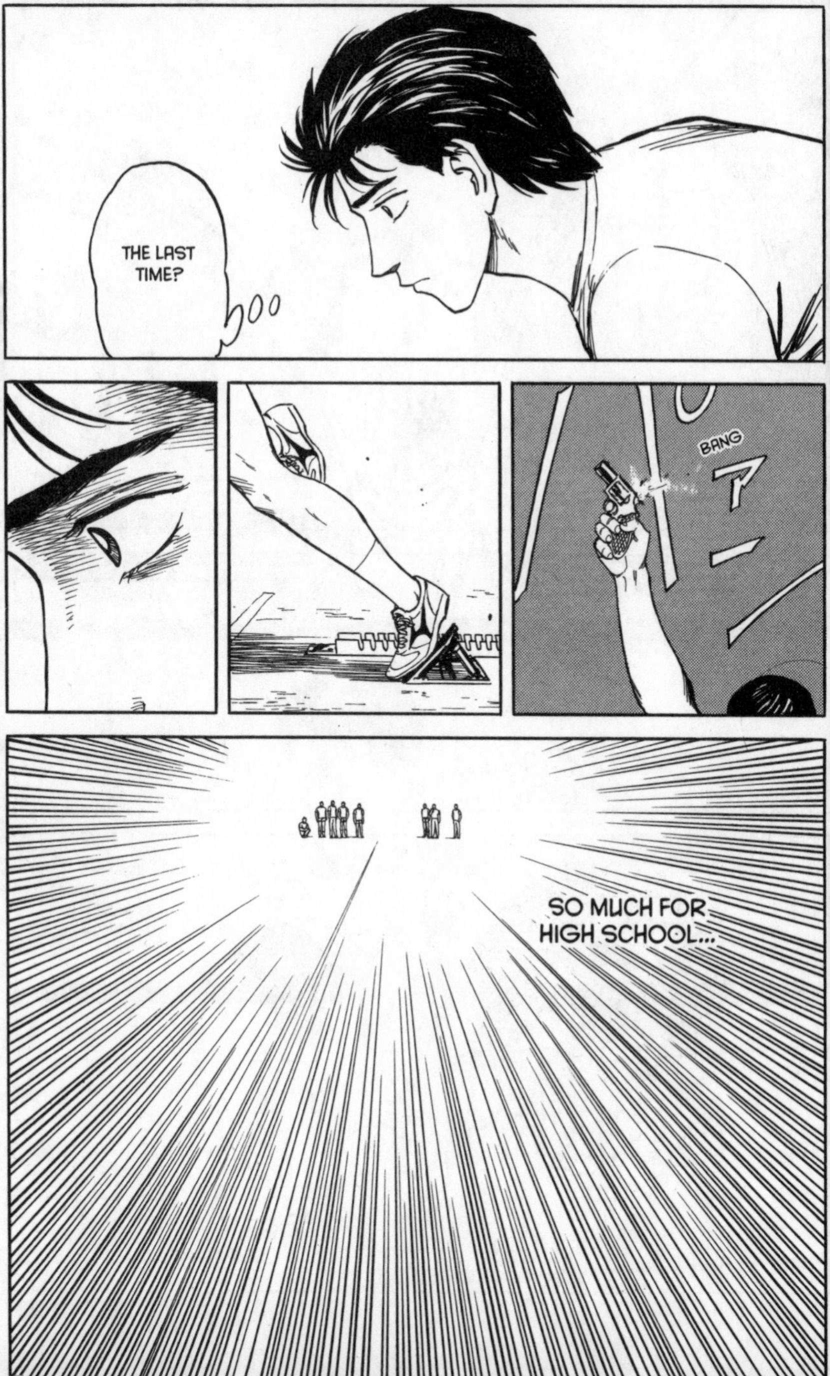
THE LAST TIME?
BANG
アー
SO MUCH FOR HIGH SCHOOL...

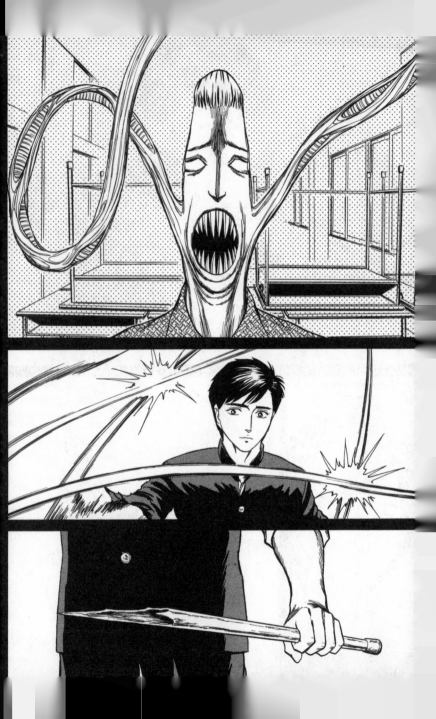

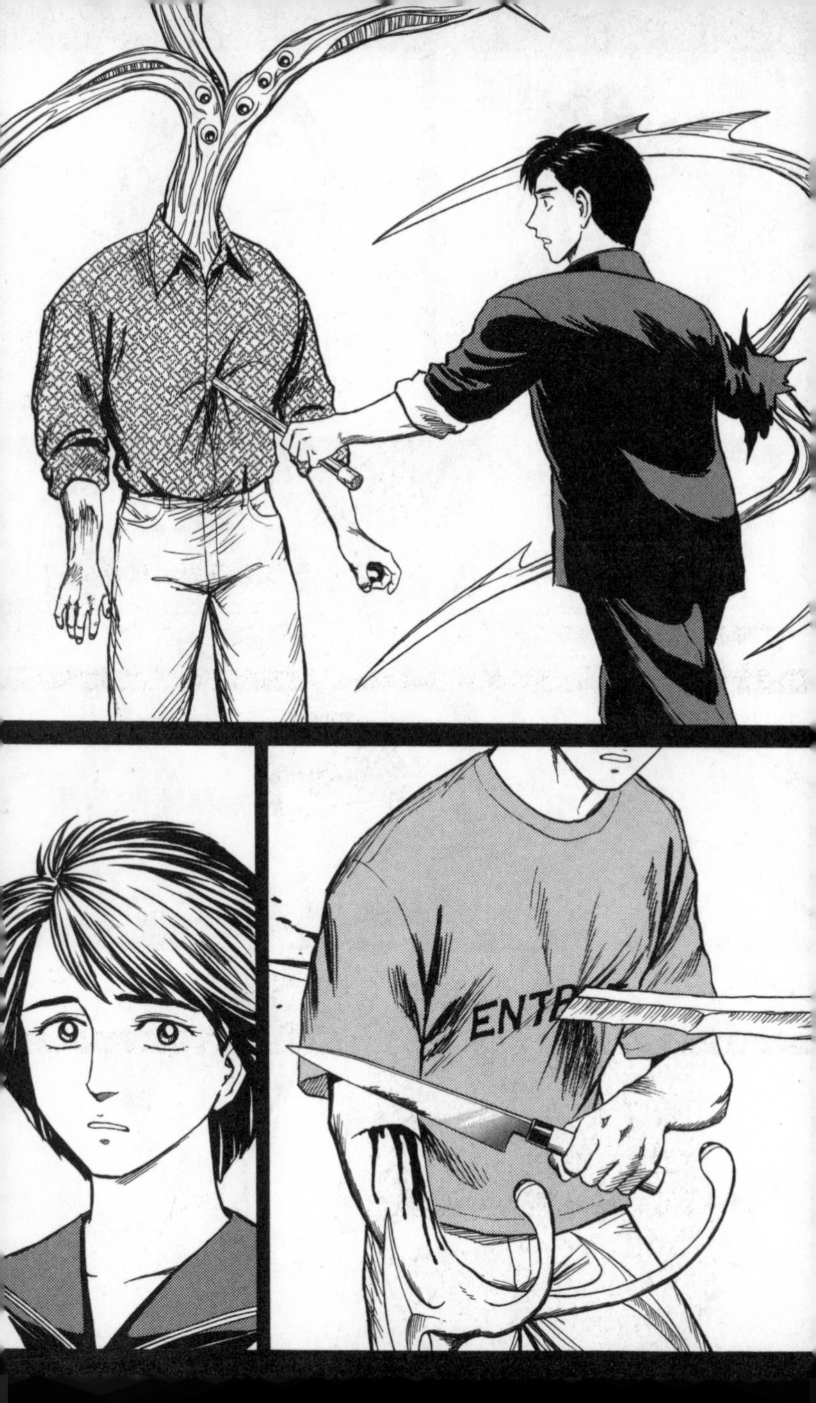

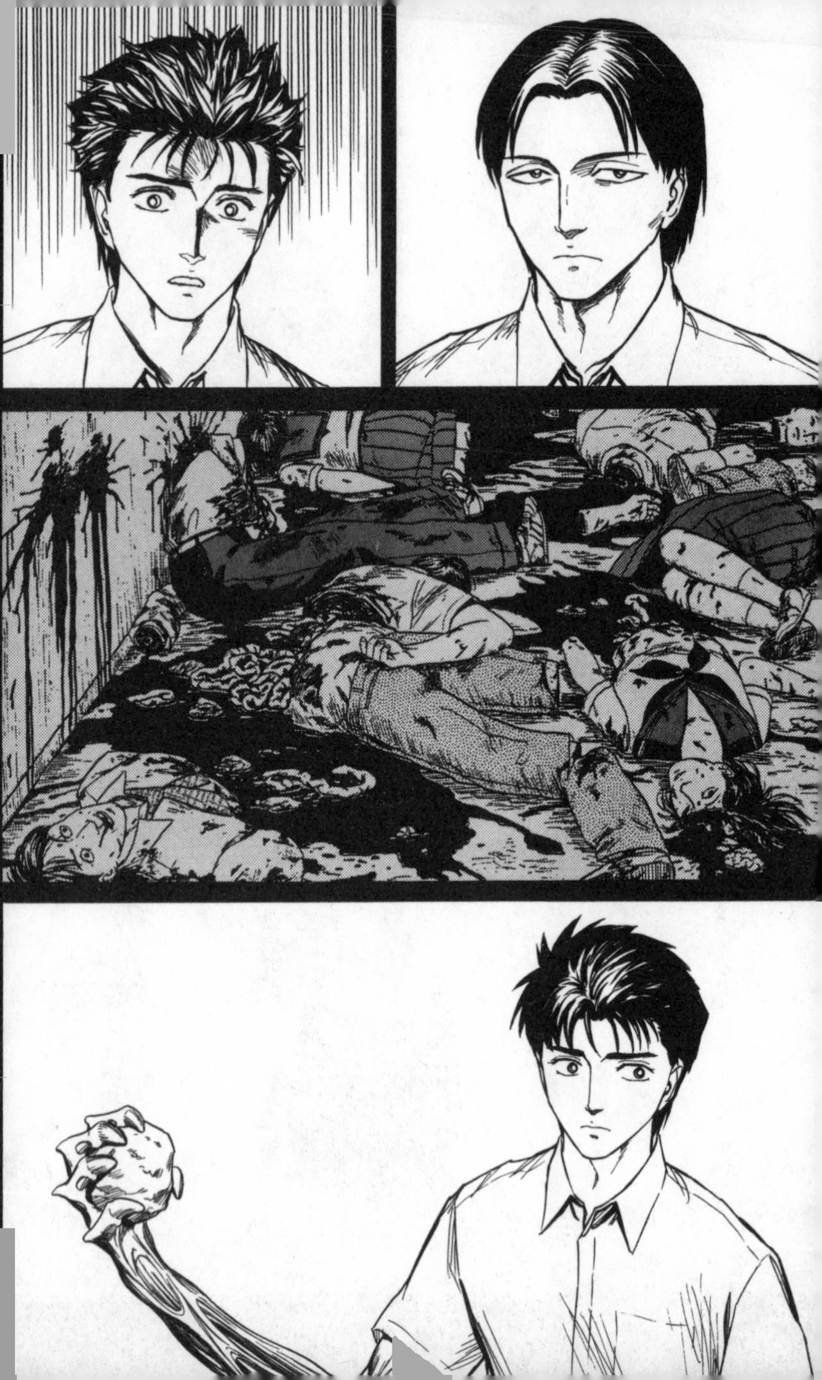

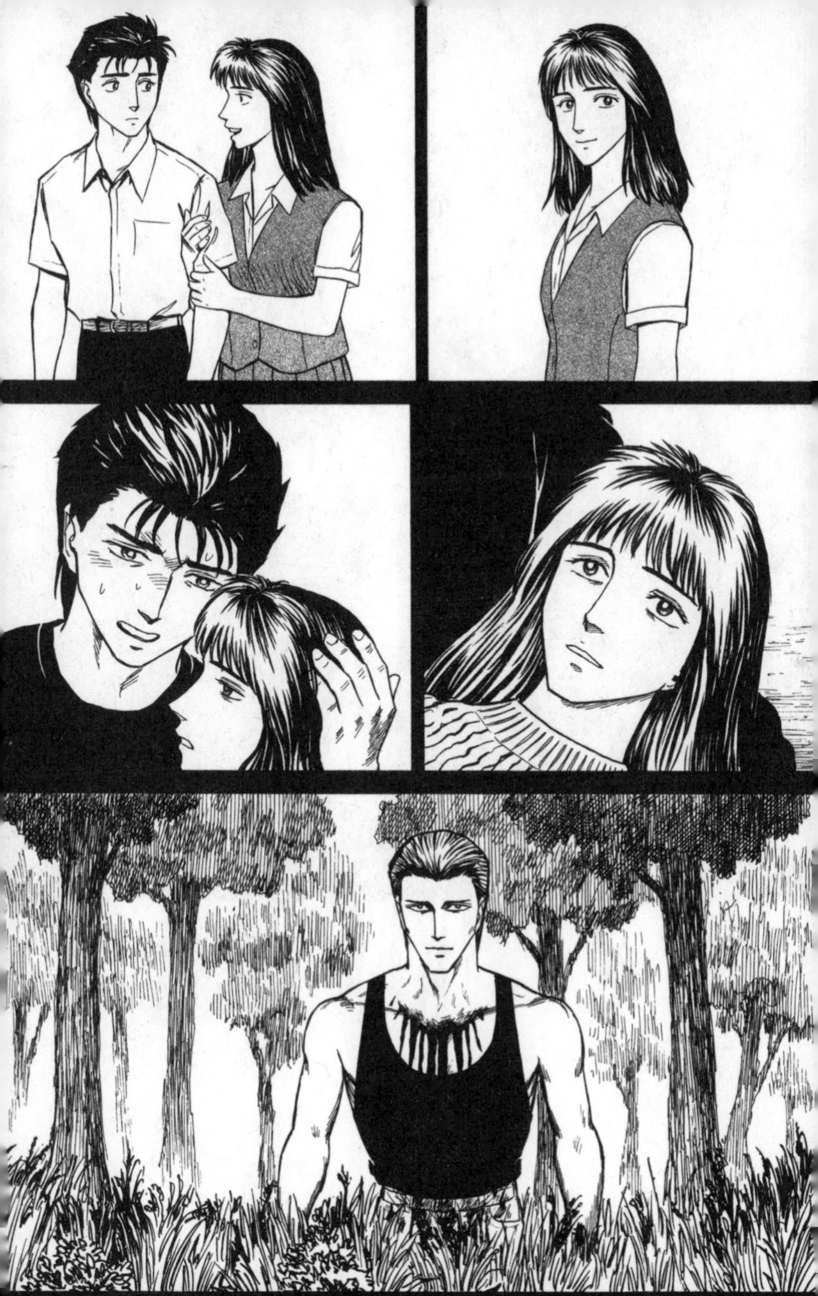

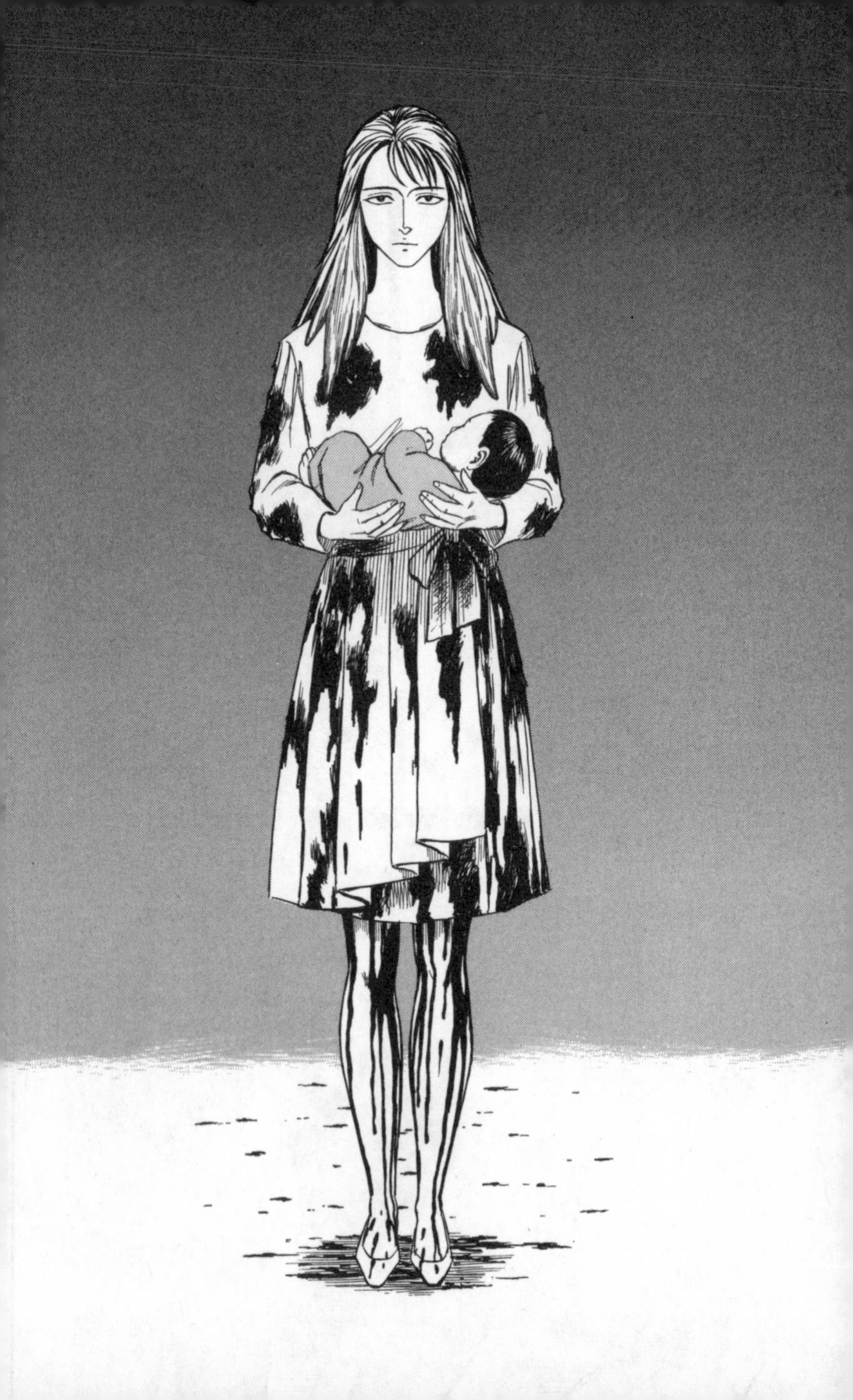

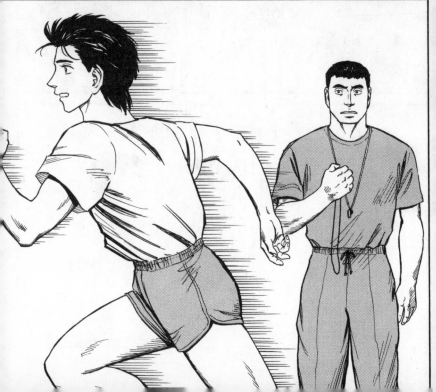

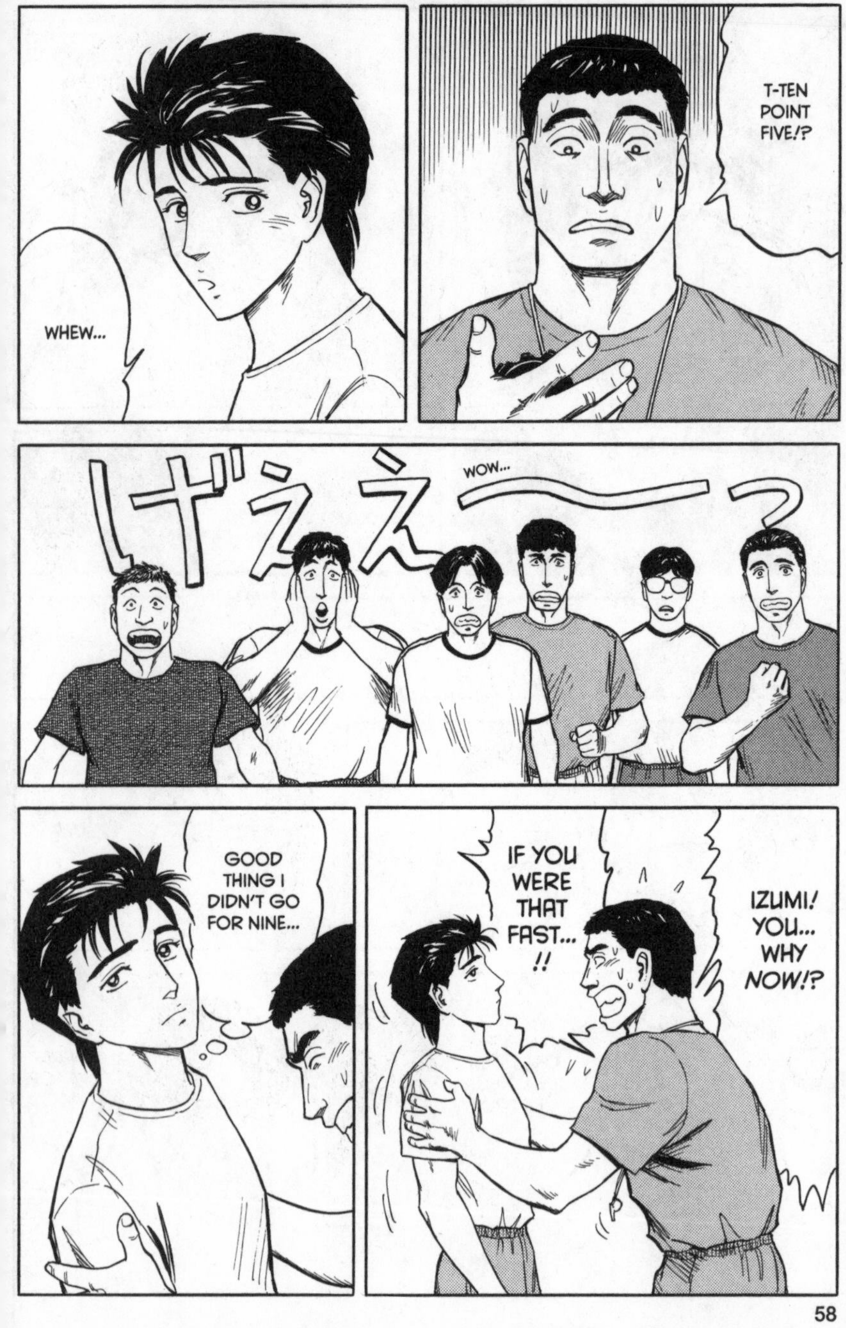
T-TEN POINT FIVE!?
WHEW...
げえぇーっ
WOW...
IZUMI! YOU... WHY NOW!?
IF YOU WERE THAT FAST...
!!
GOOD THING I DIDN'T GO FOR NINE...

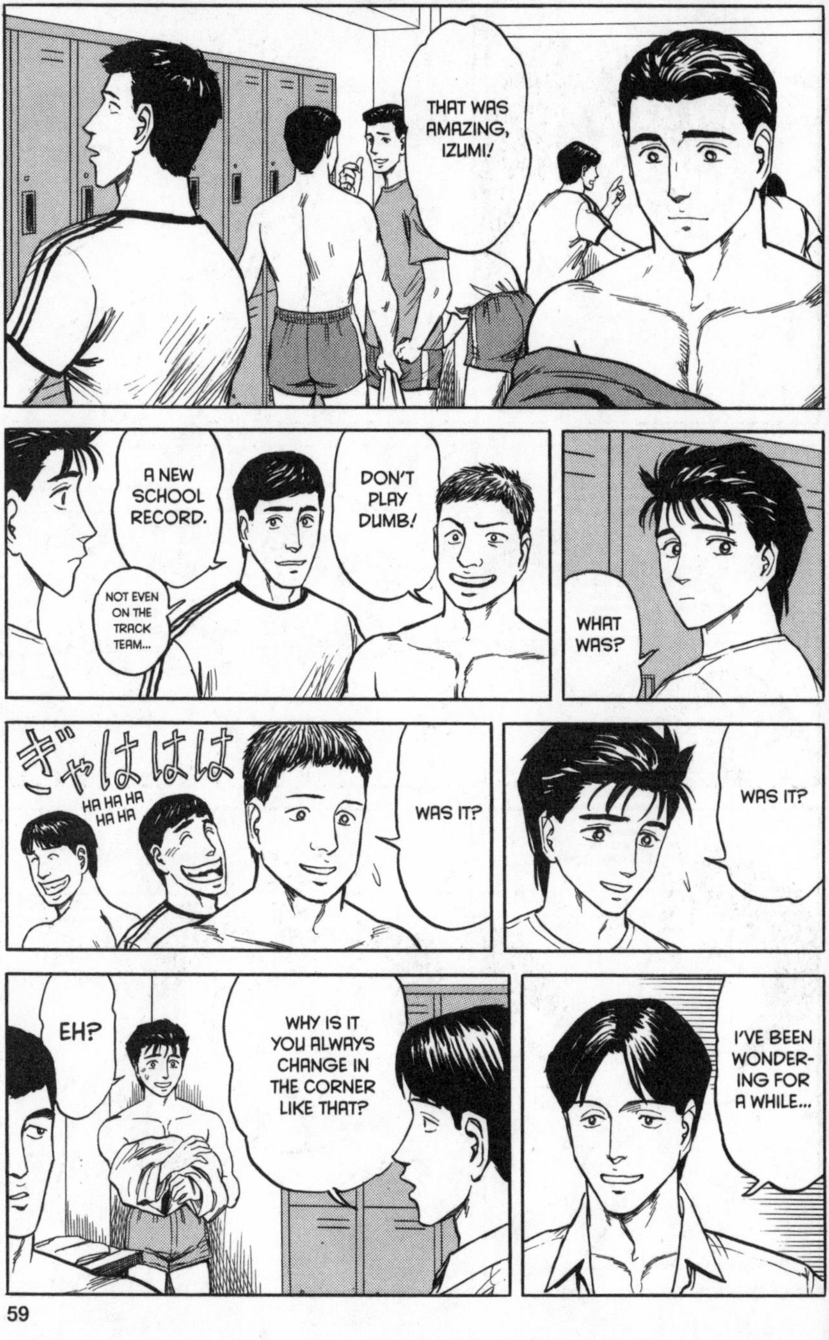
THAT WAS AMAZING, IZUMI!
WHAT WAS?
DON'T PLAY DUMB!
A NEW SCHOOL RECORD.
NOT EVEN ON THE TRACK TEAM...
WAS IT?
WAS IT?
ぎゃははは
HA HA HA HA HA
I'VE BEEN WONDER-ING FOR A WHILE...
WHY IS IT YOU ALWAYS CHANGE IN THE CORNER LIKE THAT?
EH?

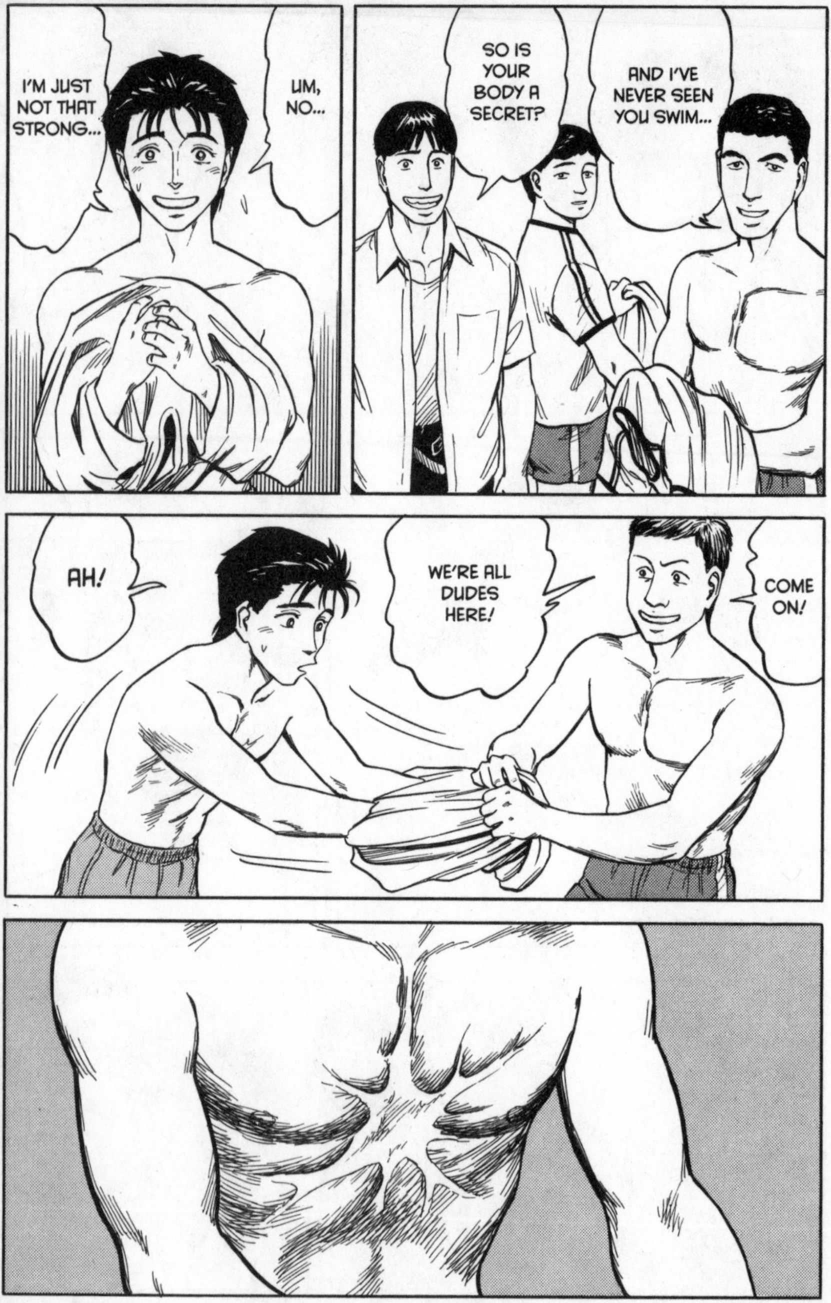
AND I'VE NEVER SEEN YOU SWIM...
SO IS YOUR BODY A SECRET?
UM, NO...
I'M JUST NOT THAT STRONG...
COME ON!
WE'RE ALL DUDES HERE!
AH!

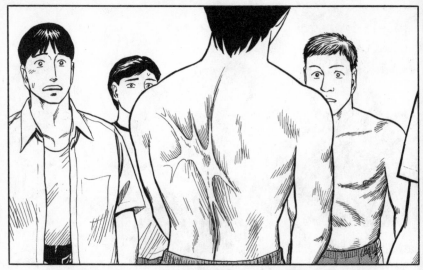

E-EXCUSE
ME.

NAH...

WELL...

OH,
UM...

SMACK

TWIT.

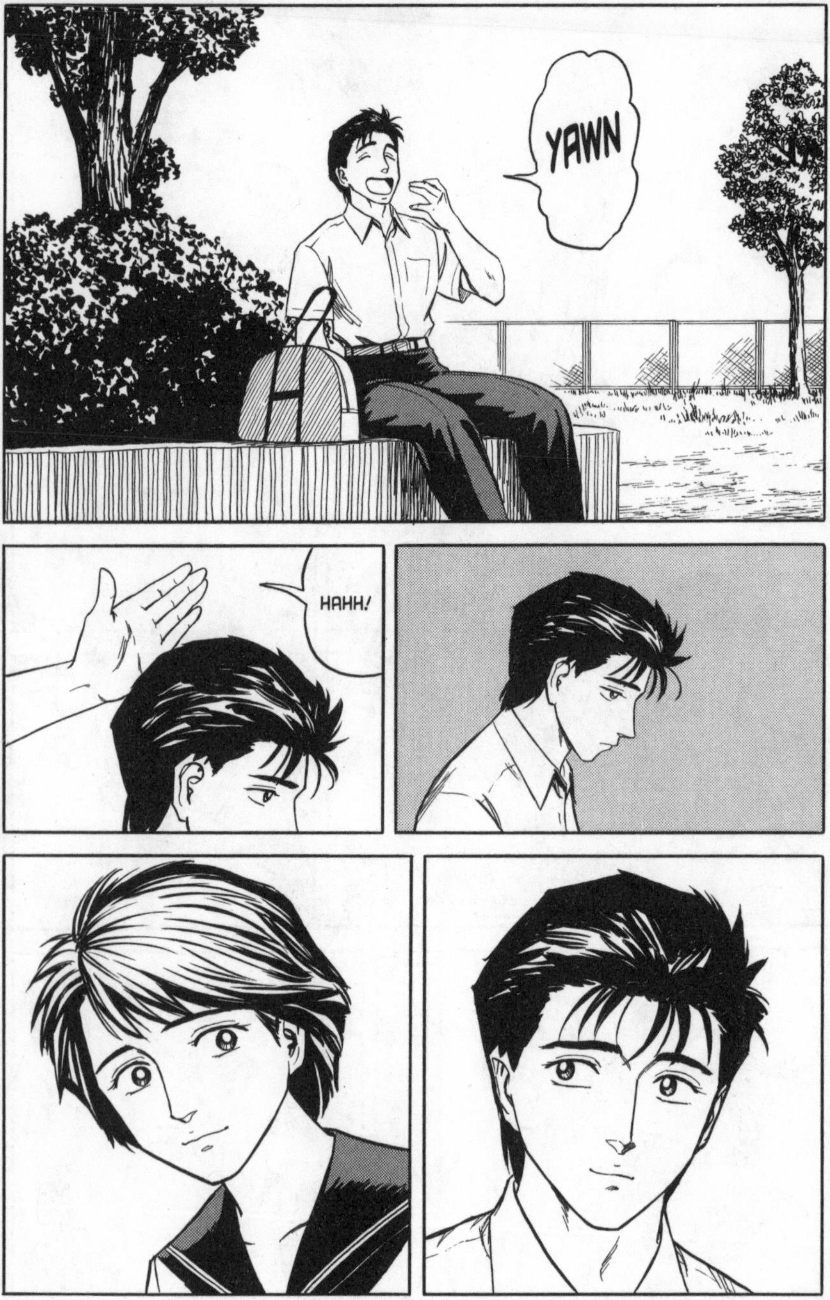
YAWN
HAHH!

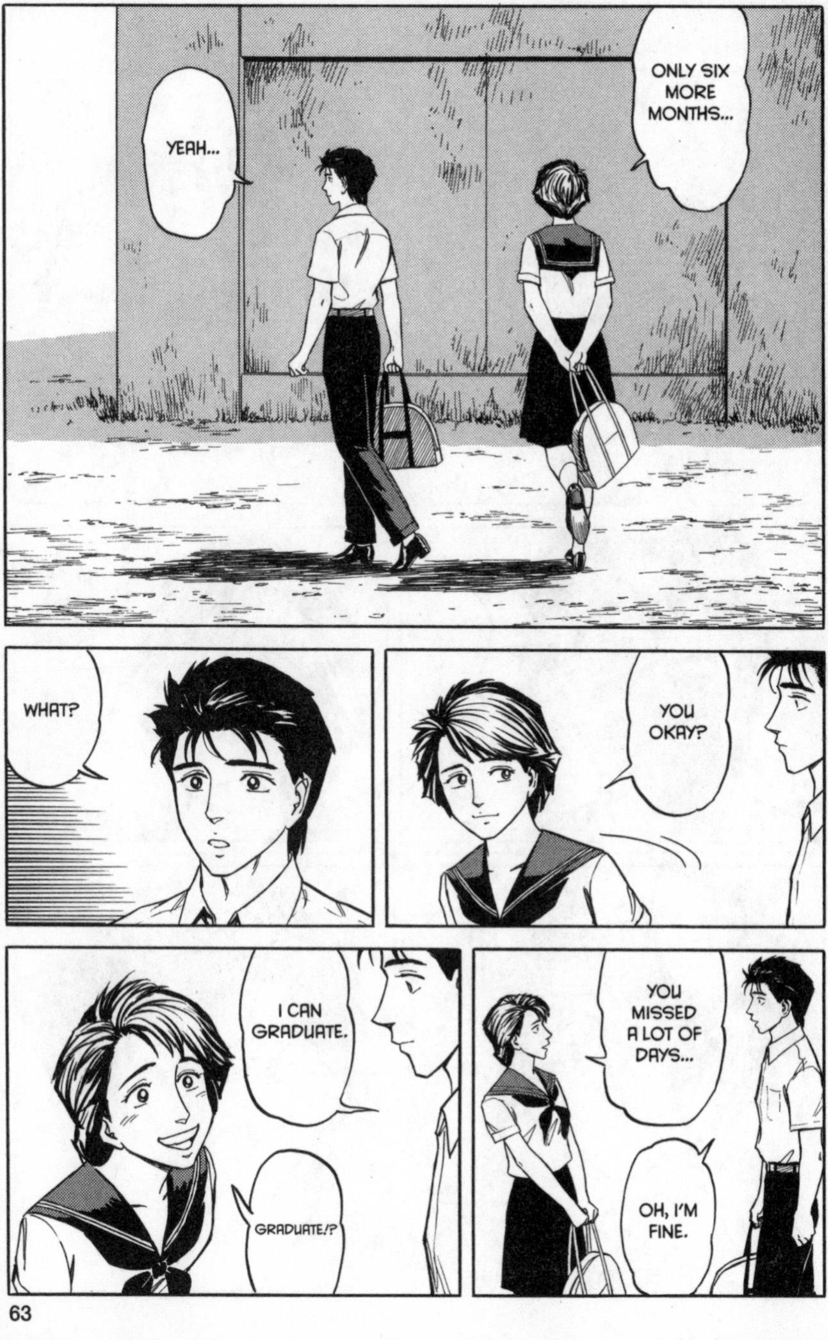
ONLY SIX MORE MONTHS...
YEAH...
YOU OKAY?
WHAT?
YOU MISSED A LOT OF DAYS...
OH, I'M FINE.
I CAN GRADUATE.
GRADUATE!?

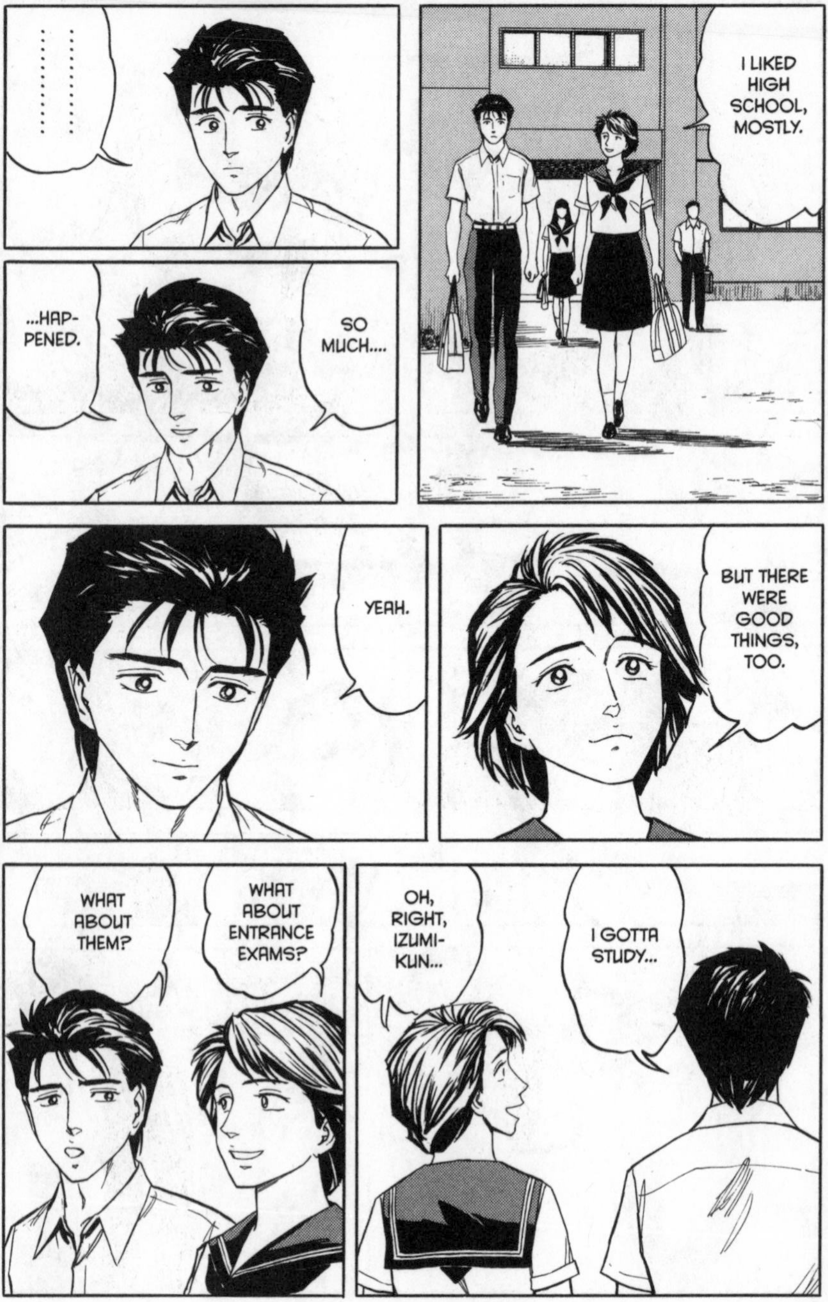
I LIKED HIGH SCHOOL, MOSTLY.
......
SO MUCH....
...HAP-PENED.
BUT THERE WERE GOOD THINGS, TOO.
YEAH.
I GOTTA STUDY...
OH, RIGHT, IZUMI-KUN...
WHAT ABOUT ENTRANCE EXAMS?
WHAT ABOUT THEM?

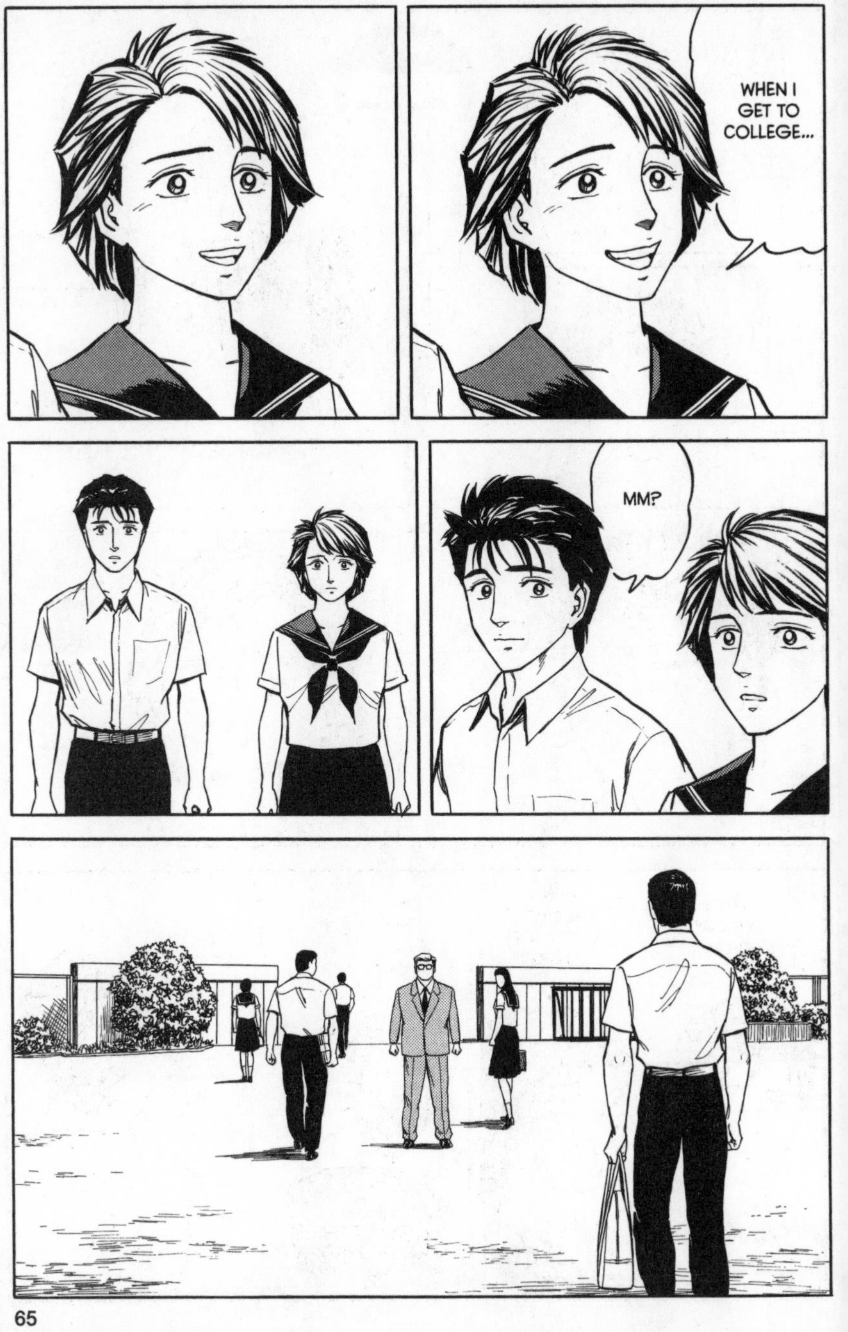
WHEN I GET TO COLLEGE...
MM?

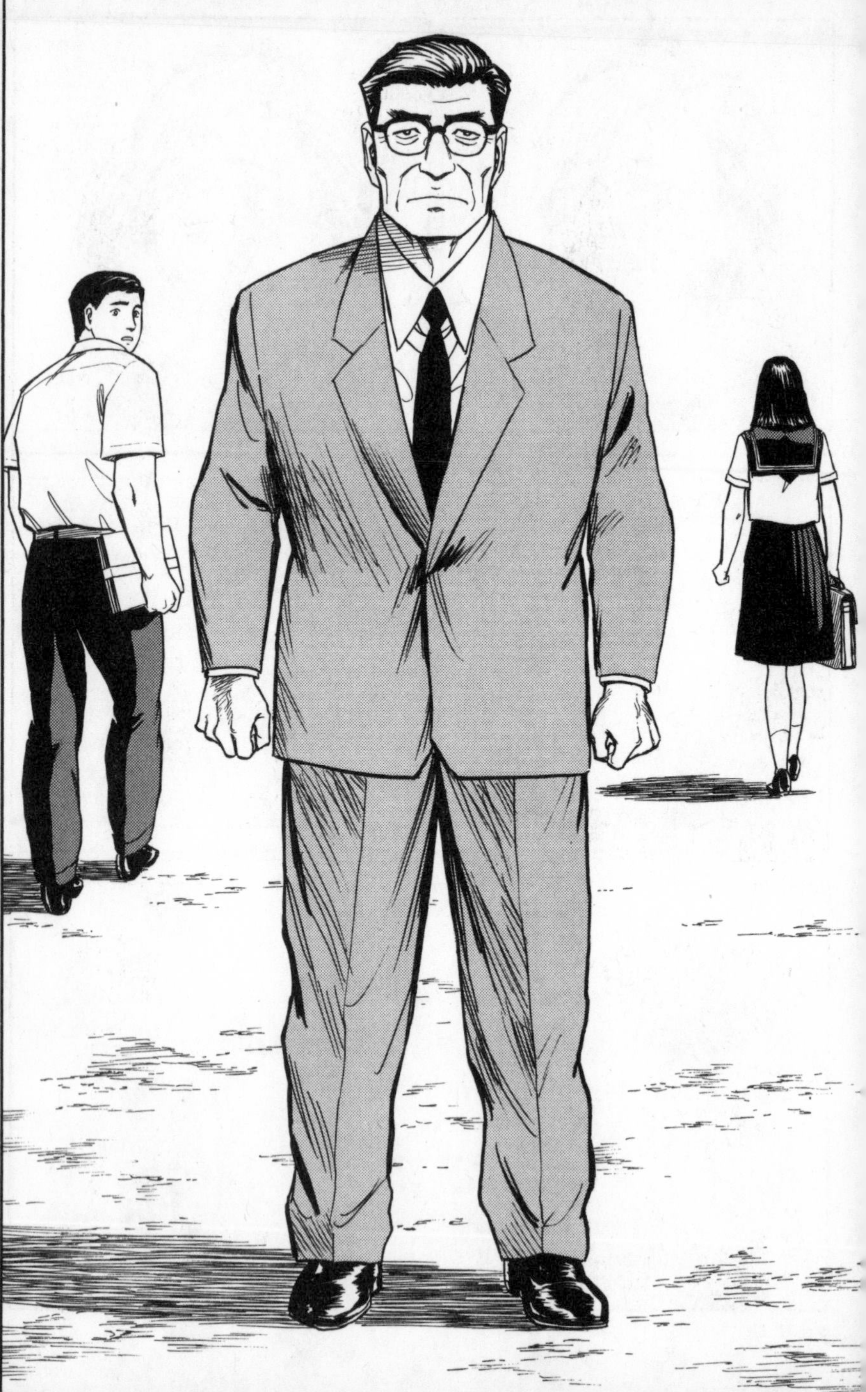

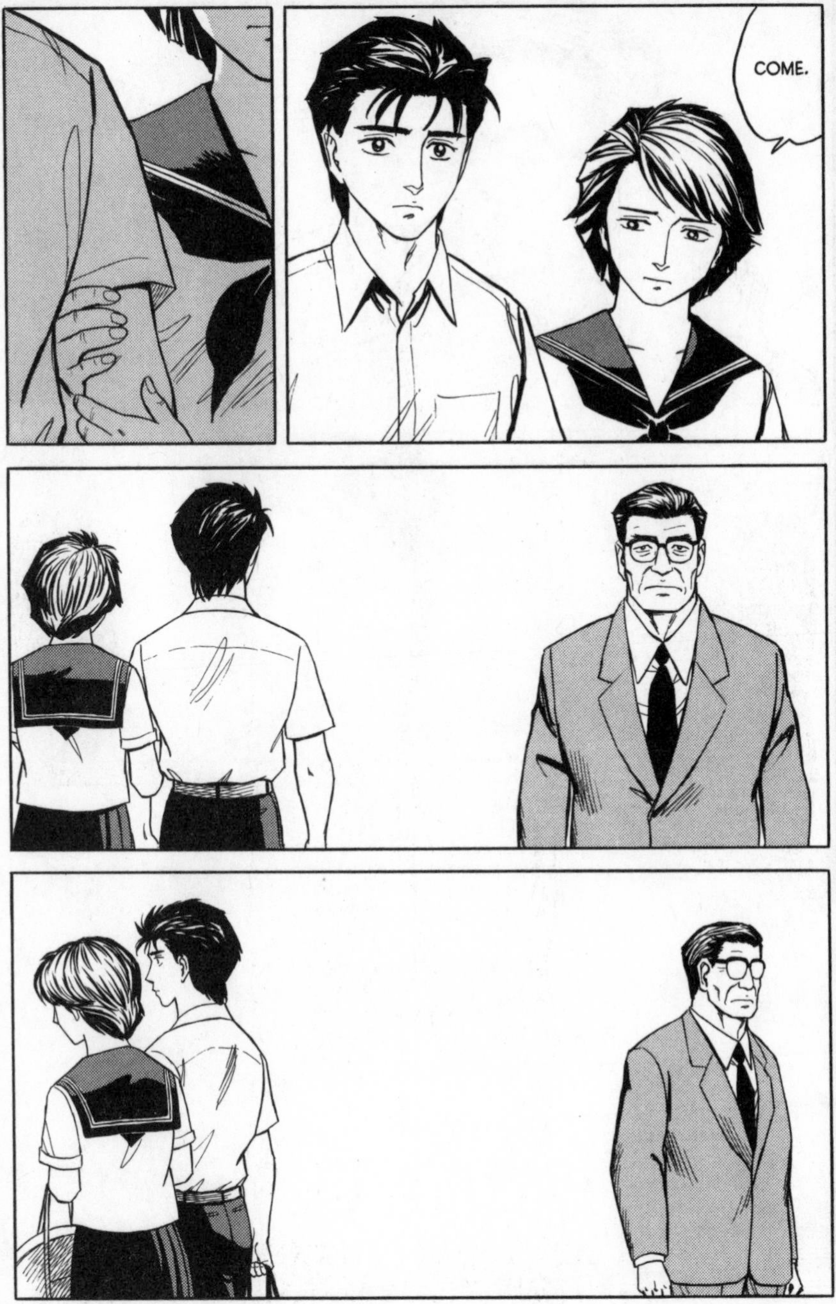
COME.

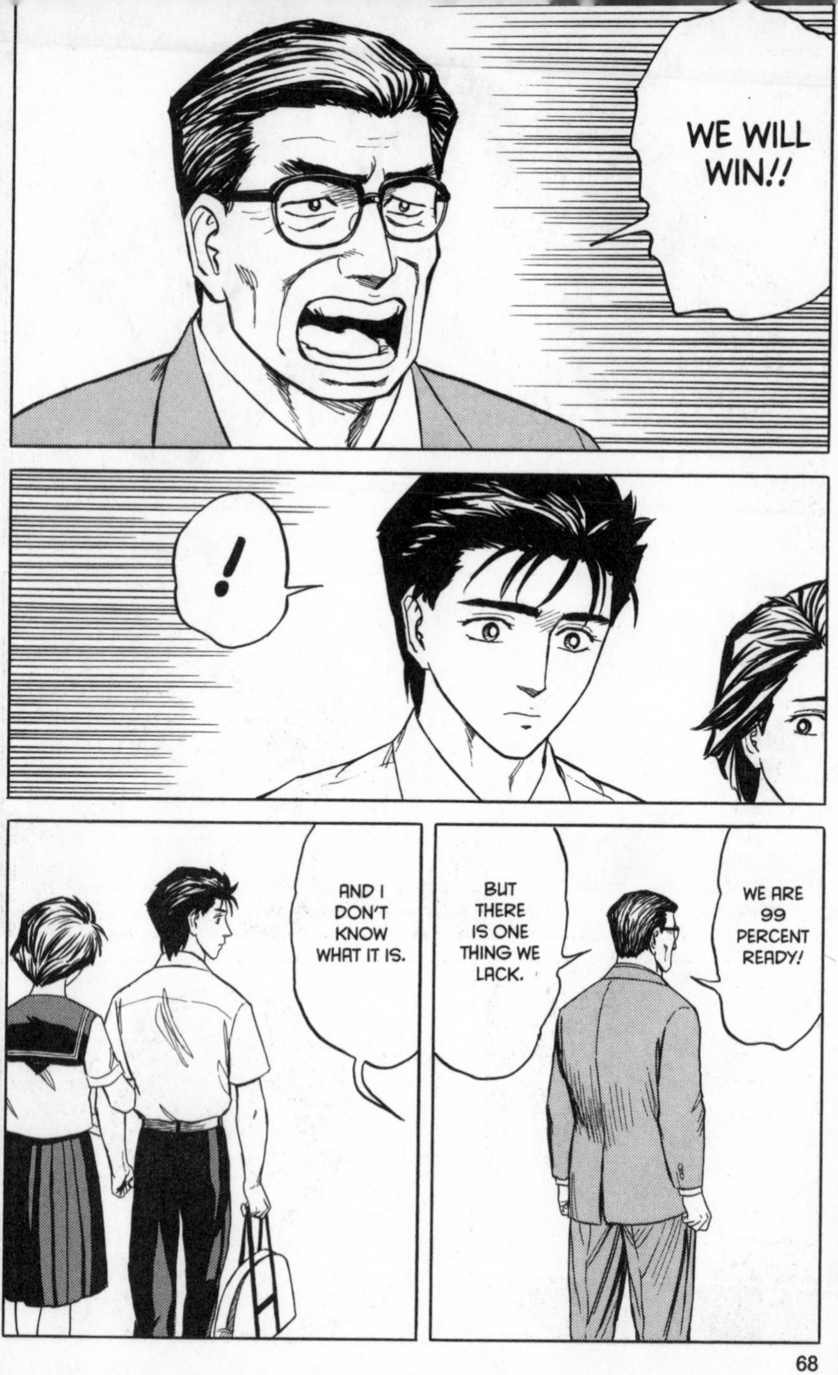
WE WILL WIN!!
!
WE ARE 99 PERCENT READY!
BUT THERE IS ONE THING WE LACK.
AND I DON'T KNOW WHAT IT IS.

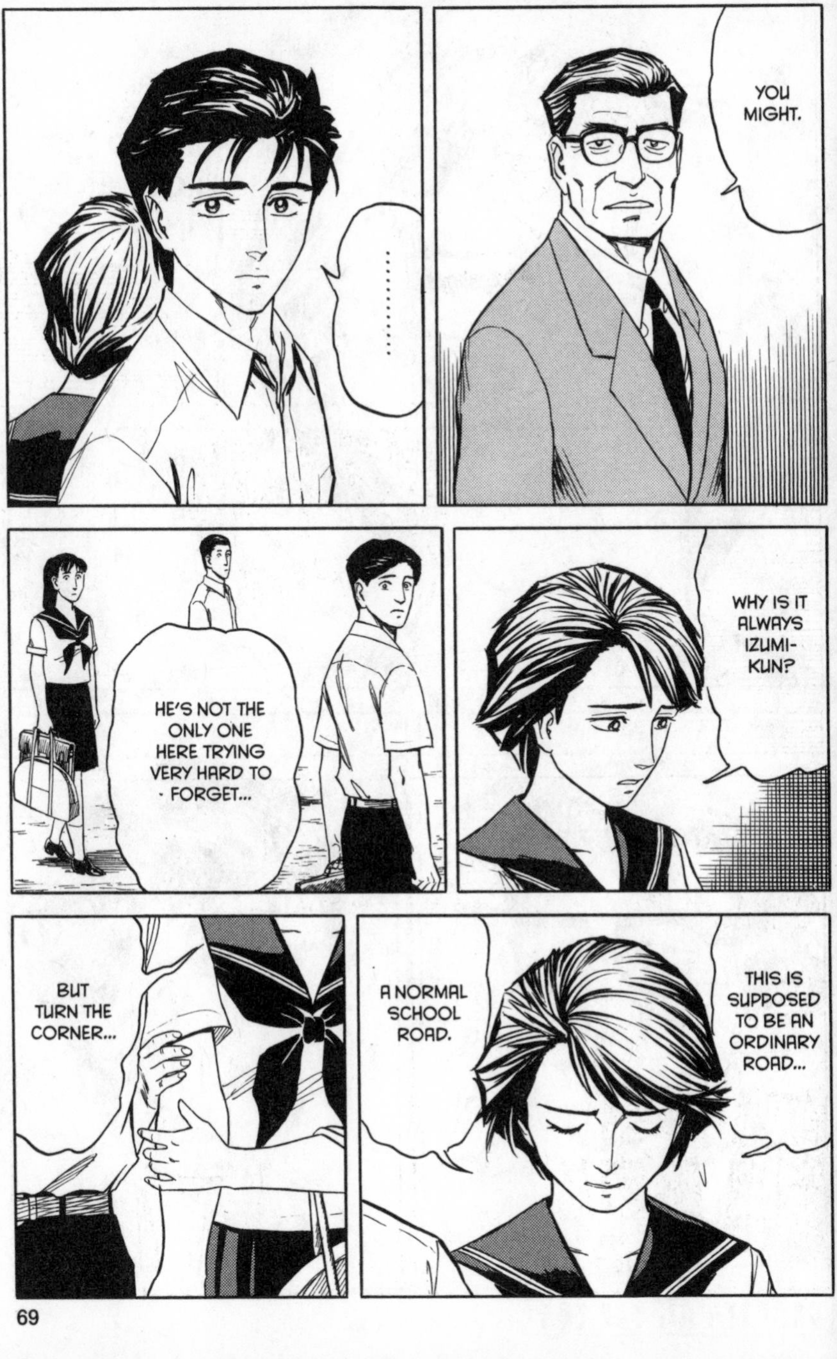
YOU MIGHT.
......
WHY IS IT ALWAYS IZUMI-KUN?
HE'S NOT THE ONLY ONE HERE TRYING VERY HARD TO FORGET...
THIS IS SUPPOSED TO BE AN ORDINARY ROAD...
A NORMAL SCHOOL ROAD.
BUT TURN THE CORNER...

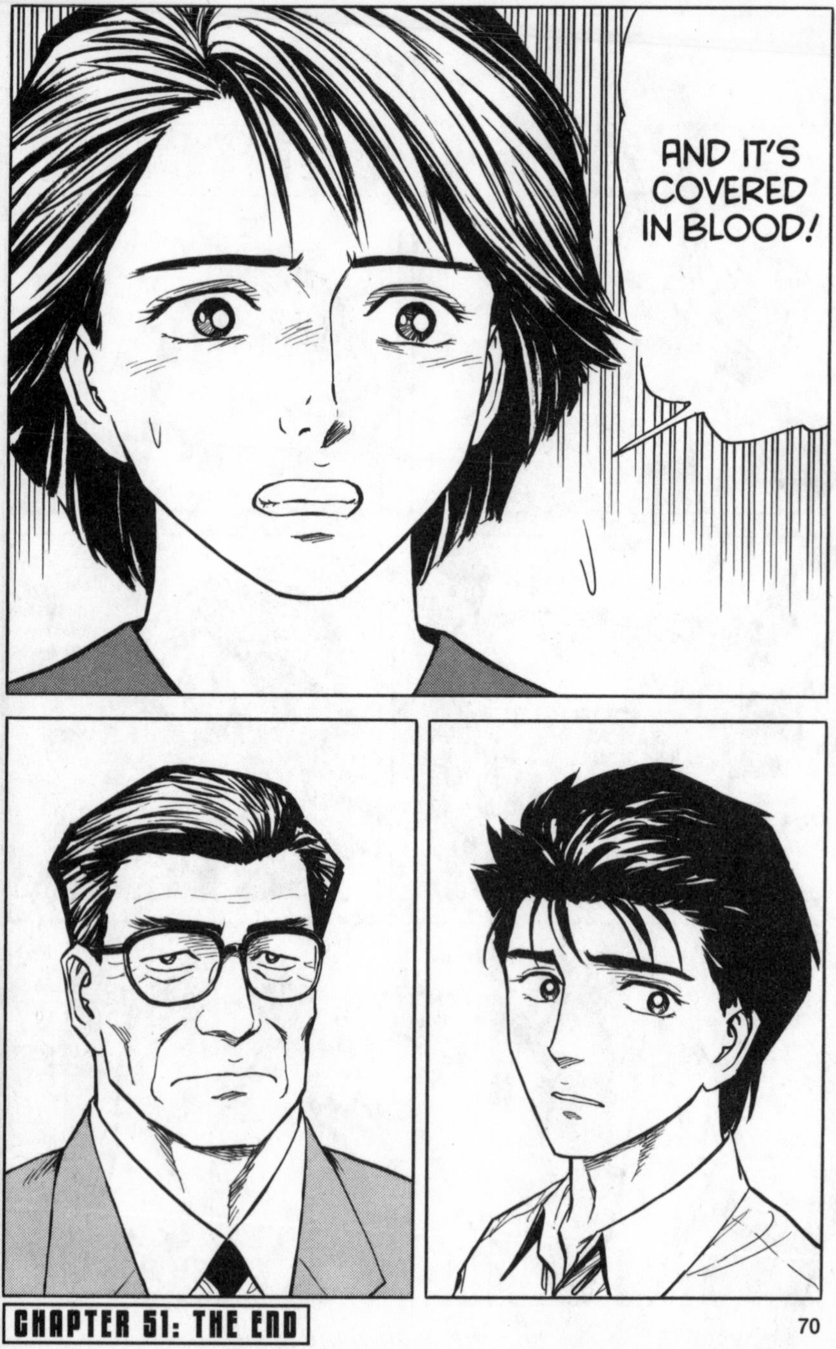
AND IT'S COVERED IN BLOOD!

CHAPTER 51: THE END

CHAPTER 52: SURROUNDED

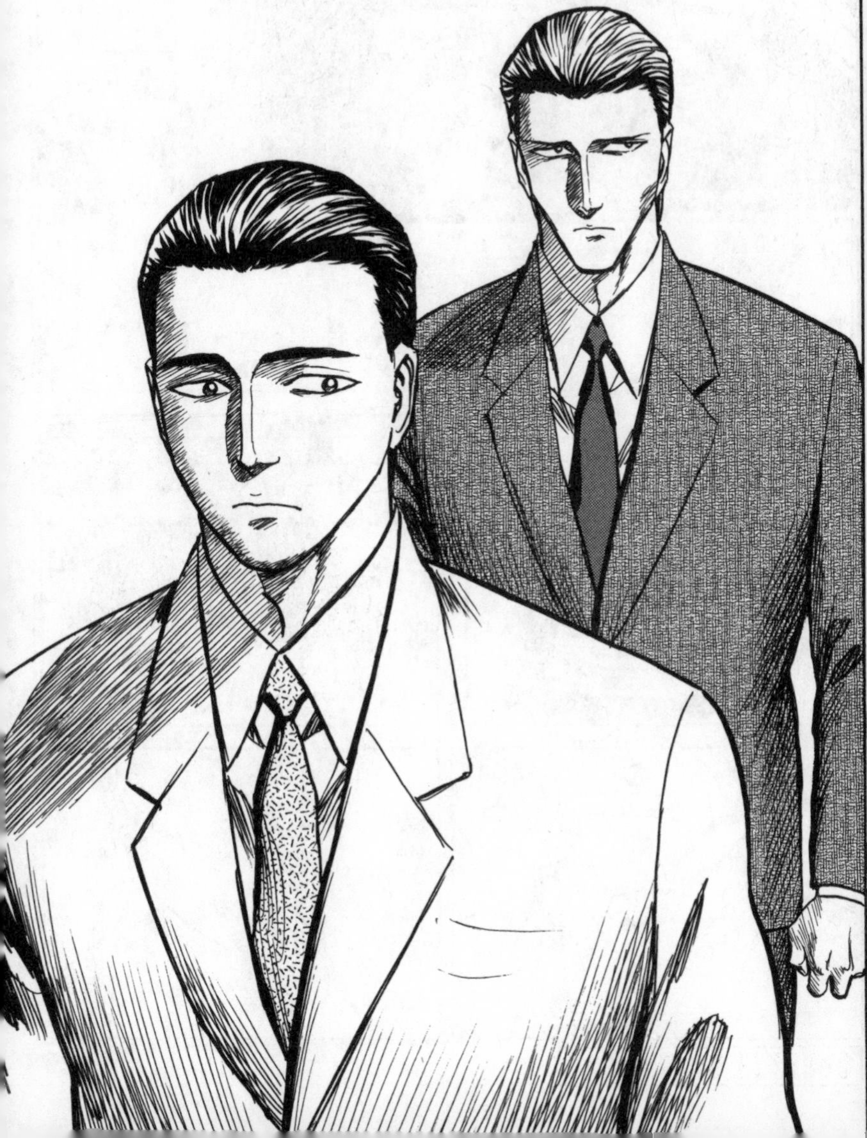

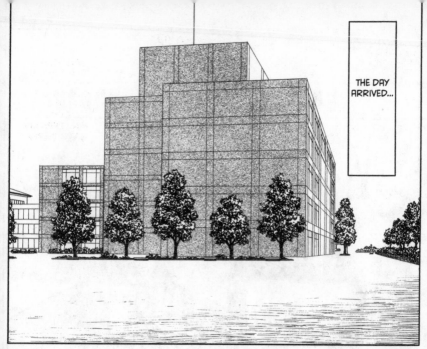

THE DAY ARRIVED...

VROOM...

SCREECH

TKK TKK

72

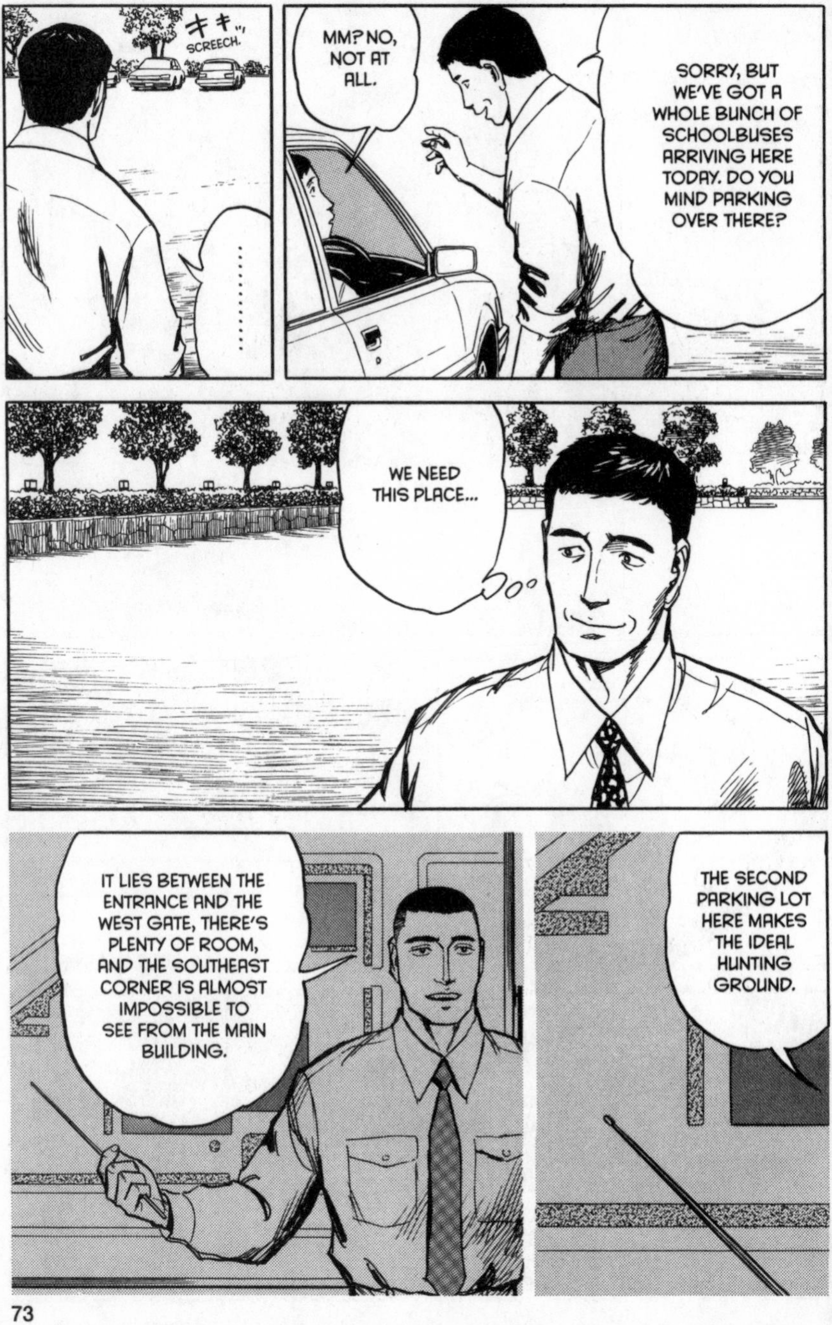

SORRY, BUT WE'VE GOT A WHOLE BUNCH OF SCHOOLBUSES ARRIVING HERE TODAY. DO YOU MIND PARKING OVER THERE?
MM? NO, NOT AT ALL.
キキ
SCREECH.
......
WE NEED THIS PLACE...
THE SECOND PARKING LOT HERE MAKES THE IDEAL HUNTING GROUND.
IT LIES BETWEEN THE ENTRANCE AND THE WEST GATE, THERE'S PLENTY OF ROOM, AND THE SOUTHEAST CORNER IS ALMOST IMPOSSIBLE TO SEE FROM THE MAIN BUILDING.

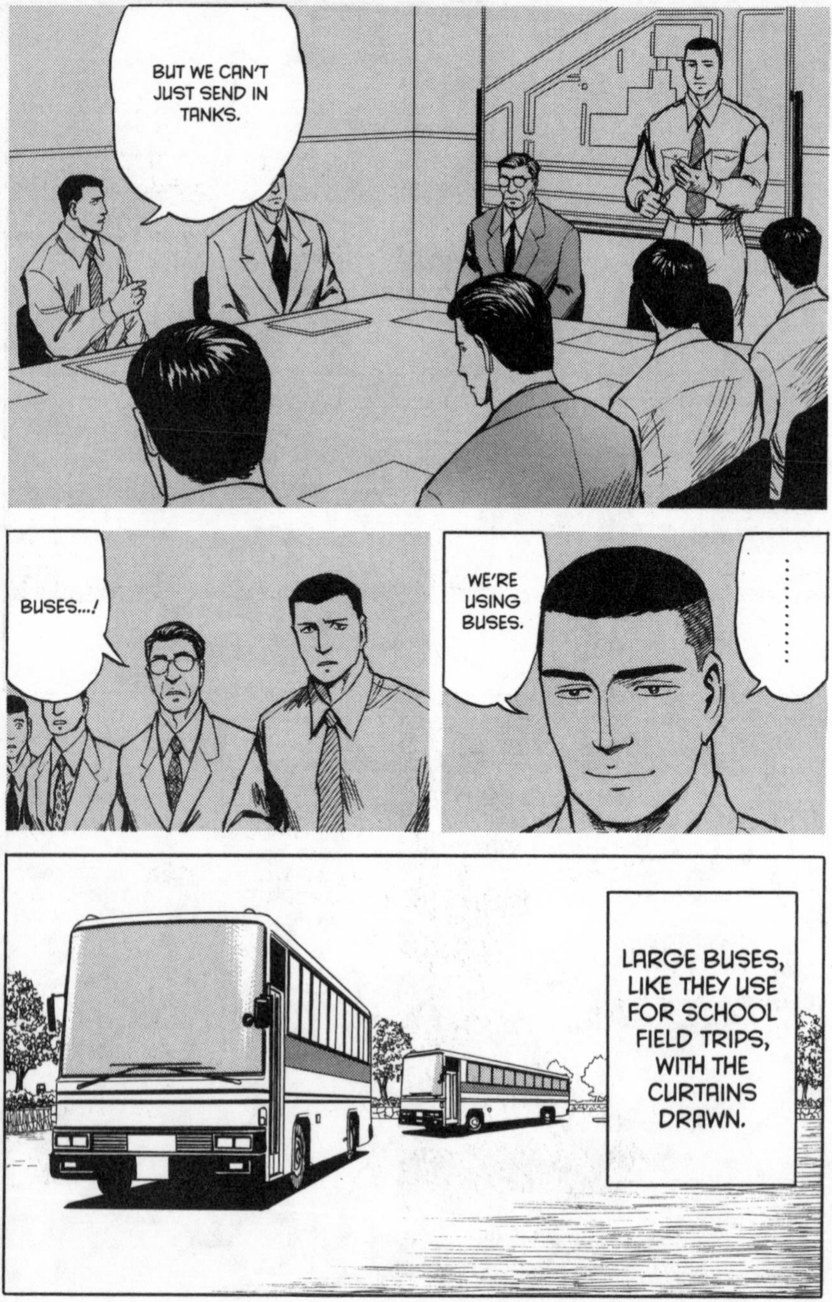
BUT WE CAN'T JUST SEND IN TANKS.
....
WE'RE USING BUSES.
BUSES...!
LARGE BUSES, LIKE THEY USE FOR SCHOOL FIELD TRIPS, WITH THE CURTAINS DRAWN.

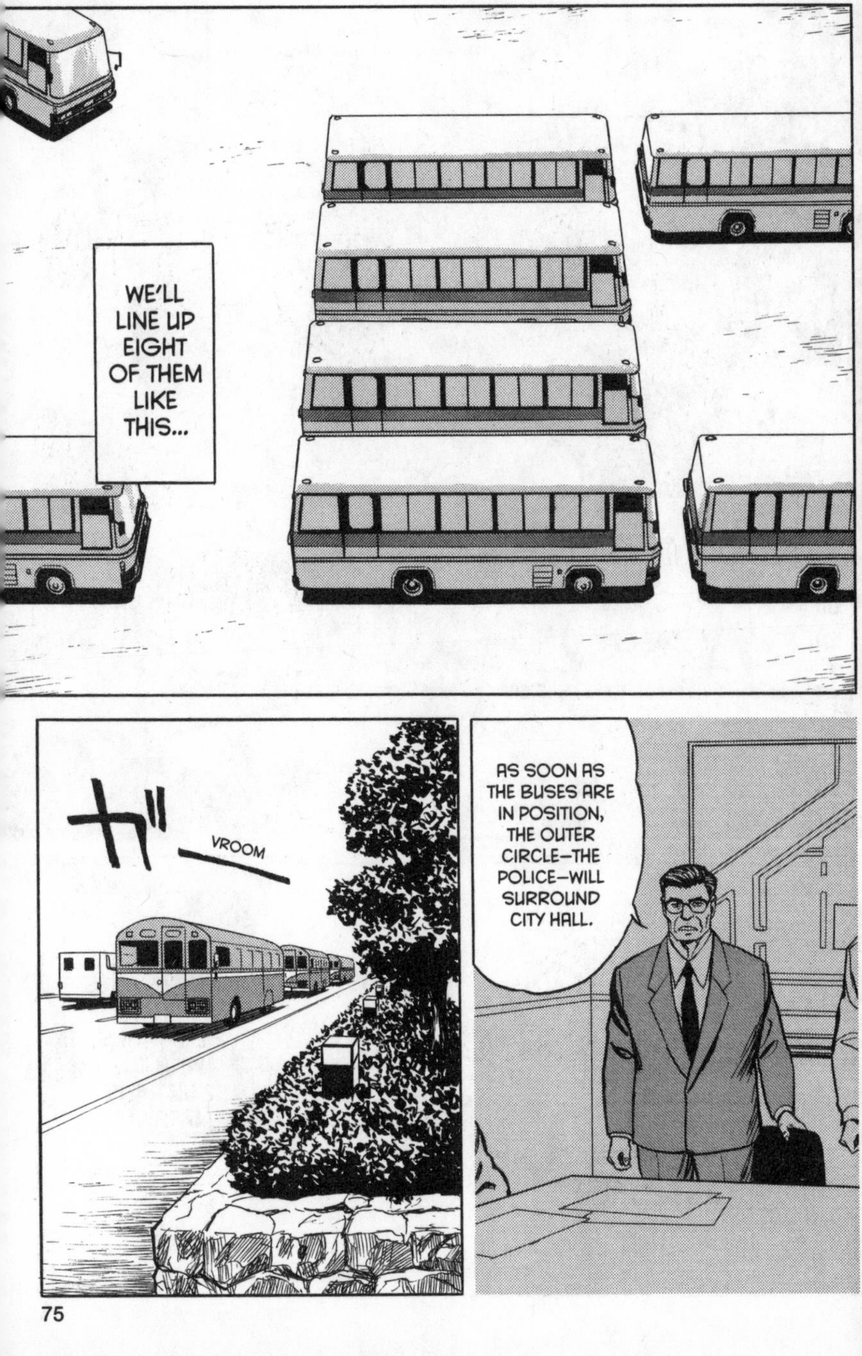
WE'LL LINE UP EIGHT OF THEM LIKE THIS...
AS SOON AS THE BUSES ARE IN POSITION, THE OUTER CIRCLE—THE POLICE—WILL SURROUND CITY HALL.
ガー
VROOM

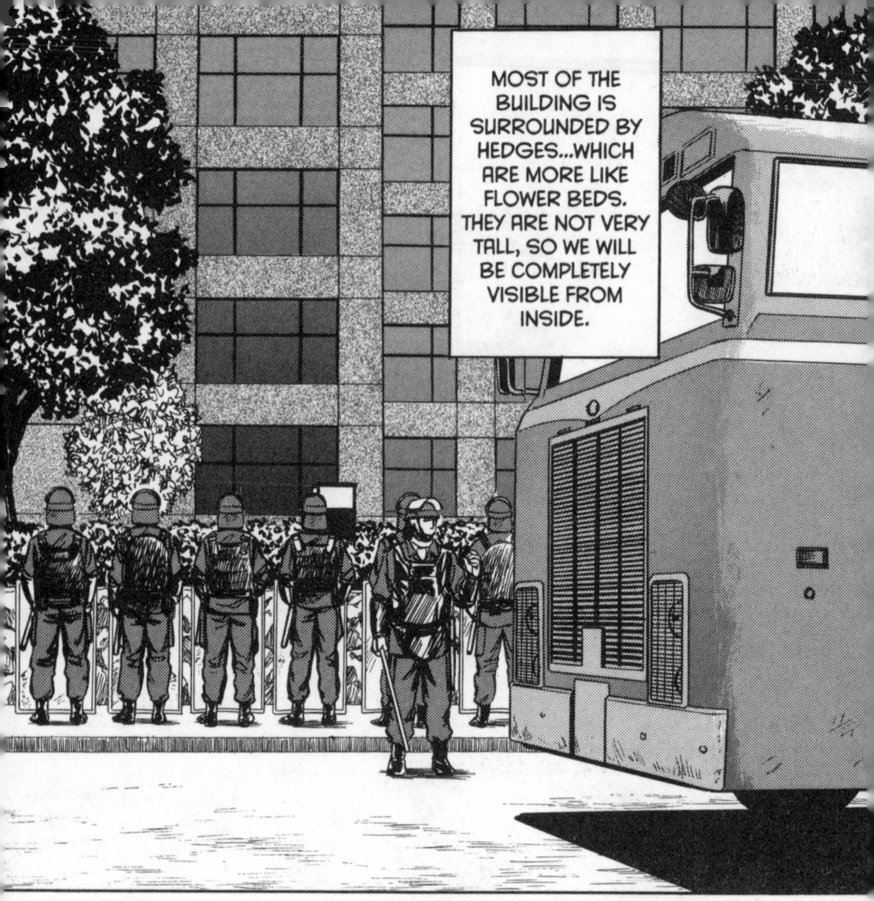
MOST OF THE BUILDING IS SURROUNDED BY HEDGES...WHICH ARE MORE LIKE FLOWER BEDS. THEY ARE NOT VERY TALL, SO WE WILL BE COMPLETELY VISIBLE FROM INSIDE.

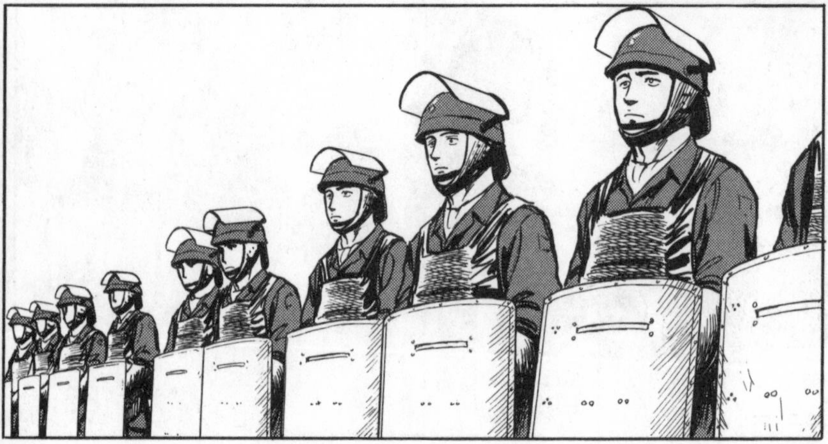

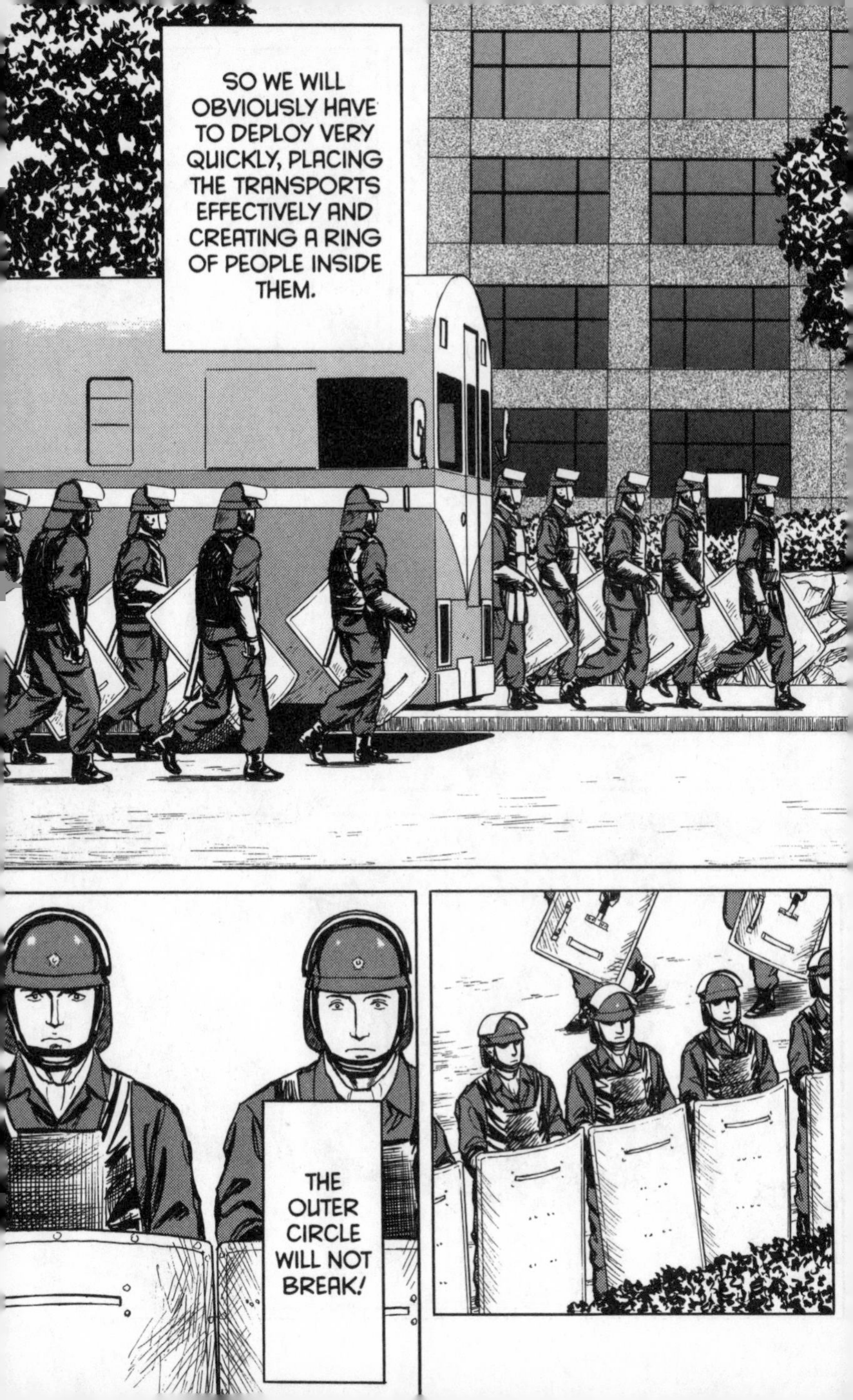
SO WE WILL OBVIOUSLY HAVE TO DEPLOY VERY QUICKLY, PLACING THE TRANSPORTS EFFECTIVELY AND CREATING A RING OF PEOPLE INSIDE THEM.
THE OUTER CIRCLE WILL NOT BREAK!

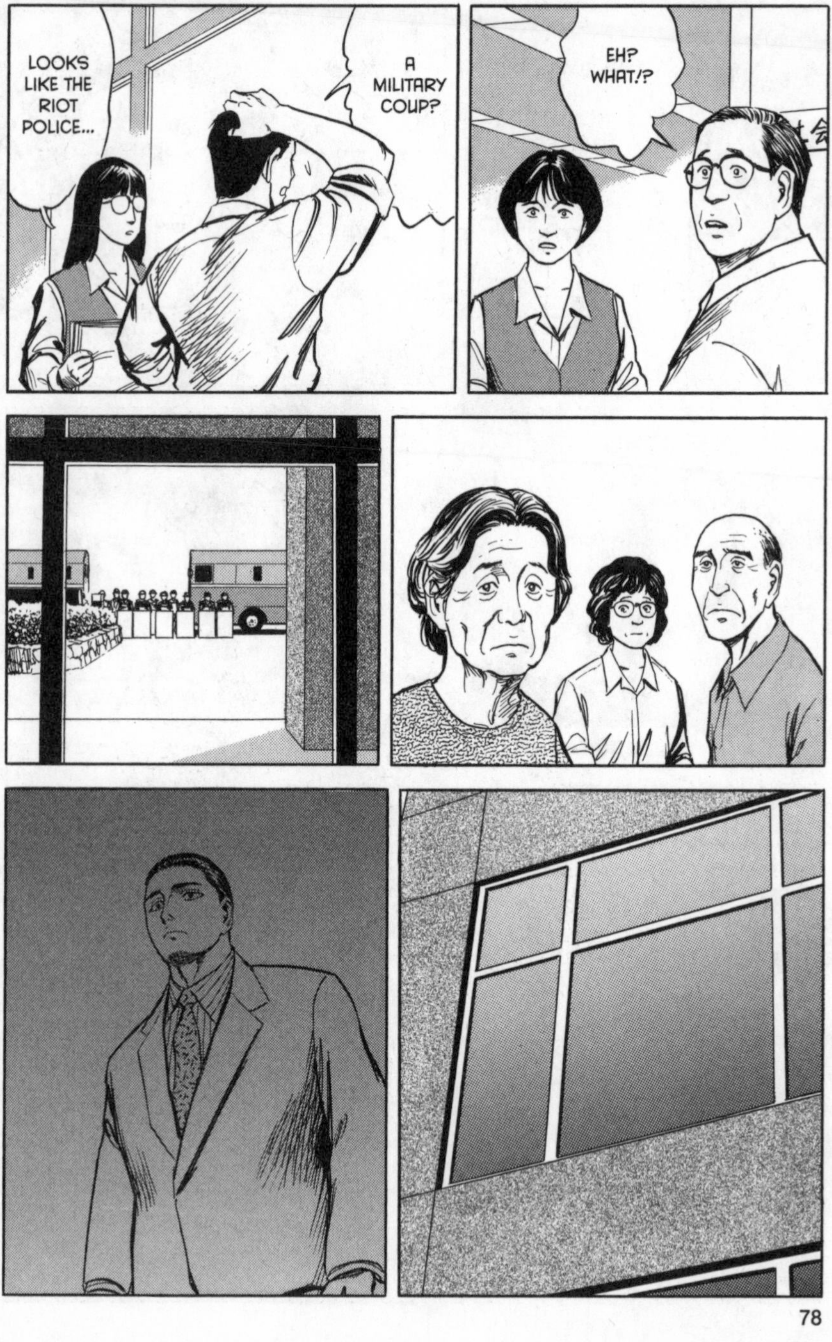
EH? WHAT!?
A MILITARY COUP?
LOOKS LIKE THE RIOT POLICE...

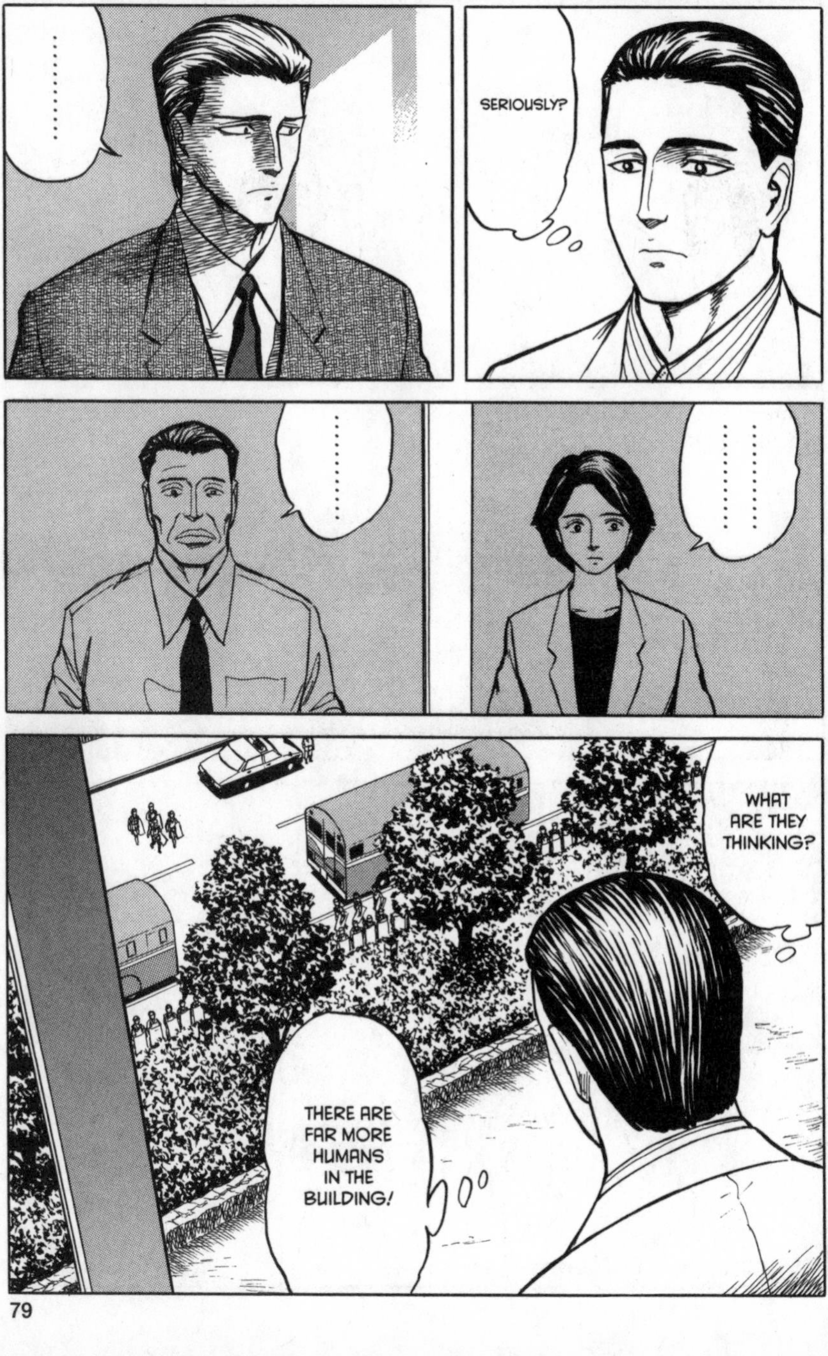
SERIOUSLY?
......
......
......
WHAT ARE THEY THINKING?
THERE ARE FAR MORE HUMANS IN THE BUILDING!

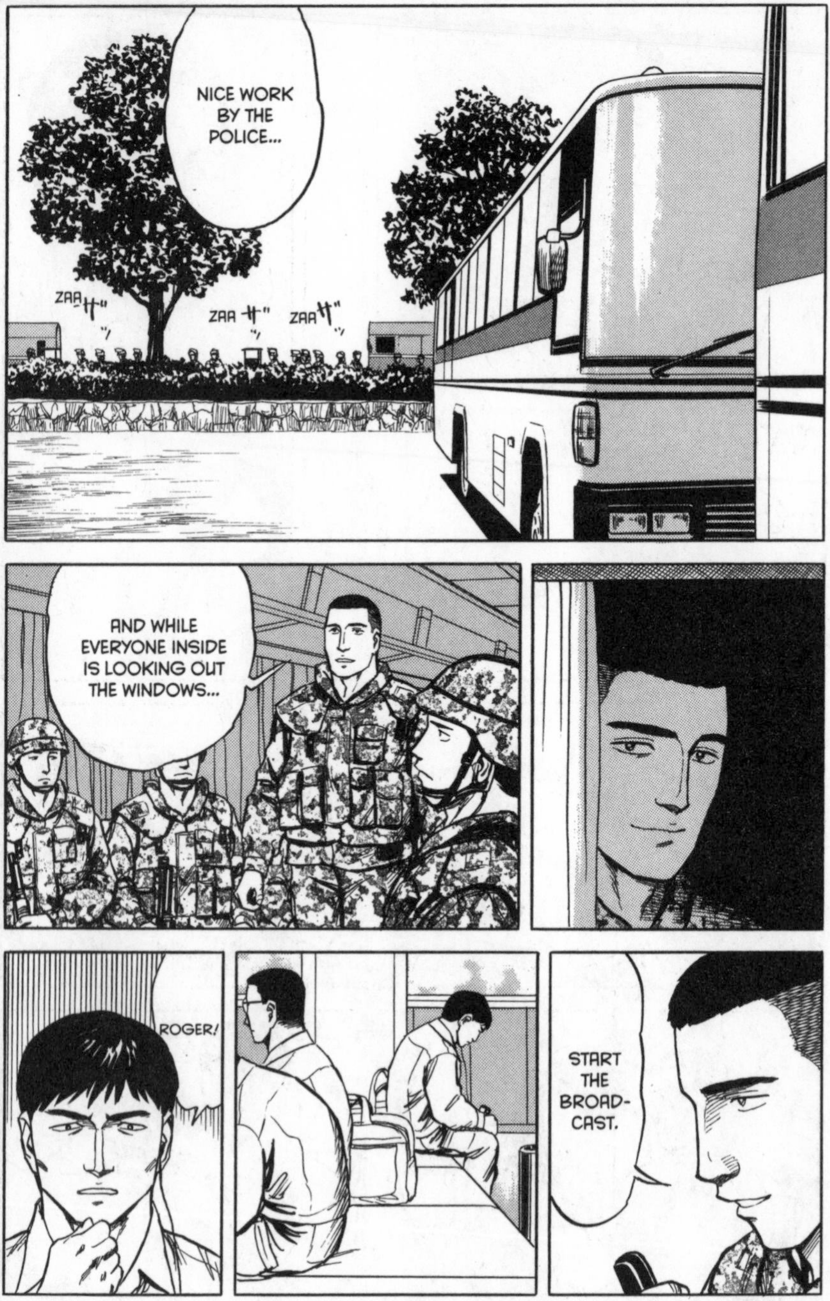
NICE WORK BY THE POLICE...
ZAA
ZAA
ZAA
AND WHILE EVERYONE INSIDE IS LOOKING OUT THE WINDOWS...
START THE BROAD-CAST.
ROGER!

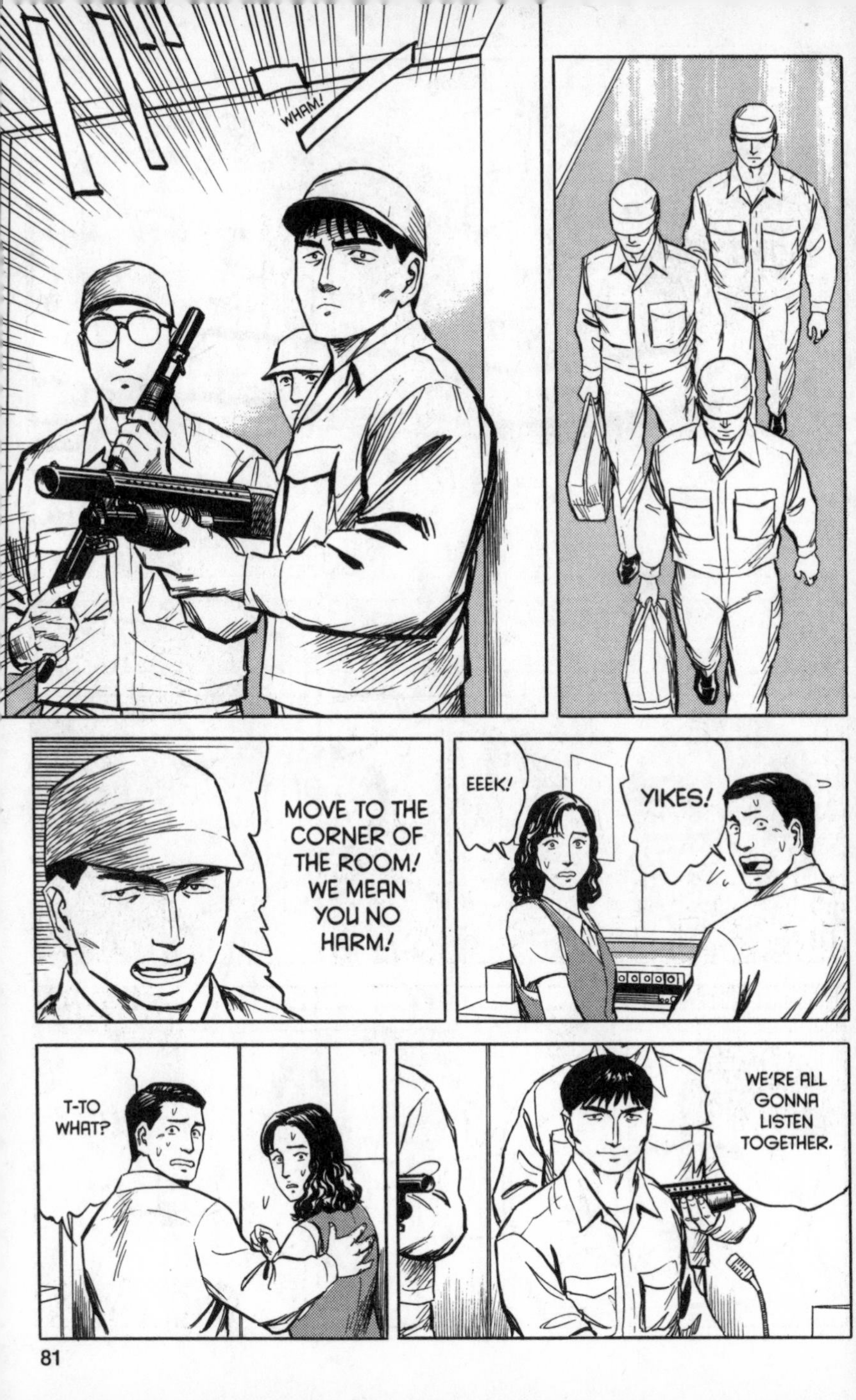
WHAM!
MOVE TO THE CORNER OF THE ROOM! WE MEAN YOU NO HARM!
EEEK!
YIKES!
T-TO WHAT?
WE'RE ALL GONNA LISTEN TOGETHER.

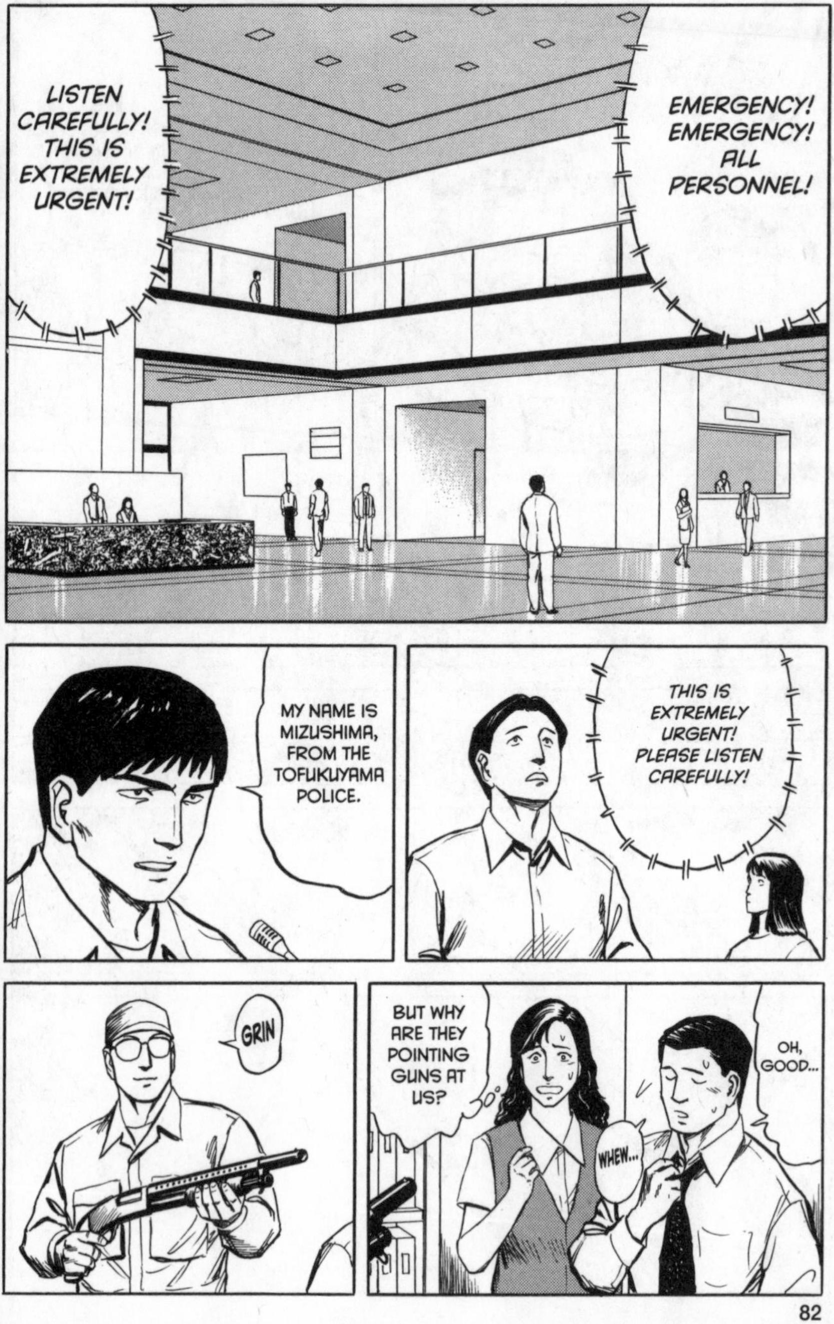
EMERGENCY! EMERGENCY! ALL PERSONNEL!
LISTEN CAREFULLY! THIS IS EXTREMELY URGENT!
THIS IS EXTREMELY URGENT! PLEASE LISTEN CAREFULLY!
MY NAME IS MIZUSHIMA, FROM THE TOFUKUYAMA POLICE.
OH, GOOD...
WHEW...
BUT WHY ARE THEY POINTING GUNS AT US?
GRIN

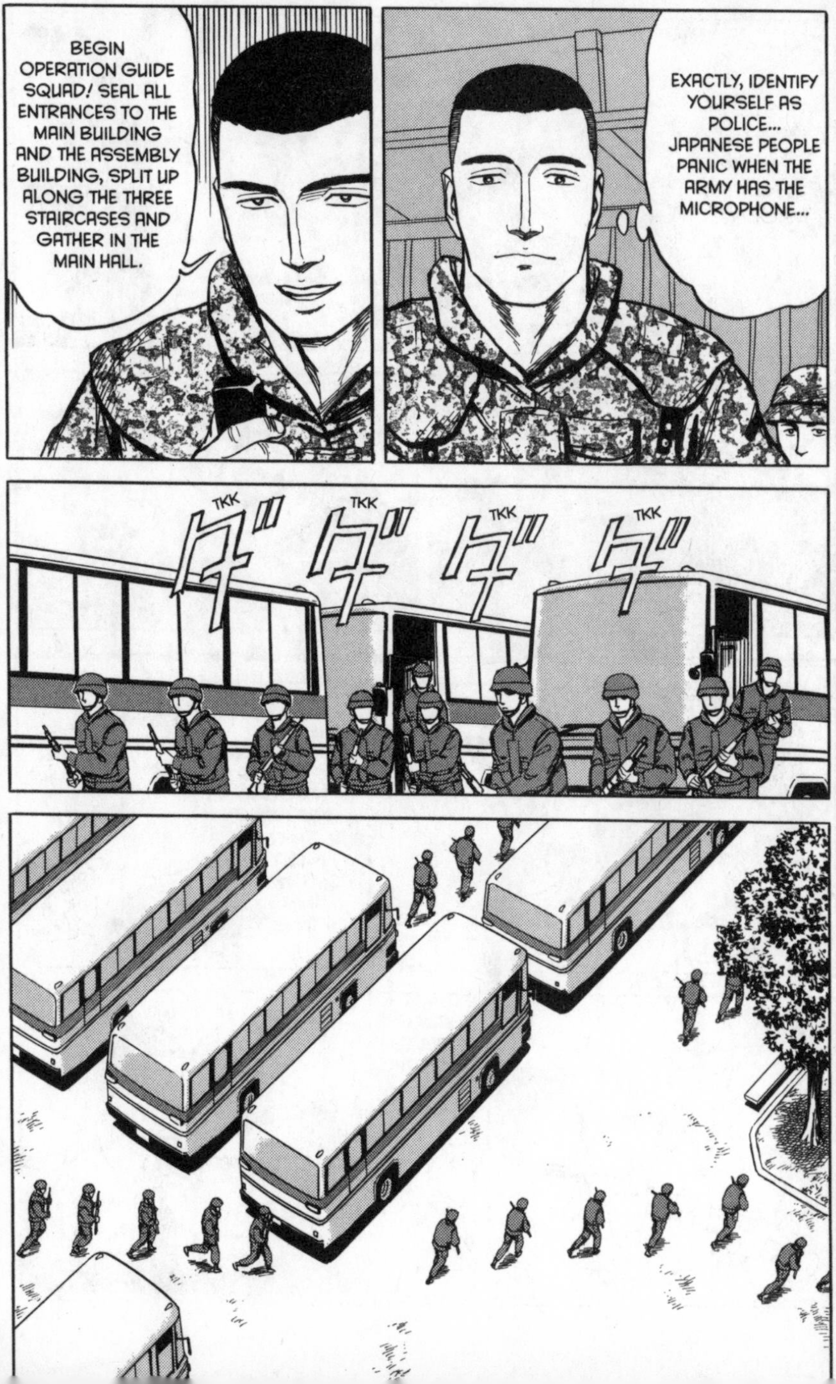
EXACTLY, IDENTIFY YOURSELF AS POLICE... JAPANESE PEOPLE PANIC WHEN THE ARMY HAS THE MICROPHONE...
BEGIN OPERATION GUIDE SQUAD! SEAL ALL ENTRANCES TO THE MAIN BUILDING AND THE ASSEMBLY BUILDING, SPLIT UP ALONG THE THREE STAIRCASES AND GATHER IN THE MAIN HALL.
TKK
TKK
TKK
TKK

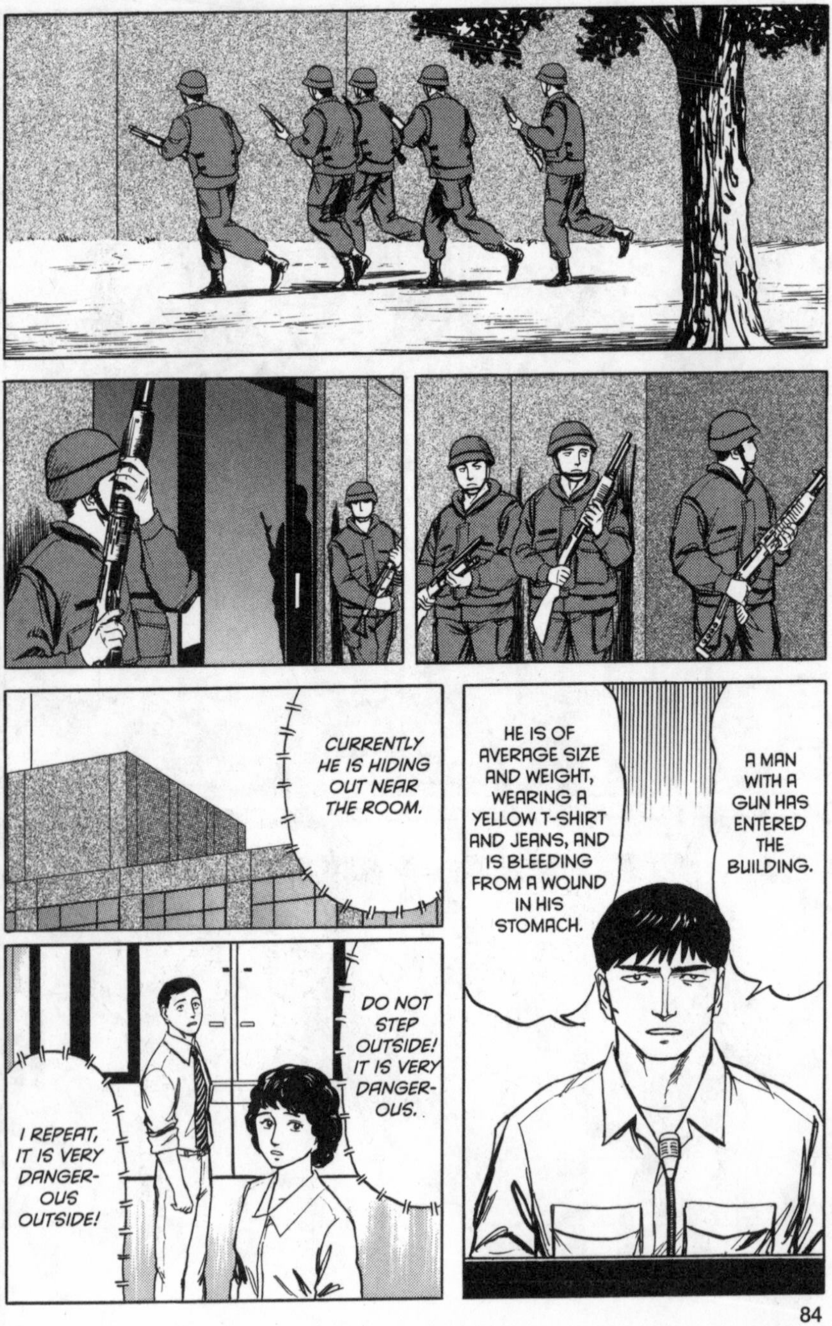
A MAN WITH A GUN HAS ENTERED THE BUILDING.
HE IS OF AVERAGE SIZE AND WEIGHT, WEARING A YELLOW T-SHIRT AND JEANS, AND IS BLEEDING FROM A WOUND IN HIS STOMACH.
CURRENTLY HE IS HIDING OUT NEAR THE ROOM.
DO NOT STEP OUTSIDE! IT IS VERY DANGEROUS.
I REPEAT, IT IS VERY DANGEROUS OUTSIDE!

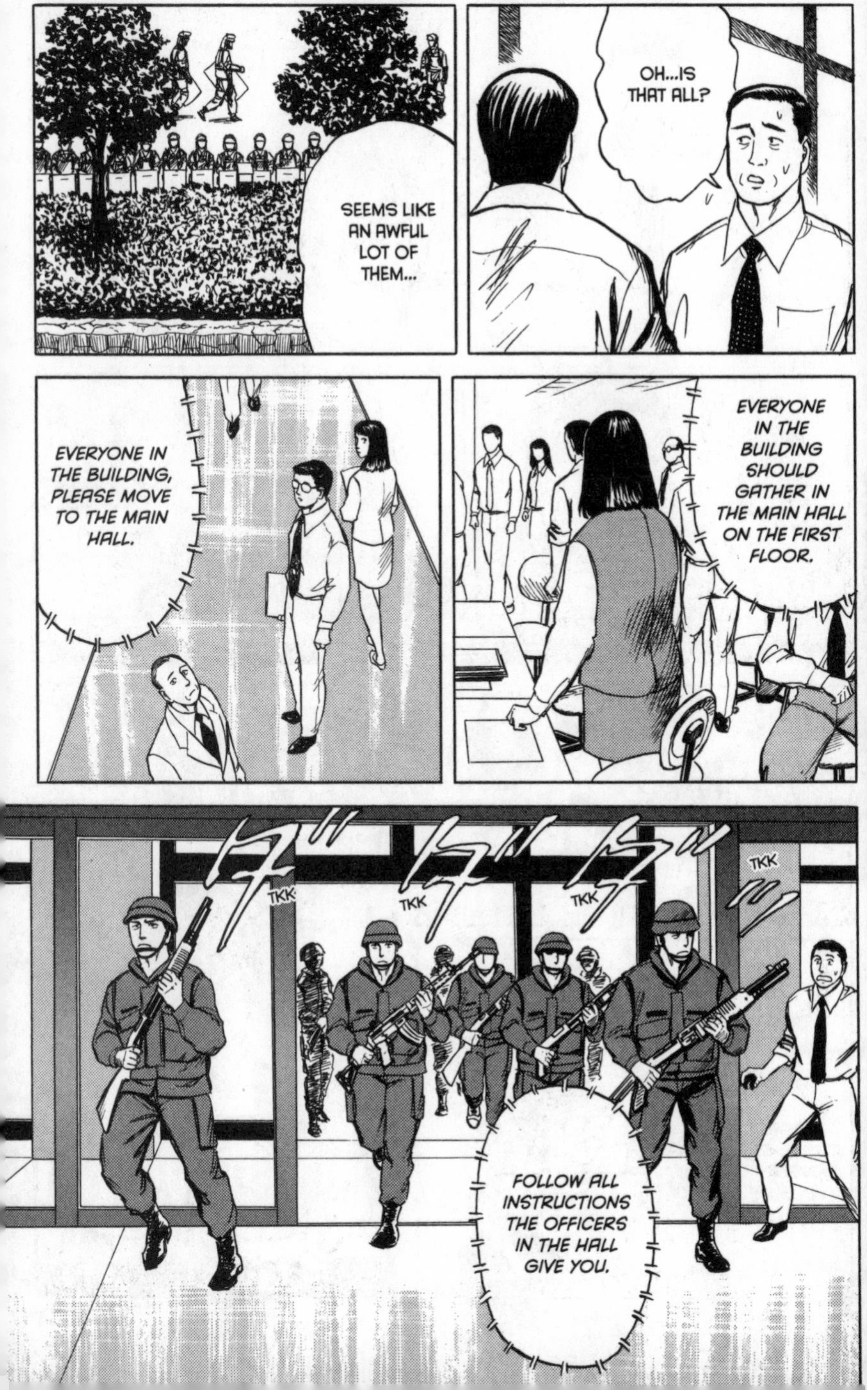
OH...IS THAT ALL?
SEEMS LIKE AN AWFUL LOT OF THEM...
EVERYONE IN THE BUILDING SHOULD GATHER IN THE MAIN HALL ON THE FIRST FLOOR.
EVERYONE IN THE BUILDING, PLEASE MOVE TO THE MAIN HALL.
TKK
TKK
TKK
TKK
FOLLOW ALL INSTRUCTIONS THE OFFICERS IN THE HALL GIVE YOU.

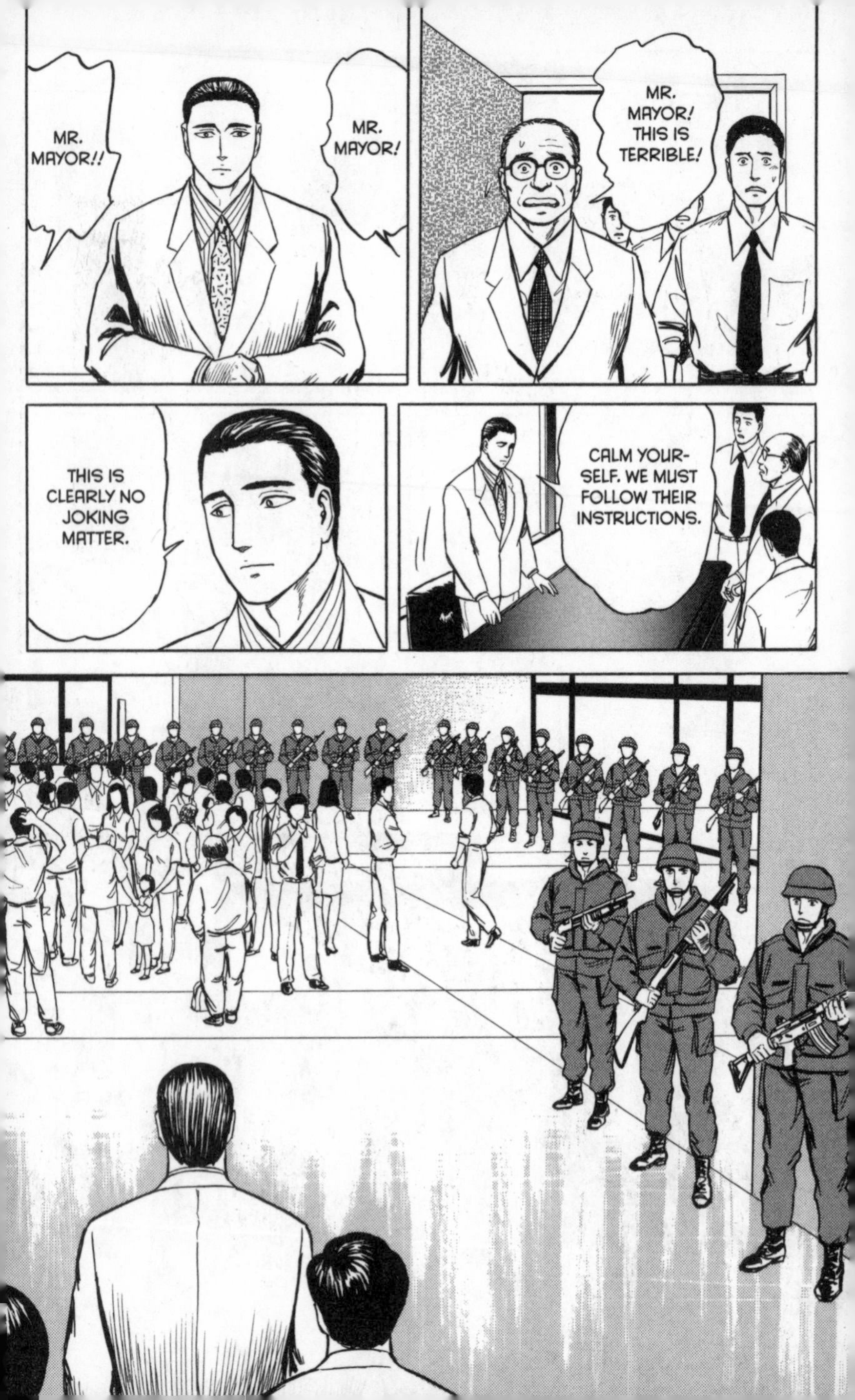
MR. MAYOR! THIS IS TERRIBLE!
MR. MAYOR!
MR. MAYOR!!
CALM YOURSELF. WE MUST FOLLOW THEIR INSTRUCTIONS.
THIS IS CLEARLY NO JOKING MATTER.

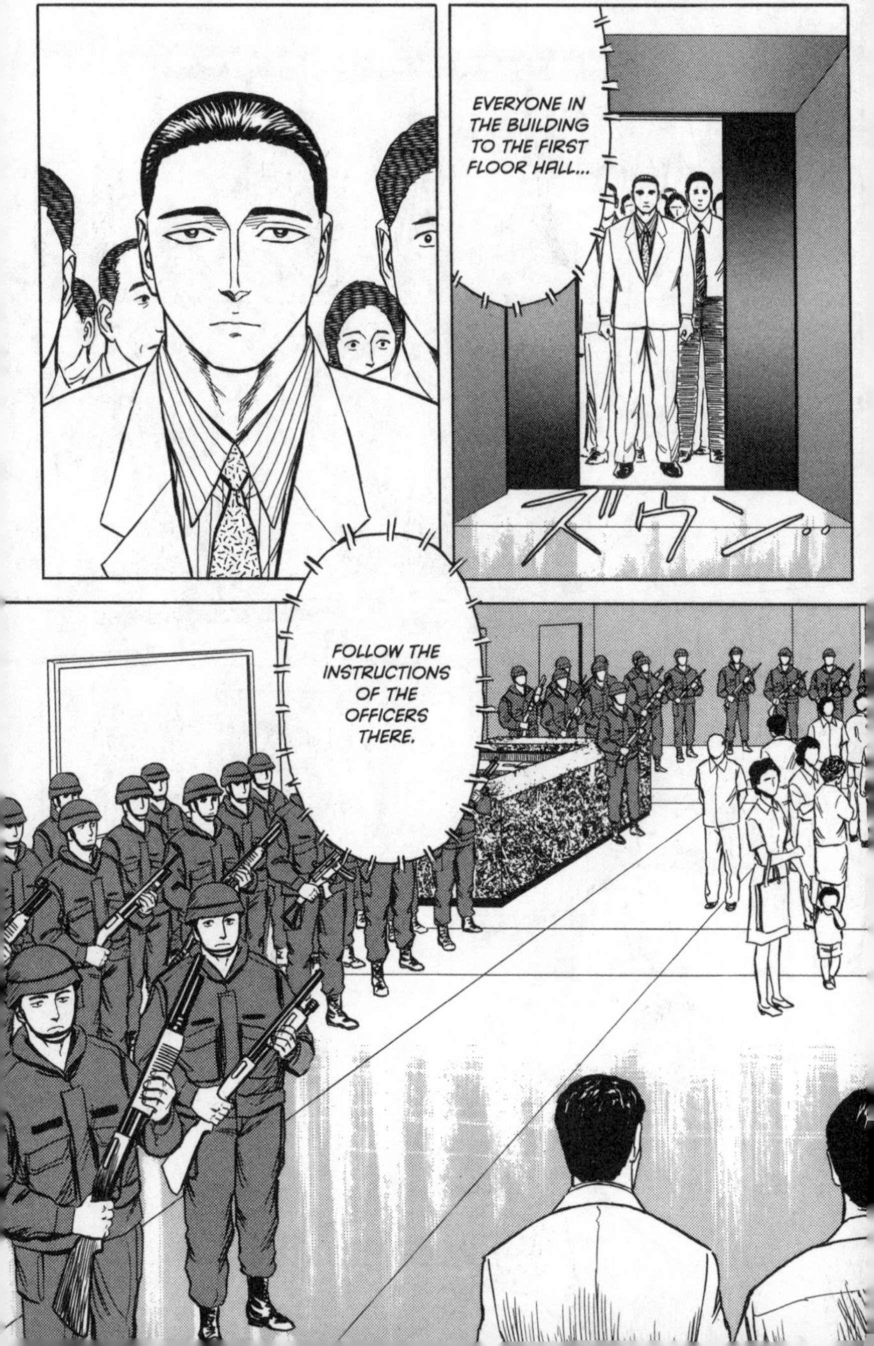
EVERYONE IN THE BUILDING TO THE FIRST FLOOR HALL...
ズウーン..
FOLLOW THE INSTRUCTIONS OF THE OFFICERS THERE.

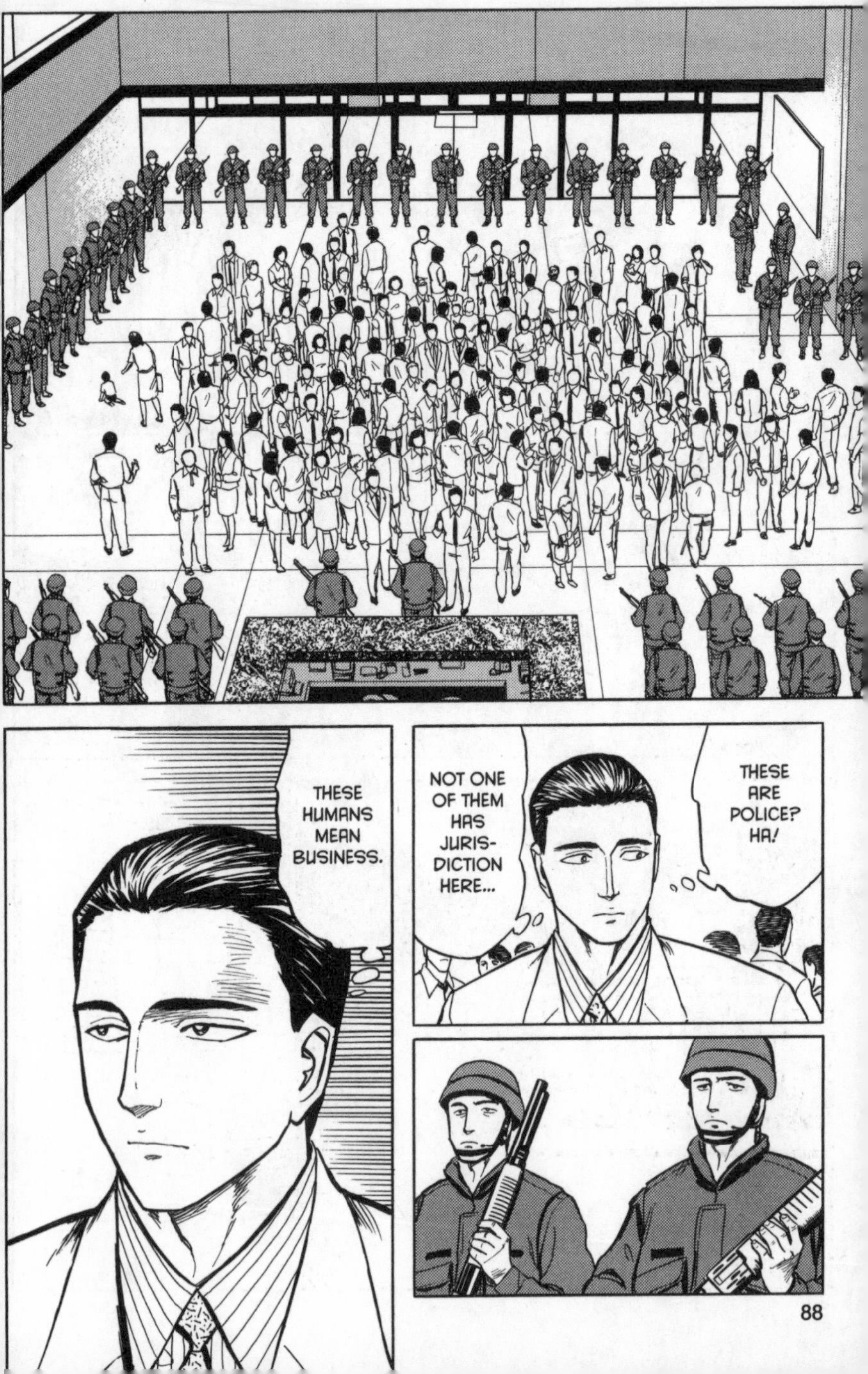
THESE ARE POLICE? HA!
NOT ONE OF THEM HAS JURIS-DICTION HERE...
THESE HUMANS MEAN BUSINESS.

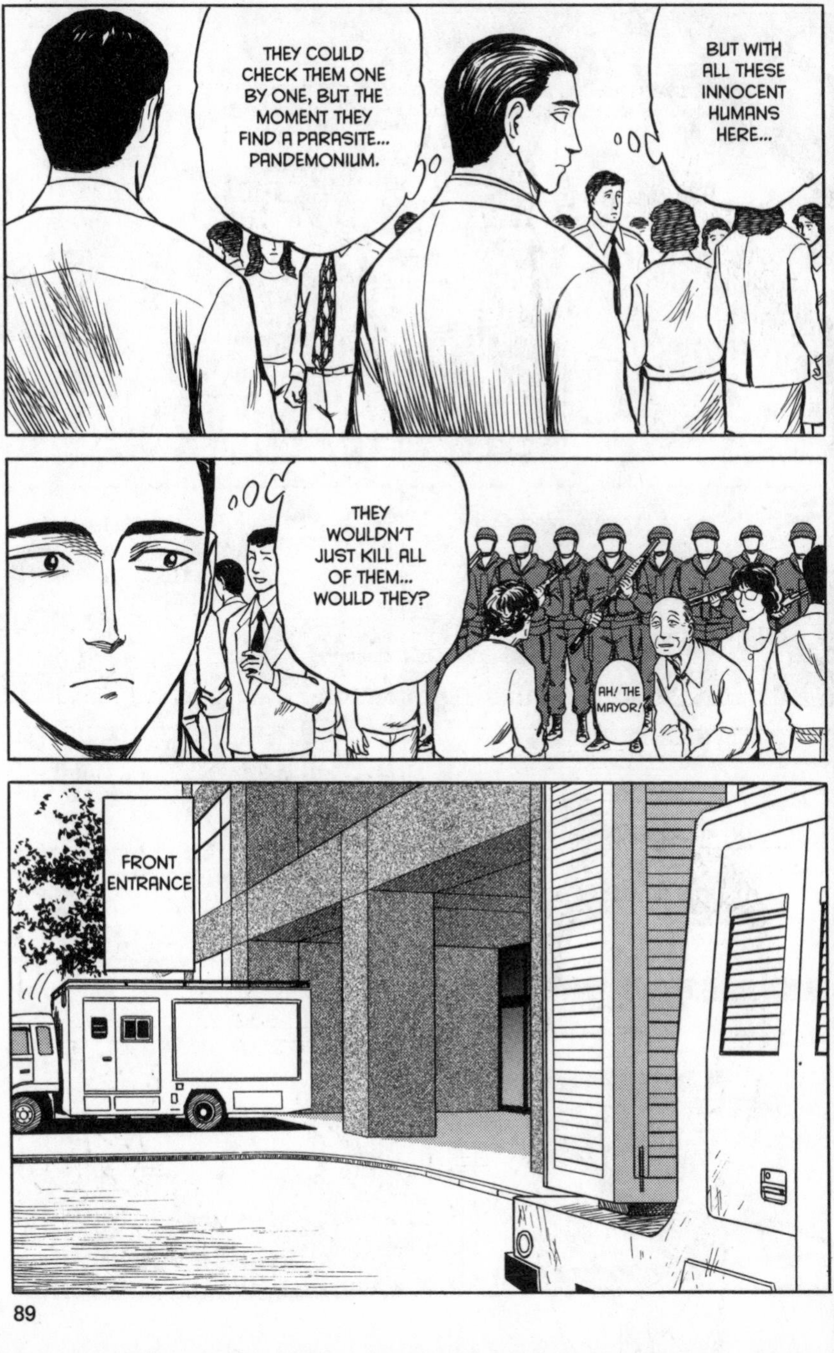
BUT WITH ALL THESE INNOCENT HUMANS HERE...
THEY COULD CHECK THEM ONE BY ONE, BUT THE MOMENT THEY FIND A PARASITE... PANDEMONIUM.
THEY WOULDN'T JUST KILL ALL OF THEM... WOULD THEY?
AH! THE MAYOR!
FRONT ENTRANCE

BACK A LITTLE MORE...STOP!
ALL FURTHER ADJUST-MENTS ARE AUTOMATIC.
WING

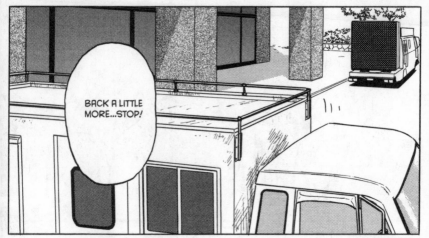

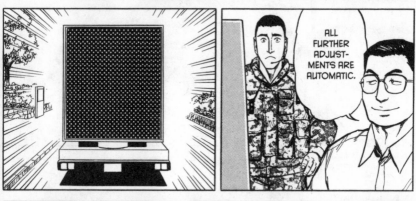

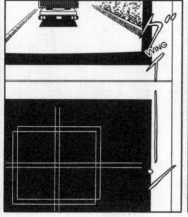

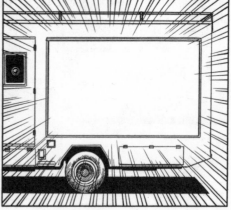

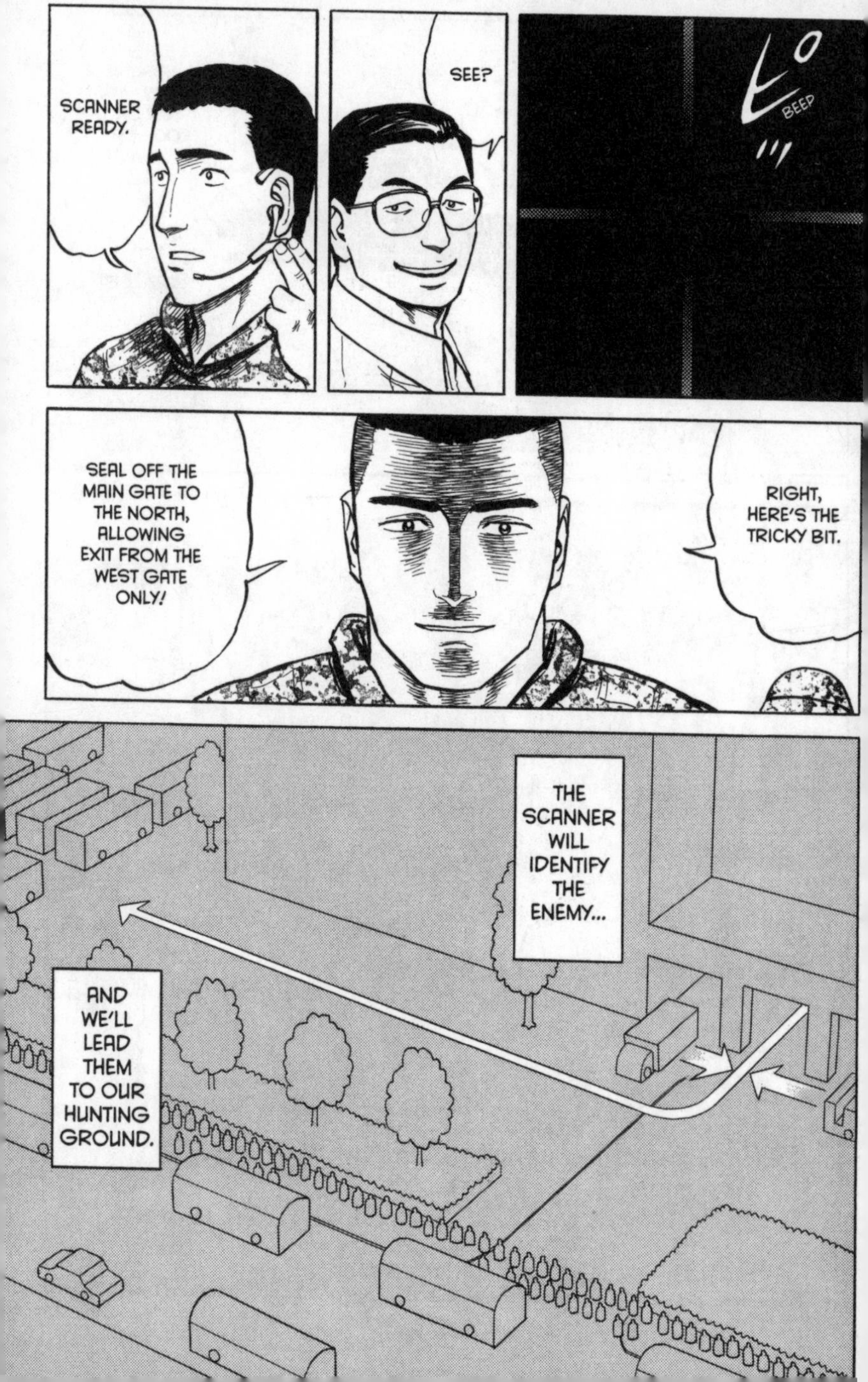
BEEP
SEE?
SCANNER READY.
RIGHT, HERE'S THE TRICKY BIT.
SEAL OFF THE MAIN GATE TO THE NORTH, ALLOWING EXIT FROM THE WEST GATE ONLY!
THE SCANNER WILL IDENTIFY THE ENEMY...
AND WE'LL LEAD THEM TO OUR HUNTING GROUND.

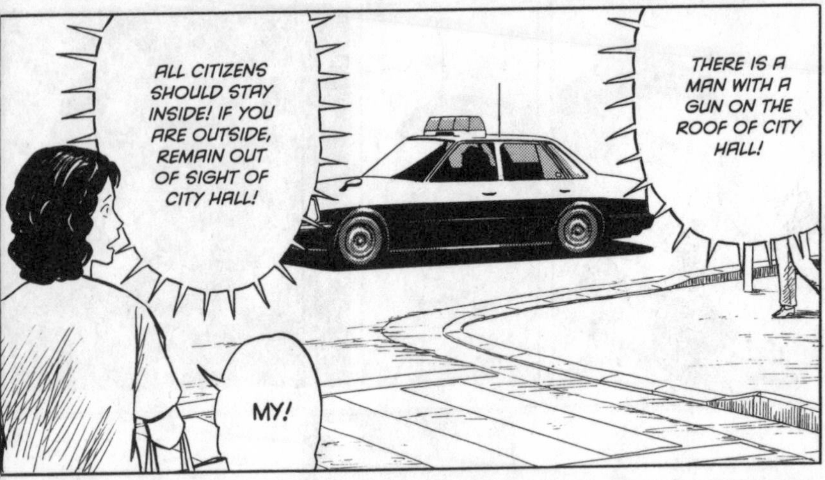
THERE IS A MAN WITH A GUN ON THE ROOF OF CITY HALL!
ALL CITIZENS SHOULD STAY INSIDE! IF YOU ARE OUTSIDE, REMAIN OUT OF SIGHT OF CITY HALL!
MY!

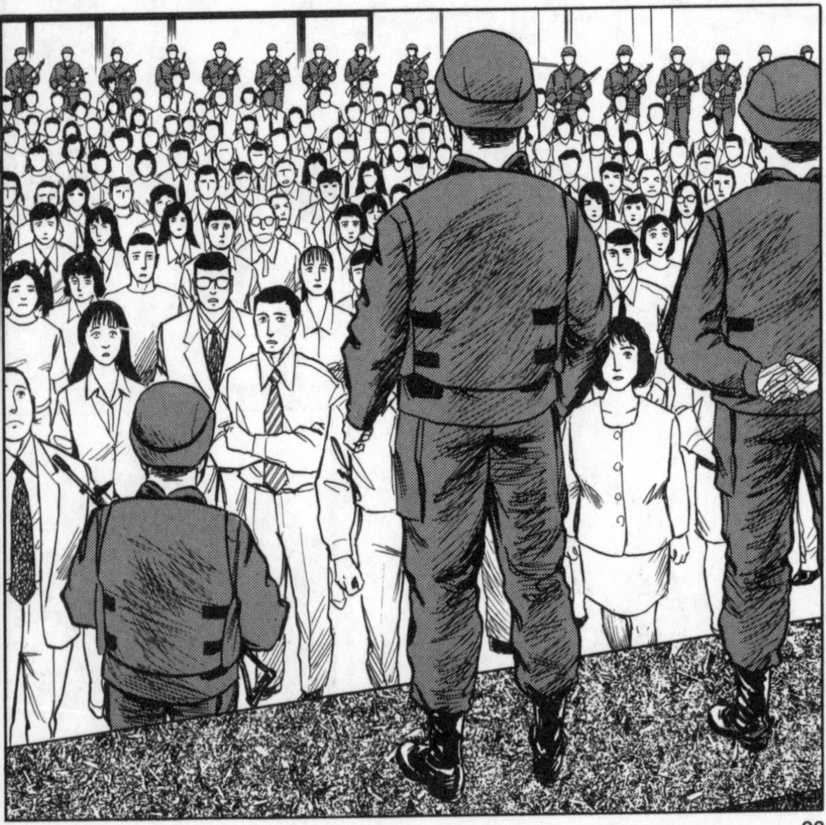

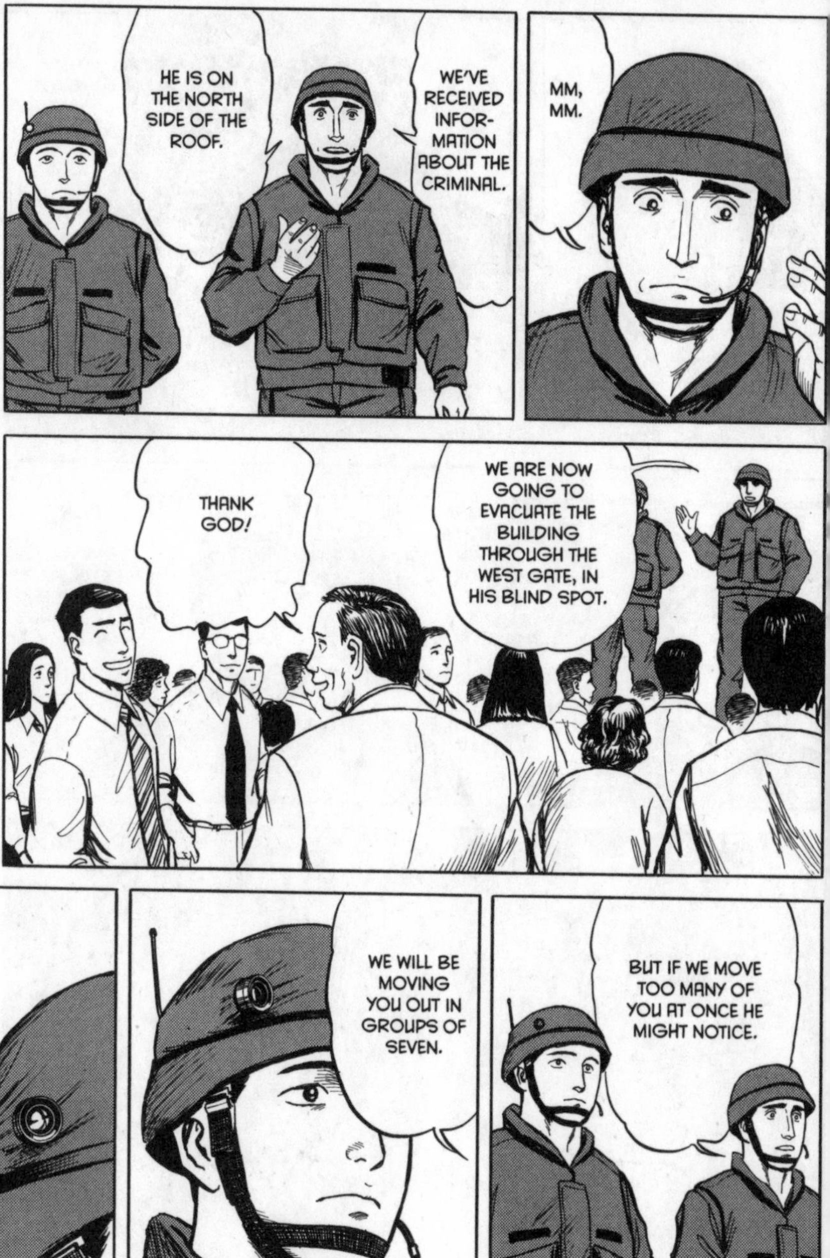
MM, MM.
WE'VE RECEIVED INFORMATION ABOUT THE CRIMINAL.
HE IS ON THE NORTH SIDE OF THE ROOF.
WE ARE NOW GOING TO EVACUATE THE BUILDING THROUGH THE WEST GATE, IN HIS BLIND SPOT.
THANK GOD!
BUT IF WE MOVE TOO MANY OF YOU AT ONCE HE MIGHT NOTICE.
WE WILL BE MOVING YOU OUT IN GROUPS OF SEVEN.

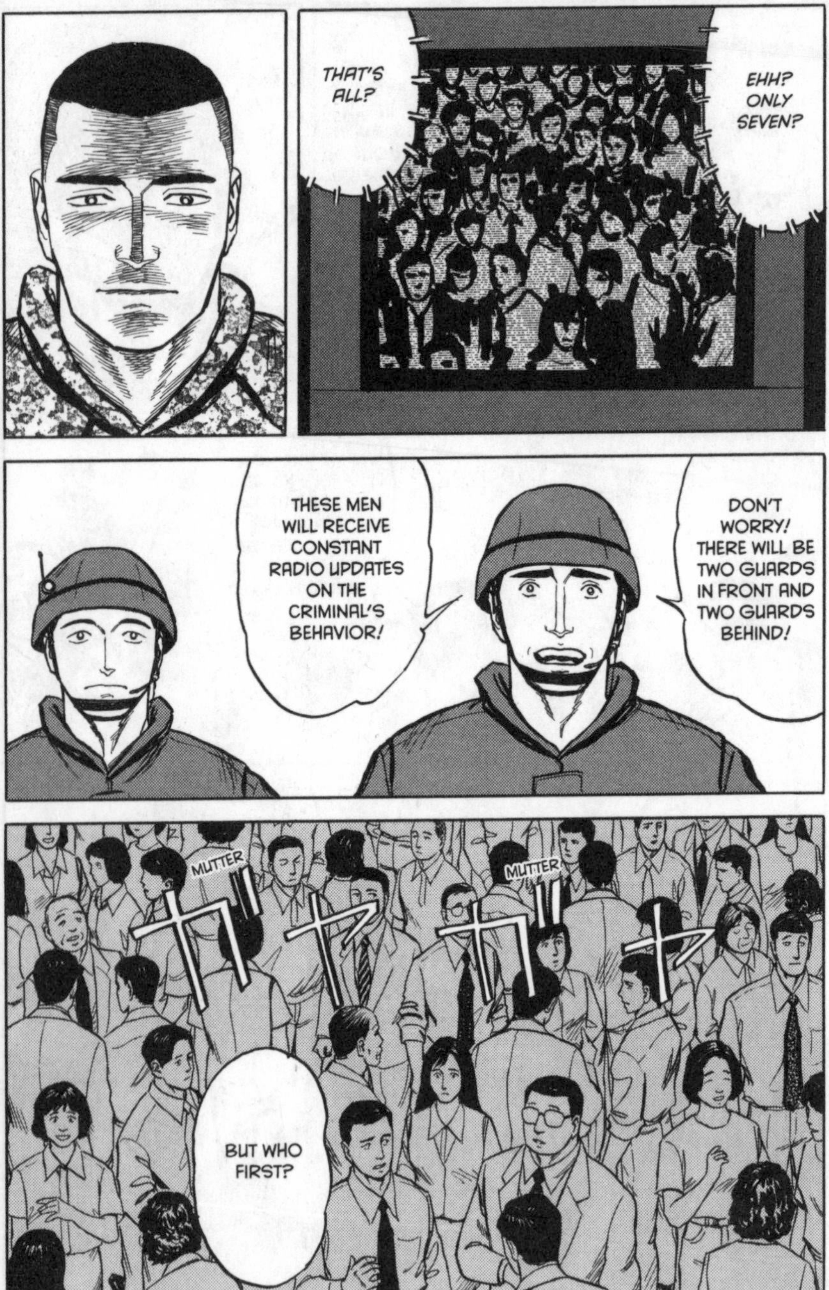
EHH? ONLY SEVEN?
THAT'S ALL?
DON'T WORRY! THERE WILL BE TWO GUARDS IN FRONT AND TWO GUARDS BEHIND!
THESE MEN WILL RECEIVE CONSTANT RADIO UPDATES ON THE CRIMINAL'S BEHAVIOR!
MUTTER
MUTTER
BUT WHO FIRST?

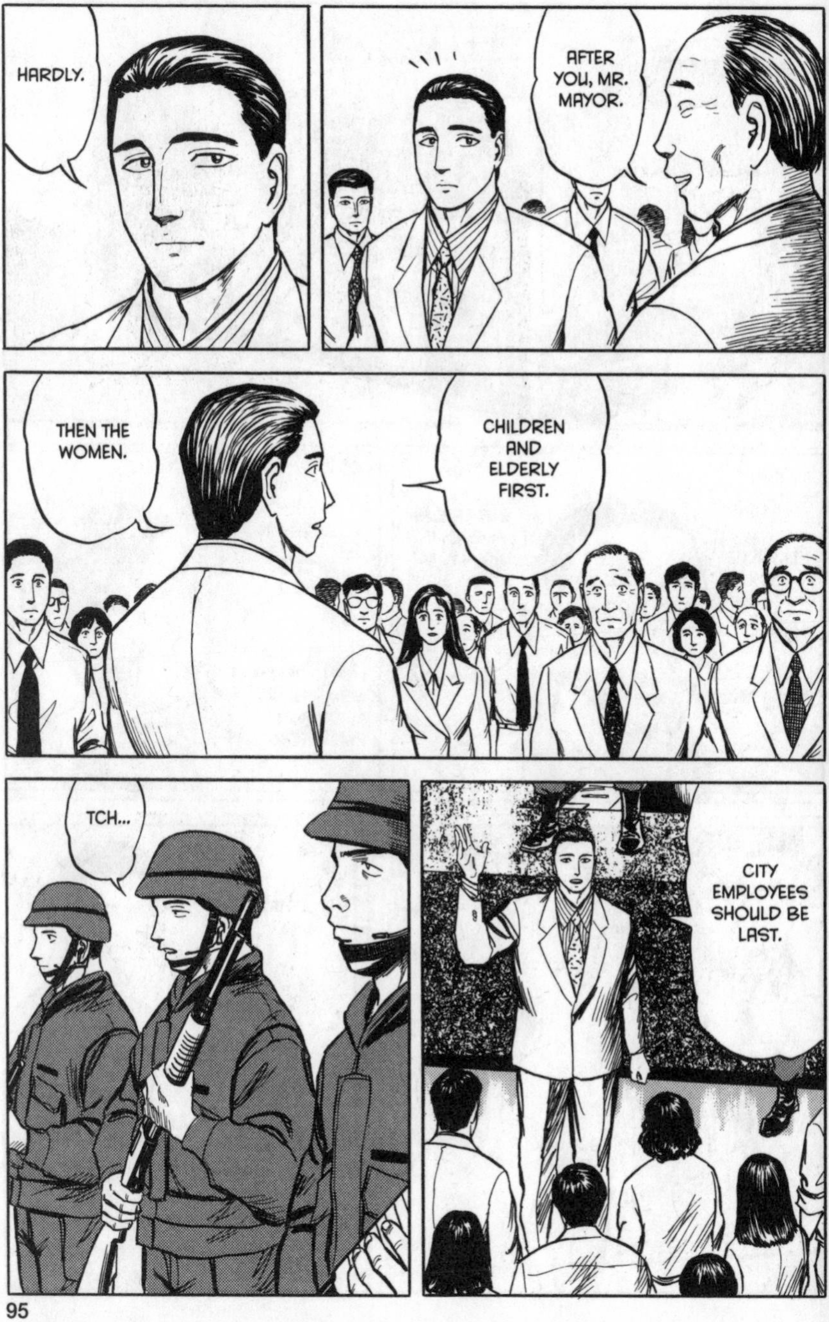
AFTER YOU, MR. MAYOR.
HARDLY.
CHILDREN AND ELDERLY FIRST.
THEN THE WOMEN.
CITY EMPLOYEES SHOULD BE LAST.
TCH...

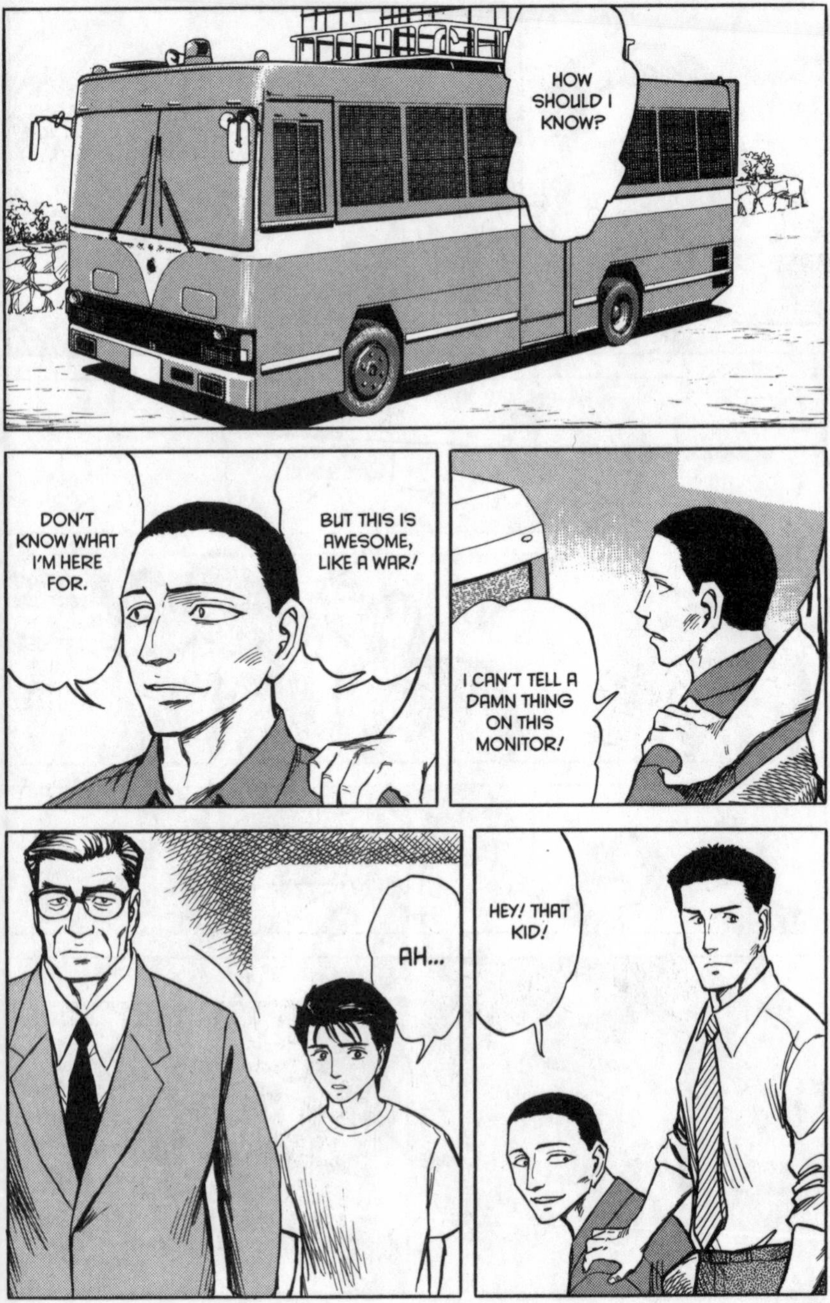
HOW SHOULD I KNOW?
I CAN'T TELL A DAMN THING ON THIS MONITOR!
BUT THIS IS AWESOME, LIKE A WAR!
DON'T KNOW WHAT I'M HERE FOR.
HEY! THAT KID!
AH...

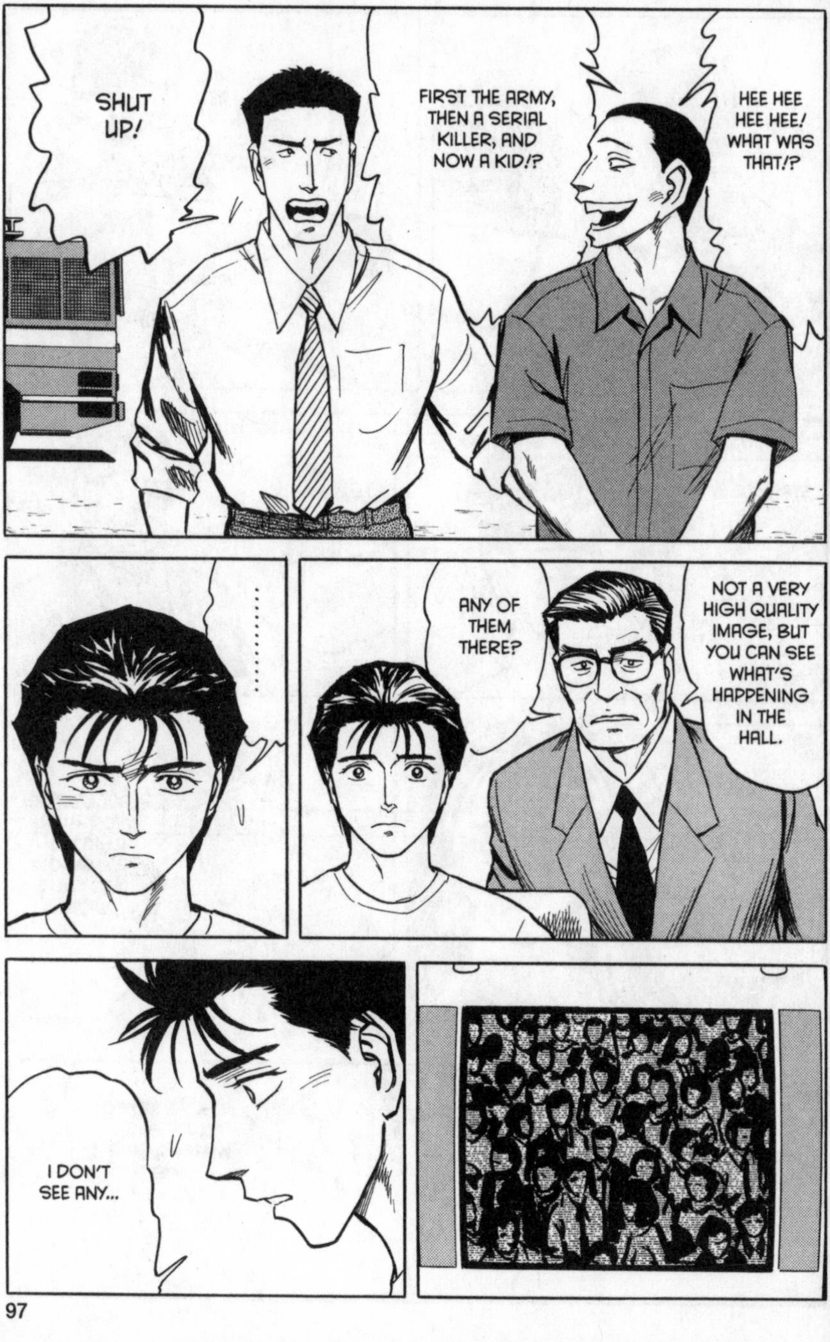
HEE HEE HEE HEE! WHAT WAS THAT!?
FIRST THE ARMY, THEN A SERIAL KILLER, AND NOW A KID!?
SHUT UP!
NOT A VERY HIGH QUALITY IMAGE, BUT YOU CAN SEE WHAT'S HAPPENING IN THE HALL.
ANY OF THEM THERE?
......
I DON'T SEE ANY...

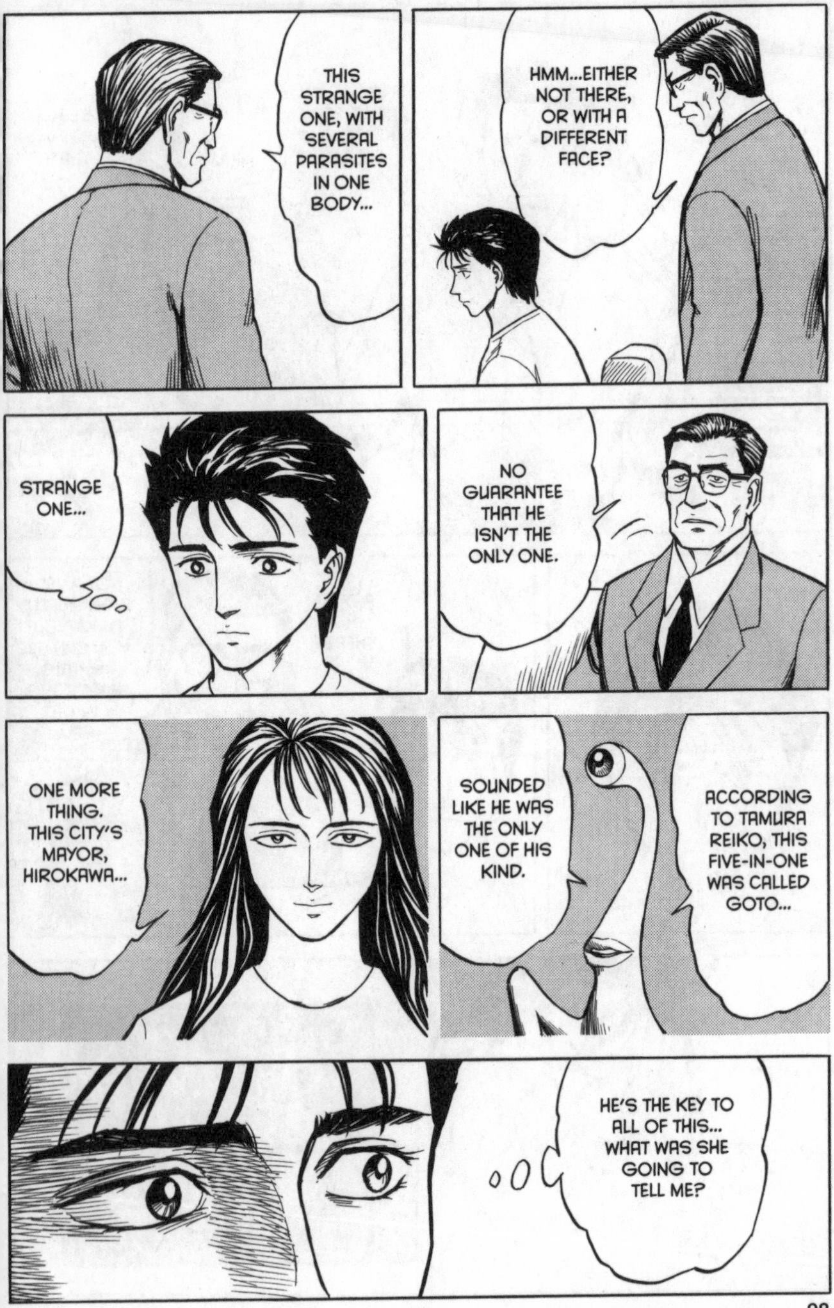
HMM...EITHER NOT THERE, OR WITH A DIFFERENT FACE?
THIS STRANGE ONE, WITH SEVERAL PARASITES IN ONE BODY...
NO GUARANTEE THAT HE ISN'T THE ONLY ONE.
STRANGE ONE...
ACCORDING TO TAMURA REIKO, THIS FIVE-IN-ONE WAS CALLED GOTO...
SOUNDED LIKE HE WAS THE ONLY ONE OF HIS KIND.
ONE MORE THING. THIS CITY'S MAYOR, HIROKAWA...
HE'S THE KEY TO ALL OF THIS... WHAT WAS SHE GOING TO TELL ME?

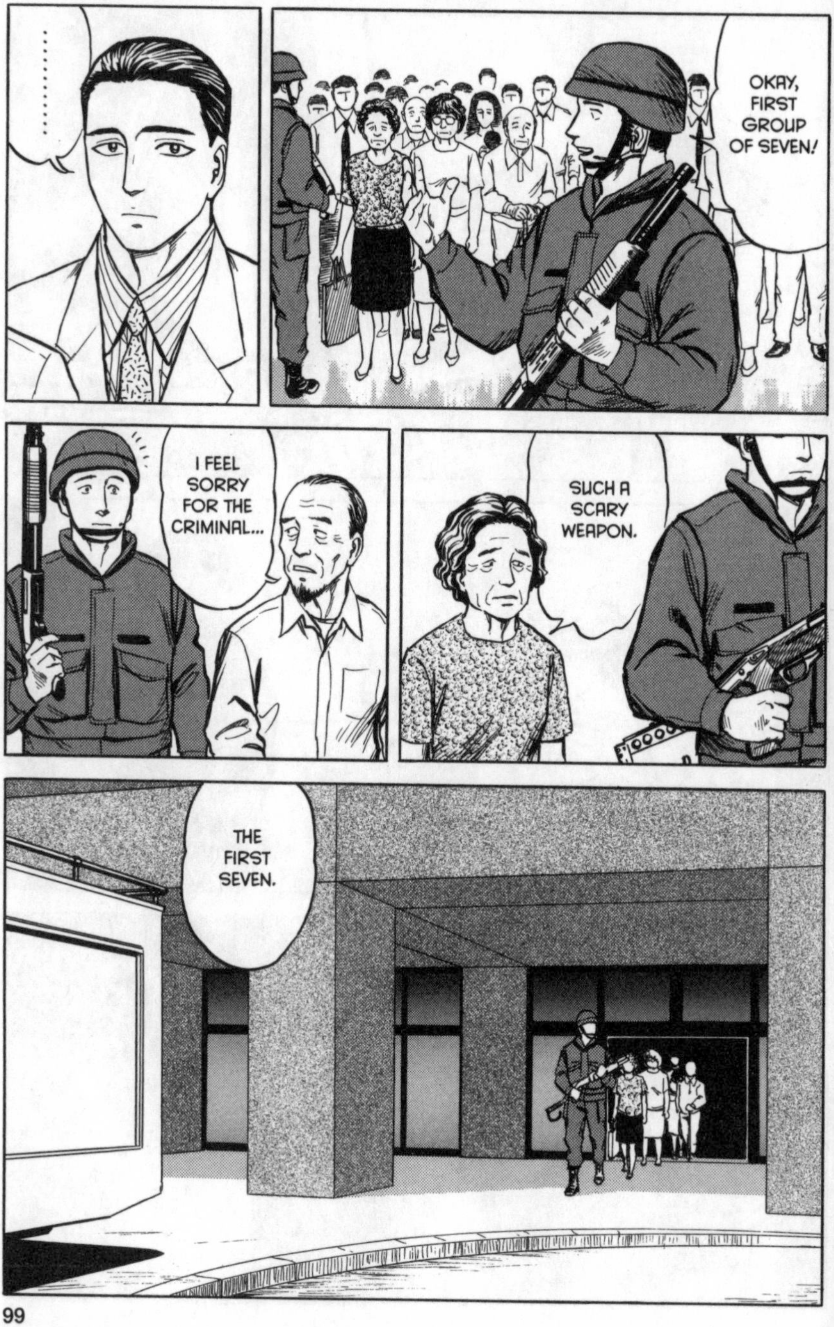

OKAY, FIRST GROUP OF SEVEN!
......
SUCH A SCARY WEAPON.
I FEEL SORRY FOR THE CRIMINAL...
THE FIRST SEVEN.

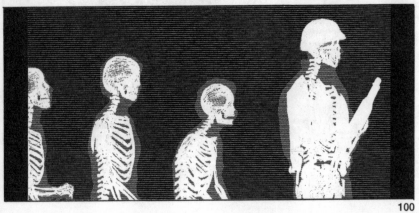

CLEAR.

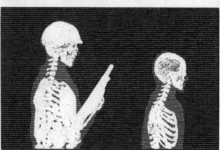

ALL HUMAN.

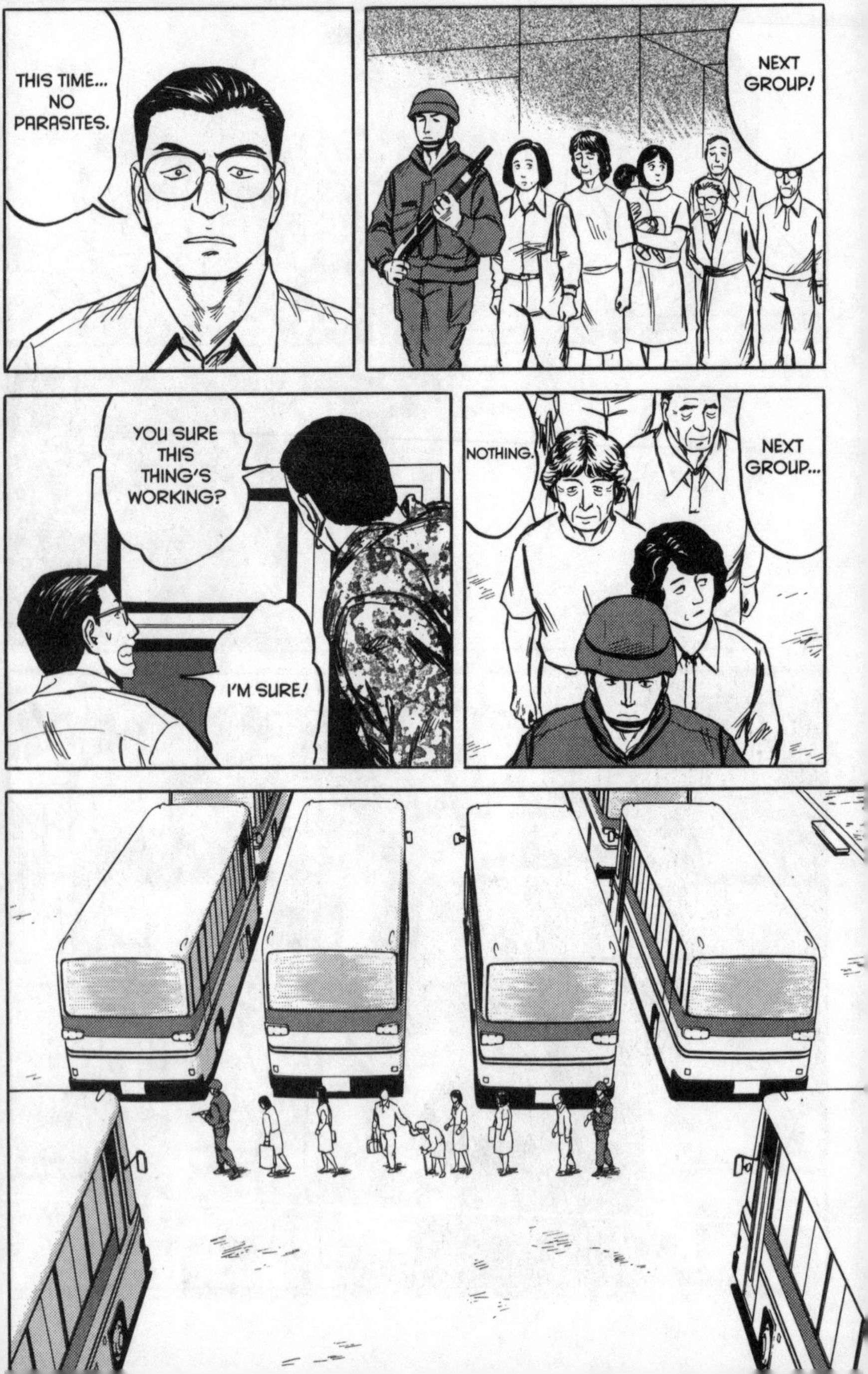
NEXT GROUP!
THIS TIME... NO PARASITES.
NEXT GROUP...
NOTHING.
YOU SURE THIS THING'S WORKING?
I'M SURE!

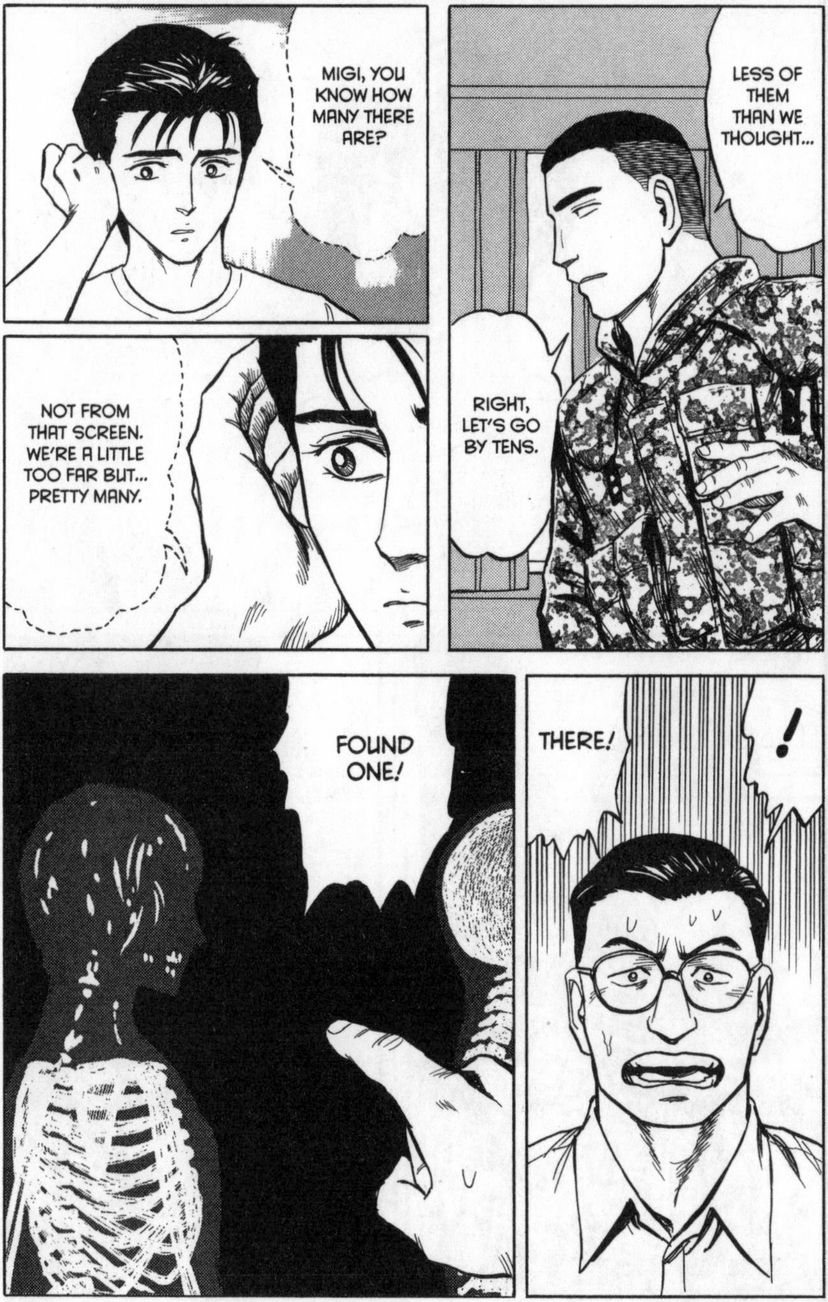
LESS OF THEM THAN WE THOUGHT...
RIGHT, LET'S GO BY TENS.
MIGI, YOU KNOW HOW MANY THERE ARE?
NOT FROM THAT SCREEN. WE'RE A LITTLE TOO FAR BUT... PRETTY MANY.
!
THERE!
FOUND ONE!

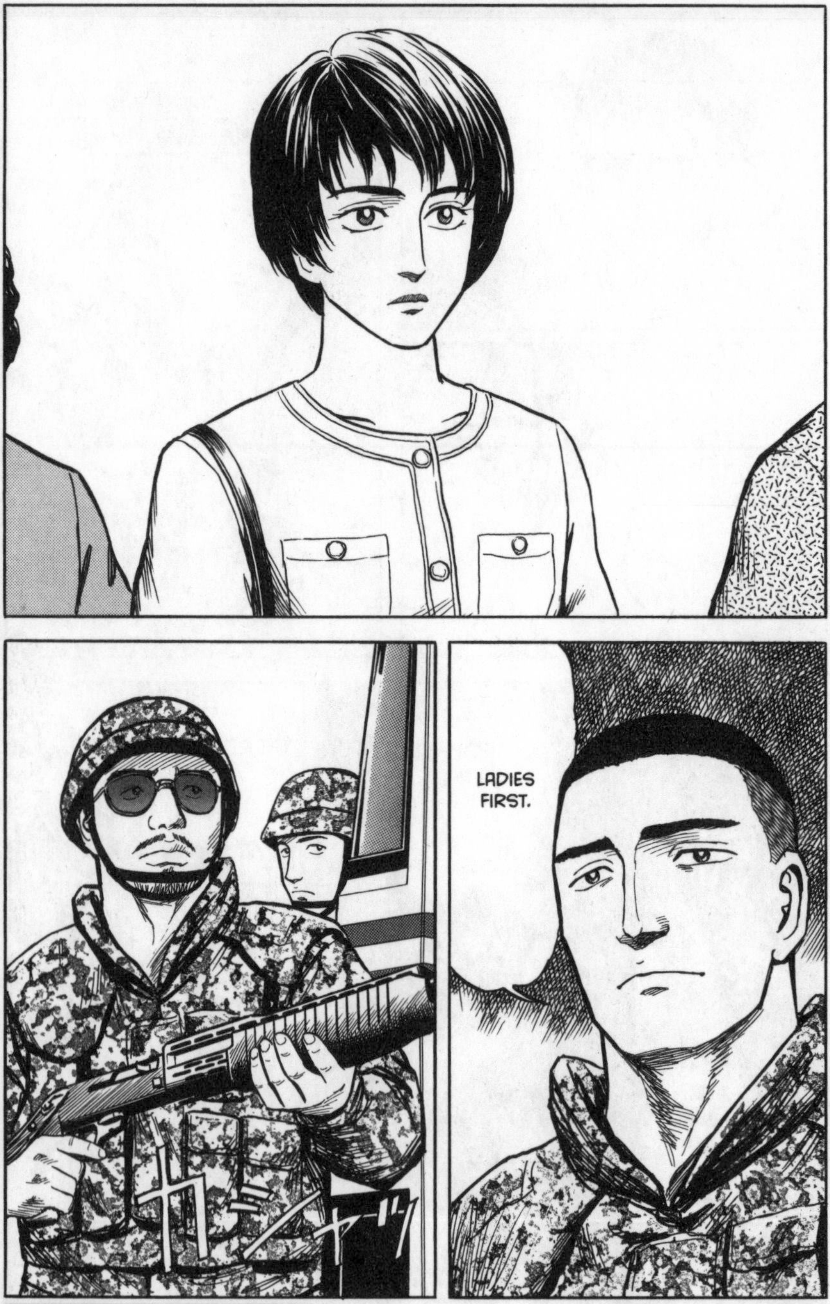
LADIES
FIRST.

CHAPTER 52: THE END

CHAPTER 53: FUSE

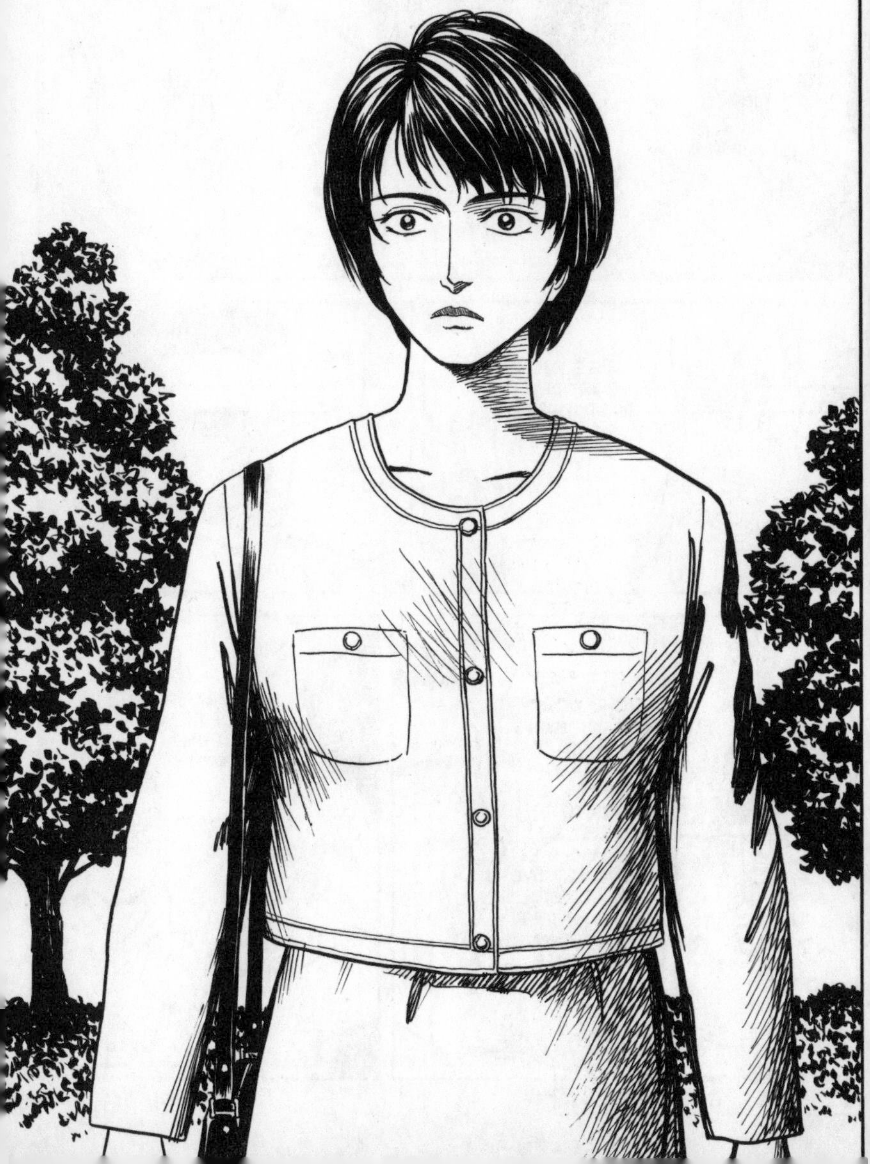

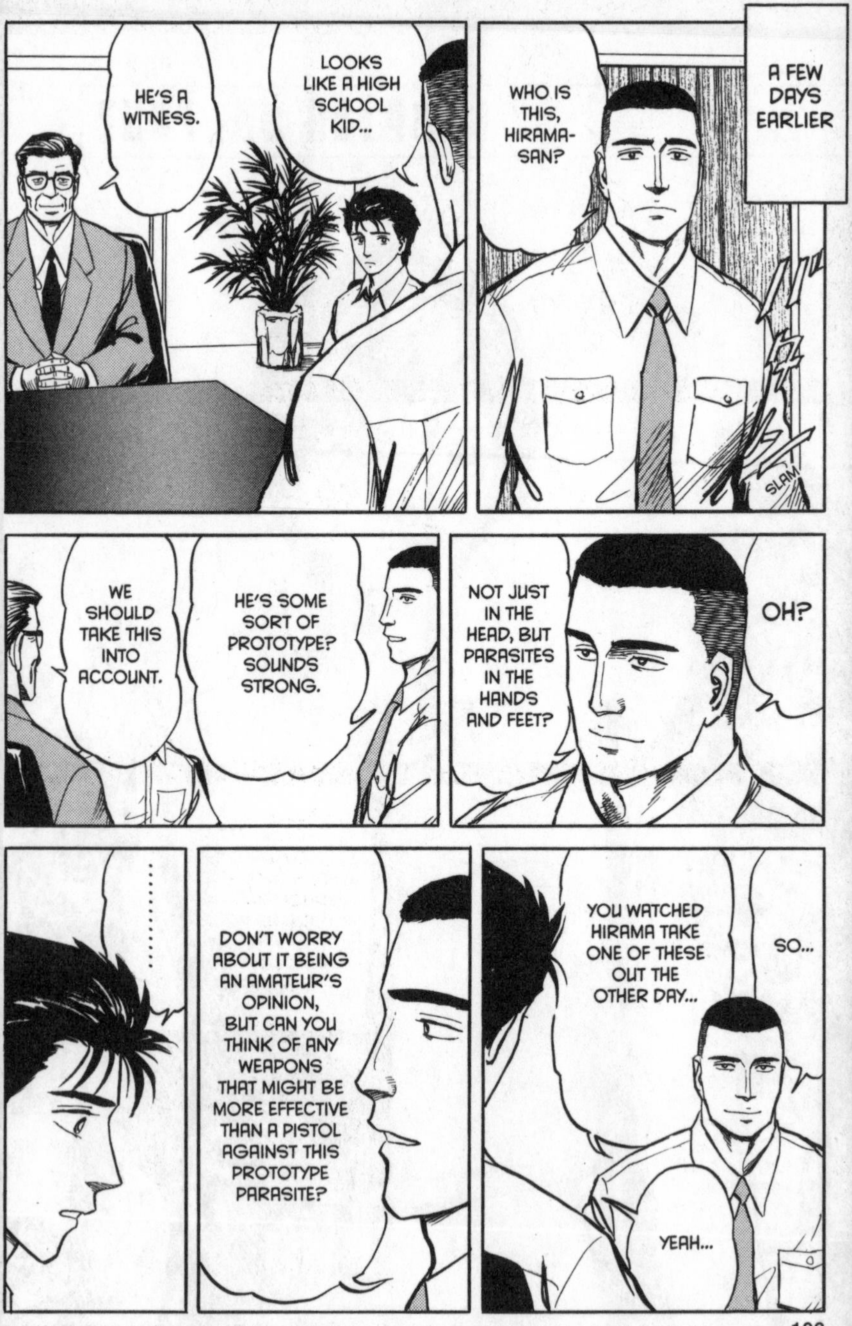
A FEW DAYS EARLIER
WHO IS THIS, HIRAMA-SAN?
SLAM
LOOKS LIKE A HIGH SCHOOL KID...
HE'S A WITNESS.
OH?
NOT JUST IN THE HEAD, BUT PARASITES IN THE HANDS AND FEET?
HE'S SOME SORT OF PROTOTYPE? SOUNDS STRONG.
WE SHOULD TAKE THIS INTO ACCOUNT.
SO...
YOU WATCHED HIRAMA TAKE ONE OF THESE OUT THE OTHER DAY...
YEAH...
DON'T WORRY ABOUT IT BEING AN AMATEUR'S OPINION, BUT CAN YOU THINK OF ANY WEAPONS THAT MIGHT BE MORE EFFECTIVE THAN A PISTOL AGAINST THIS PROTOTYPE PARASITE?
....

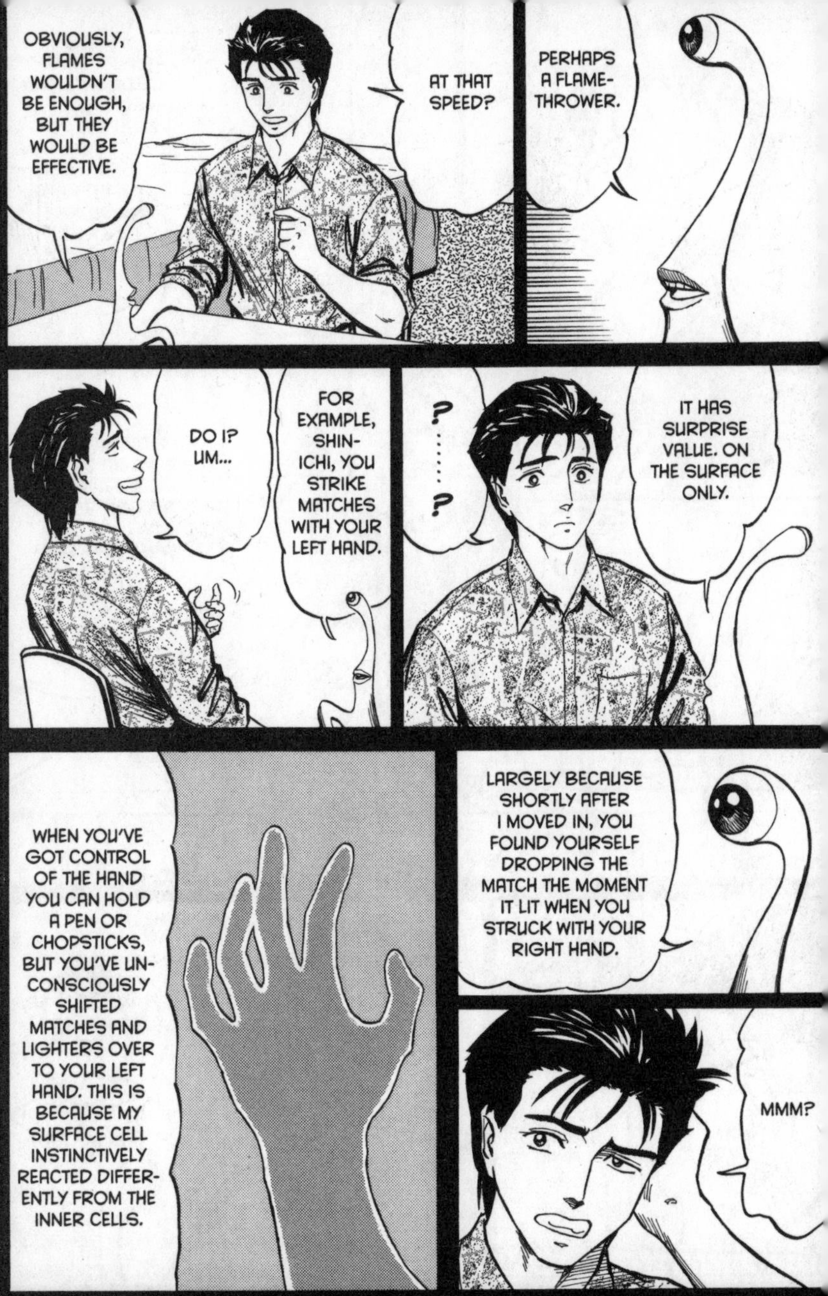
PERHAPS A FLAME-THROWER.
AT THAT SPEED?
OBVIOUSLY, FLAMES WOULDN'T BE ENOUGH, BUT THEY WOULD BE EFFECTIVE.
IT HAS SURPRISE VALUE. ON THE SURFACE ONLY.
?......?
FOR EXAMPLE, SHIN-ICHI, YOU STRIKE MATCHES WITH YOUR LEFT HAND.
DO I? UM...
LARGELY BECAUSE SHORTLY AFTER I MOVED IN, YOU FOUND YOURSELF DROPPING THE MATCH THE MOMENT IT LIT WHEN YOU STRUCK WITH YOUR RIGHT HAND.
MMM?
WHEN YOU'VE GOT CONTROL OF THE HAND YOU CAN HOLD A PEN OR CHOPSTICKS, BUT YOU'VE UN-CONSCIOUSLY SHIFTED MATCHES AND LIGHTERS OVER TO YOUR LEFT HAND. THIS IS BECAUSE MY SURFACE CELL INSTINCTIVELY REACTED DIFFER-ENTLY FROM THE INNER CELLS.

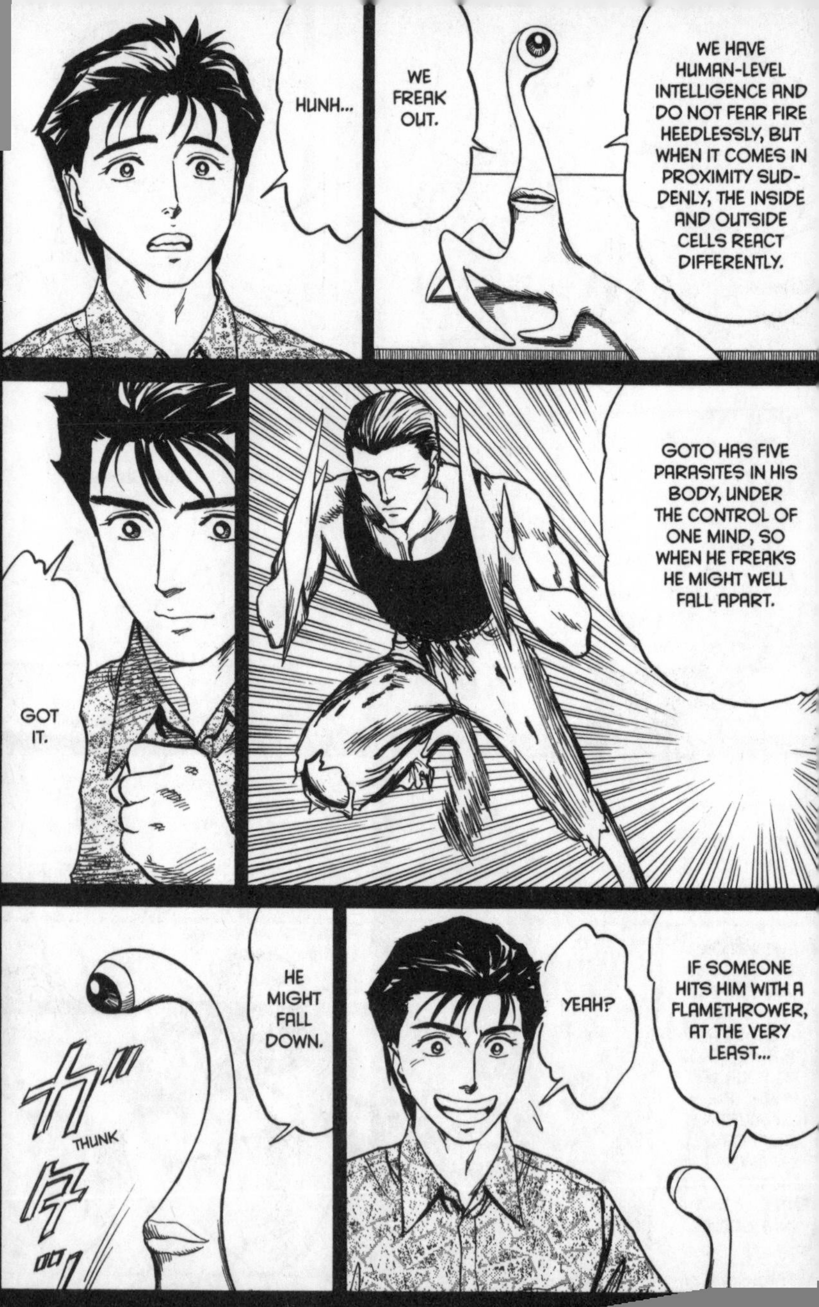
WE HAVE HUMAN-LEVEL INTELLIGENCE AND DO NOT FEAR FIRE HEEDLESSLY, BUT WHEN IT COMES IN PROXIMITY SUDDENLY, THE INSIDE AND OUTSIDE CELLS REACT DIFFERENTLY.
WE FREAK OUT.
HUNH...
GOTO HAS FIVE PARASITES IN HIS BODY, UNDER THE CONTROL OF ONE MIND, SO WHEN HE FREAKS HE MIGHT WELL FALL APART.
GOT IT.
IF SOMEONE HITS HIM WITH A FLAMETHROWER, AT THE VERY LEAST...
YEAH?
HE MIGHT FALL DOWN.
THUNK

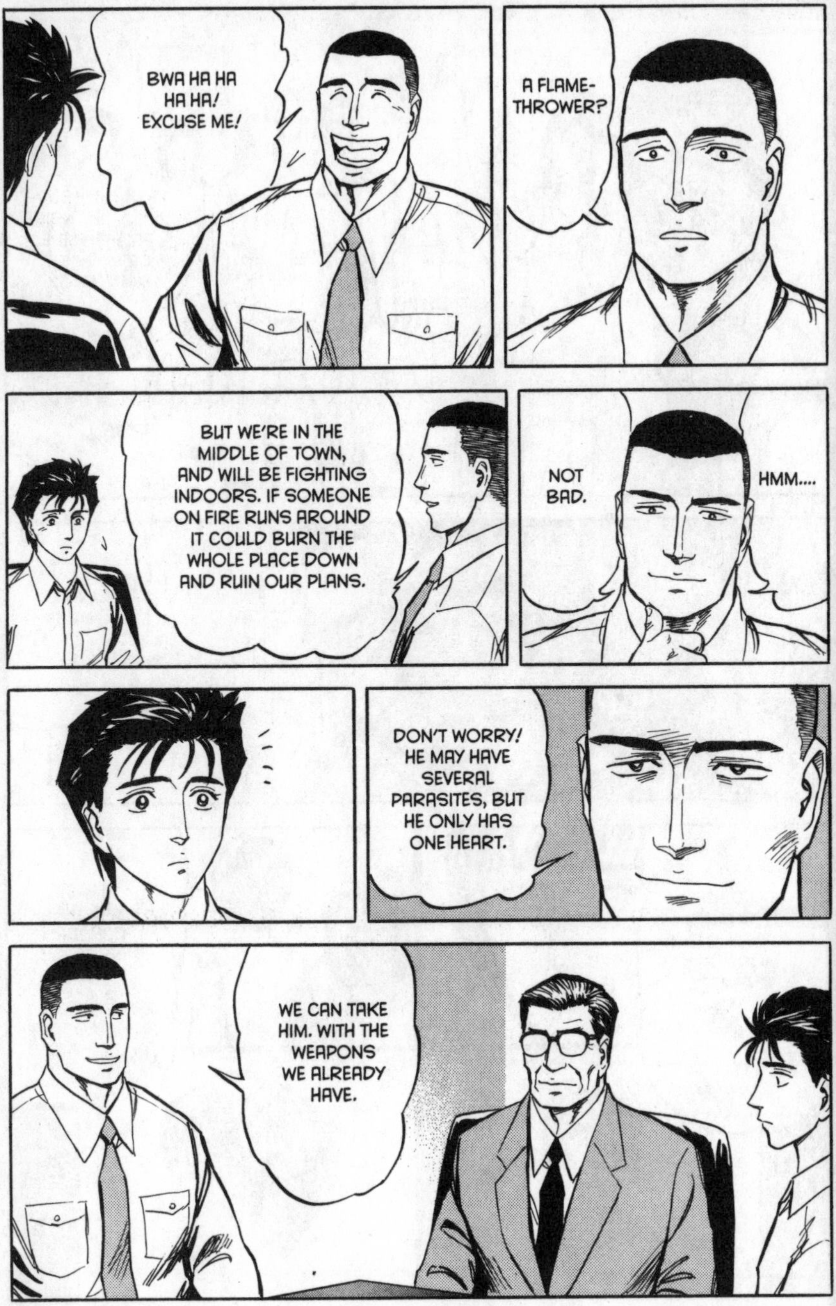
A FLAME-THROWER?
BWA HA HA HA HA! EXCUSE ME!
HMM....
NOT BAD.
BUT WE'RE IN THE MIDDLE OF TOWN, AND WILL BE FIGHTING INDOORS. IF SOMEONE ON FIRE RUNS AROUND IT COULD BURN THE WHOLE PLACE DOWN AND RUIN OUR PLANS.
DON'T WORRY! HE MAY HAVE SEVERAL PARASITES, BUT HE ONLY HAS ONE HEART.
WE CAN TAKE HIM. WITH THE WEAPONS WE ALREADY HAVE.

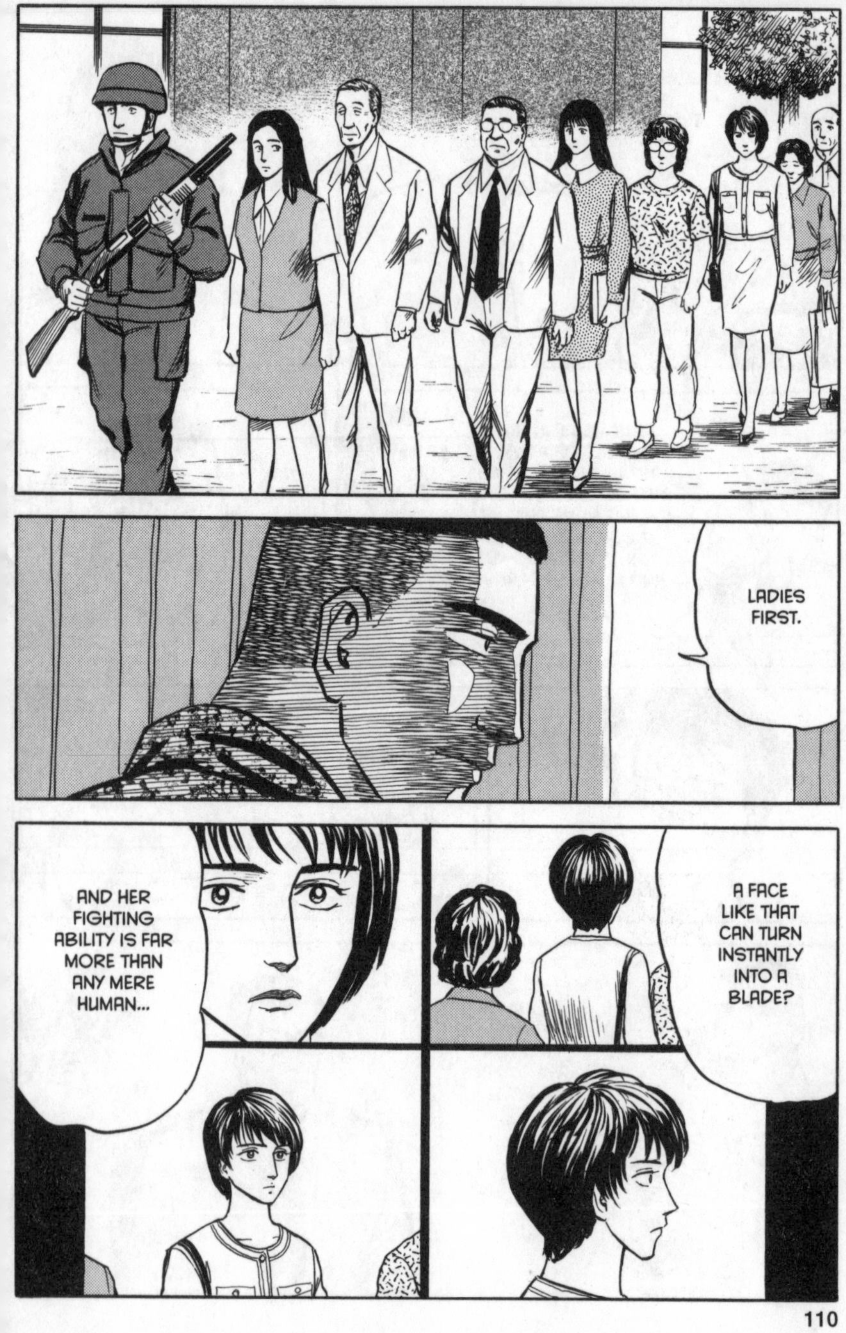
LADIES FIRST.
A FACE LIKE THAT CAN TURN INSTANTLY INTO A BLADE?
AND HER FIGHTING ABILITY IS FAR MORE THAN ANY MERE HUMAN...

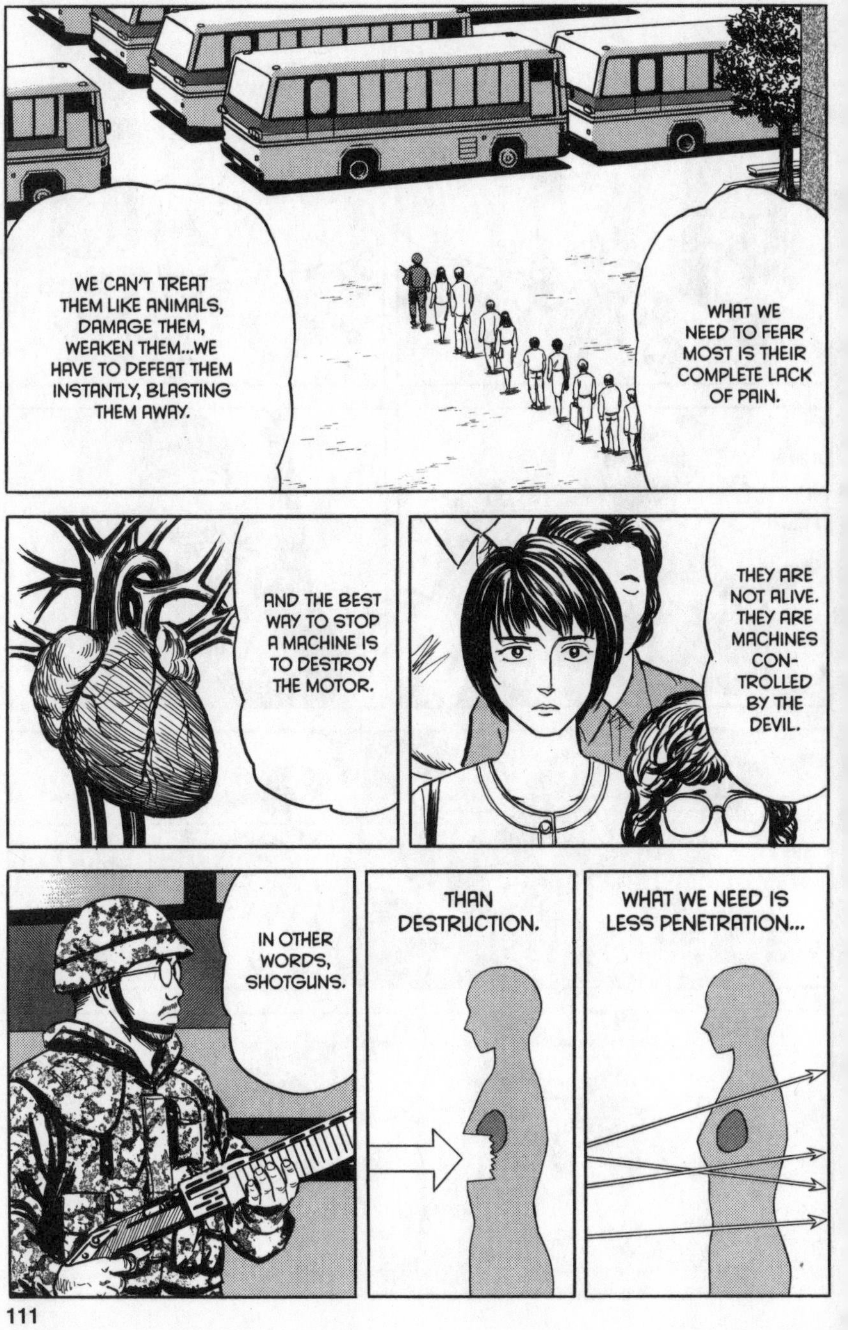
WHAT WE NEED TO FEAR MOST IS THEIR COMPLETE LACK OF PAIN.
WE CAN'T TREAT THEM LIKE ANIMALS, DAMAGE THEM, WEAKEN THEM...WE HAVE TO DEFEAT THEM INSTANTLY, BLASTING THEM AWAY.
THEY ARE NOT ALIVE. THEY ARE MACHINES CON-TROLLED BY THE DEVIL.
AND THE BEST WAY TO STOP A MACHINE IS TO DESTROY THE MOTOR.
WHAT WE NEED IS LESS PENETRATION...
THAN DESTRUCTION.
IN OTHER WORDS, SHOTGUNS.

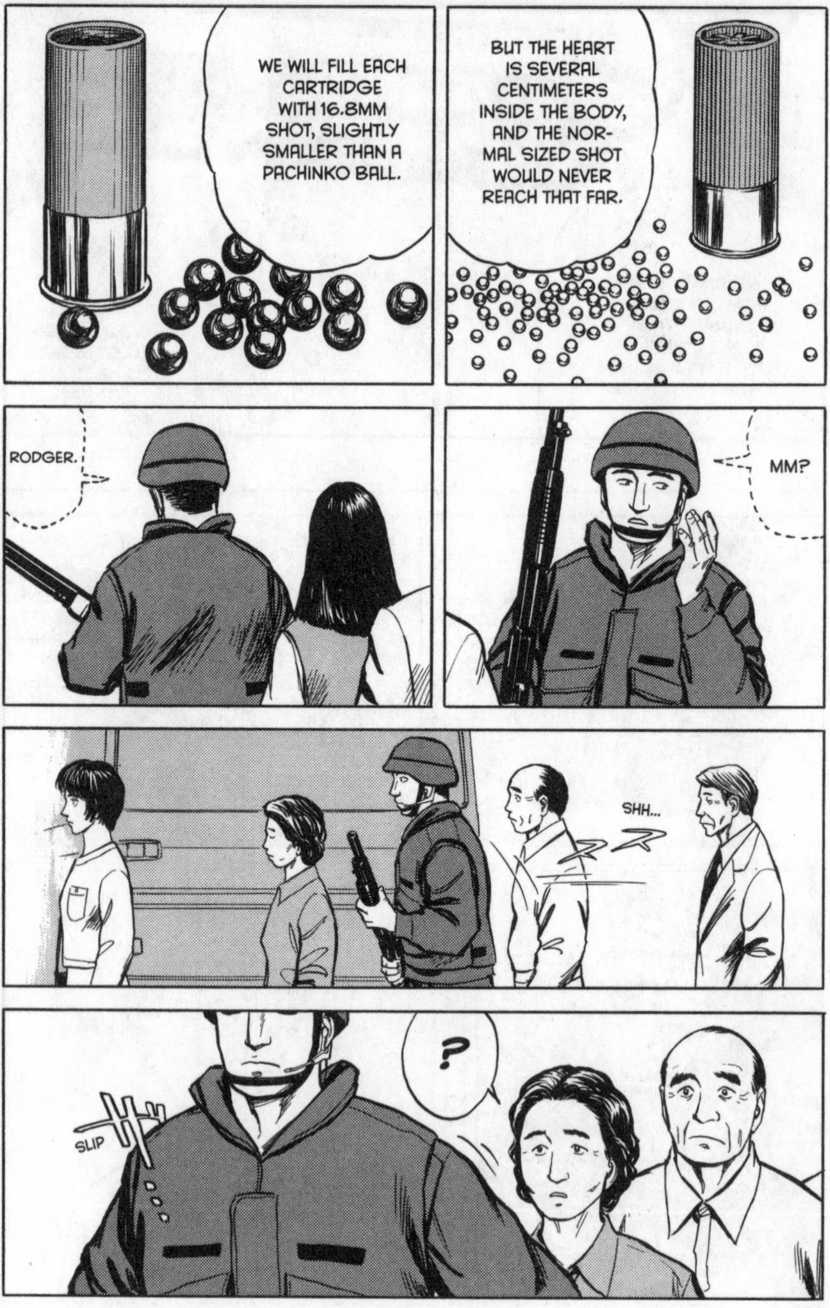
BUT THE HEART IS SEVERAL CENTIMETERS INSIDE THE BODY, AND THE NORMAL SIZED SHOT WOULD NEVER REACH THAT FAR.
WE WILL FILL EACH CARTRIDGE WITH 16.8MM SHOT, SLIGHTLY SMALLER THAN A PACHINKO BALL.
MM?
RODGER.
SHH...
?
SLIP

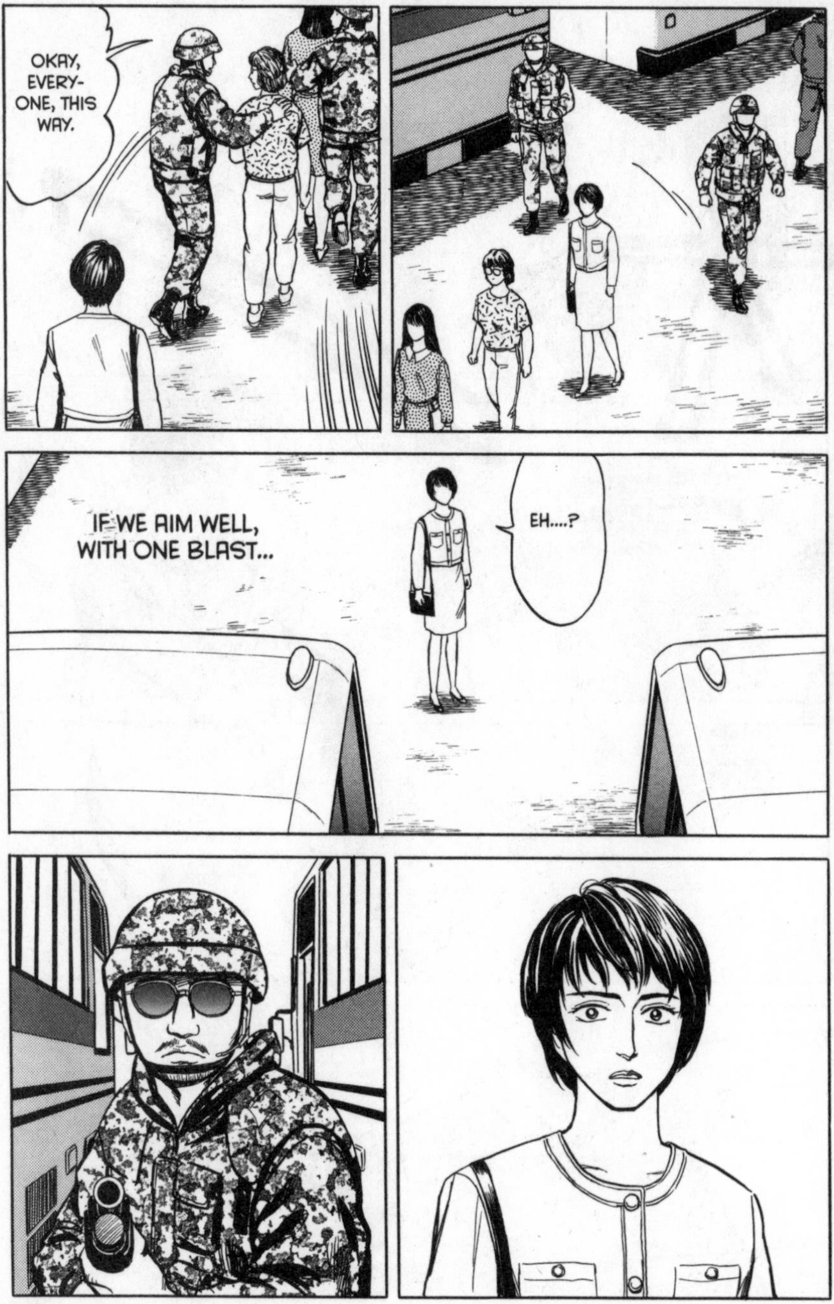
OKAY, EVERY-ONE, THIS WAY.
EH....?
IF WE AIM WELL, WITH ONE BLAST...

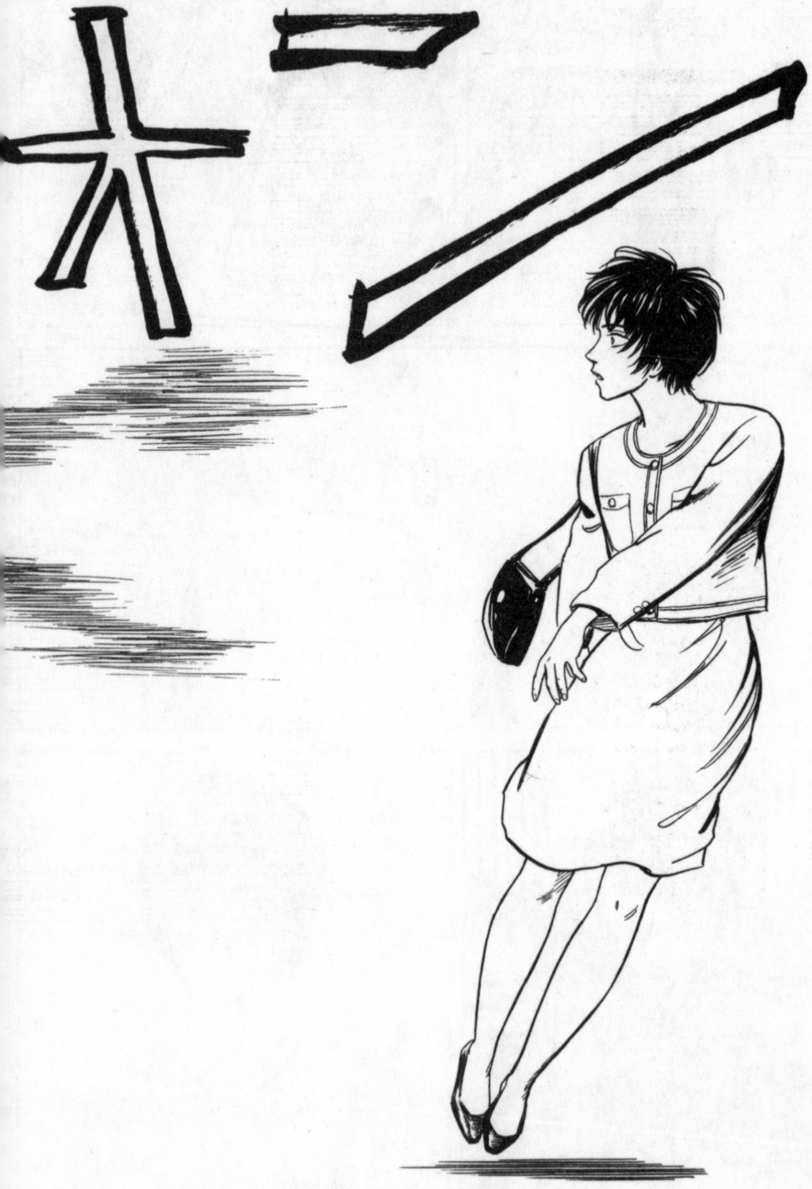
オーン

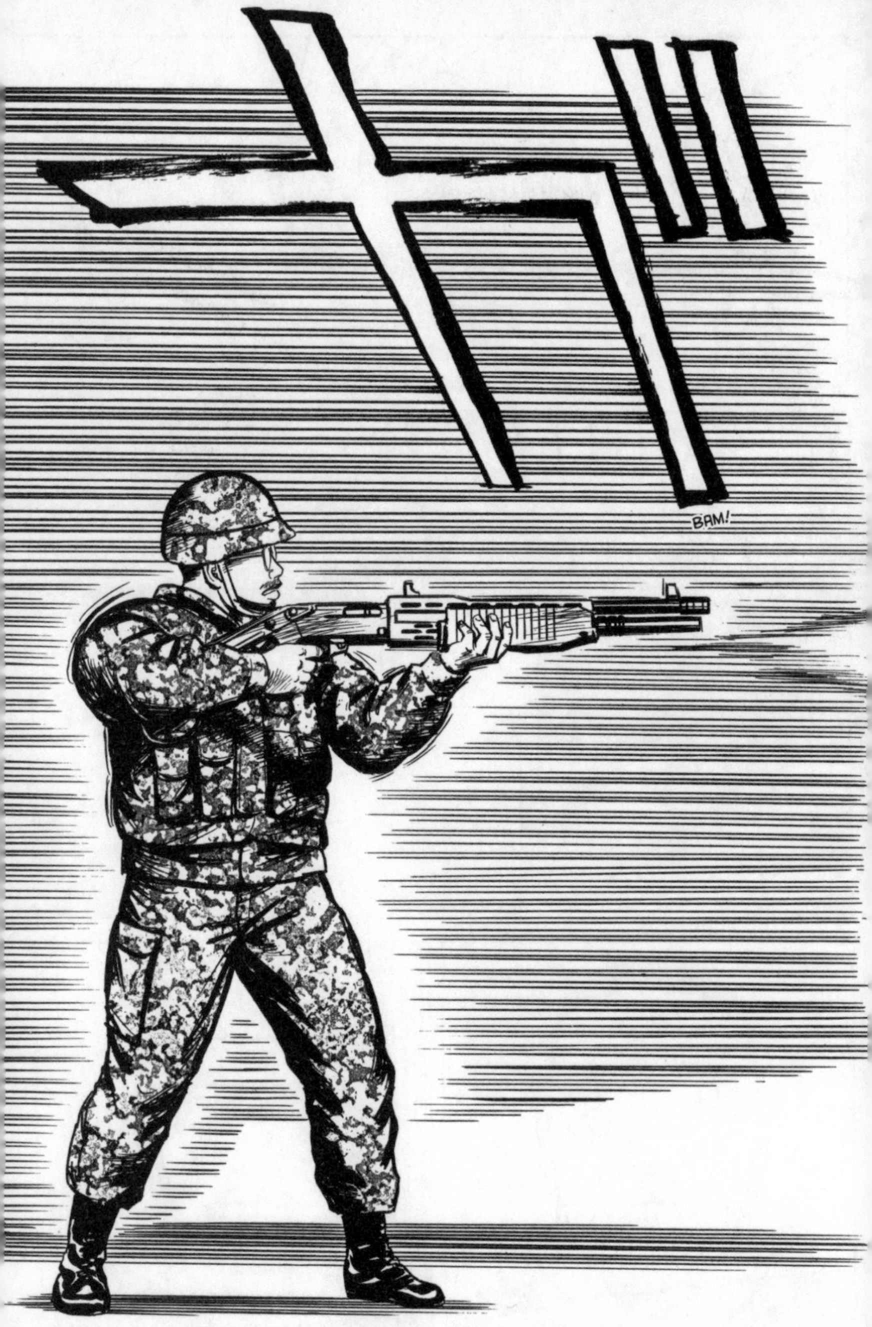
BAM!

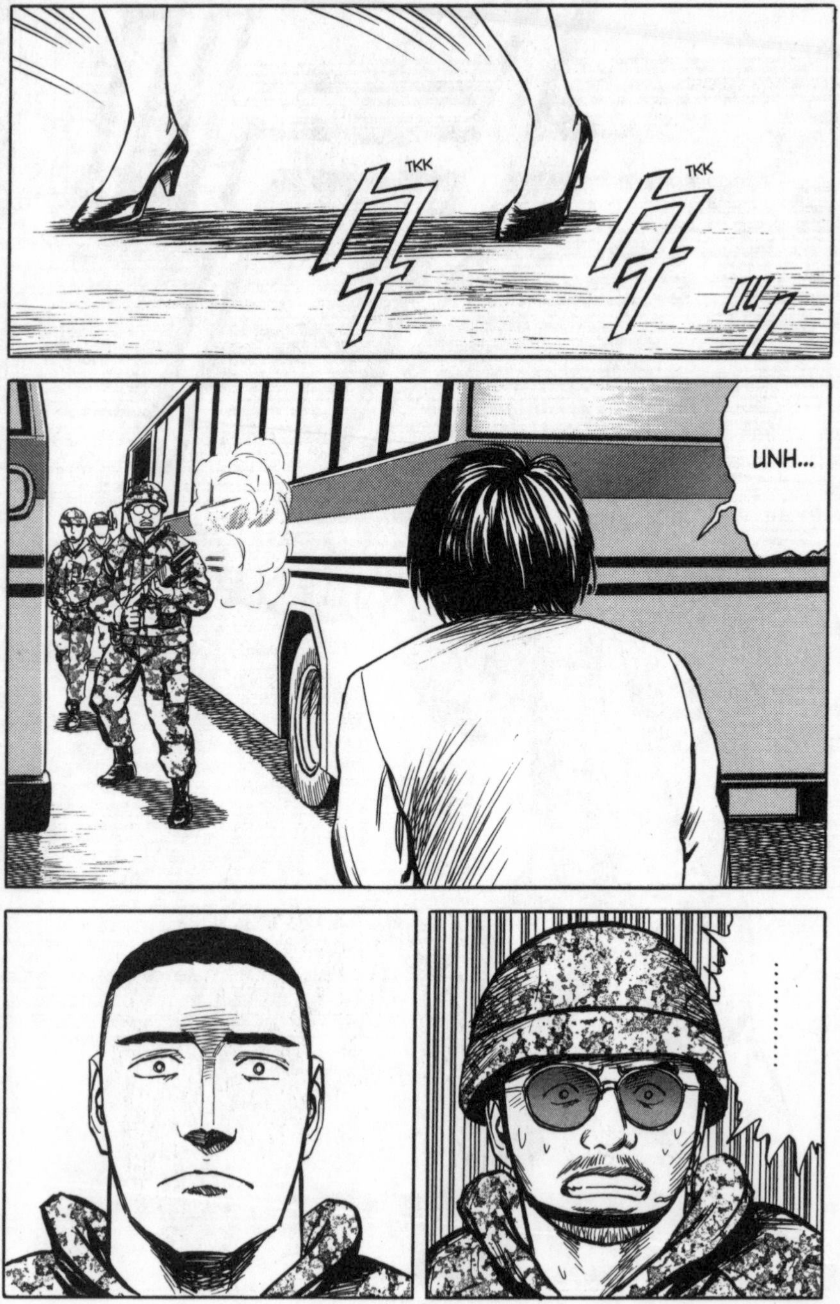
TKK
TKK
UNH...
......

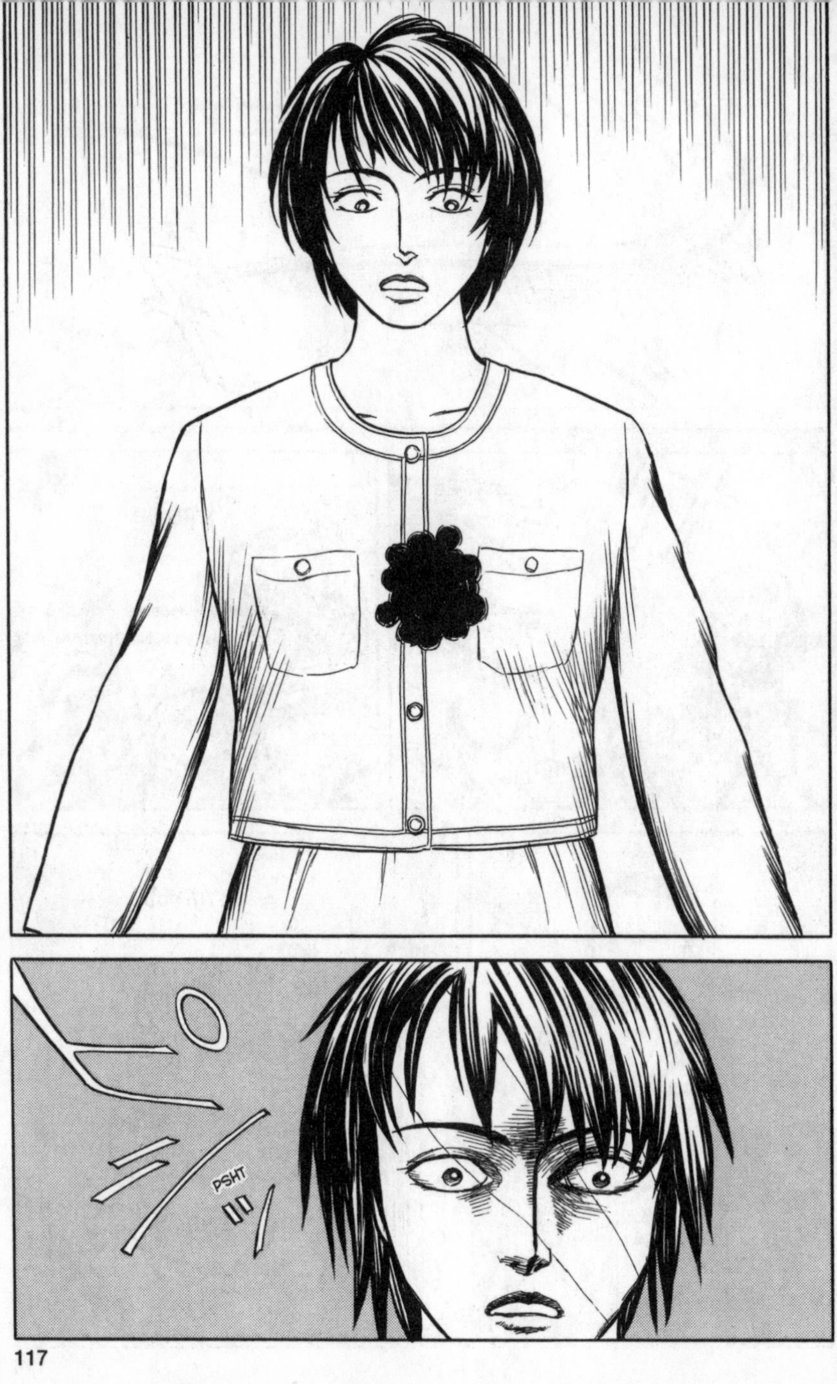
PSHT

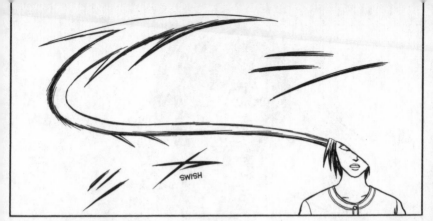

SWISH

CLUNK

AUGH!

WAIT FOR IT...

DON'T SHOOT...

YIKES!

118

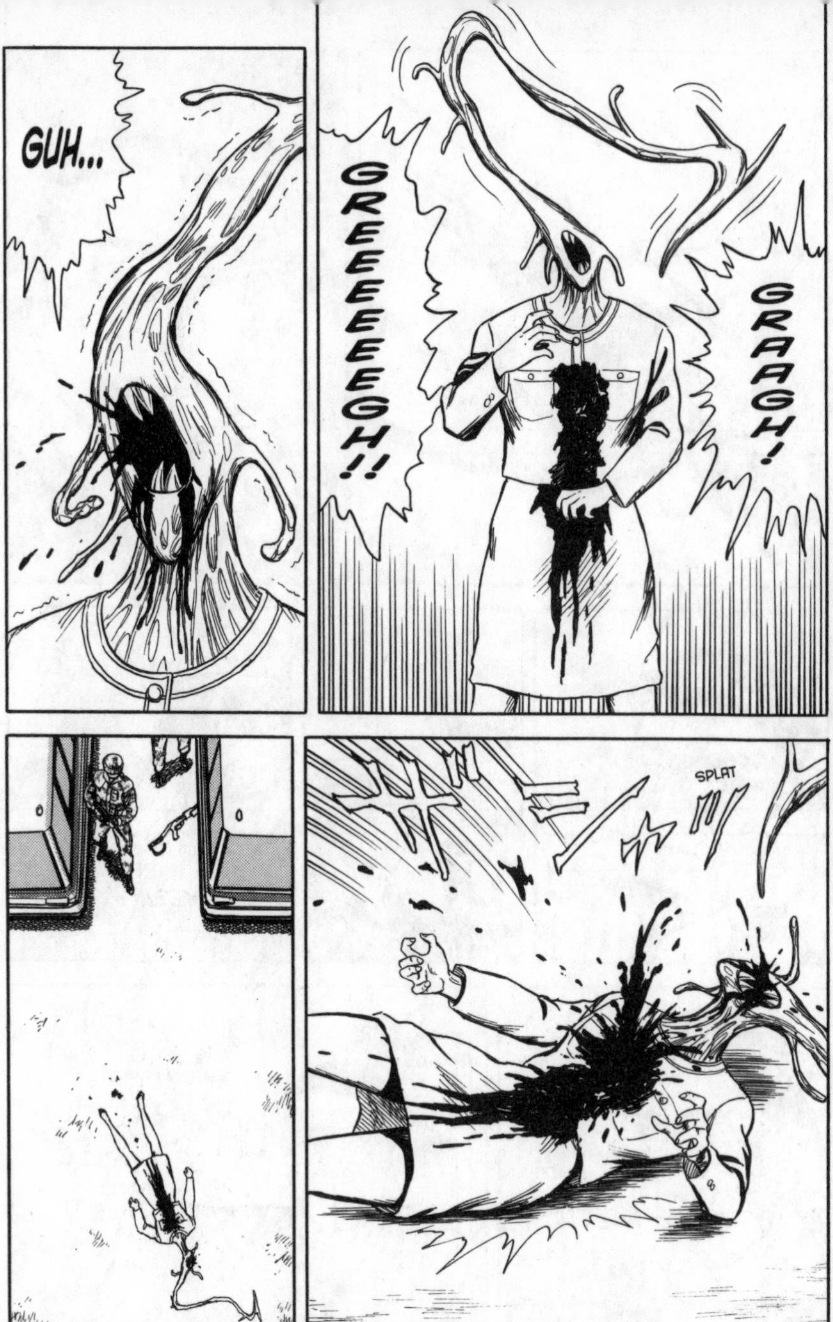
GRAAGH!
GREEEEEEGH!!
GUH...
SPLAT

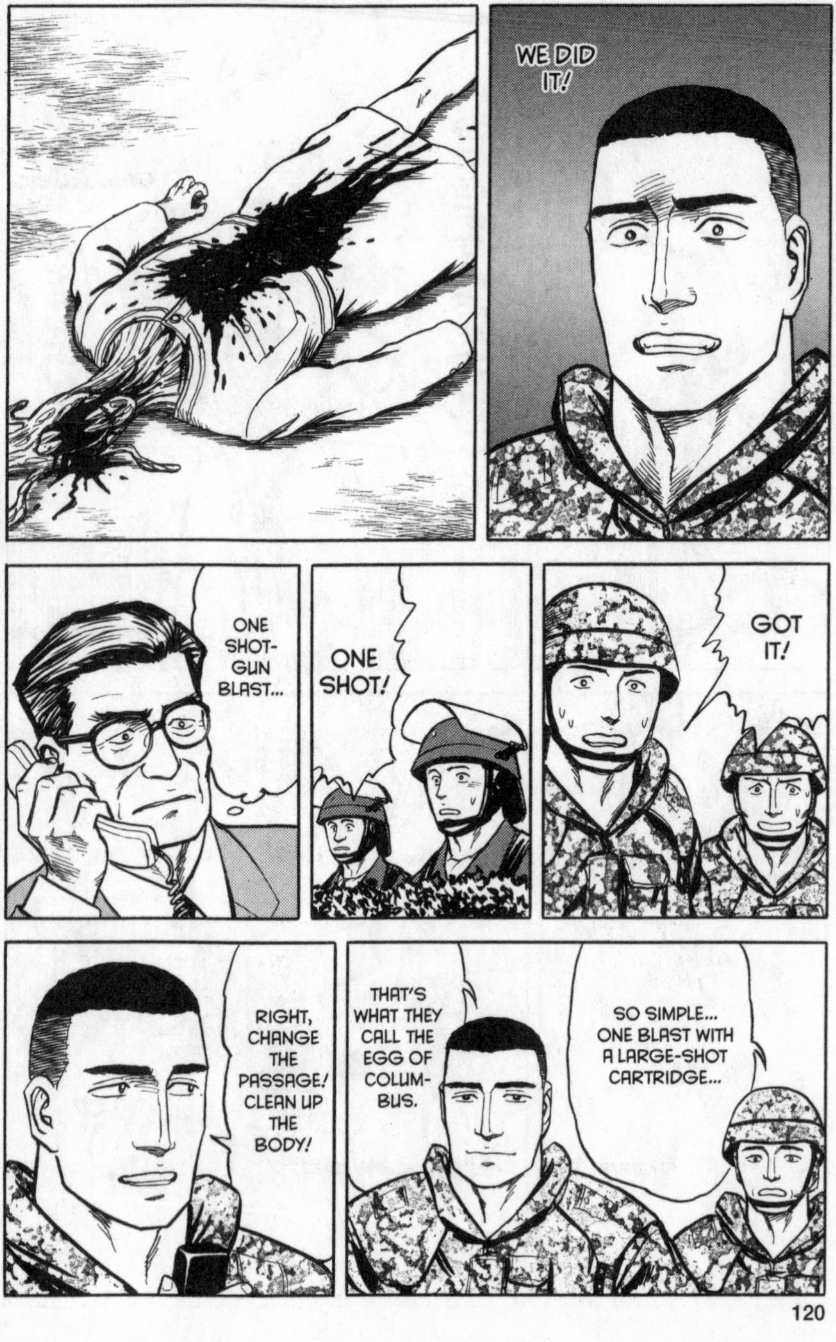
WE DID IT!
GOT IT!
ONE SHOT!
ONE SHOT-GUN BLAST...
SO SIMPLE... ONE BLAST WITH A LARGE-SHOT CARTRIDGE...
THAT'S WHAT THEY CALL THE EGG OF COLUMBUS.
RIGHT, CHANGE THE PASSAGE! CLEAN UP THE BODY!

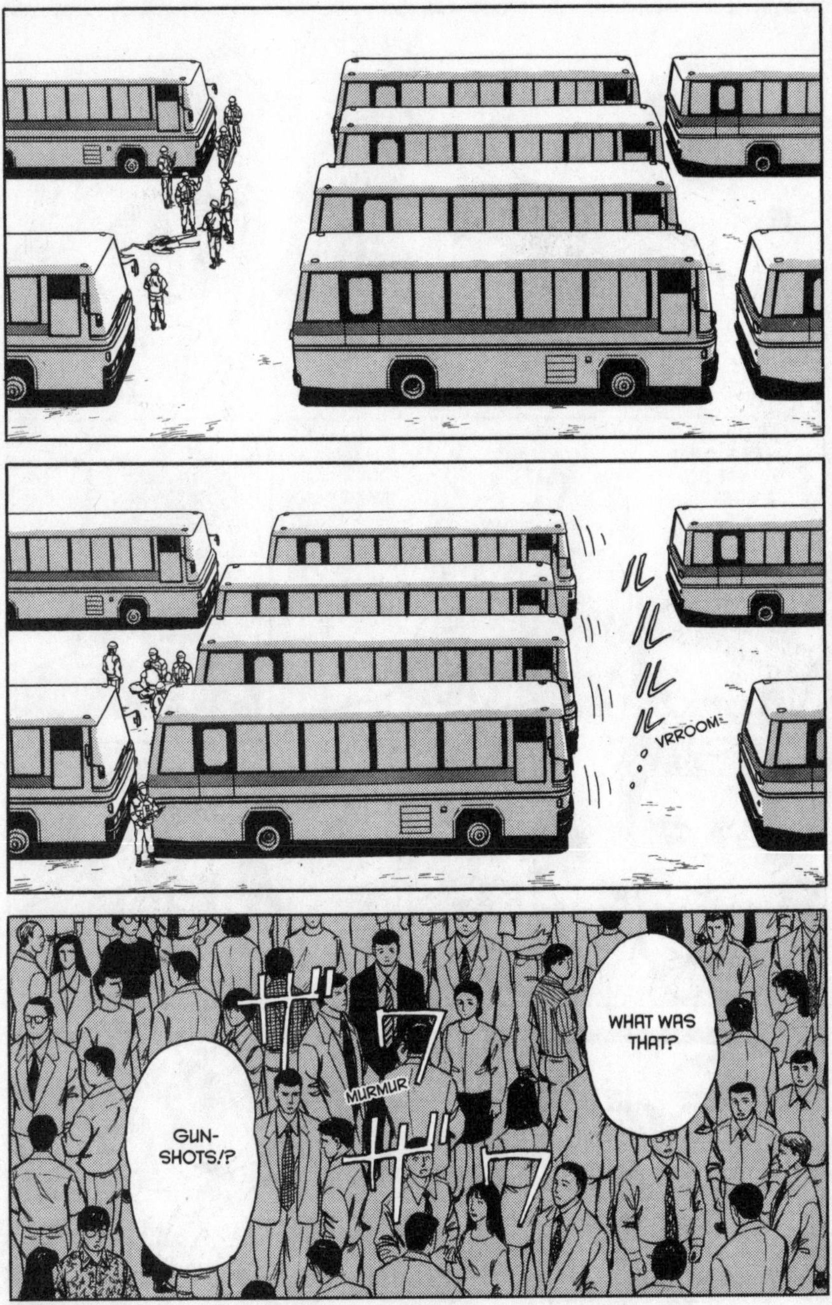
ルルルル
VRROOM
WHAT WAS THAT?
ザワ
MURMUR
ザワ
GUN-SHOTS!?

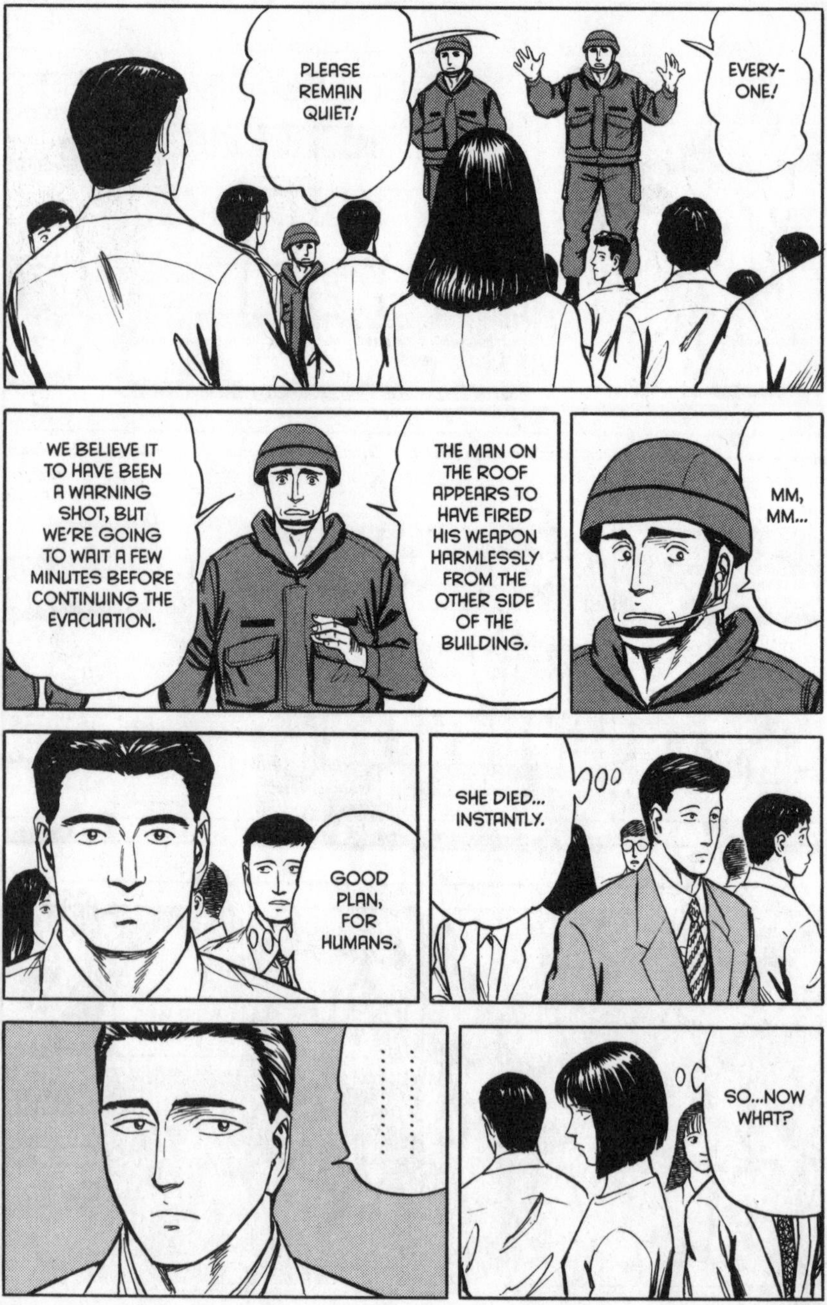
EVERY-ONE!
PLEASE REMAIN QUIET!
MM, MM...
THE MAN ON THE ROOF APPEARS TO HAVE FIRED HIS WEAPON HARMLESSLY FROM THE OTHER SIDE OF THE BUILDING.
WE BELIEVE IT TO HAVE BEEN A WARNING SHOT, BUT WE'RE GOING TO WAIT A FEW MINUTES BEFORE CONTINUING THE EVACUATION.
SHE DIED... INSTANTLY.
GOOD PLAN, FOR HUMANS.
SO...NOW WHAT?
......

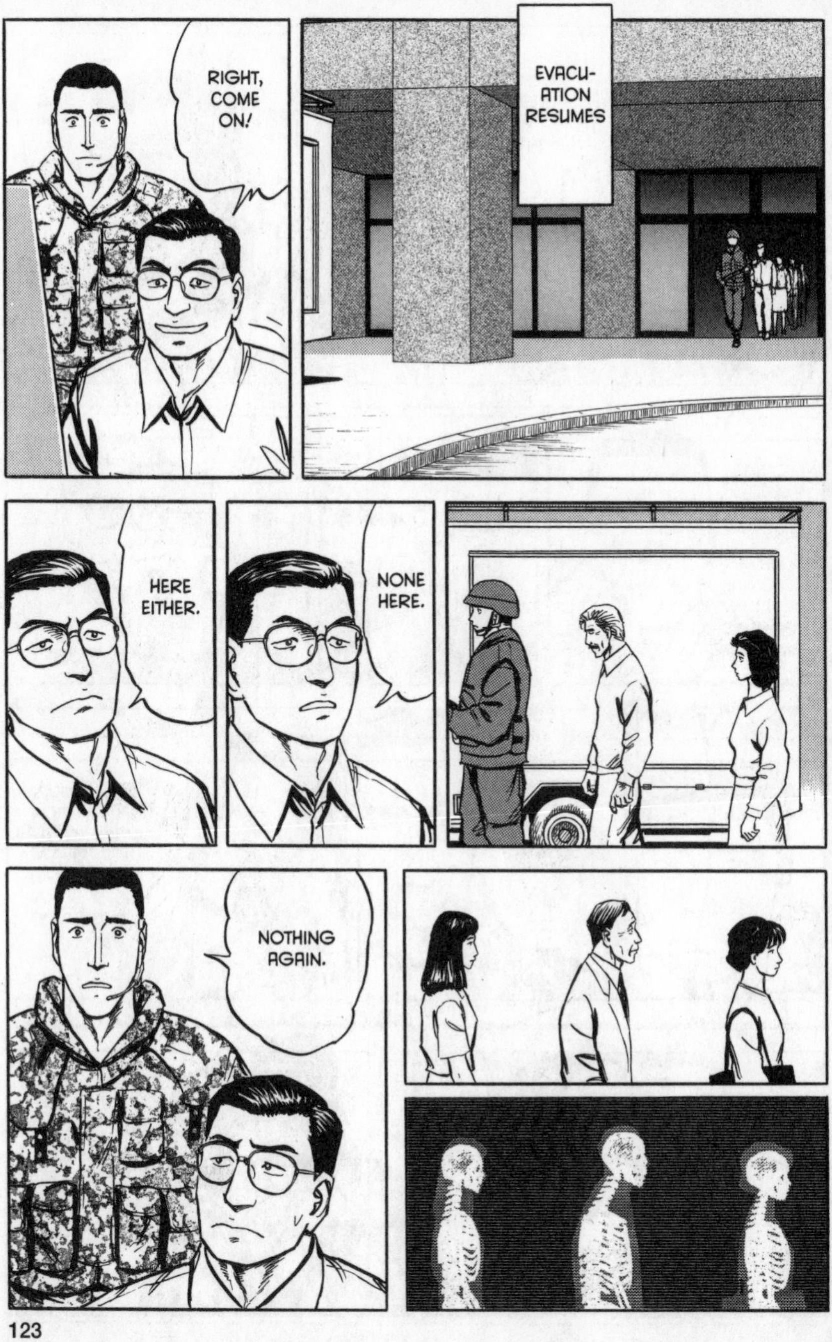
EVACU-
ATION
RESUMES
RIGHT, COME ON!
NONE HERE.
HERE EITHER.
NOTHING AGAIN.

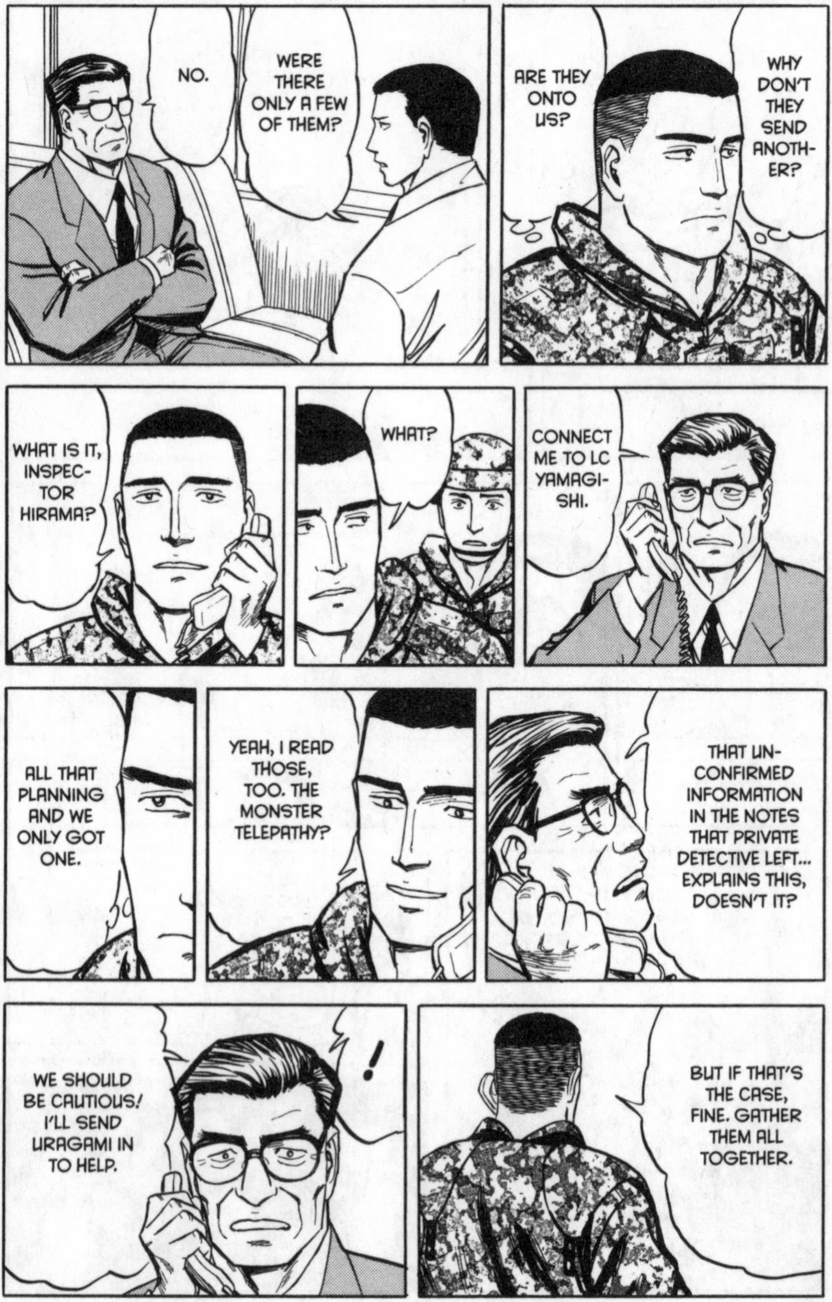
WHY DON'T THEY SEND ANOTHER?
ARE THEY ONTO US?
WERE THERE ONLY A FEW OF THEM?
NO.
CONNECT ME TO LC YAMAGISHI.
WHAT?
WHAT IS IT, INSPECTOR HIRAMA?
THAT UNCONFIRMED INFORMATION IN THE NOTES THAT PRIVATE DETECTIVE LEFT... EXPLAINS THIS, DOESN'T IT?
YEAH, I READ THOSE, TOO. THE MONSTER TELEPATHY?
ALL THAT PLANNING AND WE ONLY GOT ONE.
BUT IF THAT'S THE CASE, FINE. GATHER THEM ALL TOGETHER.
!
WE SHOULD BE CAUTIOUS! I'LL SEND URAGAMI IN TO HELP.

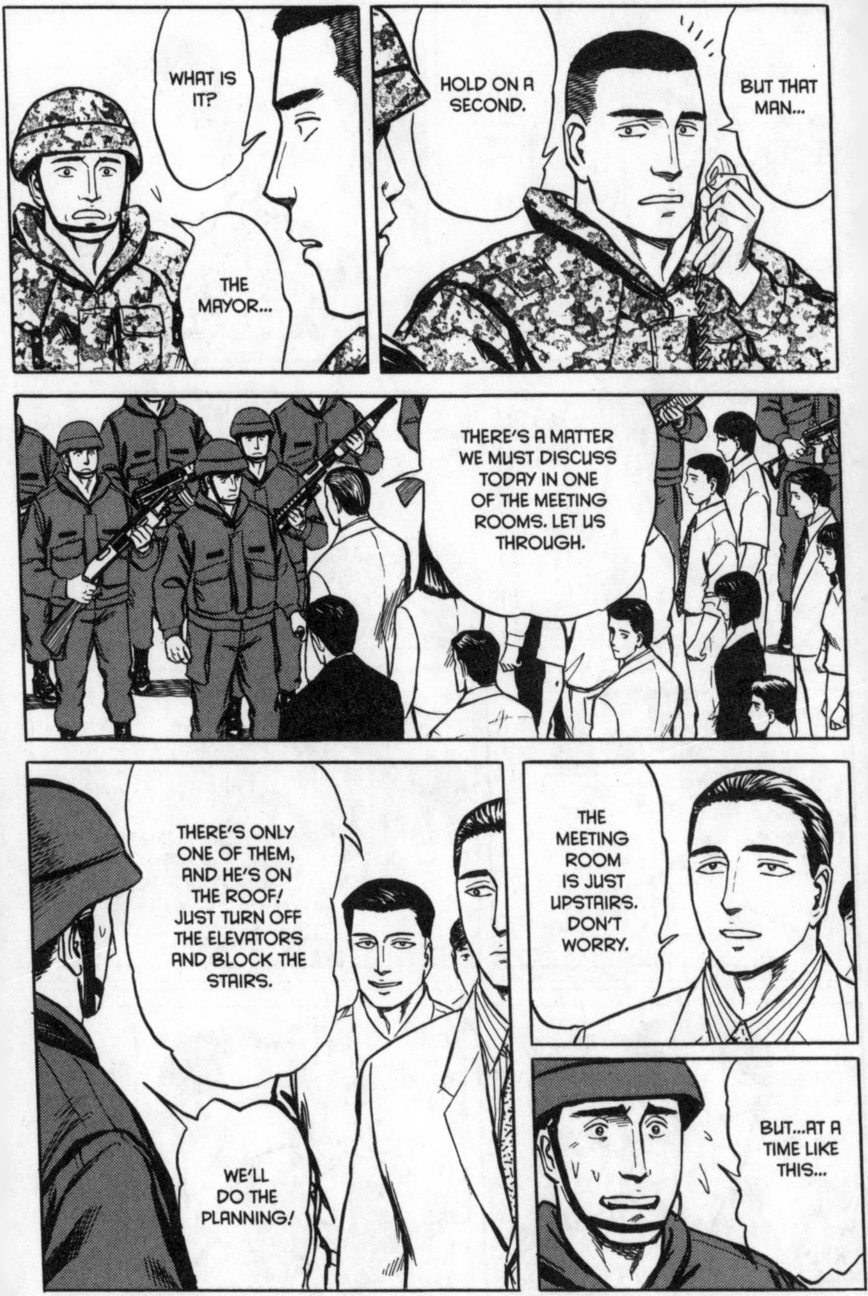
BUT THAT MAN...
HOLD ON A SECOND.
WHAT IS IT?
THE MAYOR...
THERE'S A MATTER WE MUST DISCUSS TODAY IN ONE OF THE MEETING ROOMS. LET US THROUGH.
THE MEETING ROOM IS JUST UPSTAIRS. DON'T WORRY.
BUT...AT A TIME LIKE THIS...
THERE'S ONLY ONE OF THEM, AND HE'S ON THE ROOF! JUST TURN OFF THE ELEVATORS AND BLOCK THE STAIRS.
WE'LL DO THE PLANNING!

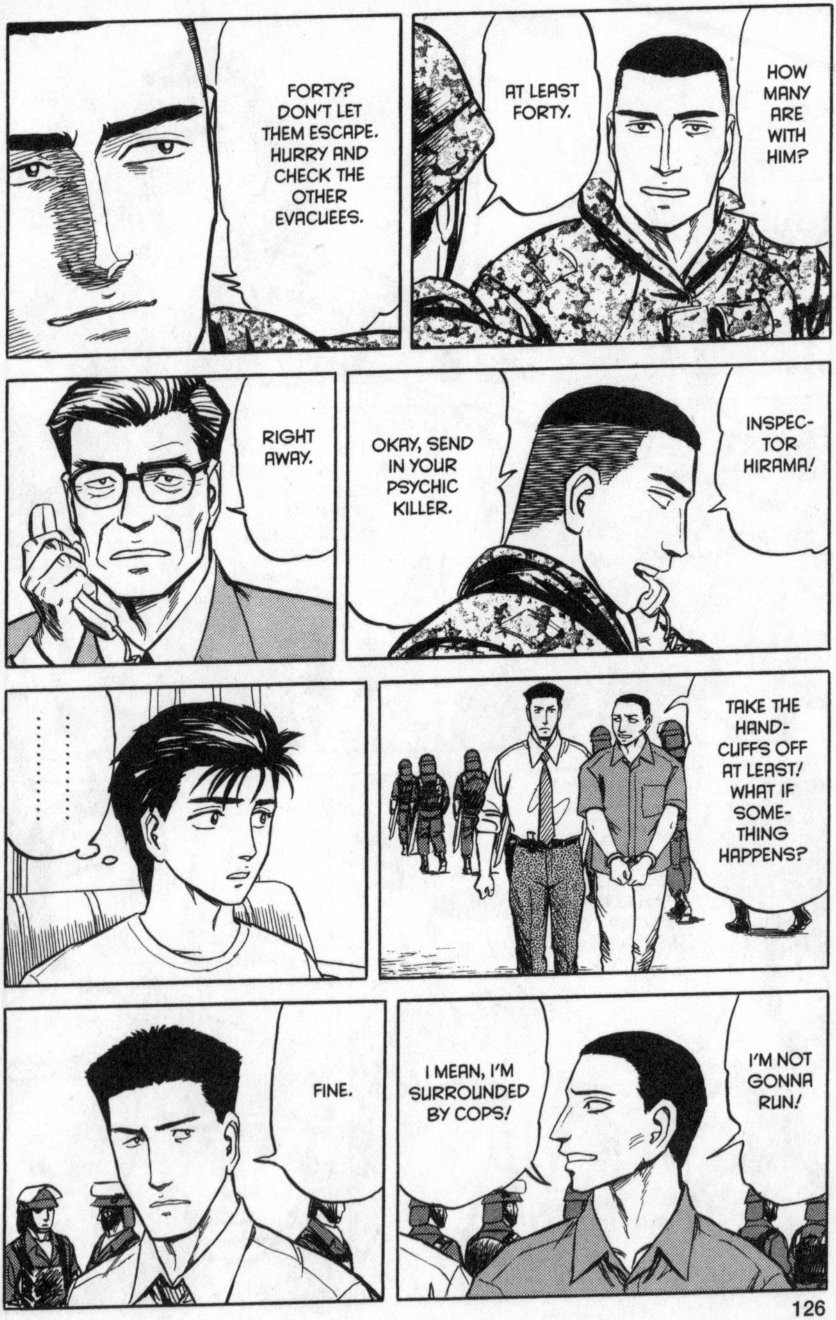
HOW MANY ARE WITH HIM?
AT LEAST FORTY.
FORTY? DON'T LET THEM ESCAPE. HURRY AND CHECK THE OTHER EVACUEES.
INSPECTOR HIRAMA!
OKAY, SEND IN YOUR PSYCHIC KILLER.
RIGHT AWAY.
TAKE THE HAND-CUFFS OFF AT LEAST! WHAT IF SOME-THING HAPPENS?
......
I'M NOT GONNA RUN!
I MEAN, I'M SURROUNDED BY COPS!
FINE.

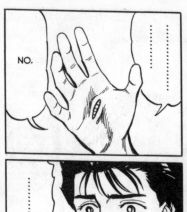

NO.

· · · · · · · ·

· · · · · · · · · · ·

WE'VE GOT TO DO MORE! WE CAN IDENTIFY THEM, TOO!

MIGI! HEY, MIGI!

PLEASE COOPERATE!!

WE CAN'T!!

IF WE'RE GOING TO DO SOMETHING, IT'LL HAVE TO BE WHILE THERE'S STILL A CROWD OF HUMANS...

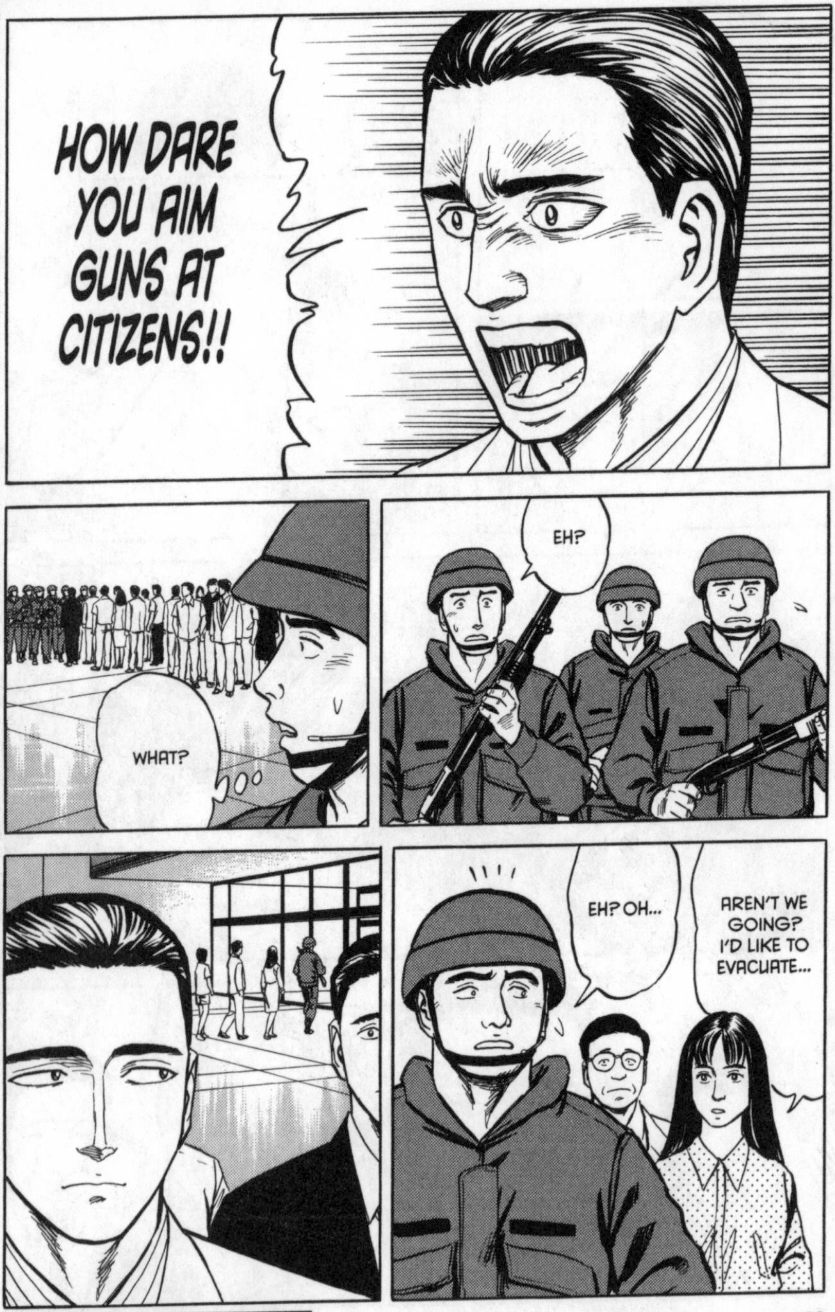
HOW DARE YOU AIM GUNS AT CITIZENS!!
EH?
WHAT?
AREN'T WE GOING? I'D LIKE TO EVACUATE...
EH? OH...

CHAPTER 53: THE END

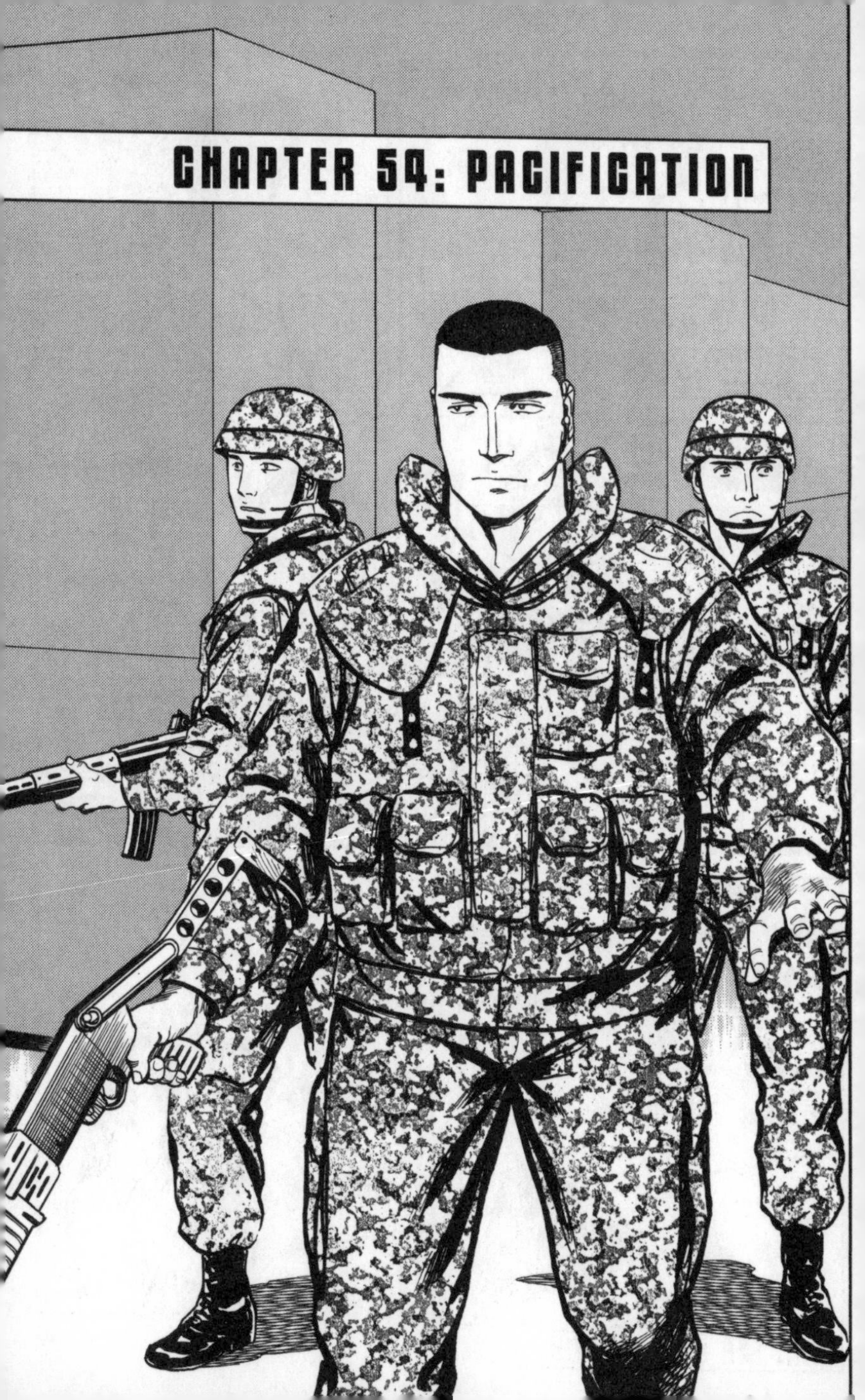
CHAPTER 54: PACIFICATION

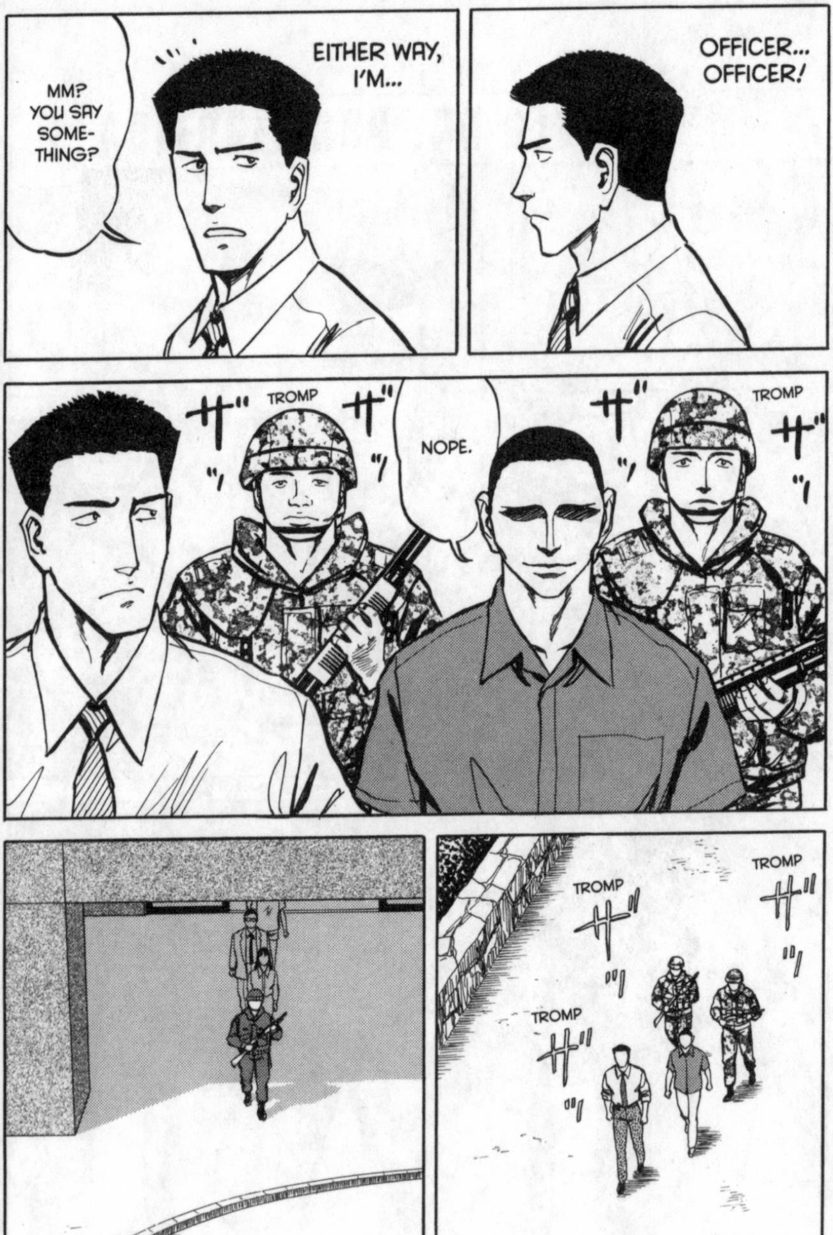

OFFICER... OFFICER!
EITHER WAY, I'M...
MM? YOU SAY SOME-THING?
TROMP
ザッ
ザッ
NOPE.
ザッ
TROMP
ザッ
TROMP
ザッ
TROMP
ザッ
TROMP
ザッ

MM? HEY, WAIT! I CAN'T TELL LIKE THIS!

OH, THIS CAR.

WAIT, STOP!

AH!

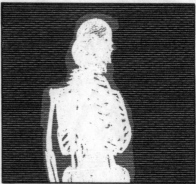

SINGLE-FILE LINE, PLEASE!

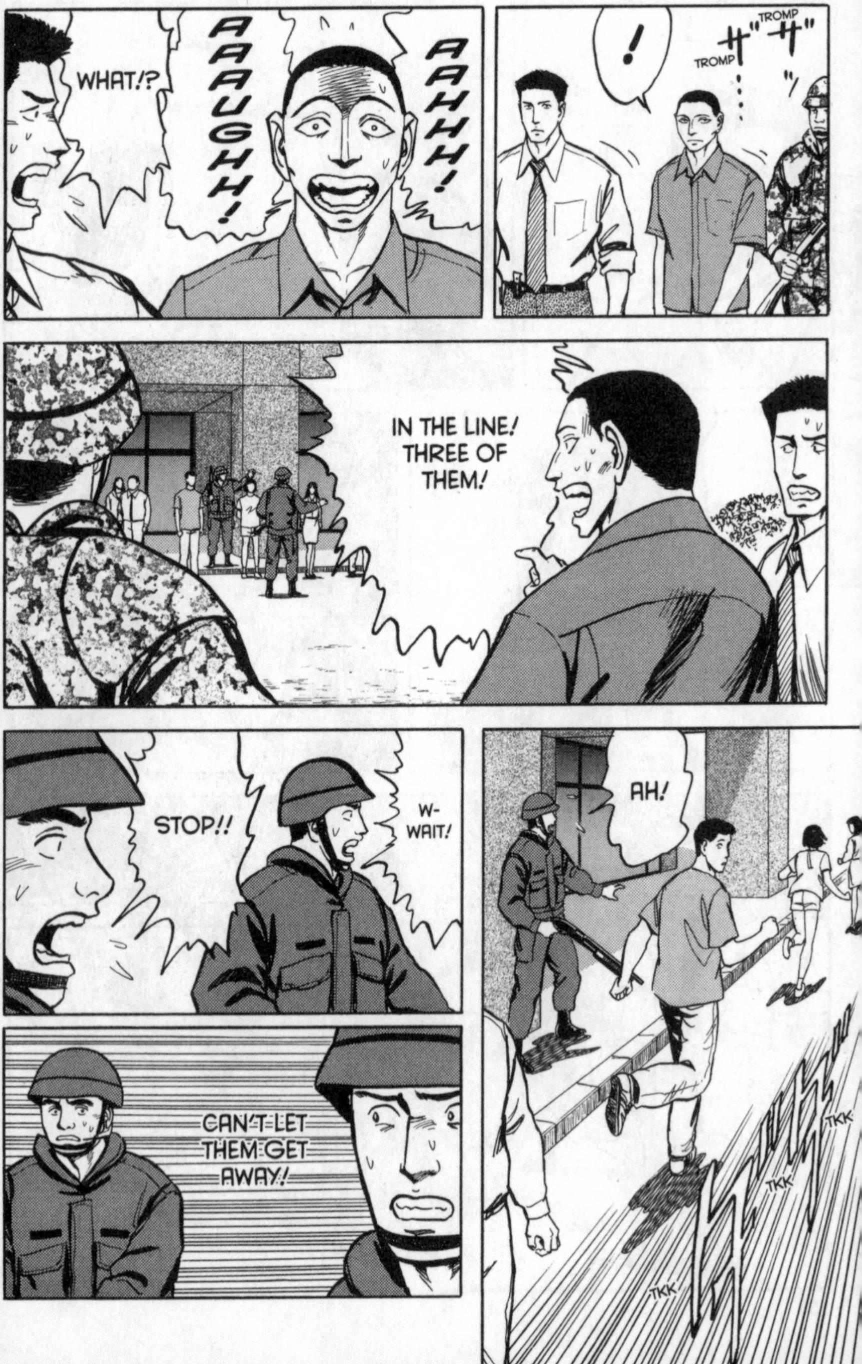
!
TROMP
TROMP
AAHHHH!
AAAUGHH!
WHAT!?
IN THE LINE! THREE OF THEM!
AH!
TKK
TKK
TKK
TKK
W- WAIT!
STOP!!
CAN'T LET THEM GET AWAY!

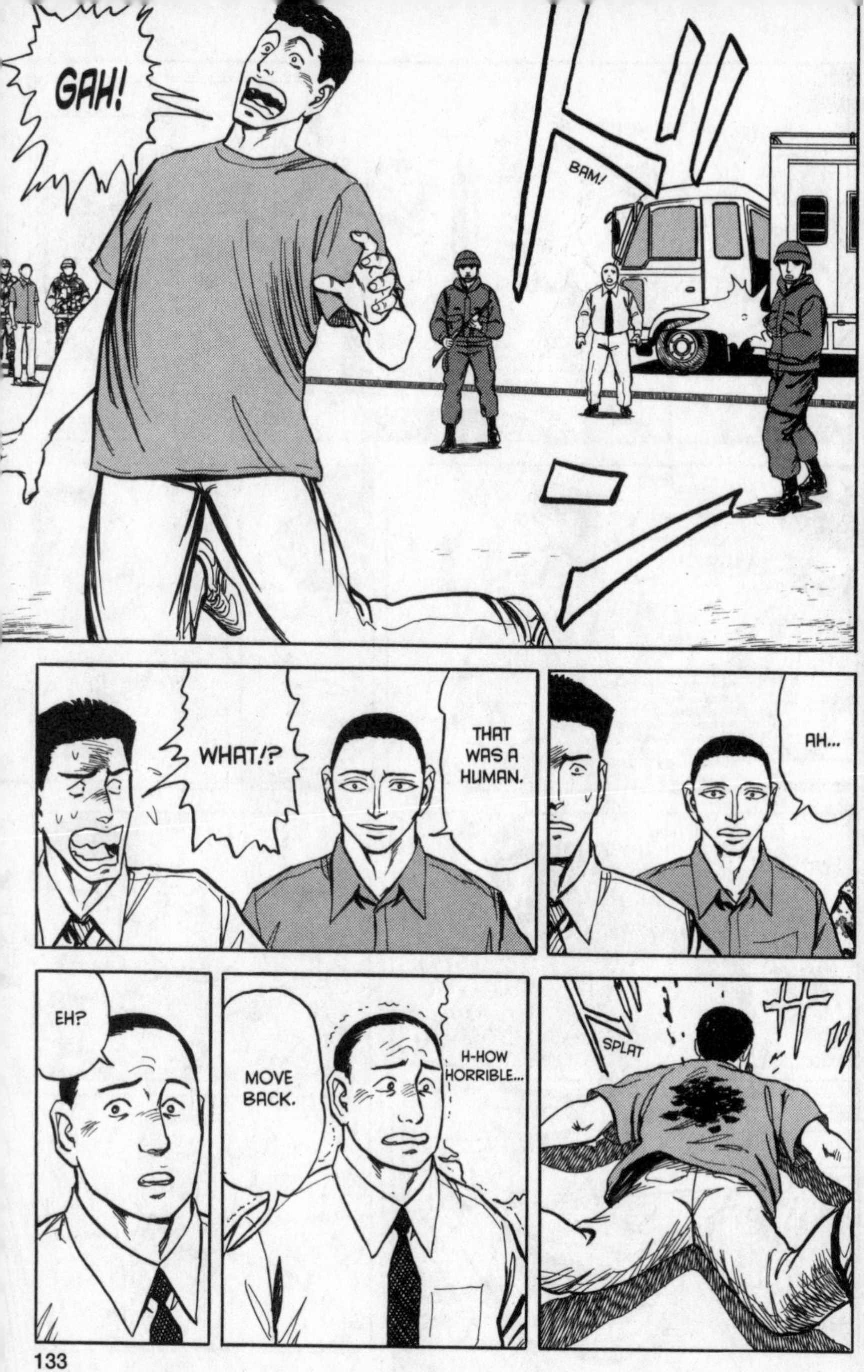
BAM!
GAH!
AH...
THAT WAS A HUMAN.
WHAT!?
SPLAT
H-HOW HORRIBLE...
MOVE BACK.
EH?

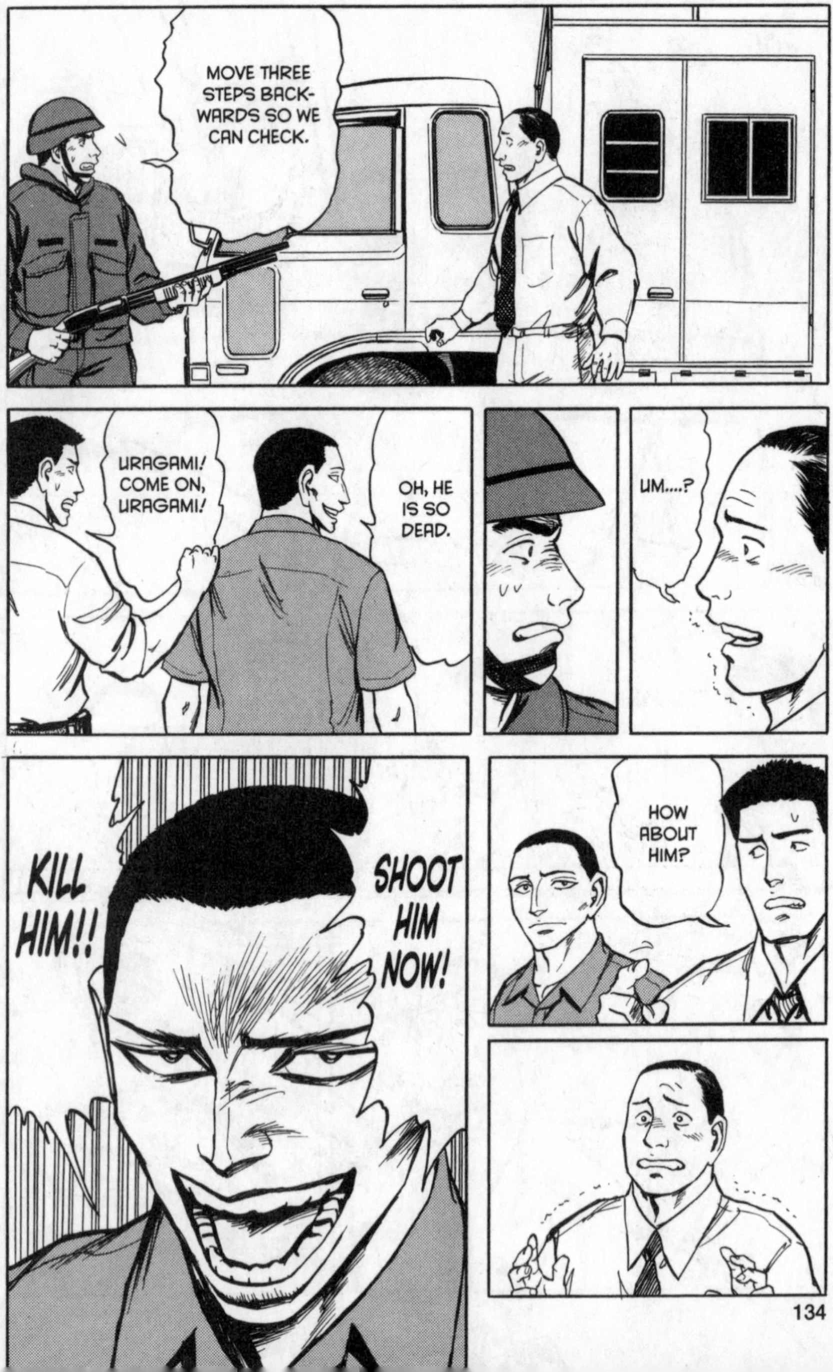
MOVE THREE STEPS BACK-WARDS SO WE CAN CHECK.
UM....?
OH, HE IS SO DEAD.
URAGAMI! COME ON, URAGAMI!
HOW ABOUT HIM?
SHOOT HIM NOW!
KILL HIM!!

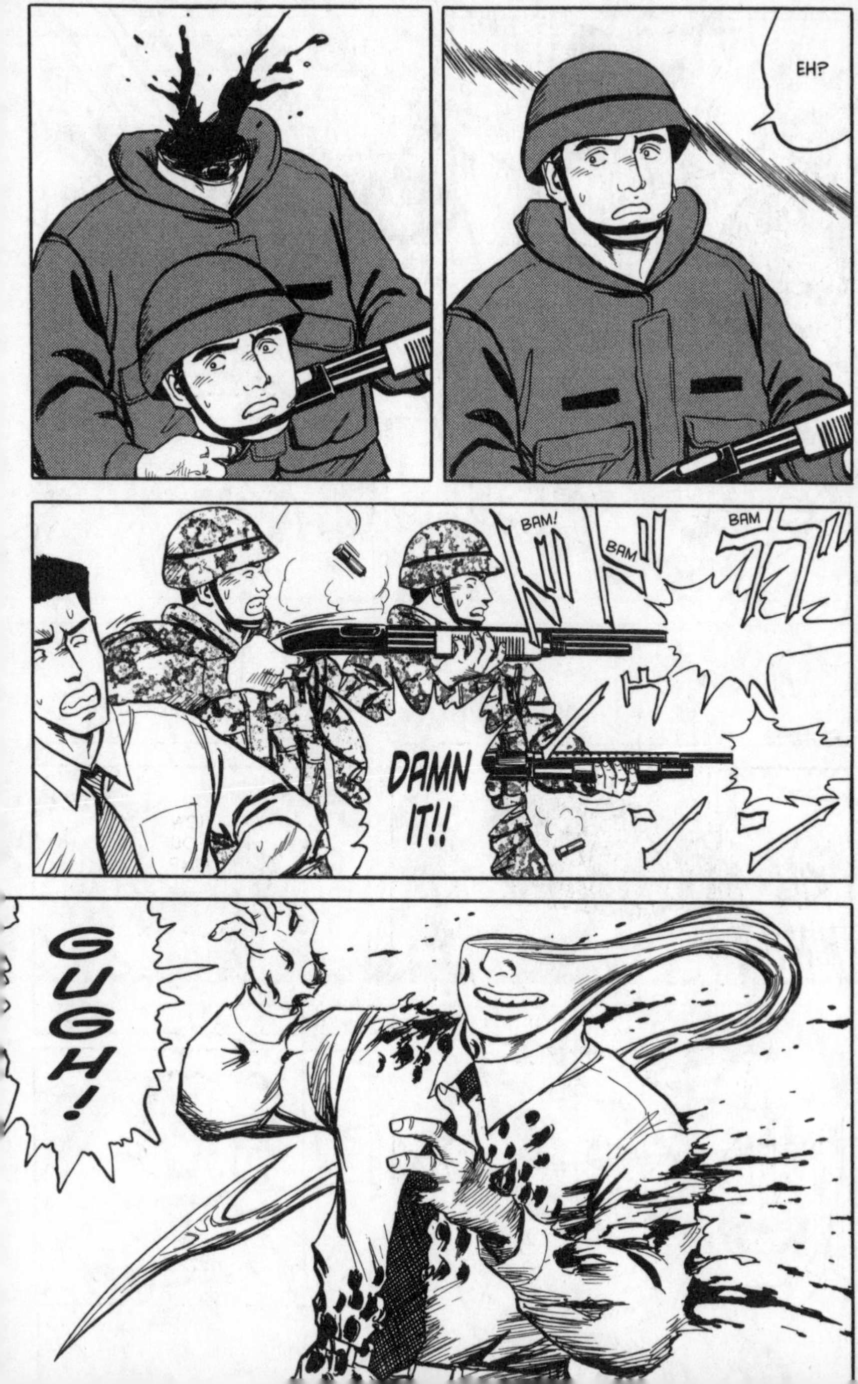
EH?
BAM!
BAM
BAM
DAMN IT!!
GUGH!

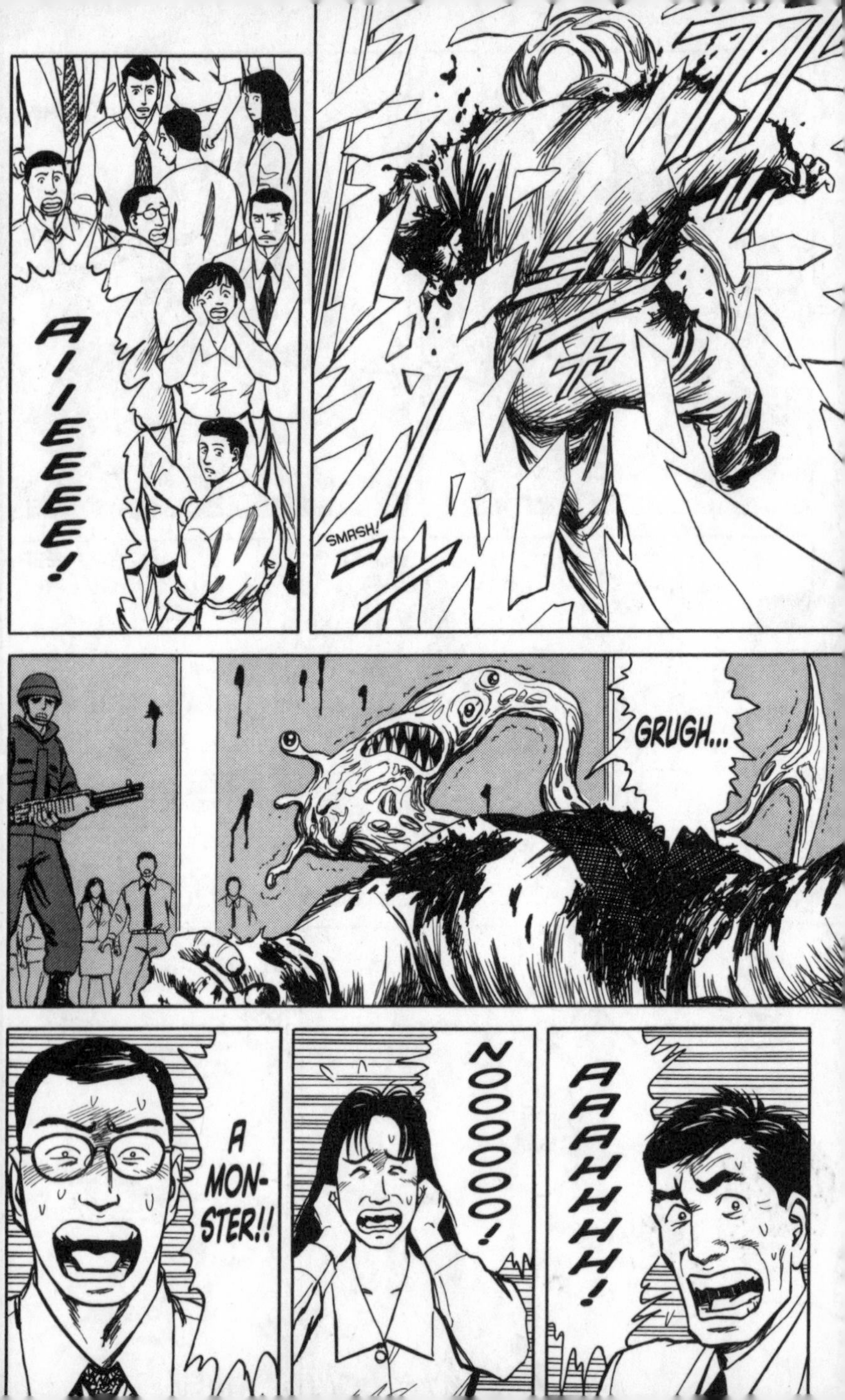
SMASH!
AIIEEEEE!
GRUGH...
AAAHHHH!
NOOOOOO!
A MON-STER!!

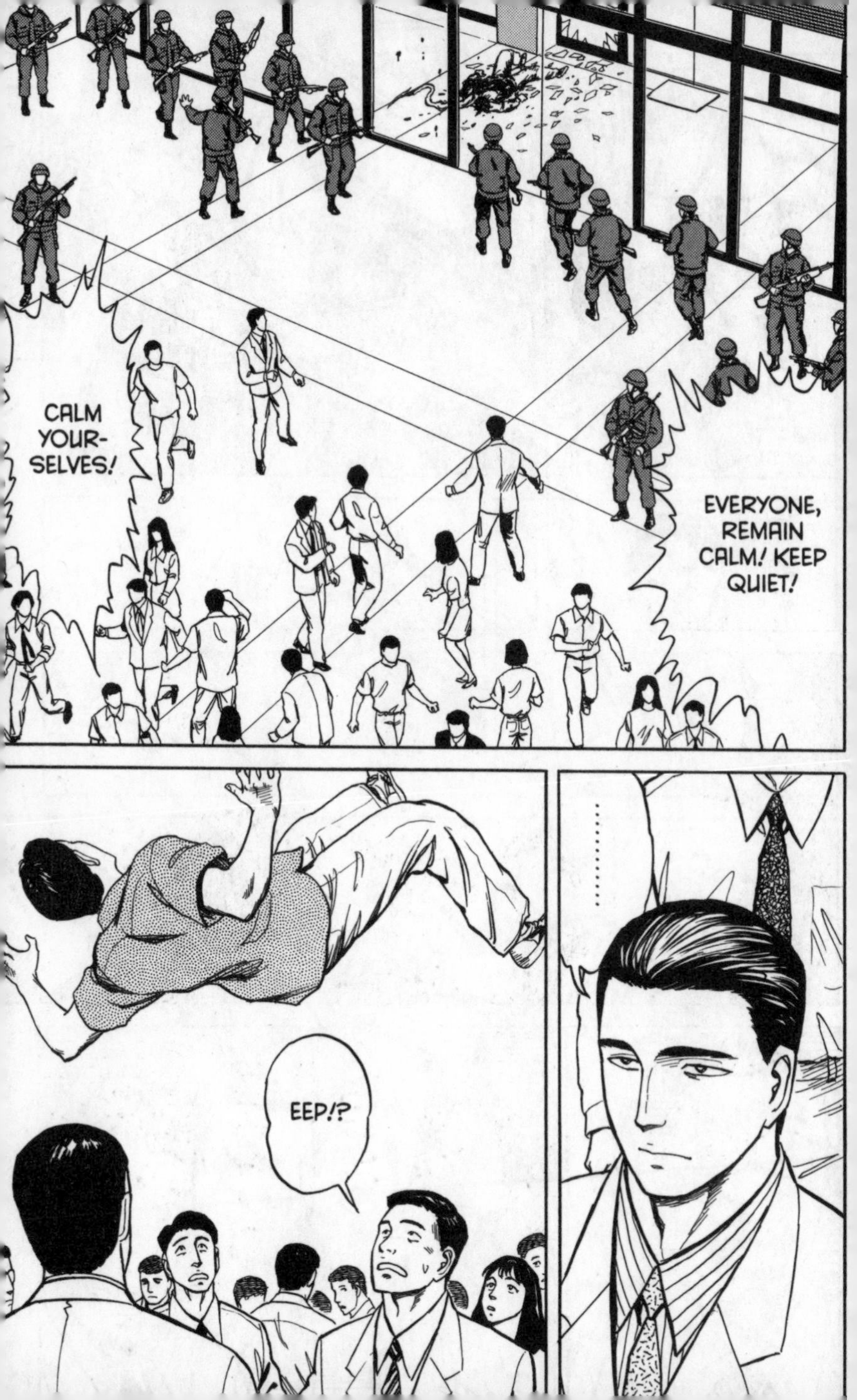
EVERYONE, REMAIN CALM! KEEP QUIET!
CALM YOUR-SELVES!
......
EEP!?

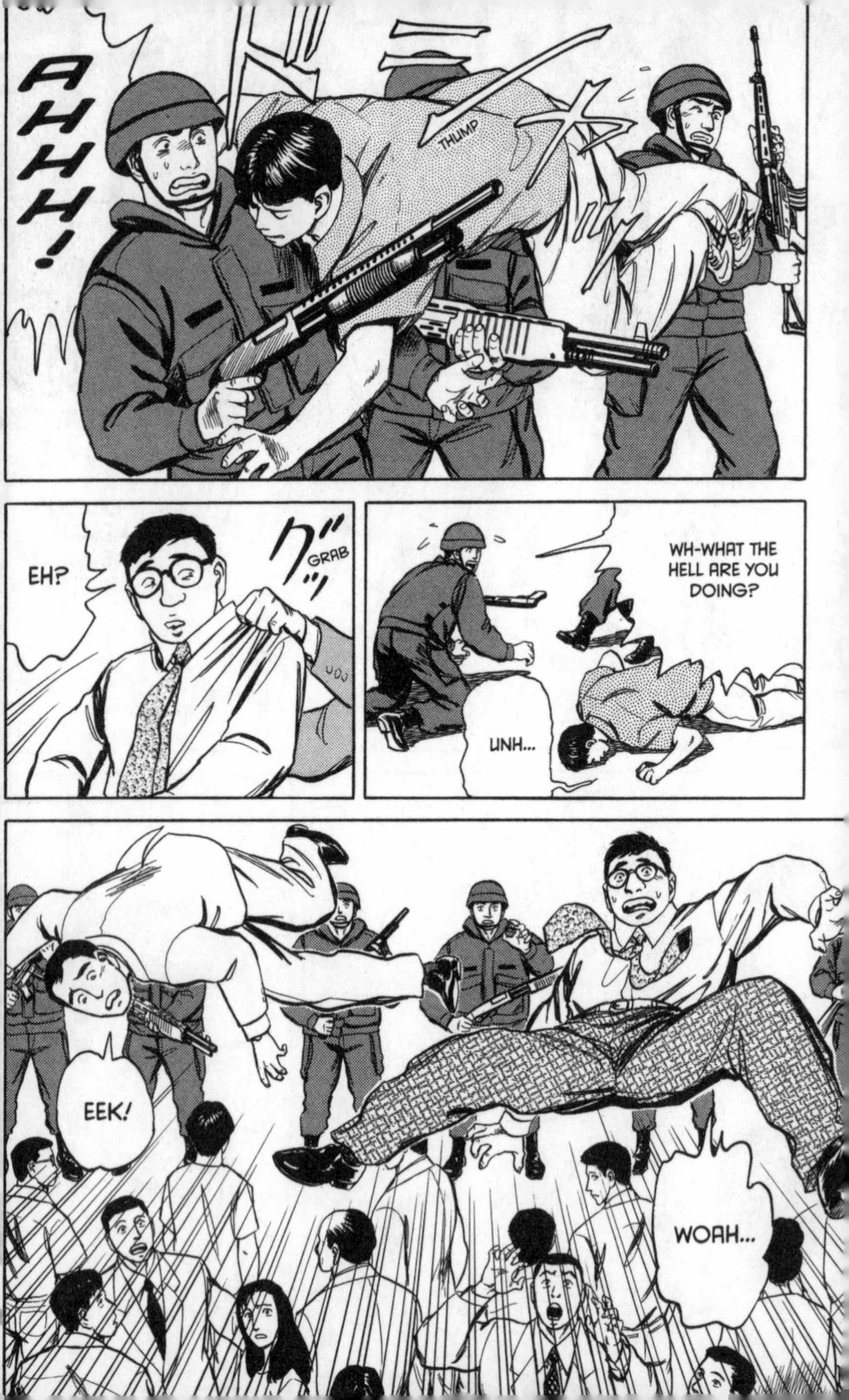
THUMP
AHHHH!
WH-WHAT THE HELL ARE YOU DOING?
UNH...
EH?
GRAB
WOAH...
EEK!

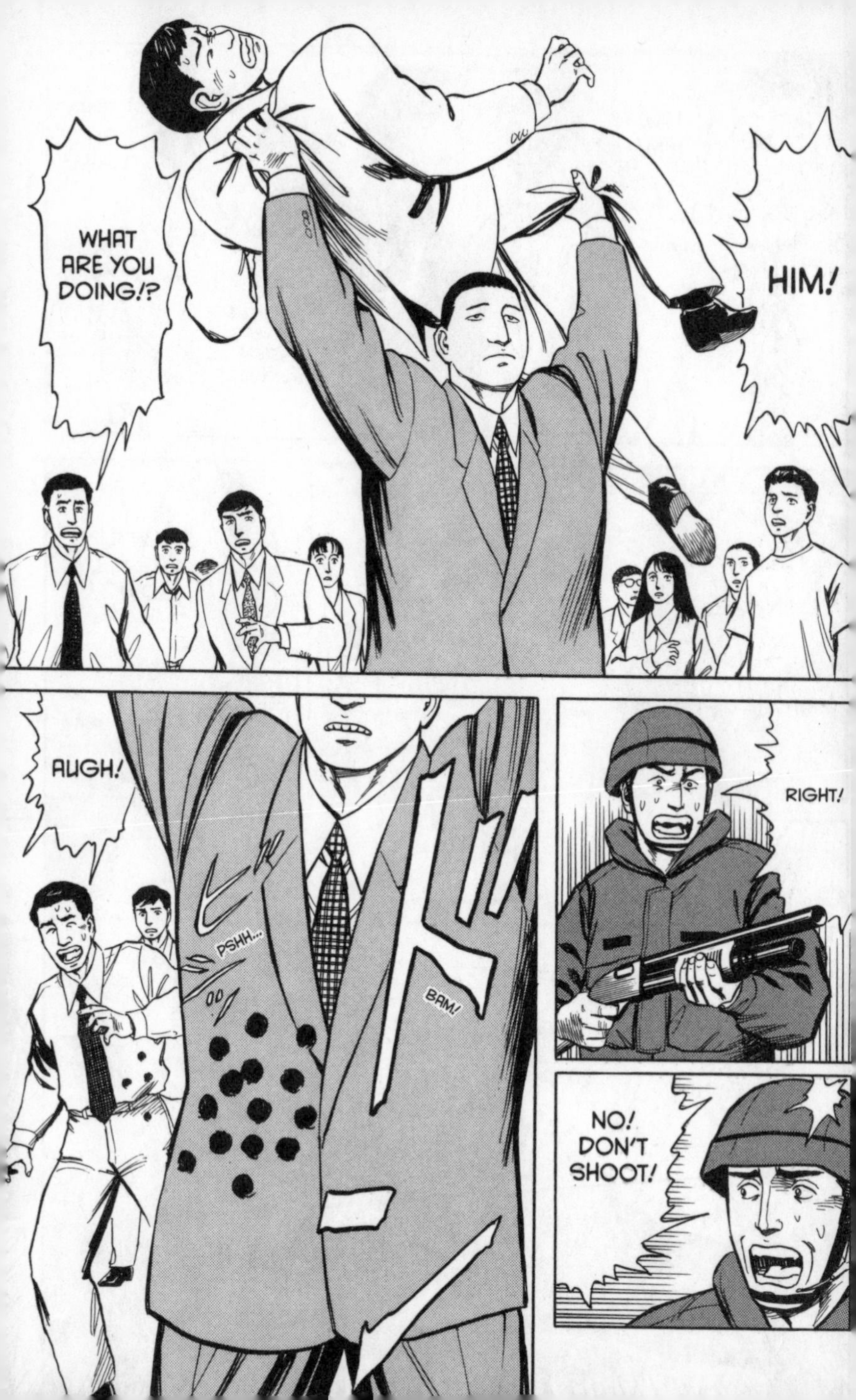
HIM!
WHAT ARE YOU DOING!?
RIGHT!
NO! DON'T SHOOT!
AUGH!
PSHH...
BAM!

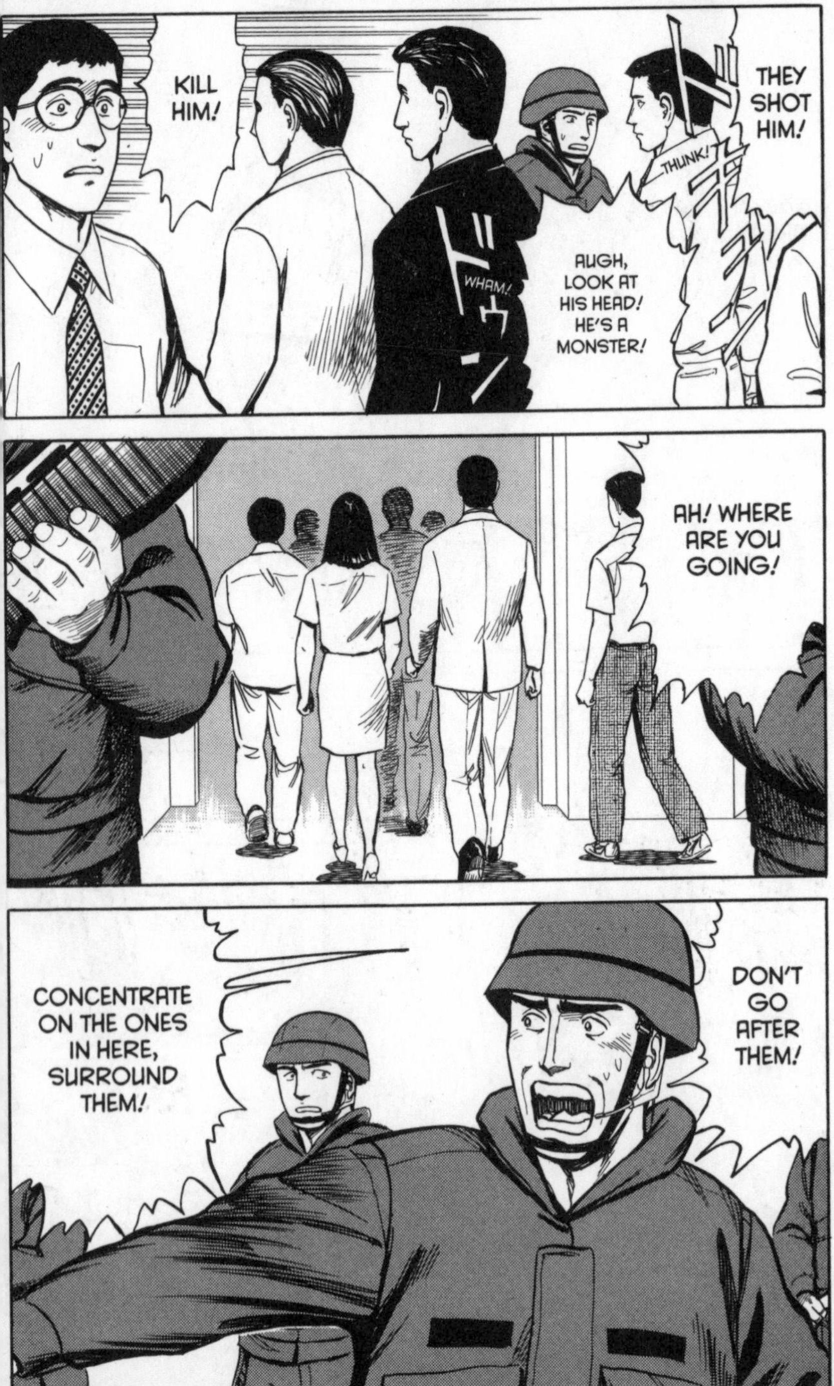
THEY SHOT HIM!
THUNK!
AUGH, LOOK AT HIS HEAD! HE'S A MONSTER!
WHAM!
KILL HIM!
AH! WHERE ARE YOU GOING!
DON'T GO AFTER THEM!
CONCENTRATE ON THE ONES IN HERE, SURROUND THEM!

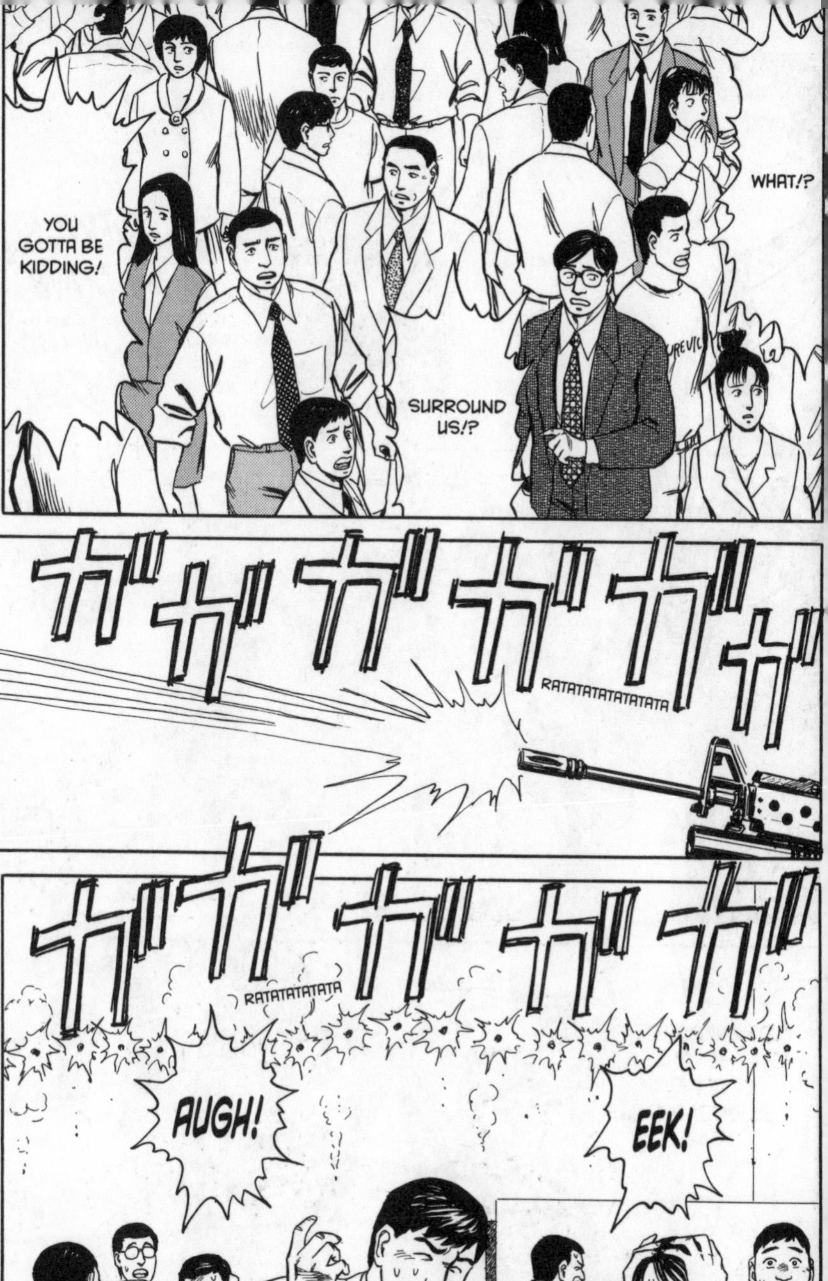
WHAT!?
SURROUND US!?
YOU GOTTA BE KIDDING!
ガガガガガガ
RATATATATATATATA
ガガガガガ
RATATATATATA
EEK!
AUGH!

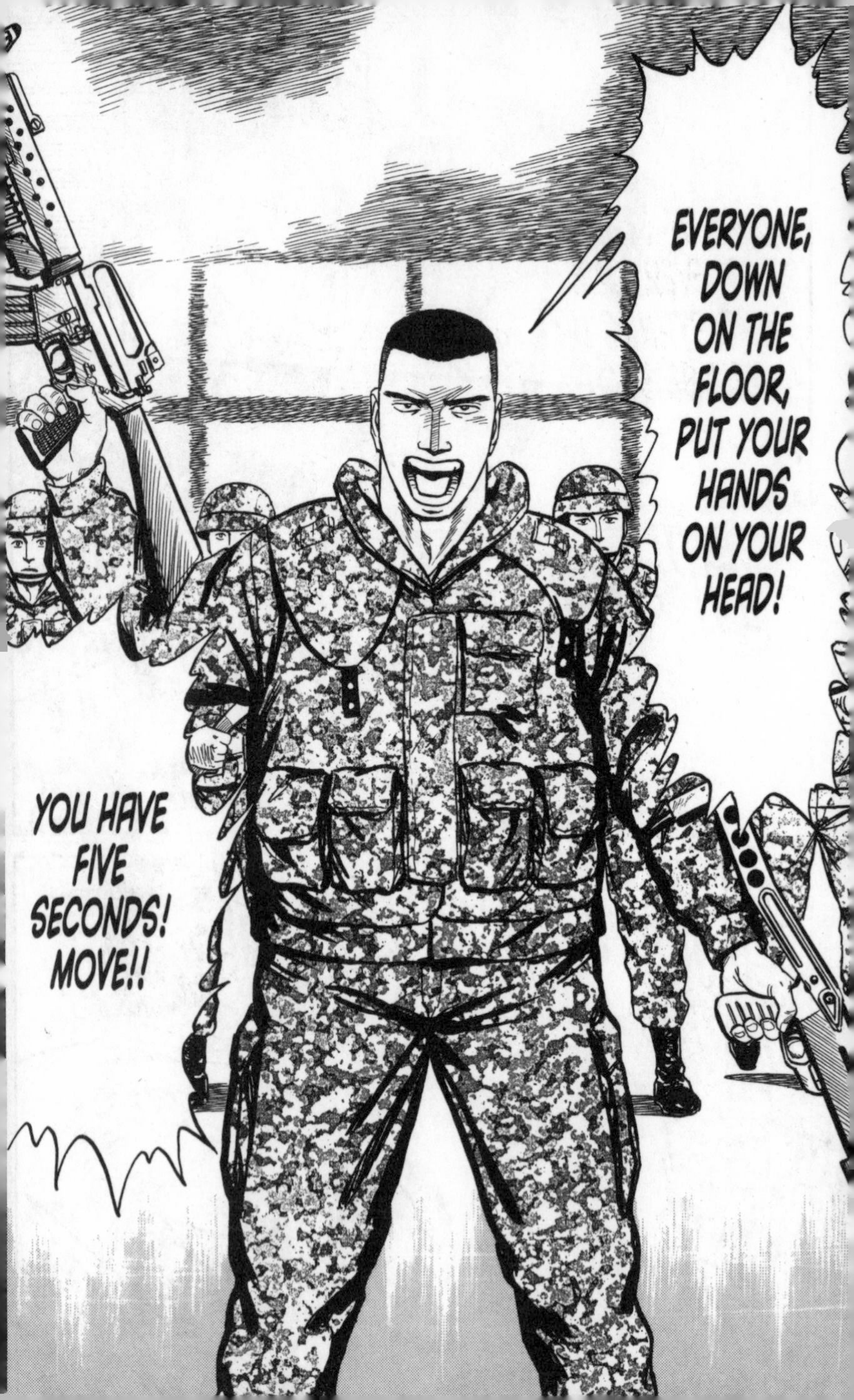
EVERYONE, DOWN ON THE FLOOR, PUT YOUR HANDS ON YOUR HEAD!
YOU HAVE FIVE SECONDS! MOVE!!

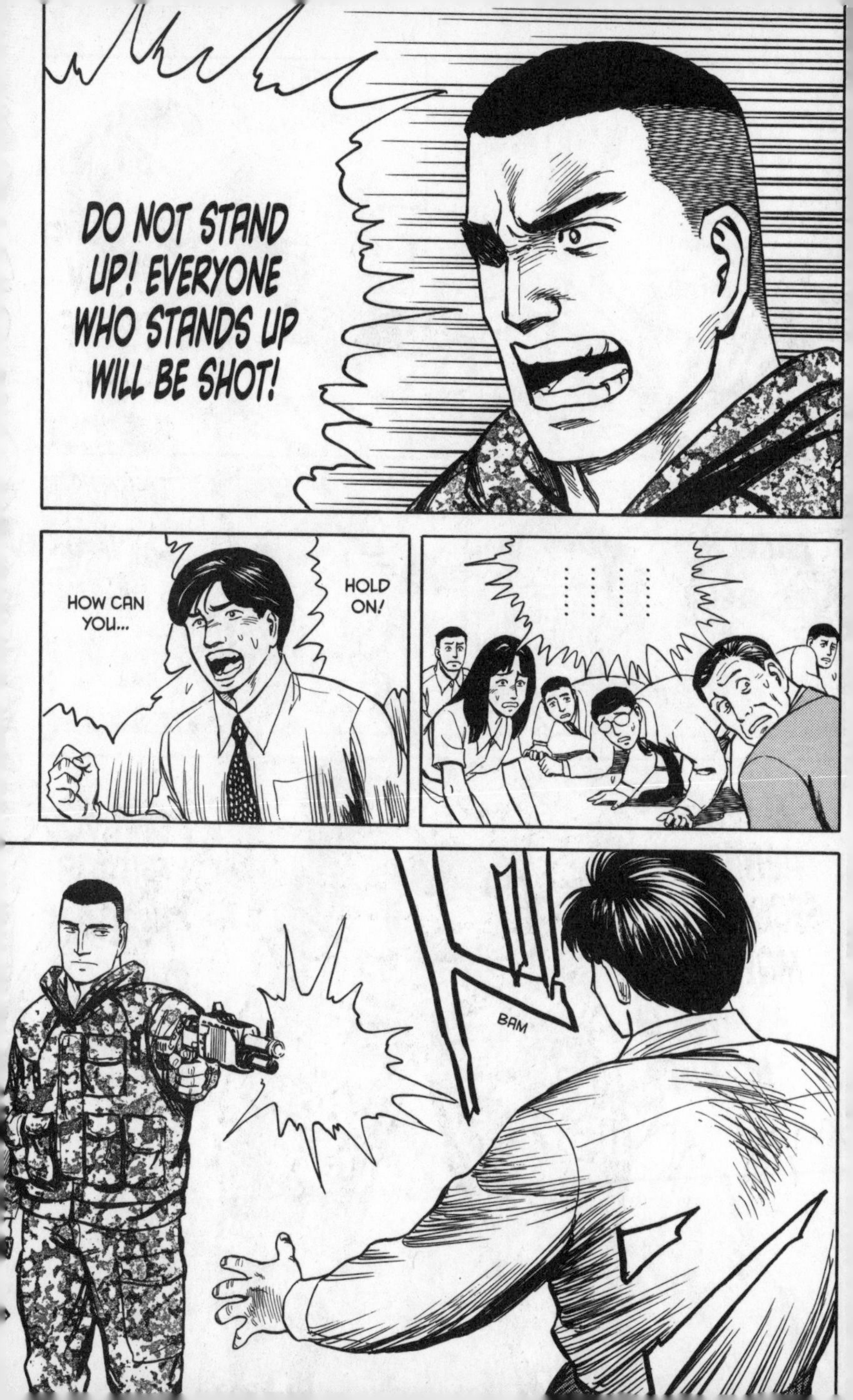
DO NOT STAND UP! EVERYONE WHO STANDS UP WILL BE SHOT!
......
HOLD ON!
HOW CAN YOU...
BAM

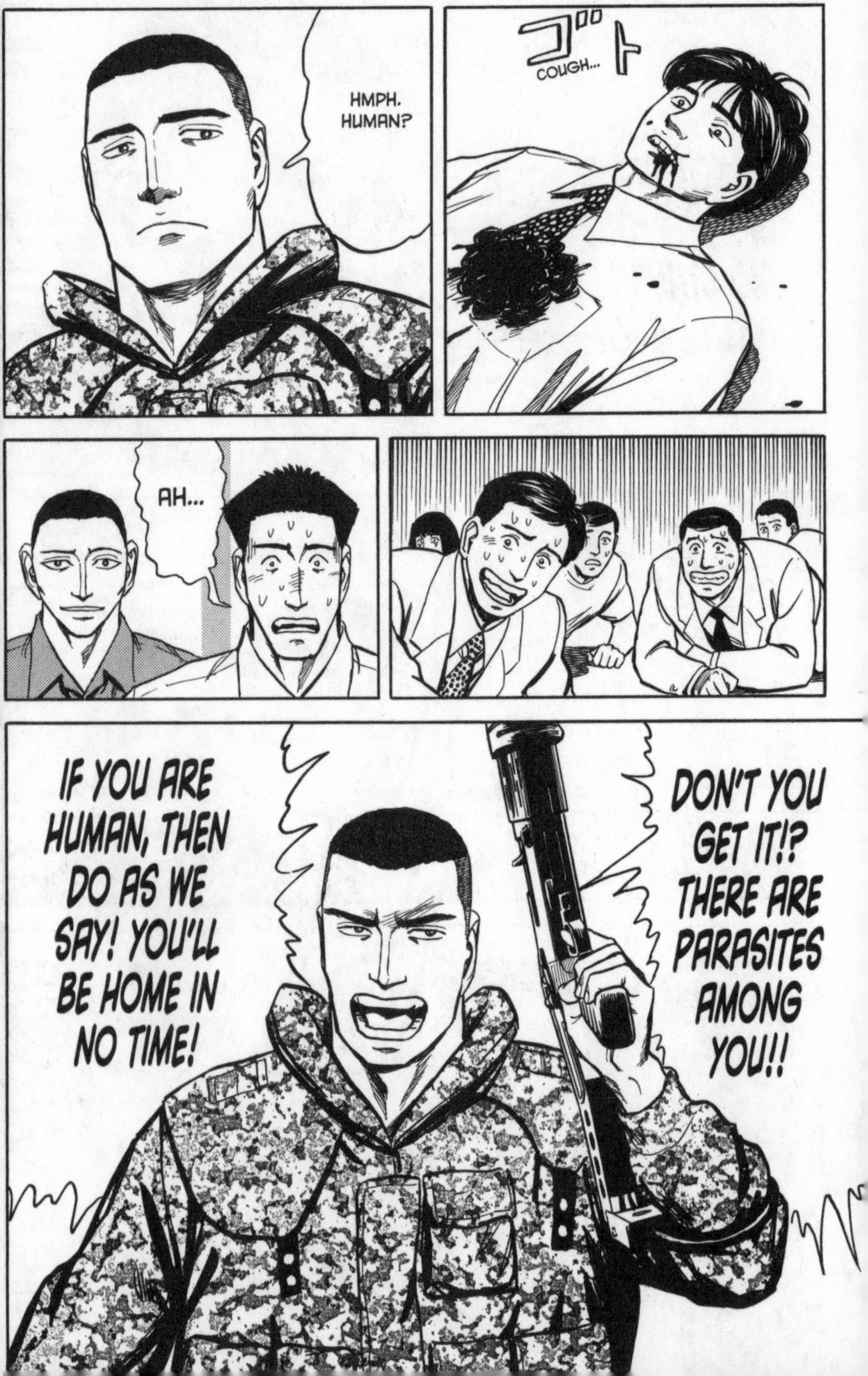
COUGH...
HMPH. HUMAN?
AH...
DON'T YOU GET IT!? THERE ARE PARASITES AMONG YOU!!
IF YOU ARE HUMAN, THEN DO AS WE SAY! YOU'LL BE HOME IN NO TIME!

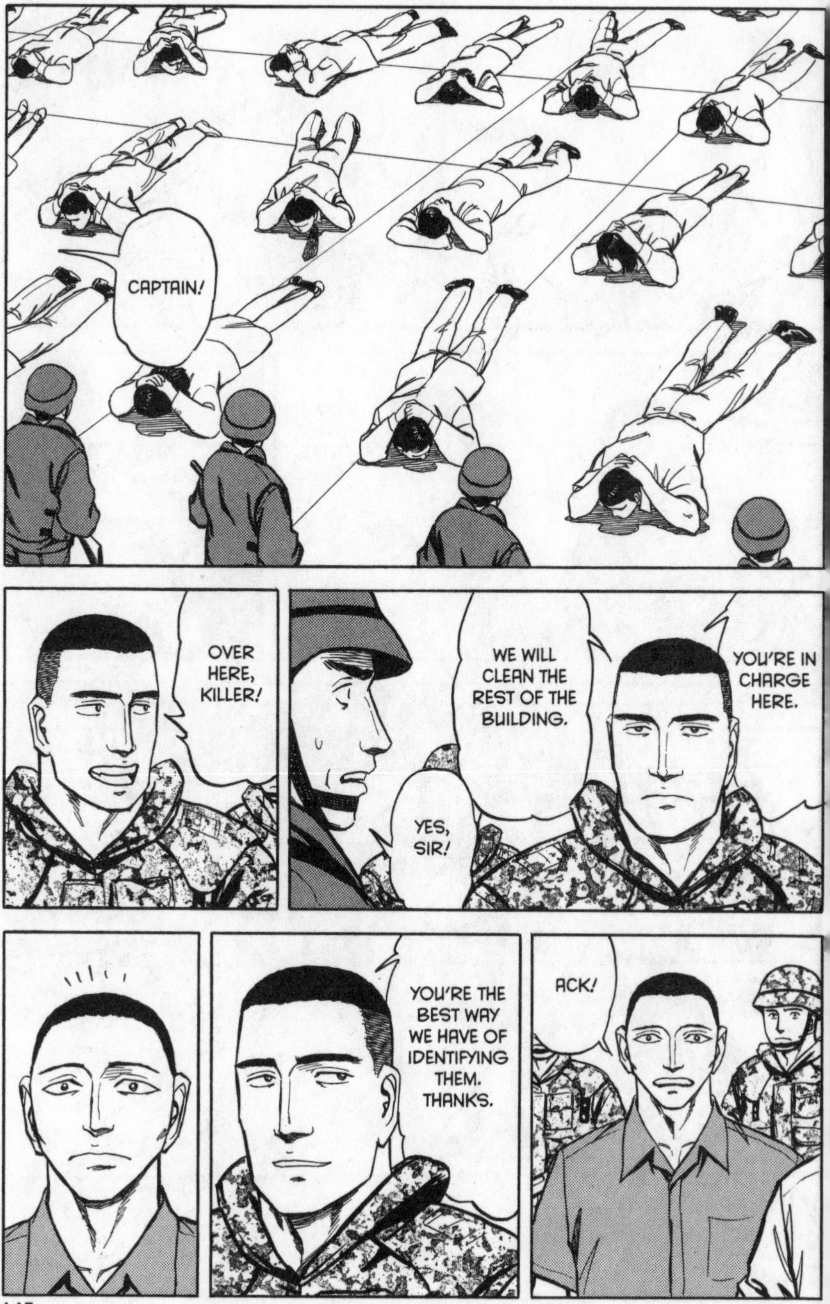
CAPTAIN!
YOU'RE IN CHARGE HERE.
WE WILL CLEAN THE REST OF THE BUILDING.
YES, SIR!
OVER HERE, KILLER!
ACK!
YOU'RE THE BEST WAY WE HAVE OF IDENTIFYING THEM. THANKS.

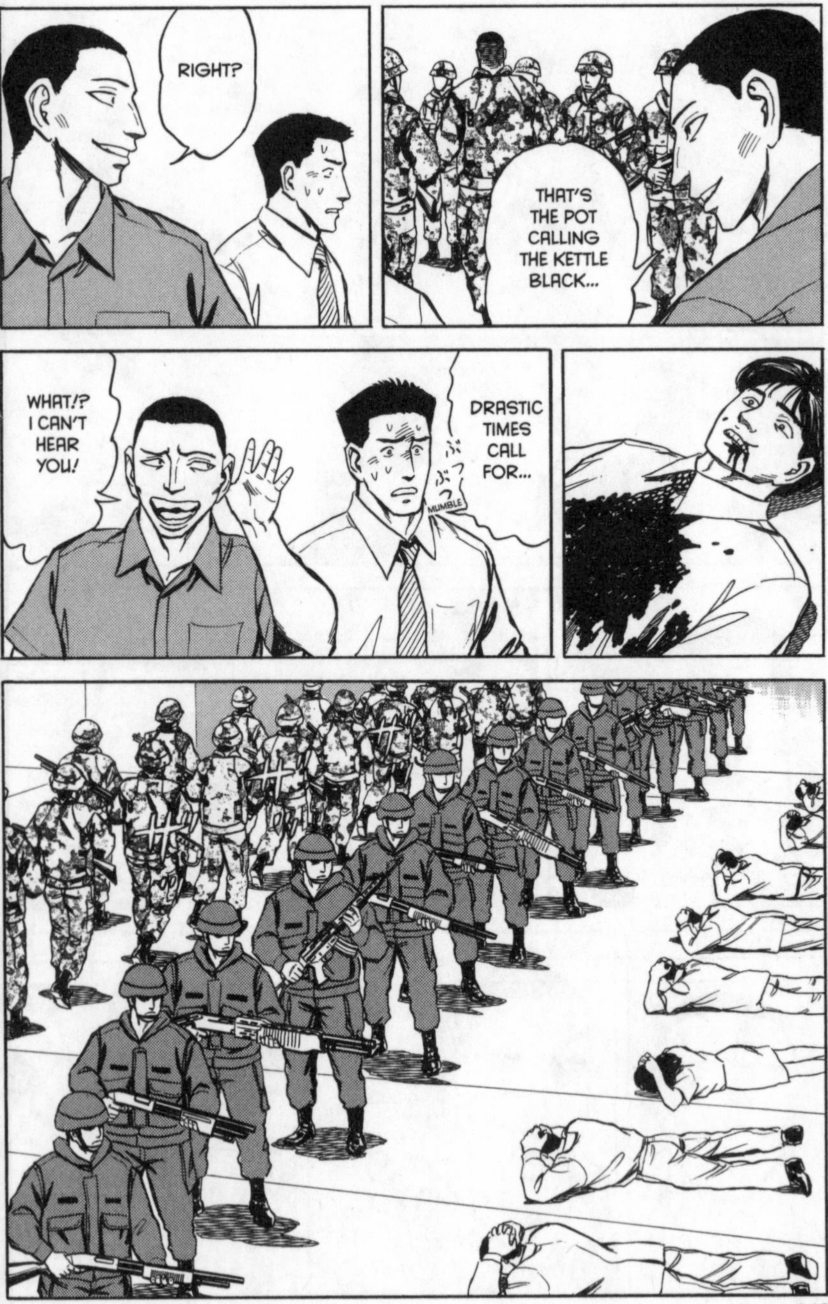
THAT'S THE POT CALLING THE KETTLE BLACK...
RIGHT?
DRASTIC TIMES CALL FOR...
ぶつぶつ
MUMBLE
WHAT!? I CAN'T HEAR YOU!

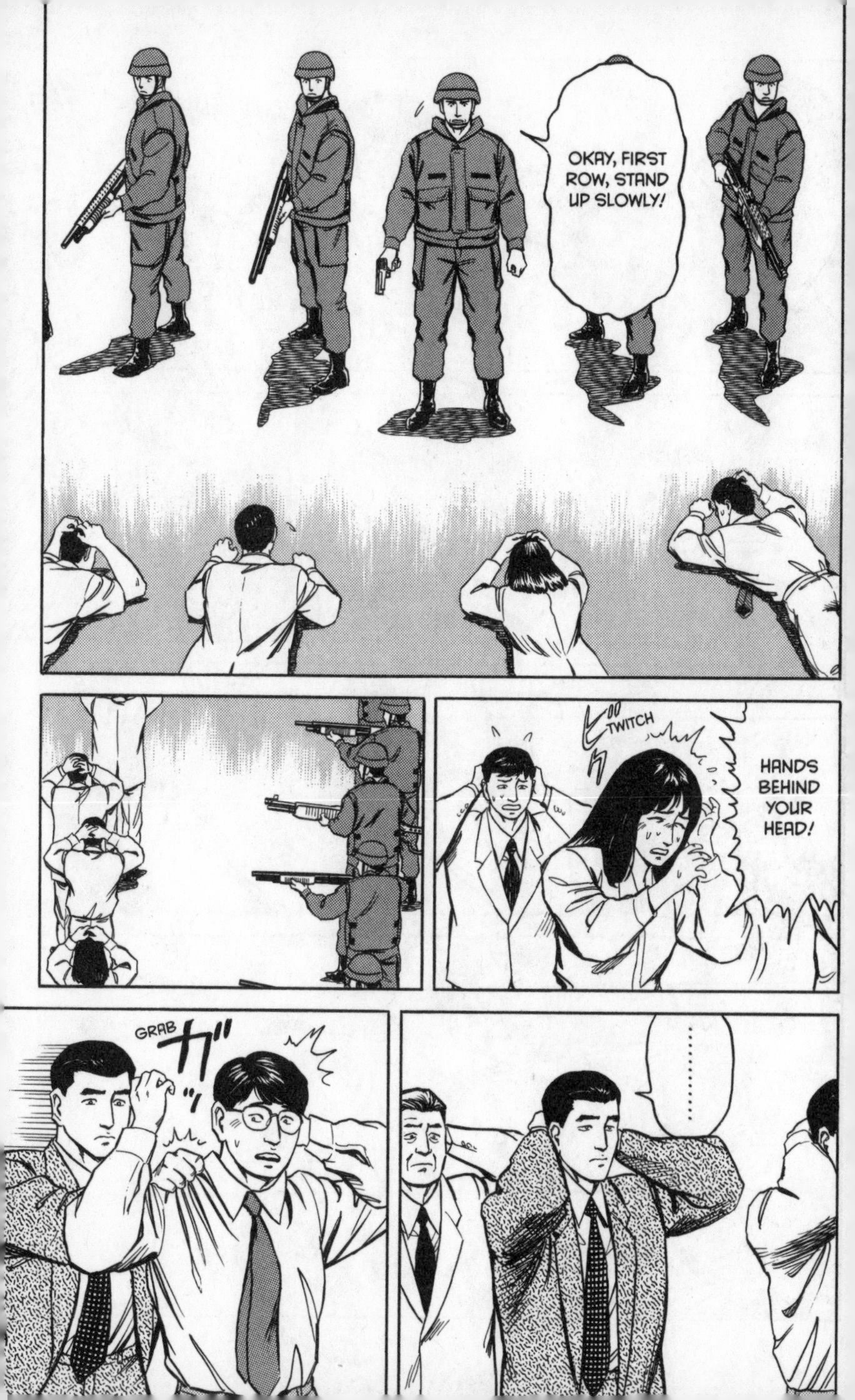
OKAY, FIRST ROW, STAND UP SLOWLY!
TWITCH
HANDS BEHIND YOUR HEAD!
......
GRAB

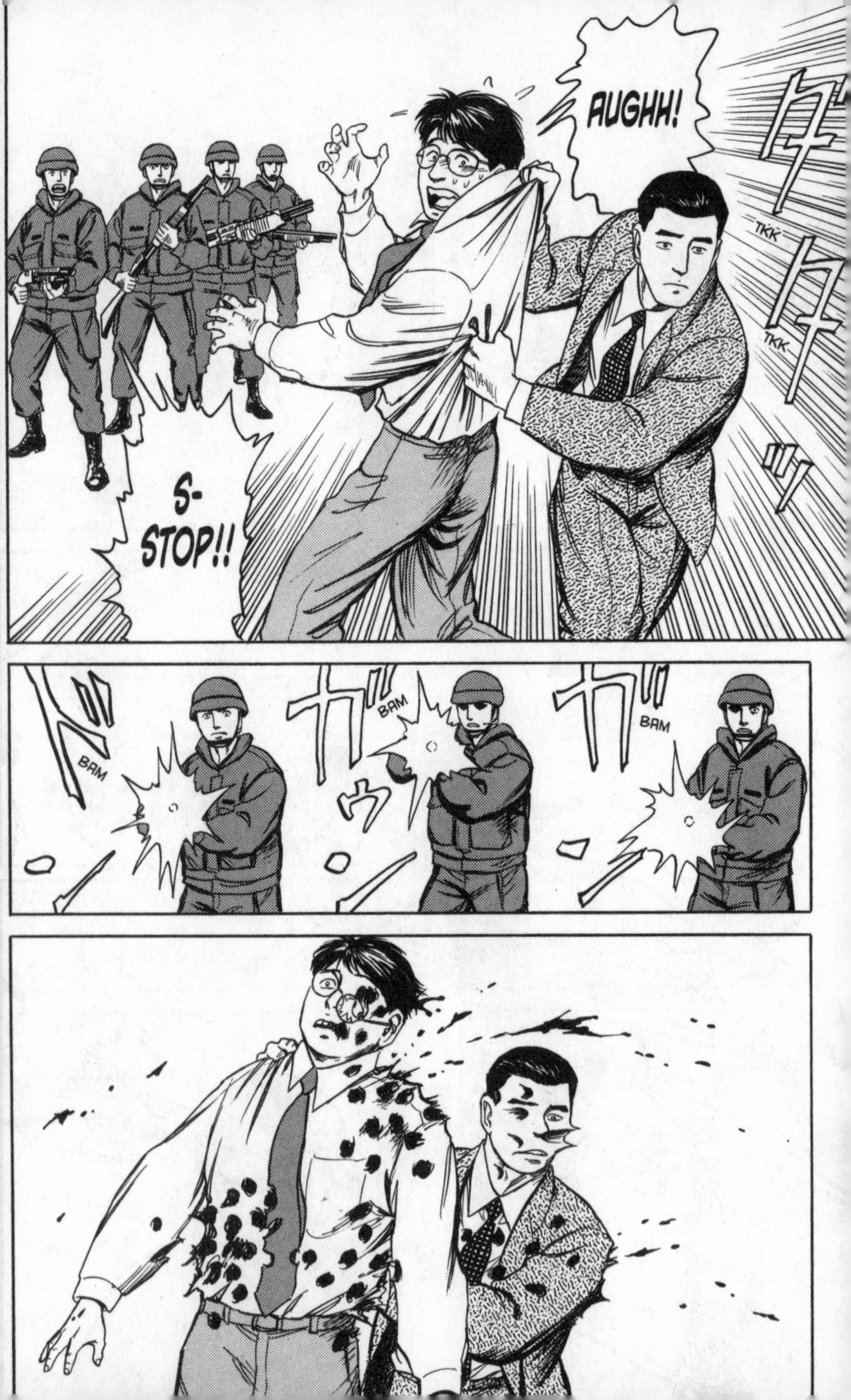
AUGHH!
TKK
TKK
S-
STOP!!
BAM
BAM
BAM

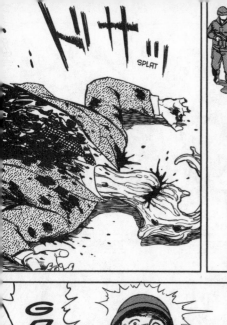

SPLAT

GUH...

BAM

BAMM!

GAH!

SLICE!

EEEK!

PLOP

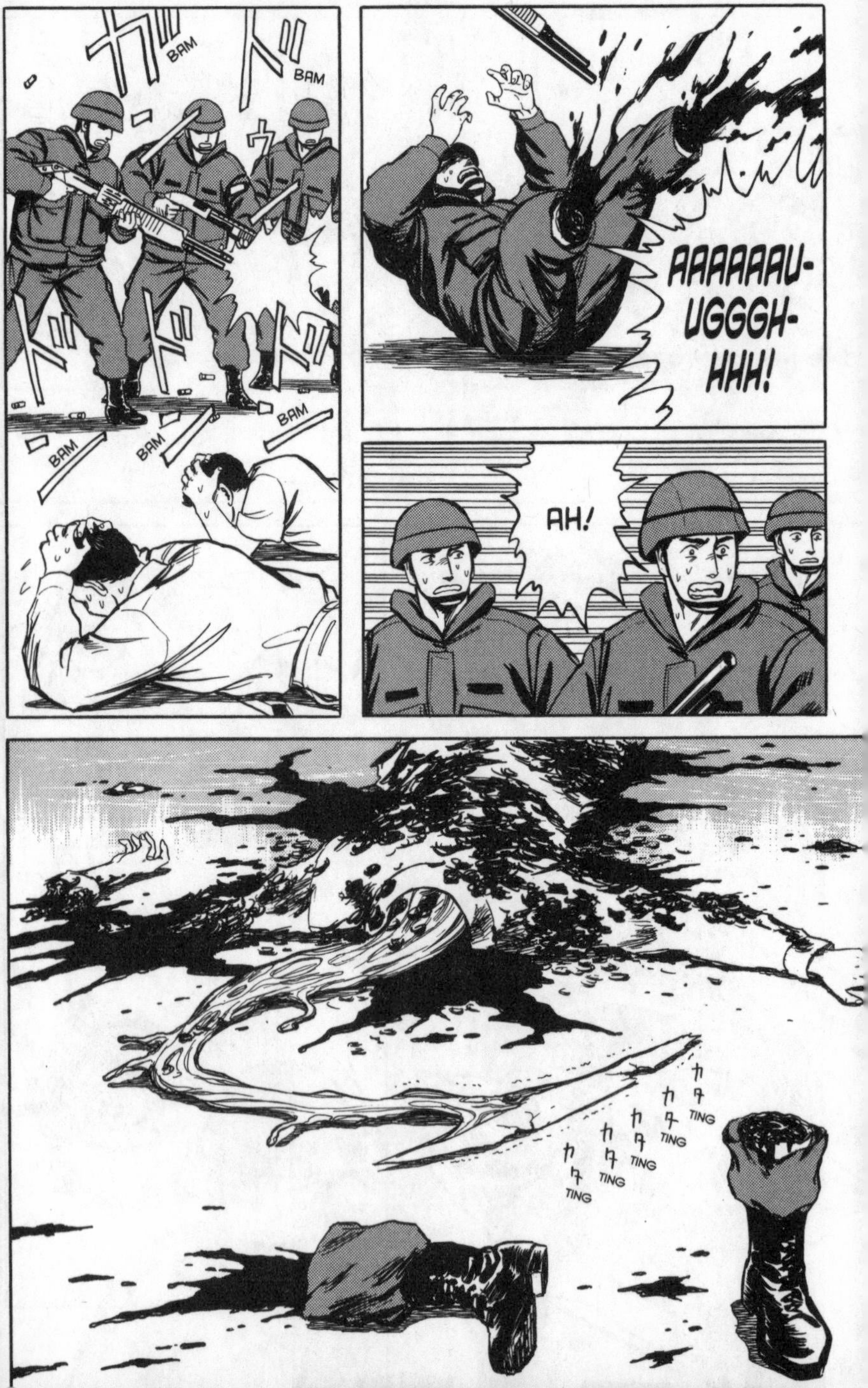
AAAAAAU-UGGGH-HHH!
AH!
BAM
BAM
BAM
BAM
BAM
TING
TING
TING
TING
TING

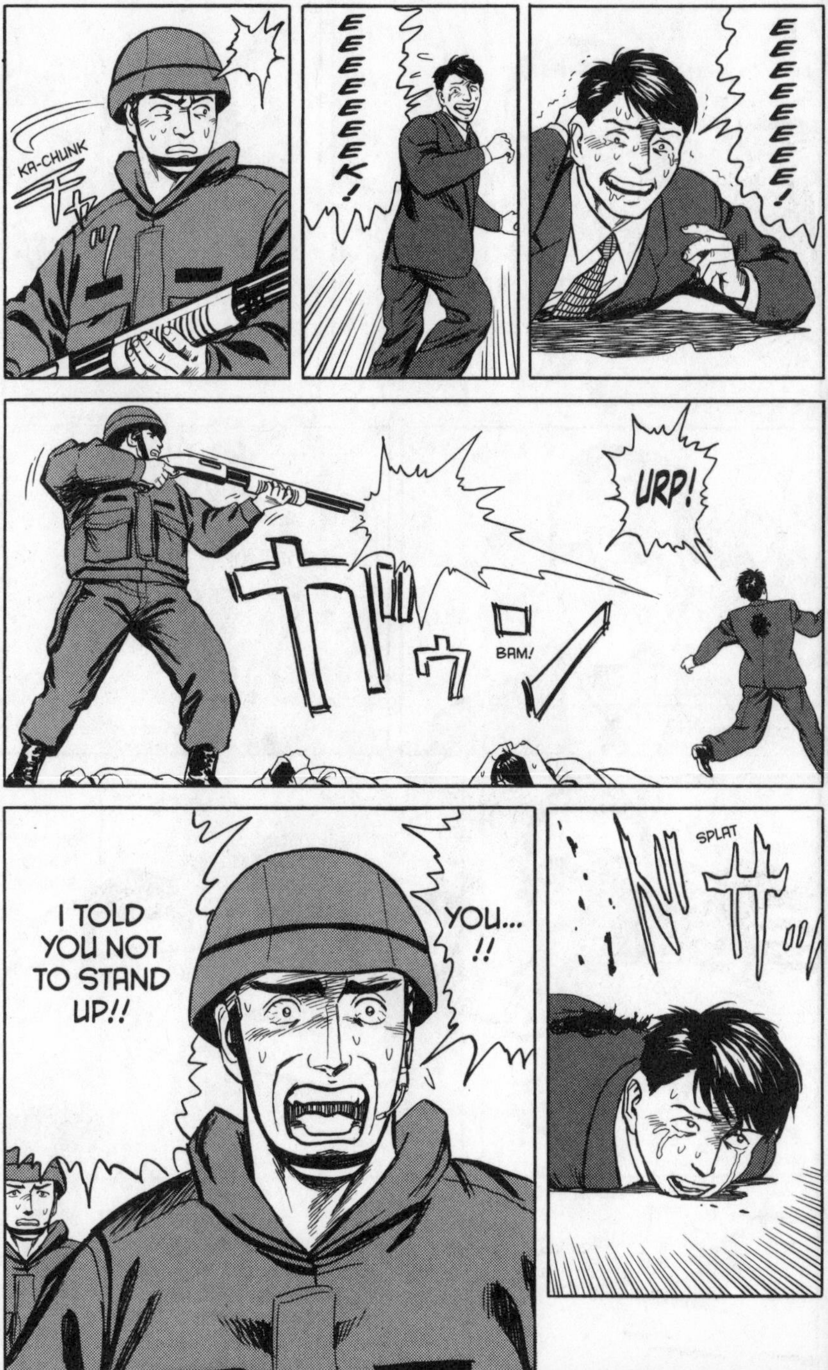
EEEEEEEE!
EEEEEEEK!
KA-CHUNK
URP!
BAM!
SPLAT
YOU... !!
I TOLD YOU NOT TO STAND UP!!

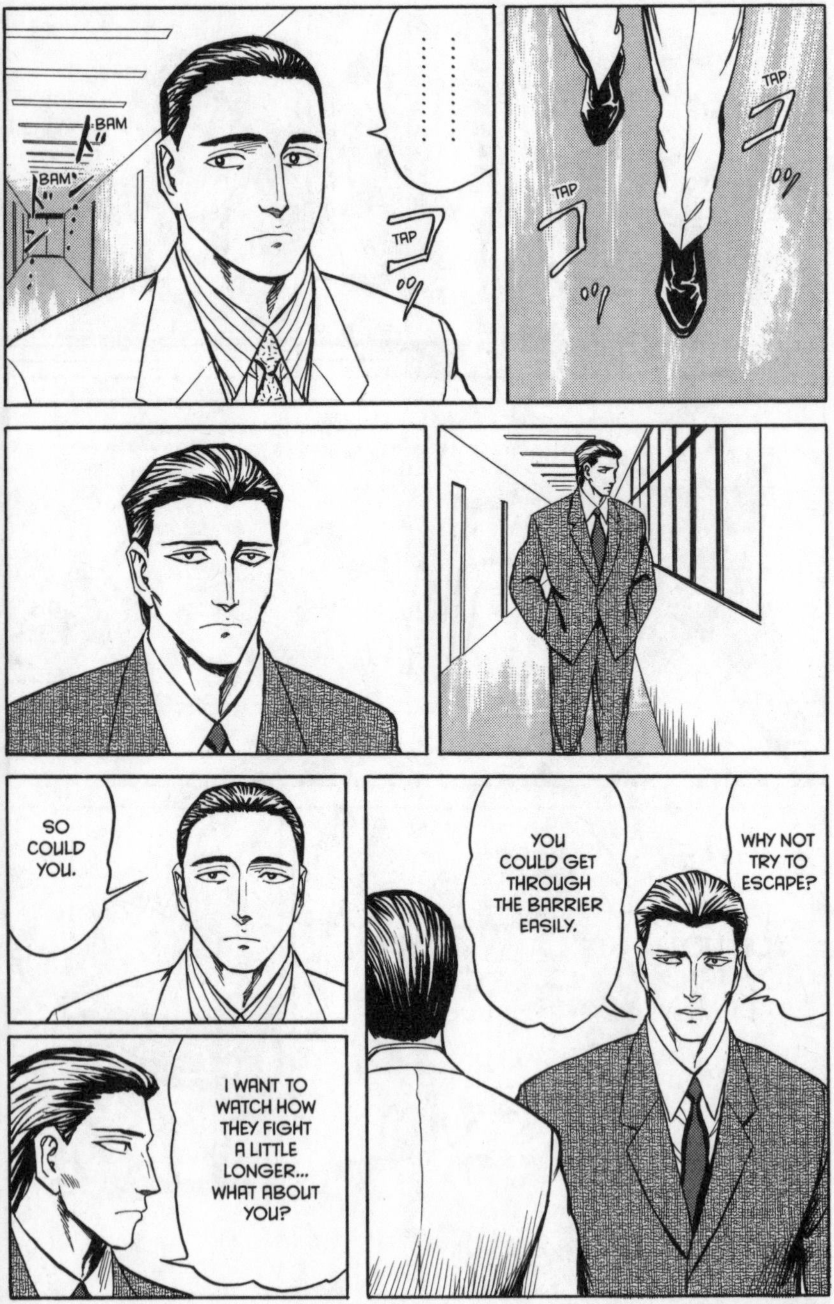
TAP
TAP
......
BAM
BAM
TAP
WHY NOT TRY TO ESCAPE?
YOU COULD GET THROUGH THE BARRIER EASILY.
SO COULD YOU.
I WANT TO WATCH HOW THEY FIGHT A LITTLE LONGER... WHAT ABOUT YOU?

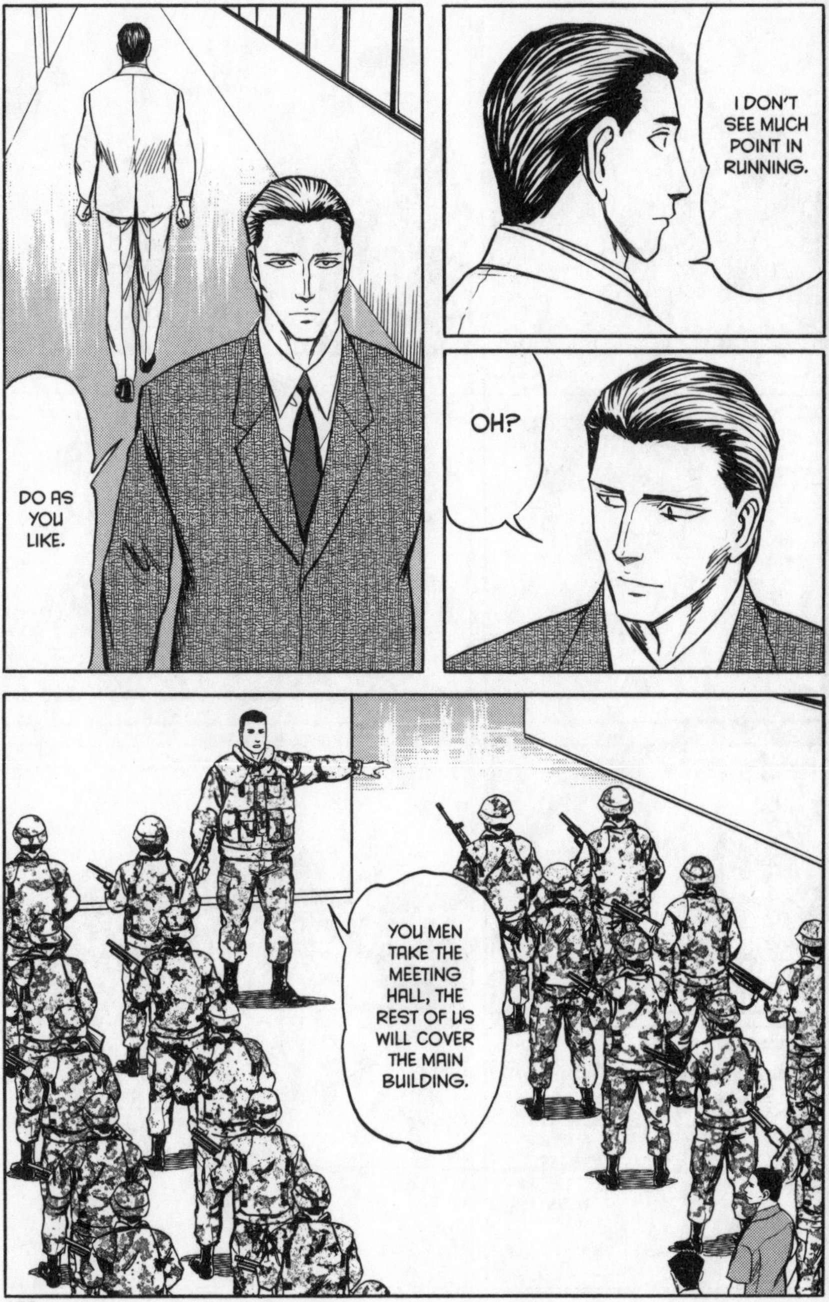
I DON'T SEE MUCH POINT IN RUNNING.
OH?
DO AS YOU LIKE.
YOU MEN TAKE THE MEETING HALL, THE REST OF US WILL COVER THE MAIN BUILDING.

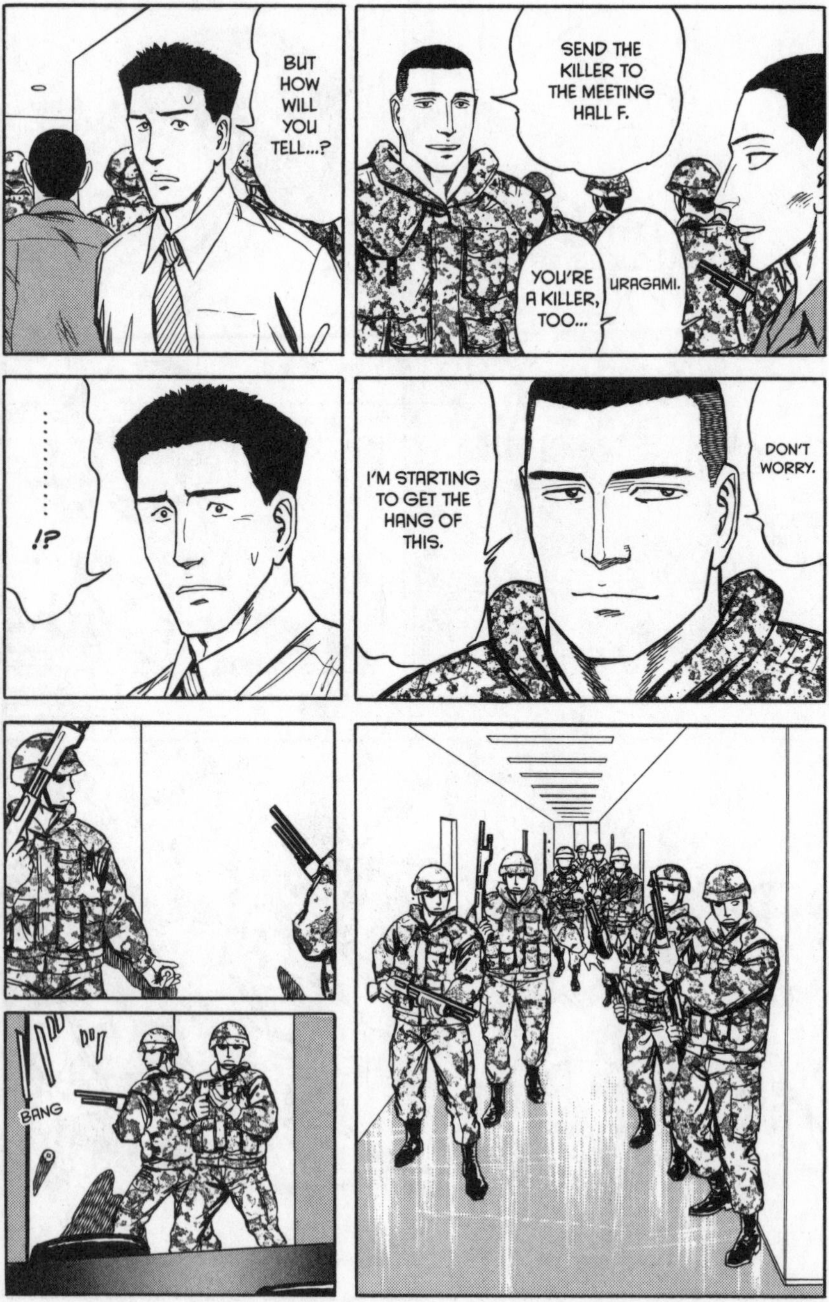
SEND THE KILLER TO THE MEETING HALL F.
URAGAMI.
YOU'RE A KILLER, TOO...
BUT HOW WILL YOU TELL...?
DON'T WORRY.
I'M STARTING TO GET THE HANG OF THIS.
......!?
BANG

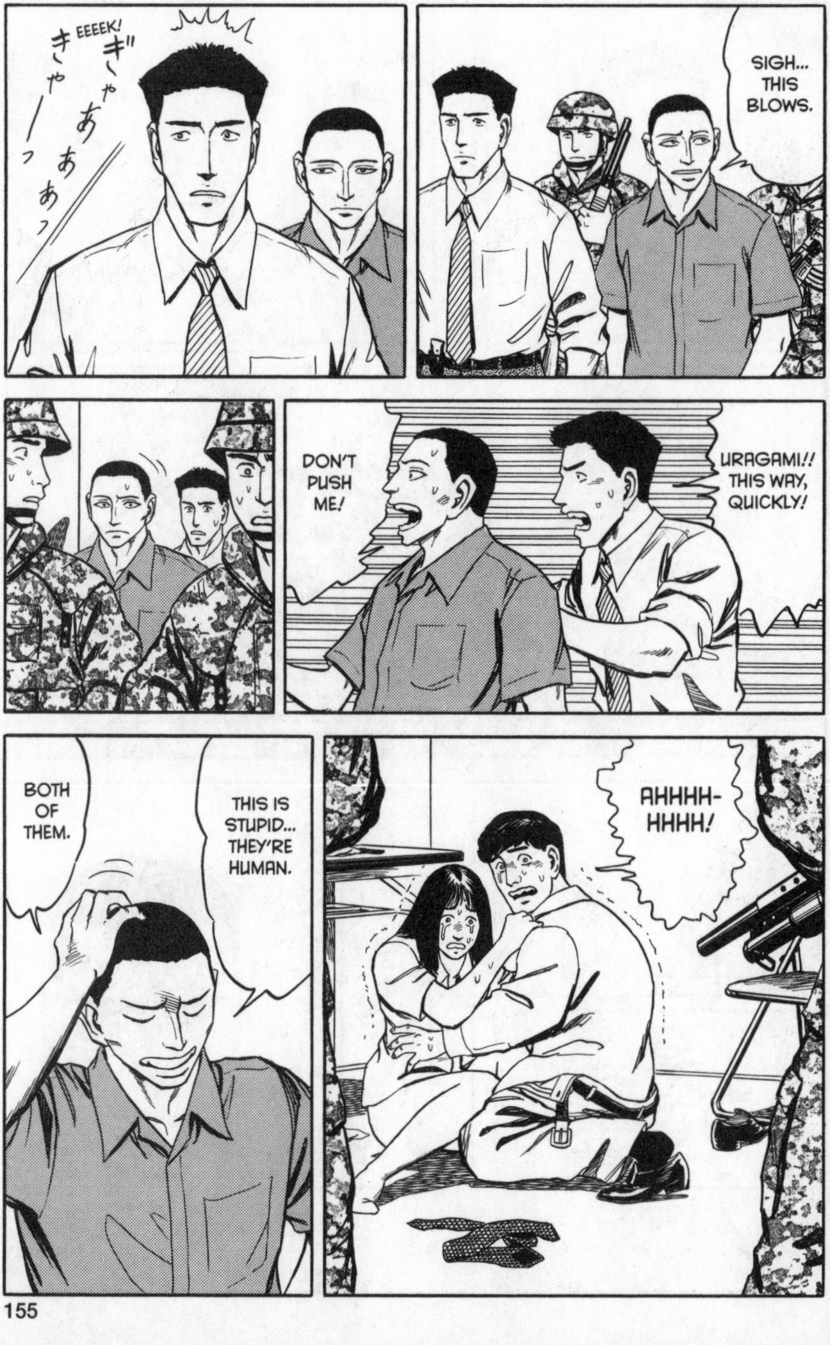
SIGH... THIS BLOWS.
EEEEK!
ぎゃあああっ
きゃーっ
URAGAMI!! THIS WAY, QUICKLY!
DON'T PUSH ME!
AHHHH-HHHH!
THIS IS STUPID... THEY'RE HUMAN.
BOTH OF THEM.

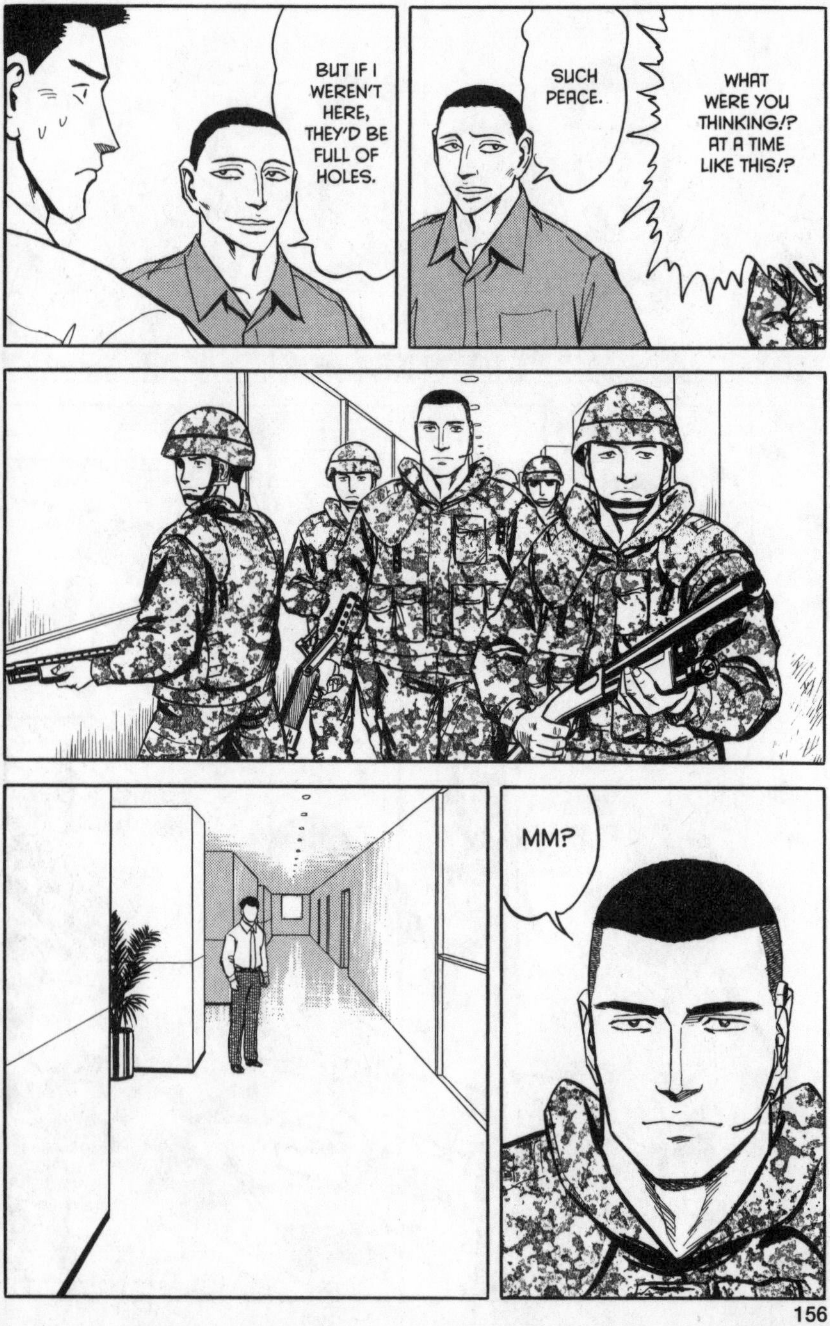
WHAT WERE YOU THINKING!? AT A TIME LIKE THIS!?
SUCH PEACE.
BUT IF I WEREN'T HERE, THEY'D BE FULL OF HOLES.
MM?

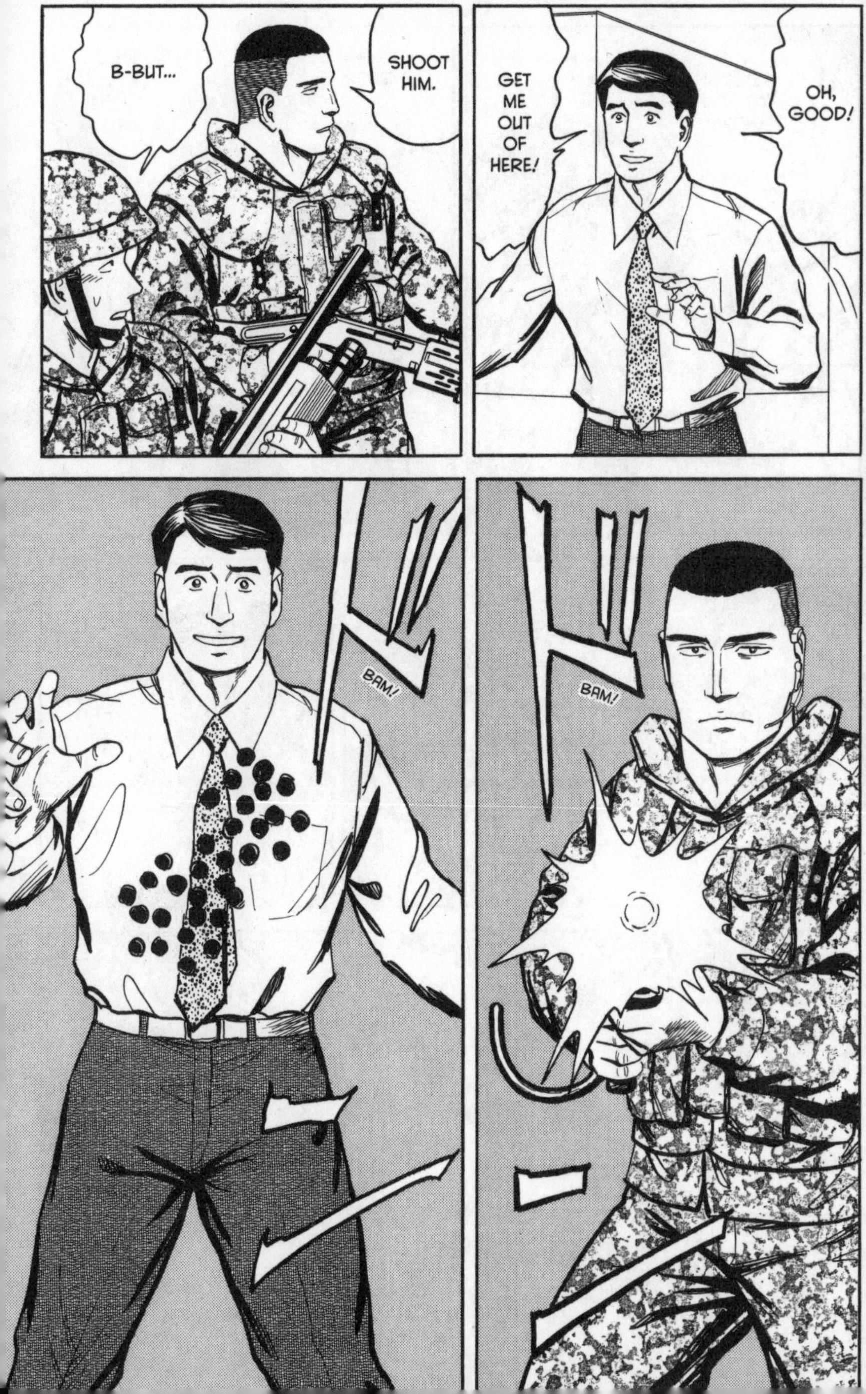
OH, GOOD!
GET ME OUT OF HERE!
SHOOT HIM.
B-BUT...
BAM!
BAM!

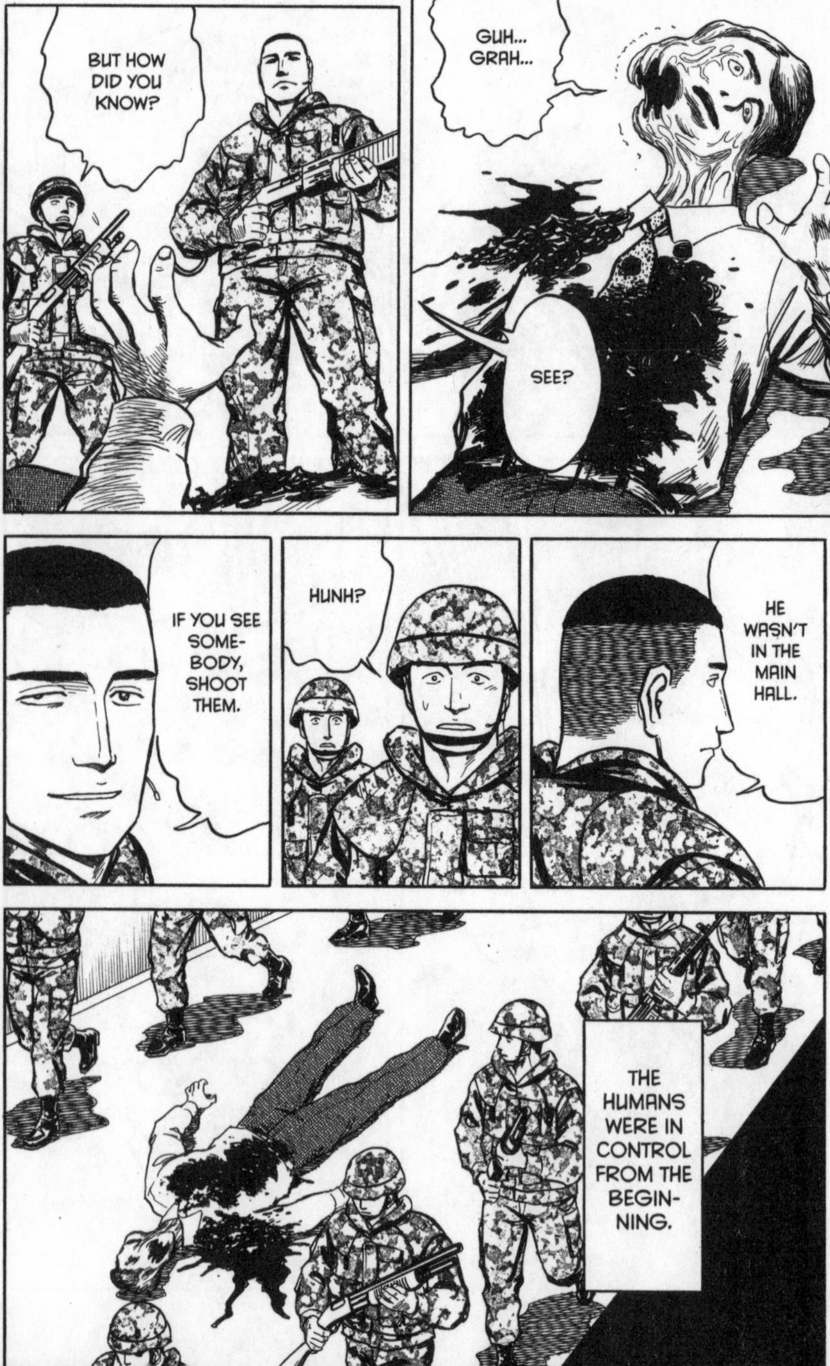
GUH... GRAH...
SEE?
BUT HOW DID YOU KNOW?
HE WASN'T IN THE MAIN HALL.
HUNH?
IF YOU SEE SOMEBODY, SHOOT THEM.
THE HUMANS WERE IN CONTROL FROM THE BEGINNING.

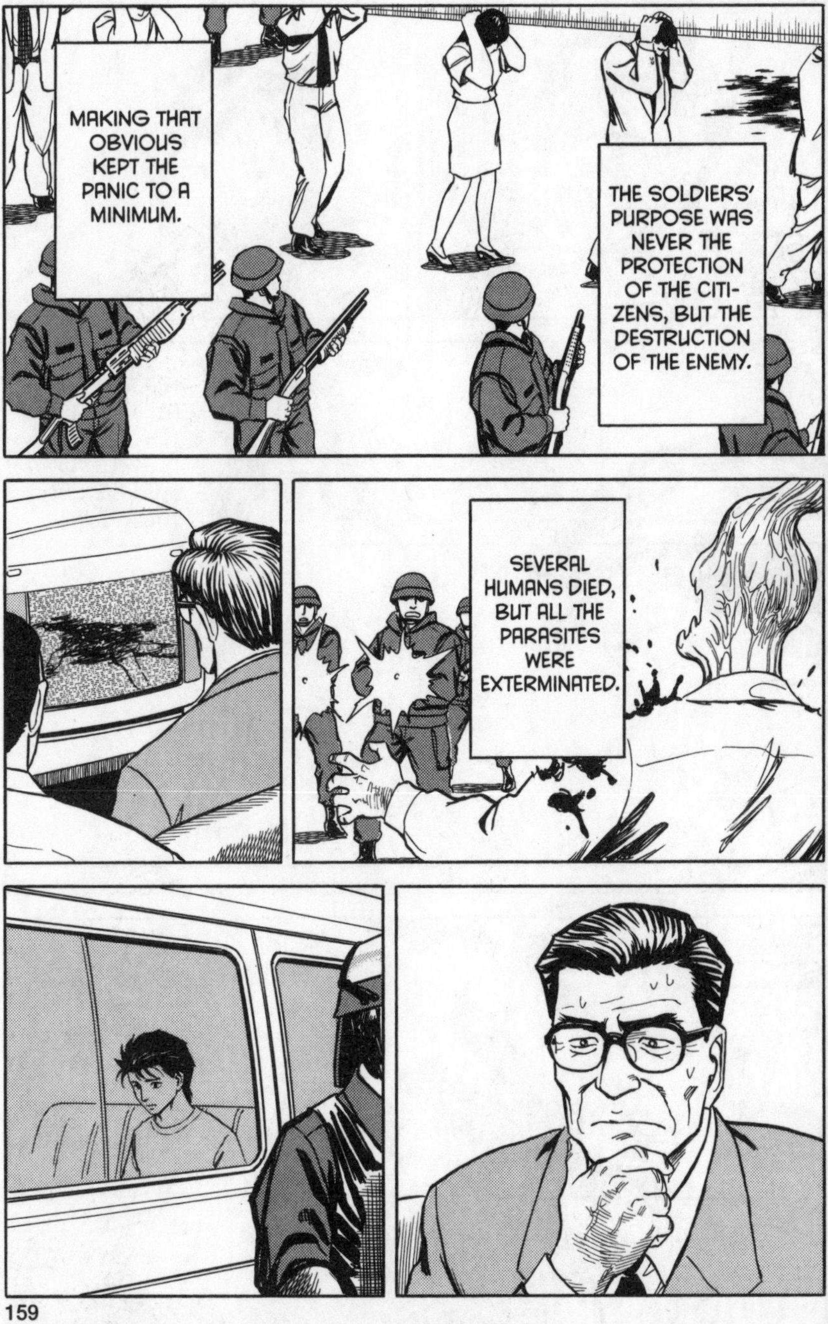
THE SOLDIERS' PURPOSE WAS NEVER THE PROTECTION OF THE CITI-ZENS, BUT THE DESTRUCTION OF THE ENEMY.
MAKING THAT OBVIOUS KEPT THE PANIC TO A MINIMUM.
SEVERAL HUMANS DIED, BUT ALL THE PARASITES WERE EXTERMINATED.

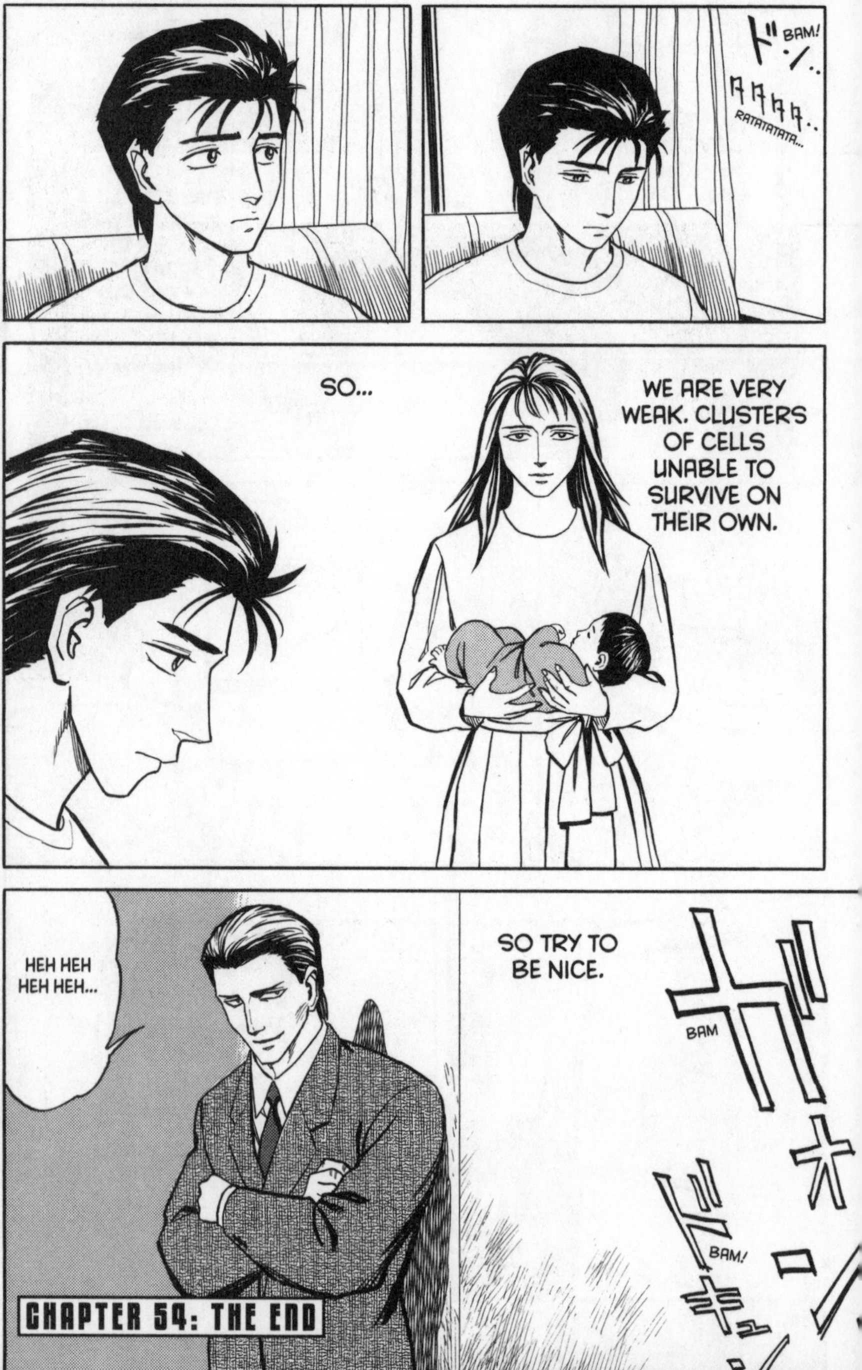
BAM!
RATATATATA...
WE ARE VERY WEAK. CLUSTERS OF CELLS UNABLE TO SURVIVE ON THEIR OWN.
SO...
SO TRY TO BE NICE.
BAM
BAM!
HEH HEH HEH HEH...
CHAPTER 54: THE END

CHAPTER 55: PARASYTE

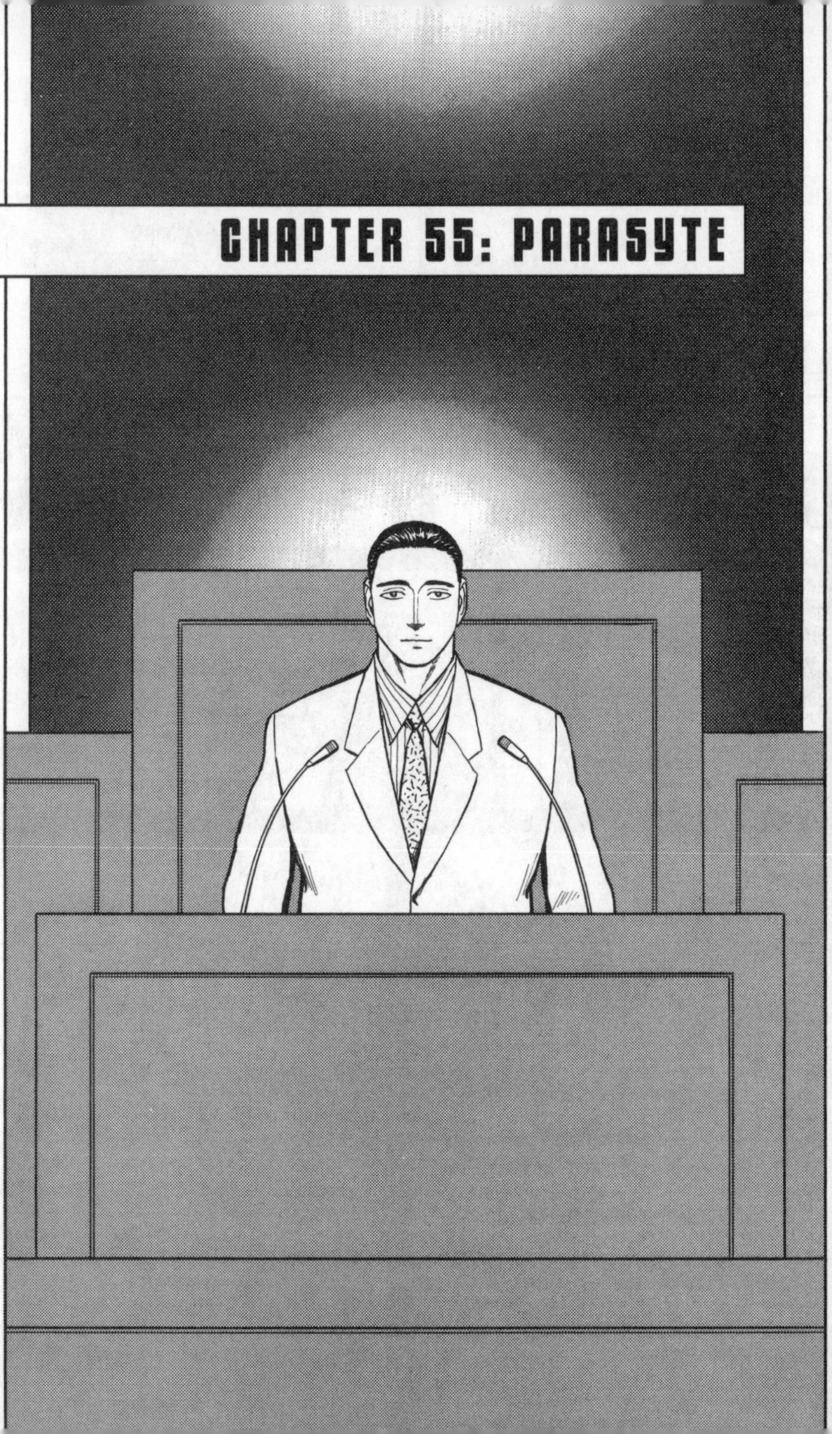

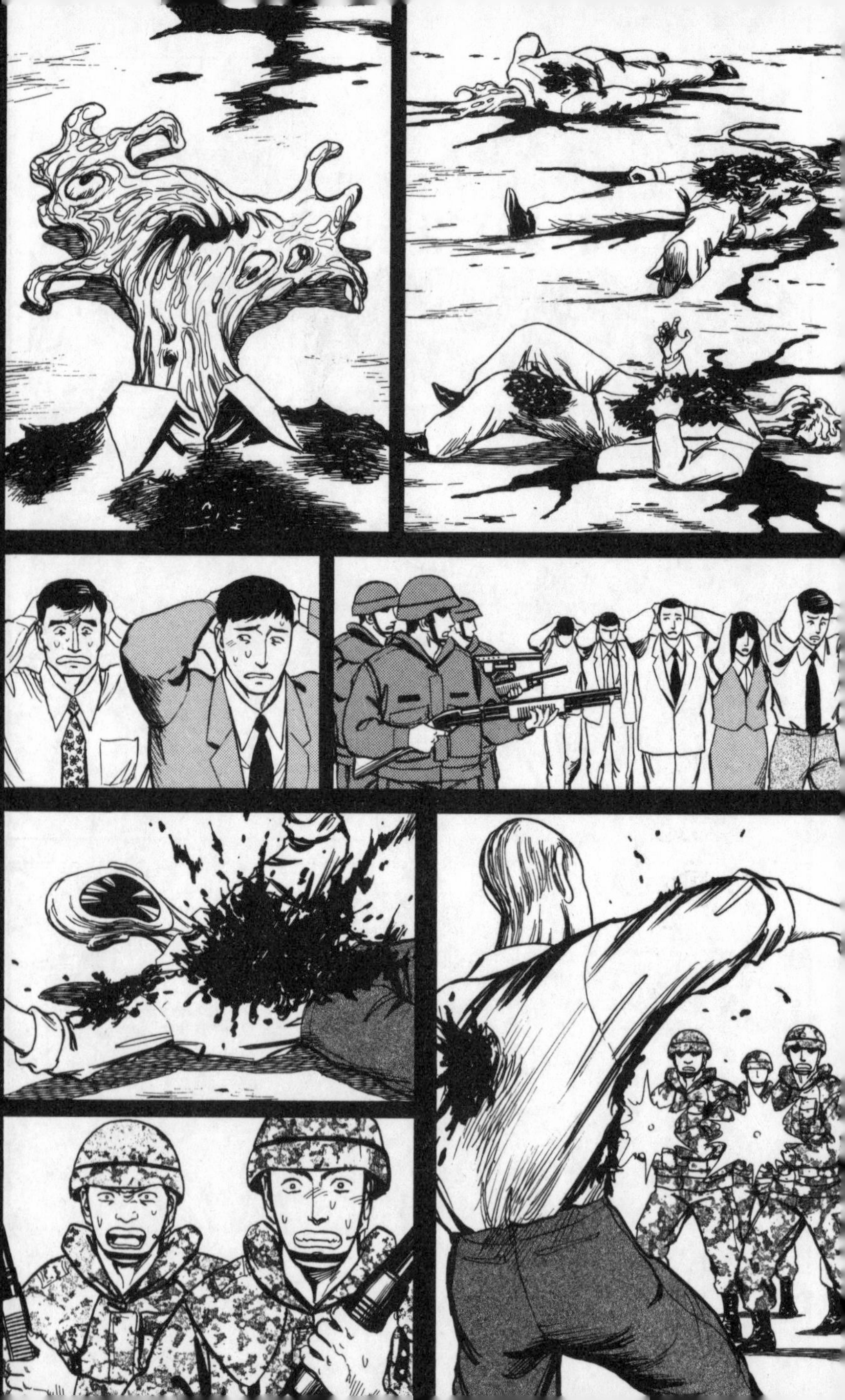

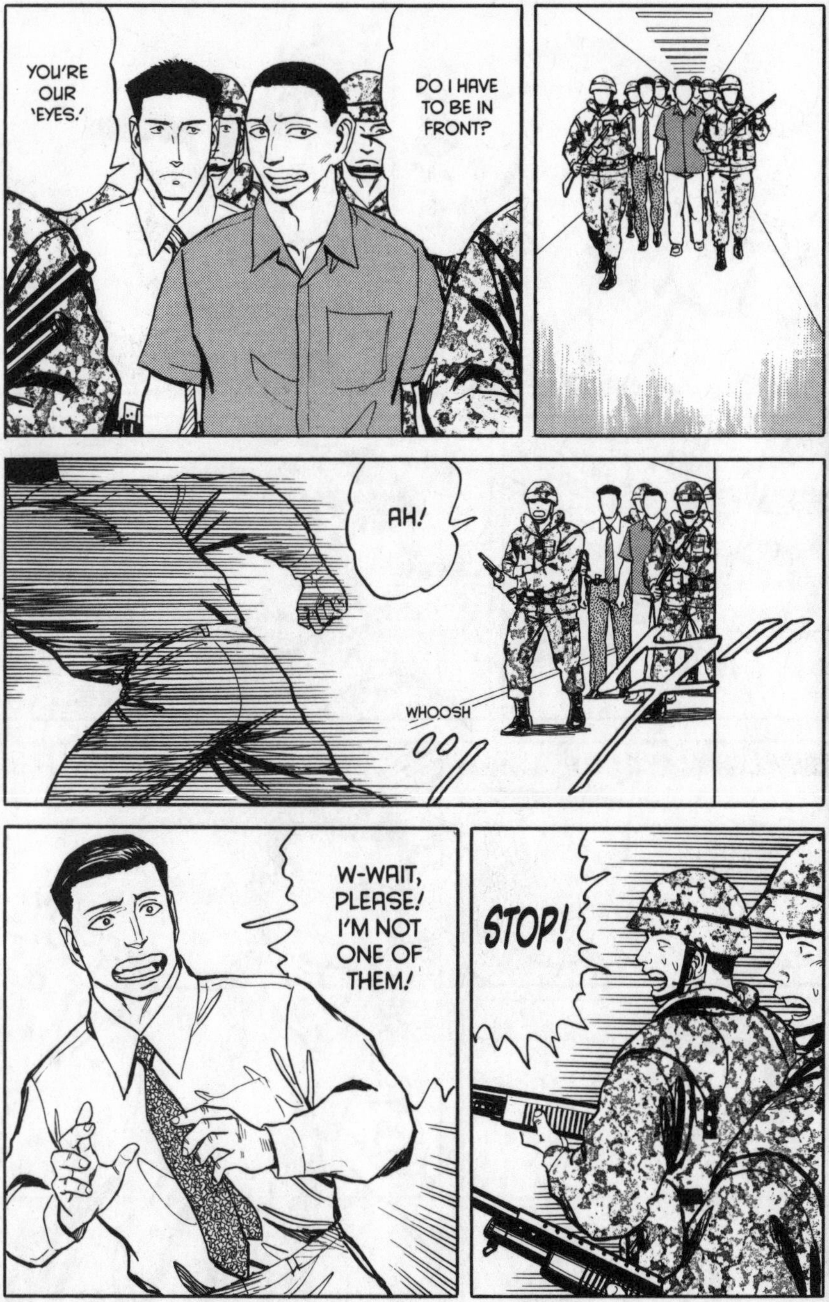
DO I HAVE TO BE IN FRONT?
YOU'RE OUR 'EYES.'
AH!
WHOOSH
STOP!
W-WAIT, PLEASE! I'M NOT ONE OF THEM!

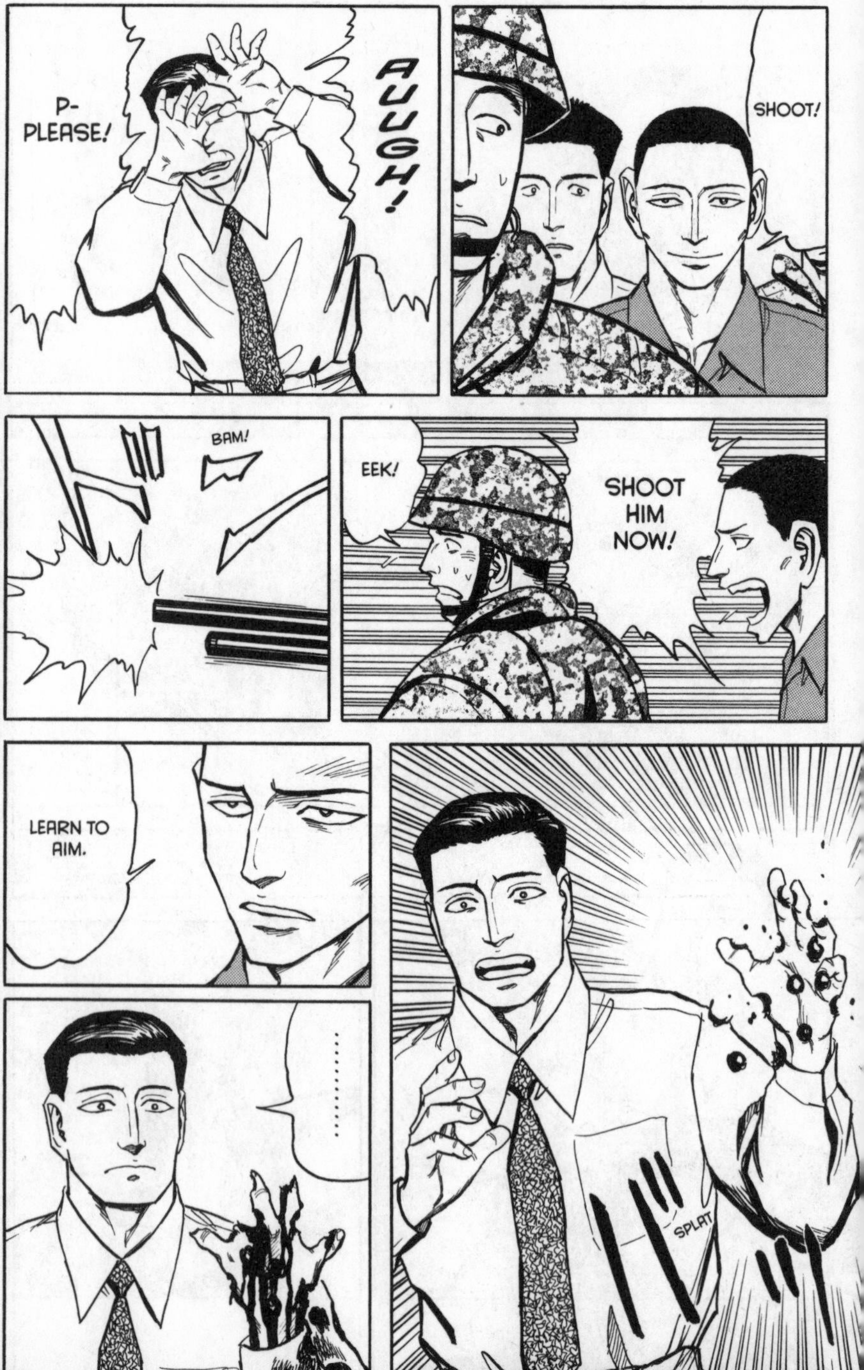
SHOOT!
AUUGH!
P-PLEASE!
SHOOT HIM NOW!
EEK!
BAM!
SPLAT
LEARN TO AIM.
......

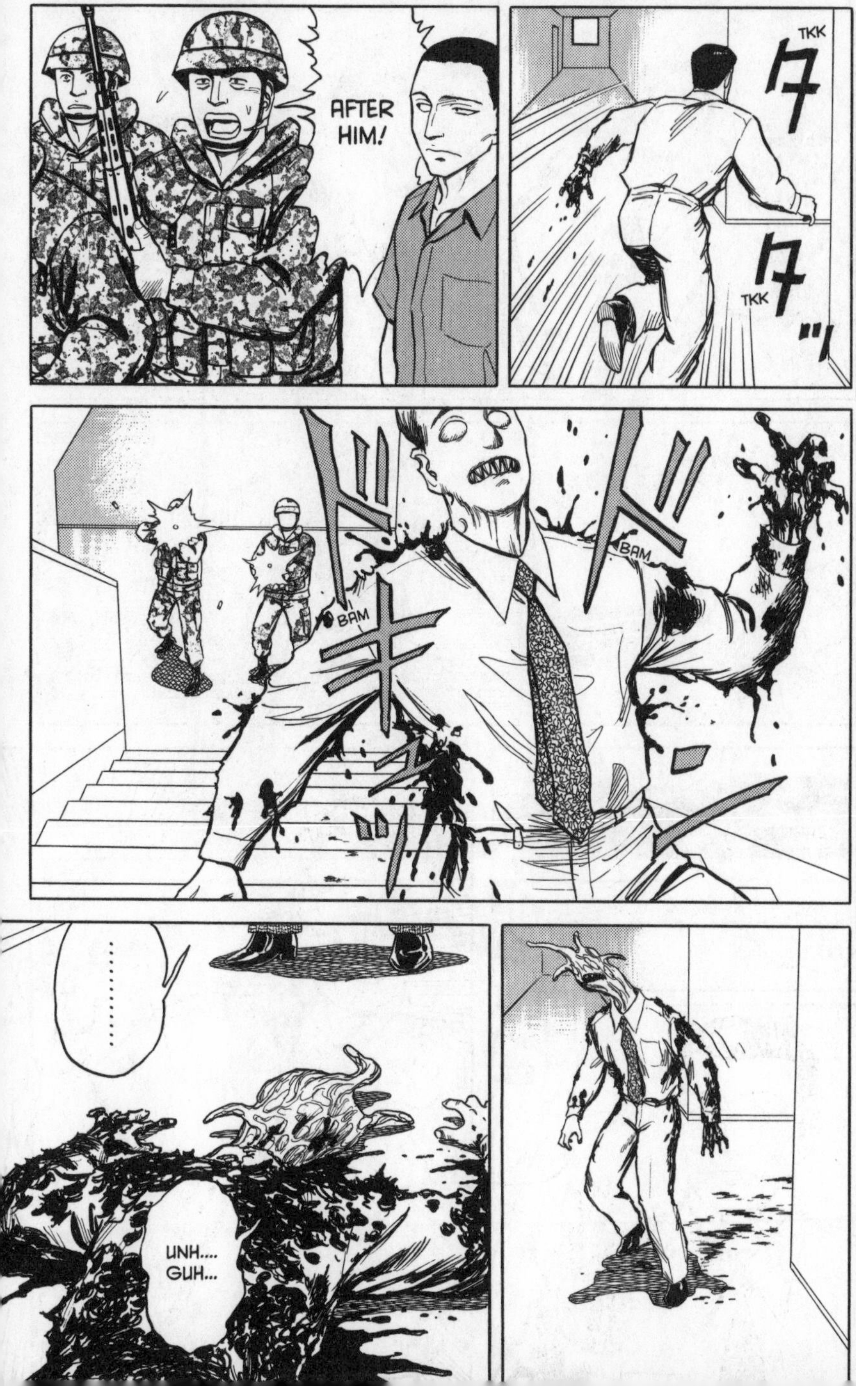
TKK
TKK
AFTER HIM!
BAM
BAM
......
UNH.... GUH...

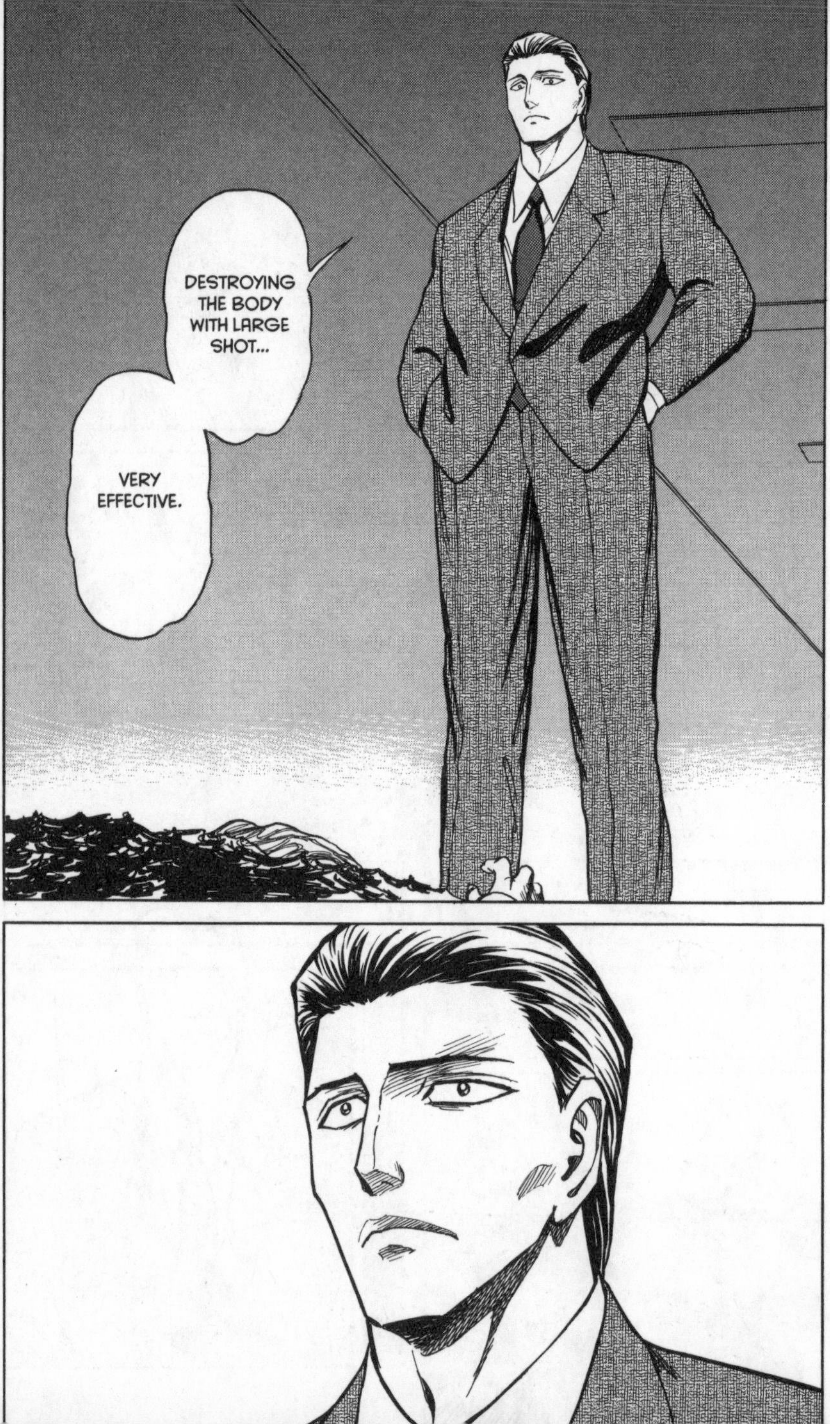
DESTROYING THE BODY WITH LARGE SHOT...
VERY EFFECTIVE.

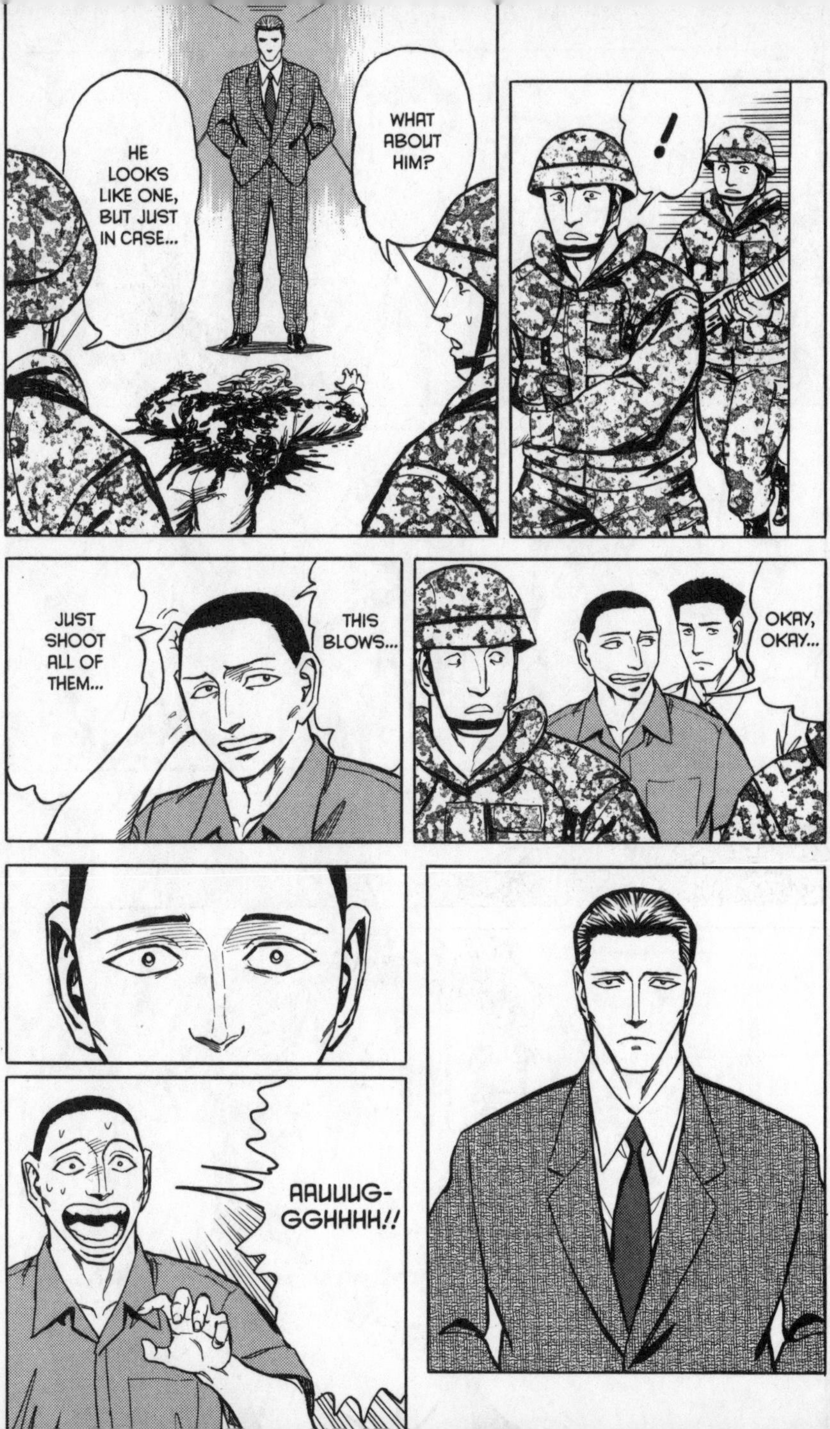
!
WHAT ABOUT HIM?
HE LOOKS LIKE ONE, BUT JUST IN CASE...
OKAY, OKAY...
THIS BLOWS...
JUST SHOOT ALL OF THEM...
AAUUUG-GGHHHH!!

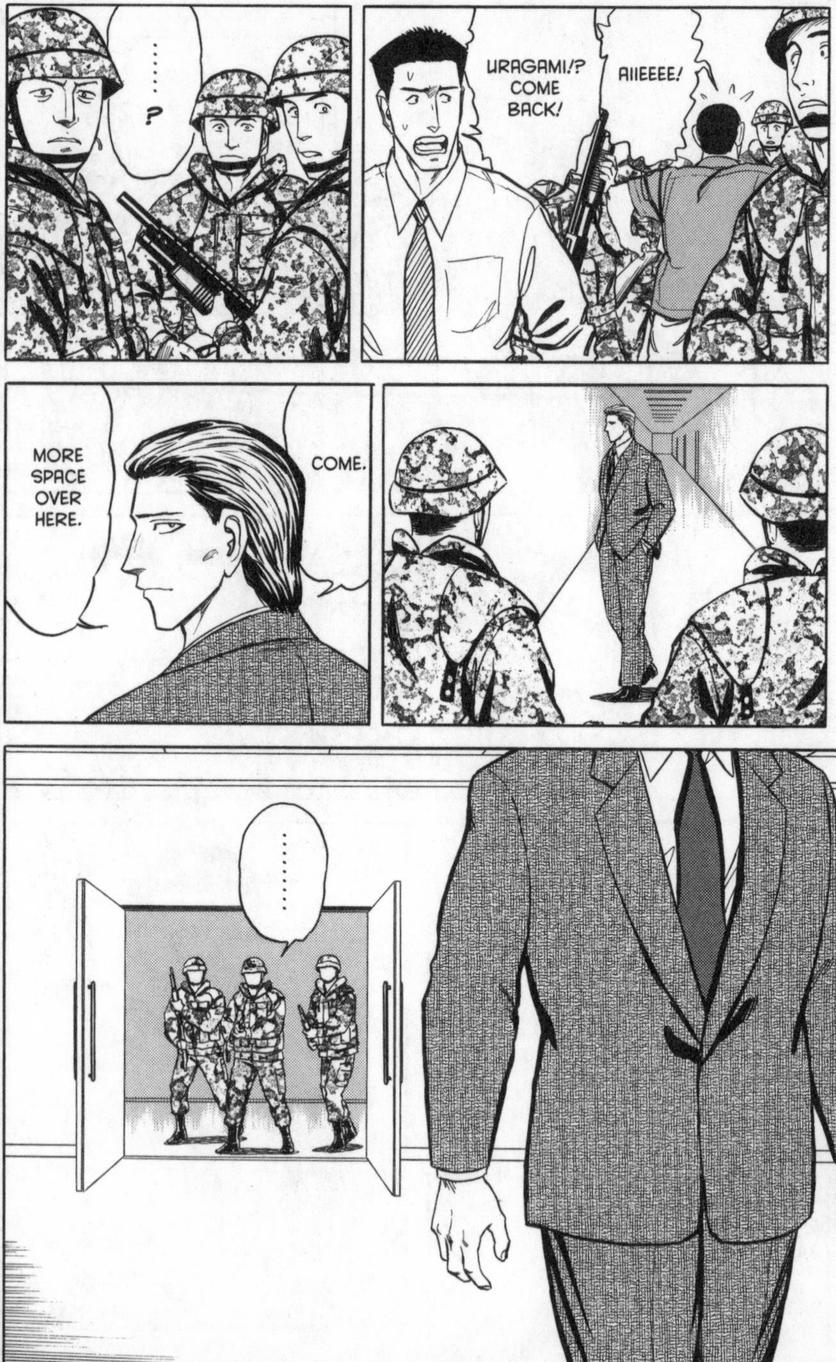
AIIEEEE!
URAGAMI!? COME BACK!
......?
COME.
MORE SPACE OVER HERE.
......

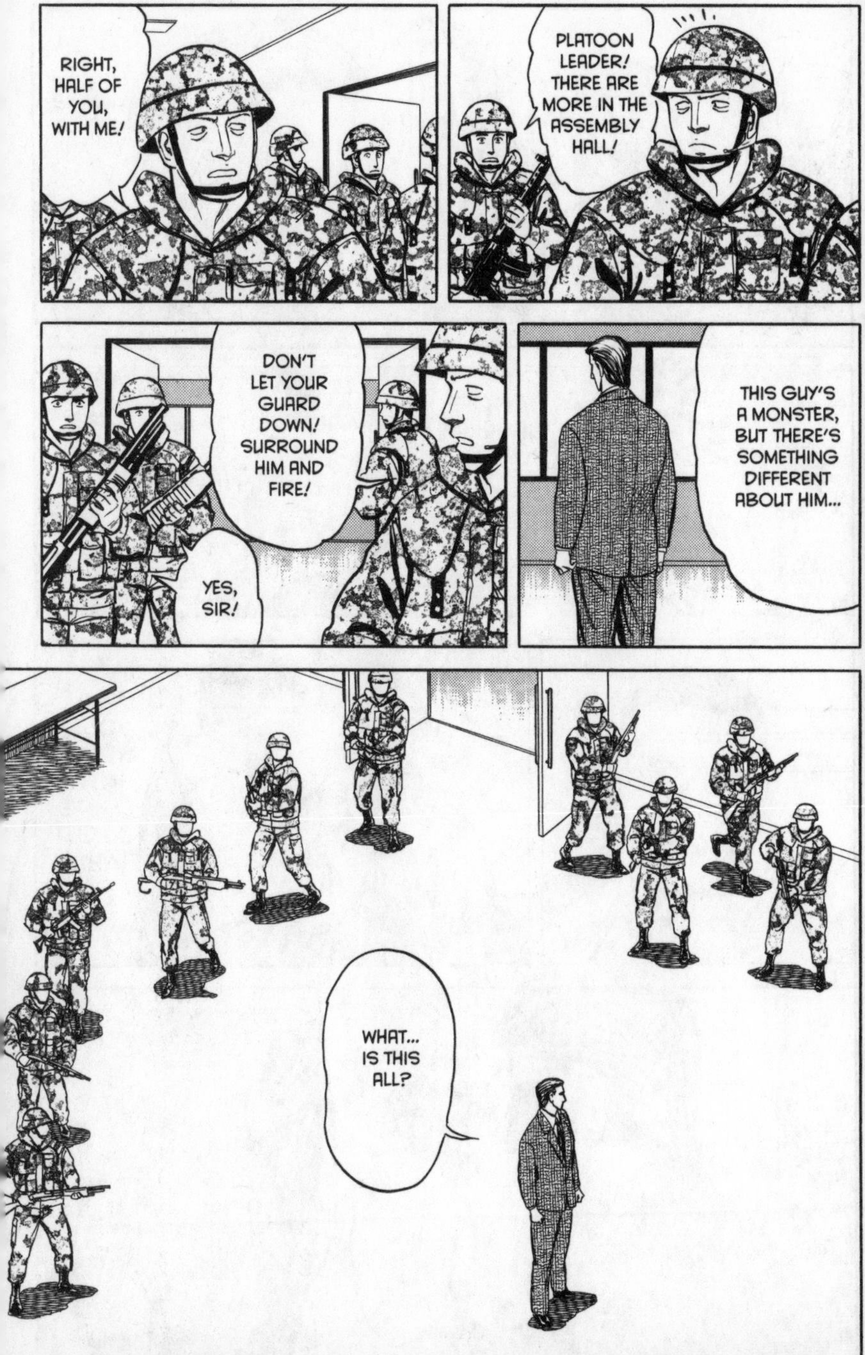
PLATOON LEADER! THERE ARE MORE IN THE ASSEMBLY HALL!
RIGHT, HALF OF YOU, WITH ME!
THIS GUY'S A MONSTER, BUT THERE'S SOMETHING DIFFERENT ABOUT HIM...
DON'T LET YOUR GUARD DOWN! SURROUND HIM AND FIRE!
YES, SIR!
WHAT... IS THIS ALL?

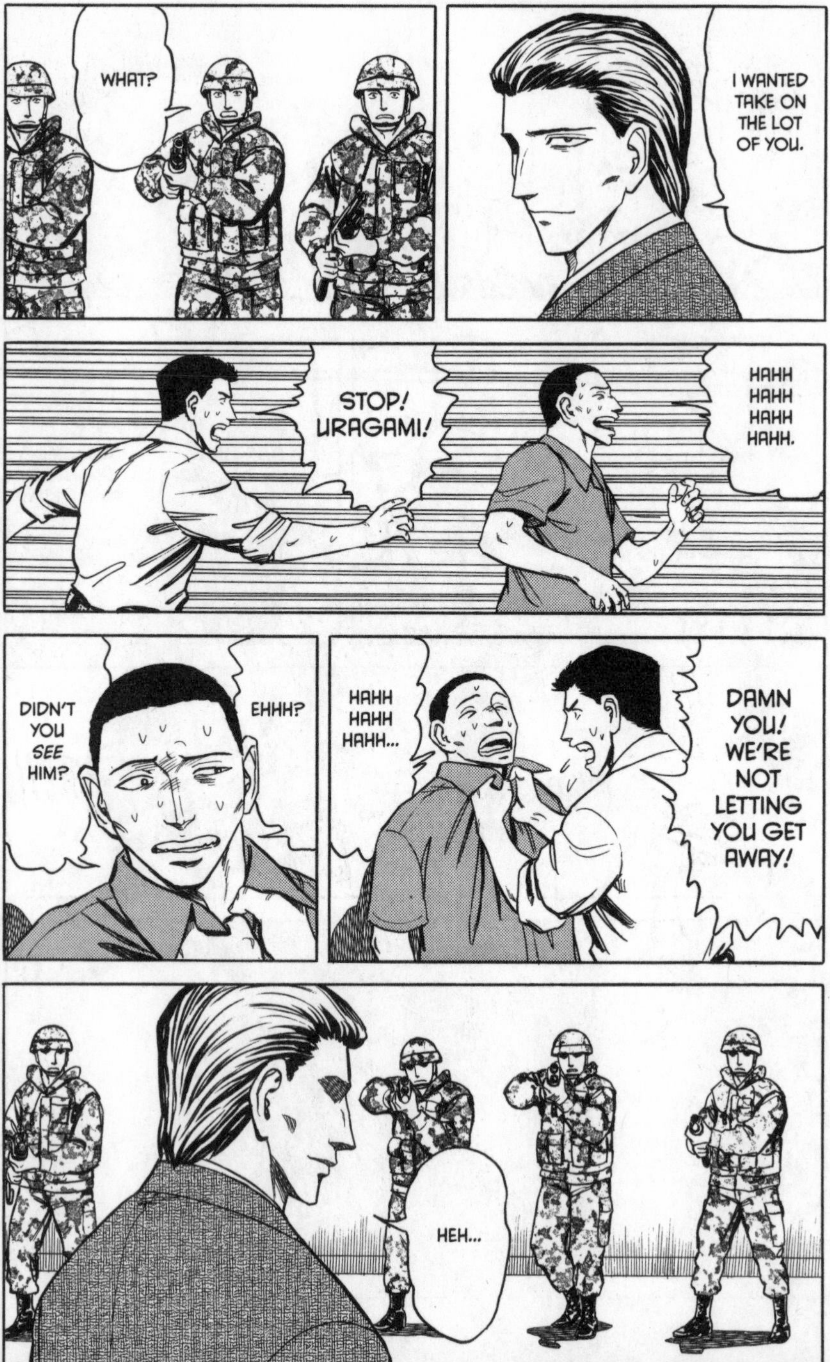
I WANTED TAKE ON THE LOT OF YOU.
WHAT?
HAHH HAHH HAHH HAHH.
STOP! URAGAMI!
DAMN YOU! WE'RE NOT LETTING YOU GET AWAY!
HAHH HAHH HAHH...
EHHH?
DIDN'T YOU *SEE* HIM?
HEH...

WHAT!?

EH? HE LOOKED... HUMAN TO YOU?

BLAM

BLAM BLAM BLAM

FIRE!!

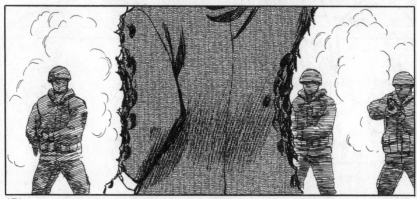

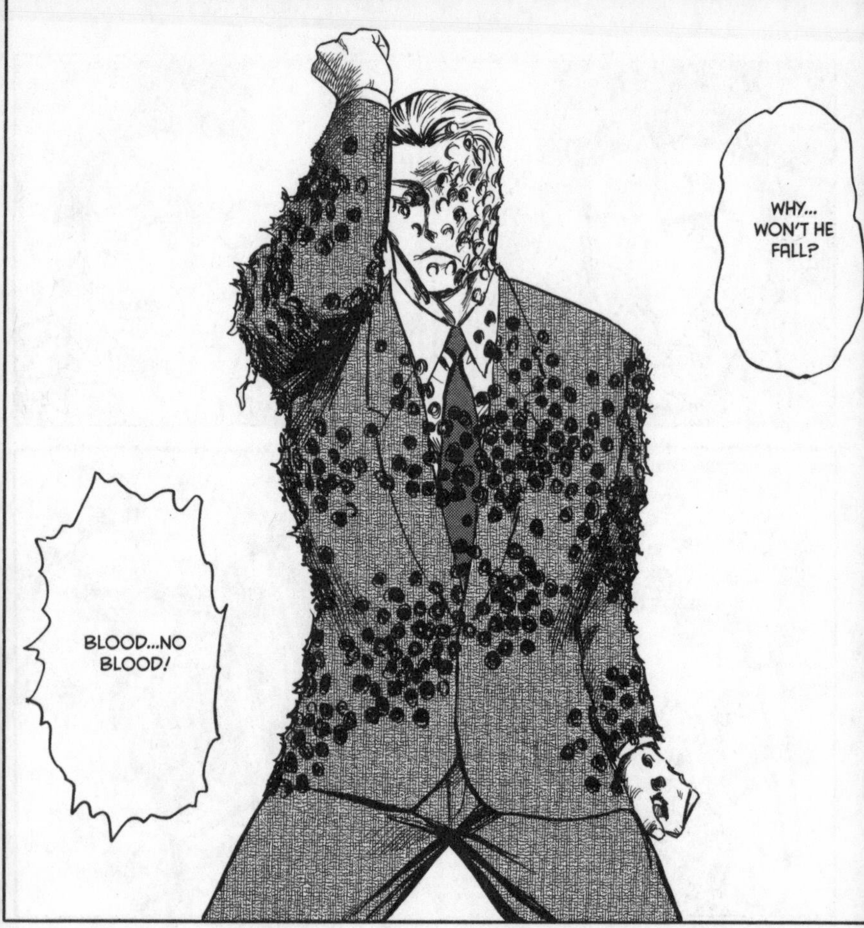
WHY... WON'T HE FALL?
BLOOD...NO BLOOD!

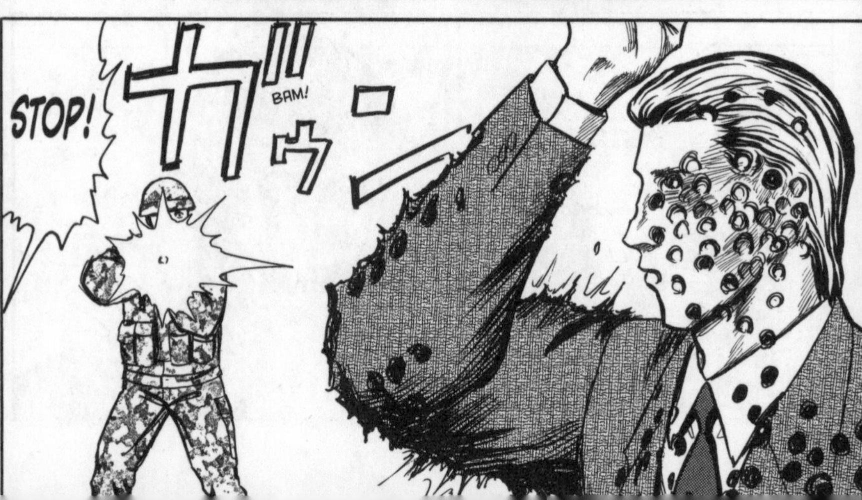
BAM!
STOP!

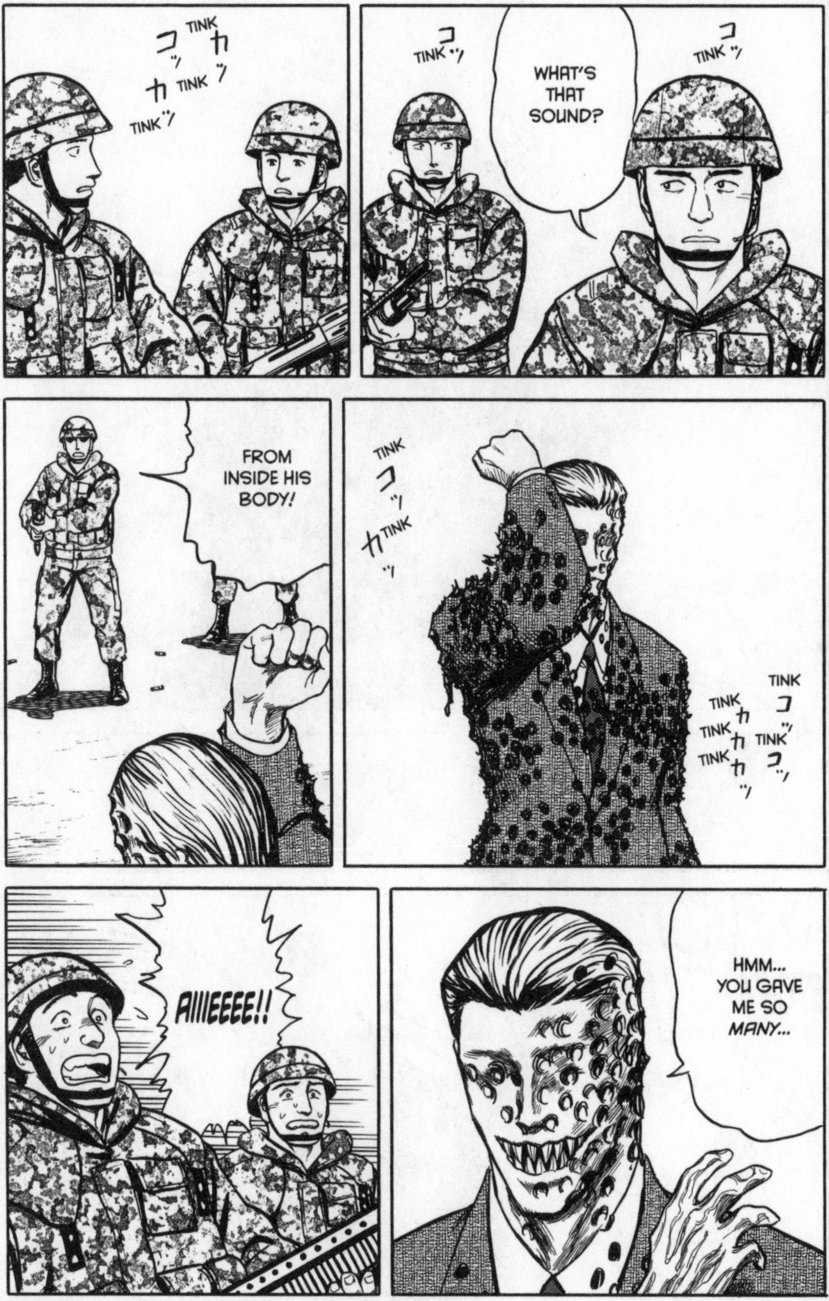
TINK コッ
WHAT'S THAT SOUND?
TINK コッ
TINK コッ TINK カッ
TINK カッ
FROM INSIDE HIS BODY!
TINK コッ TINK カッ
TINK カ TINK カ TINK カッ TINK コッ TINK コッ
HMM... YOU GAVE ME SO MANY...
AIIIEEEE!!

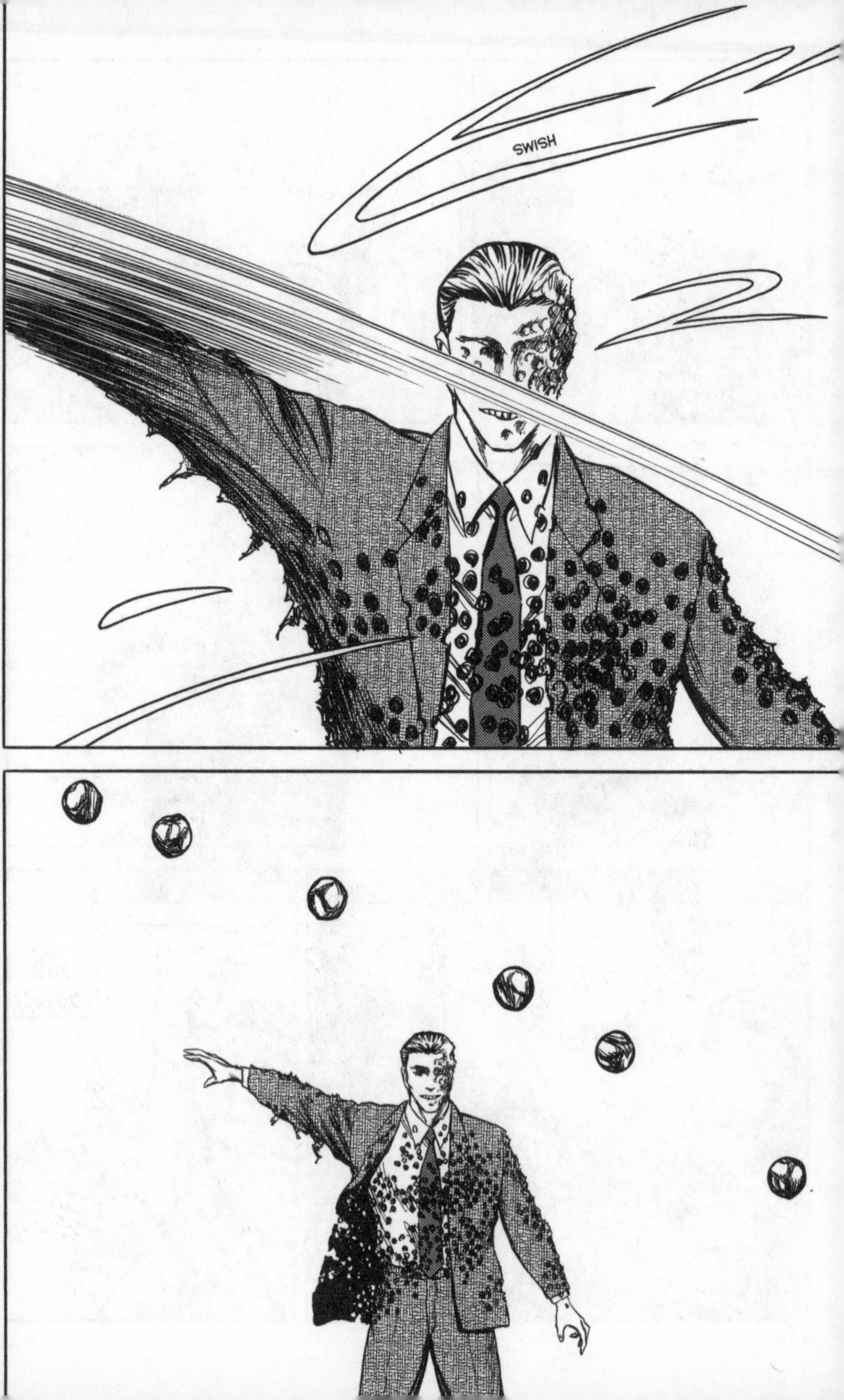
SWISH

SPLAT

ACK...

PTT

NO WAY... SHOT PELLETS!?

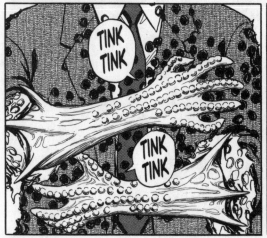

TINK TINK

TINK TINK

HIS ARMS!

175

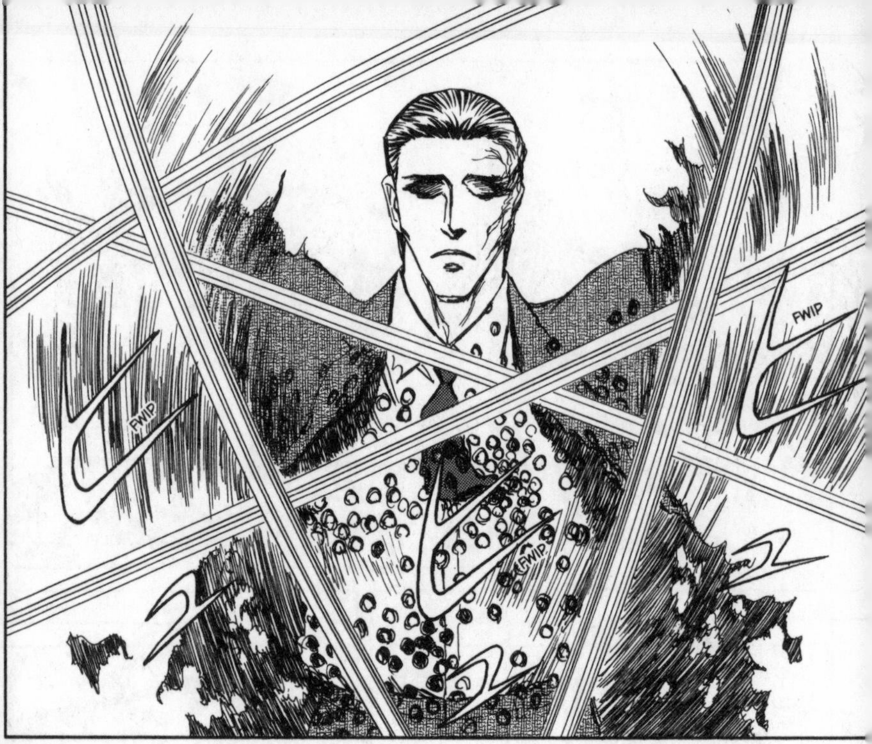
FWIP
FWIP
FWIP
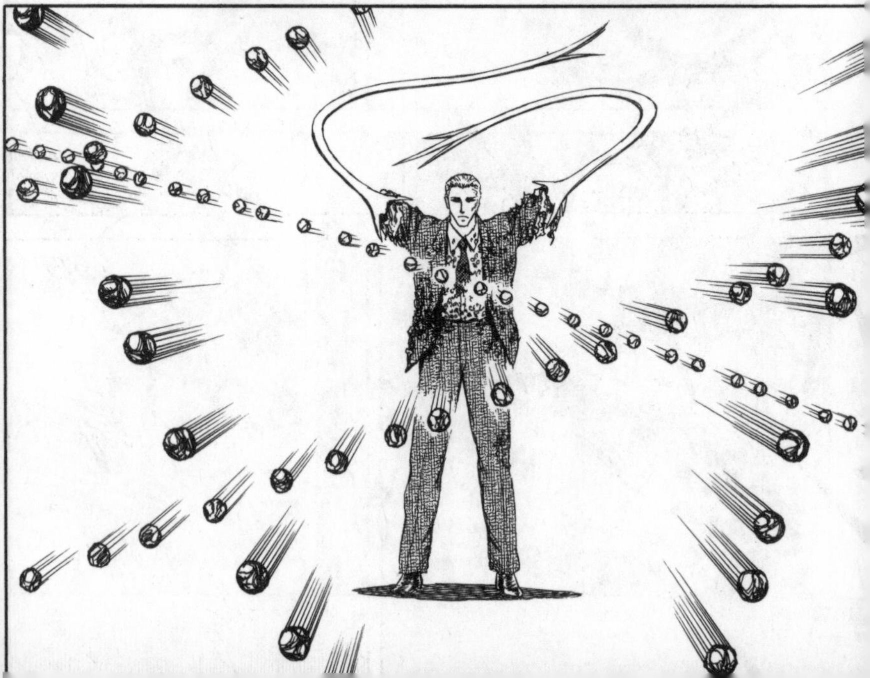

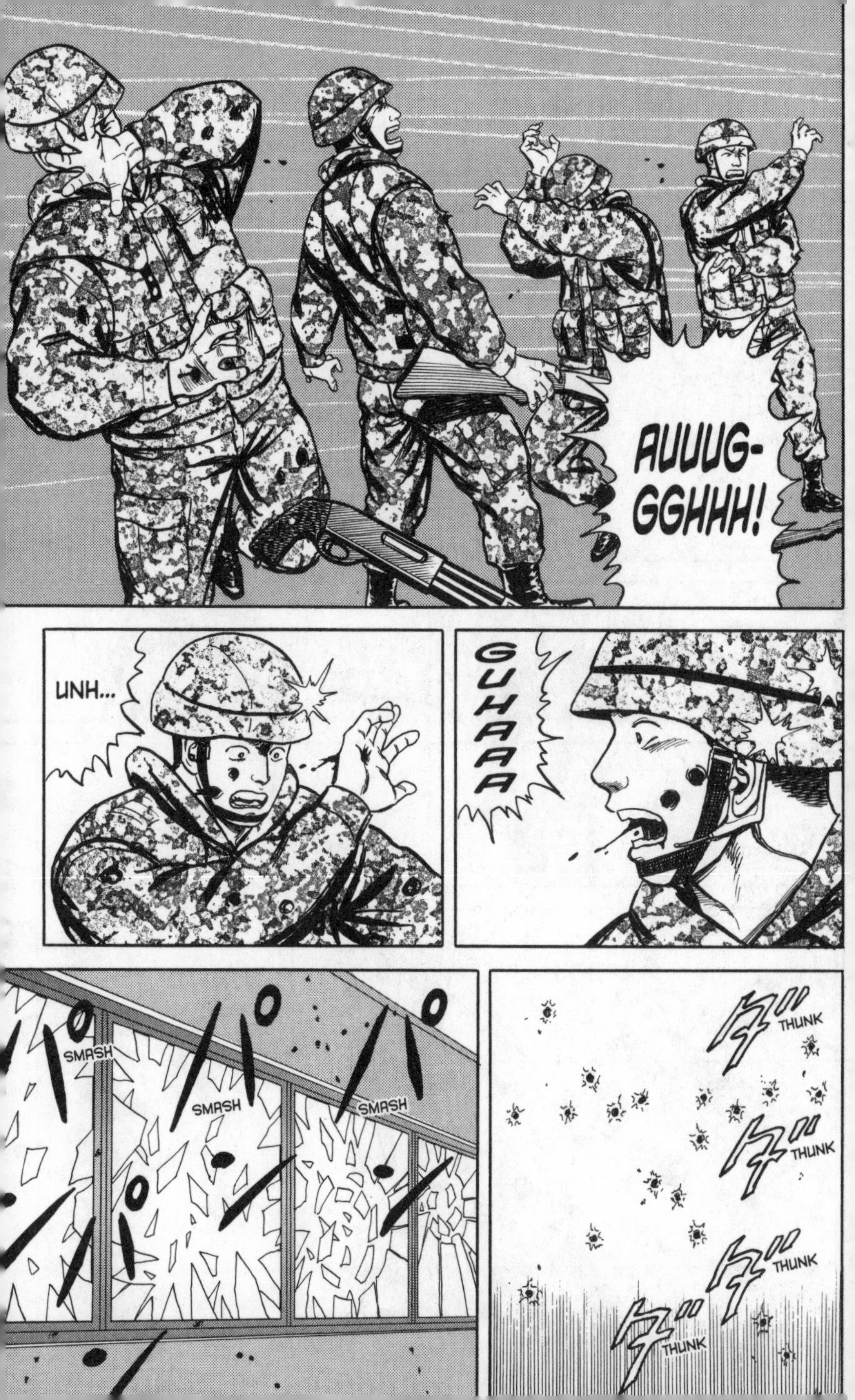
AUUUG-GGHHH!
GUHAAAA
UNH...
THUNK
THUNK
THUNK
THUNK
SMASH
SMASH
SMASH

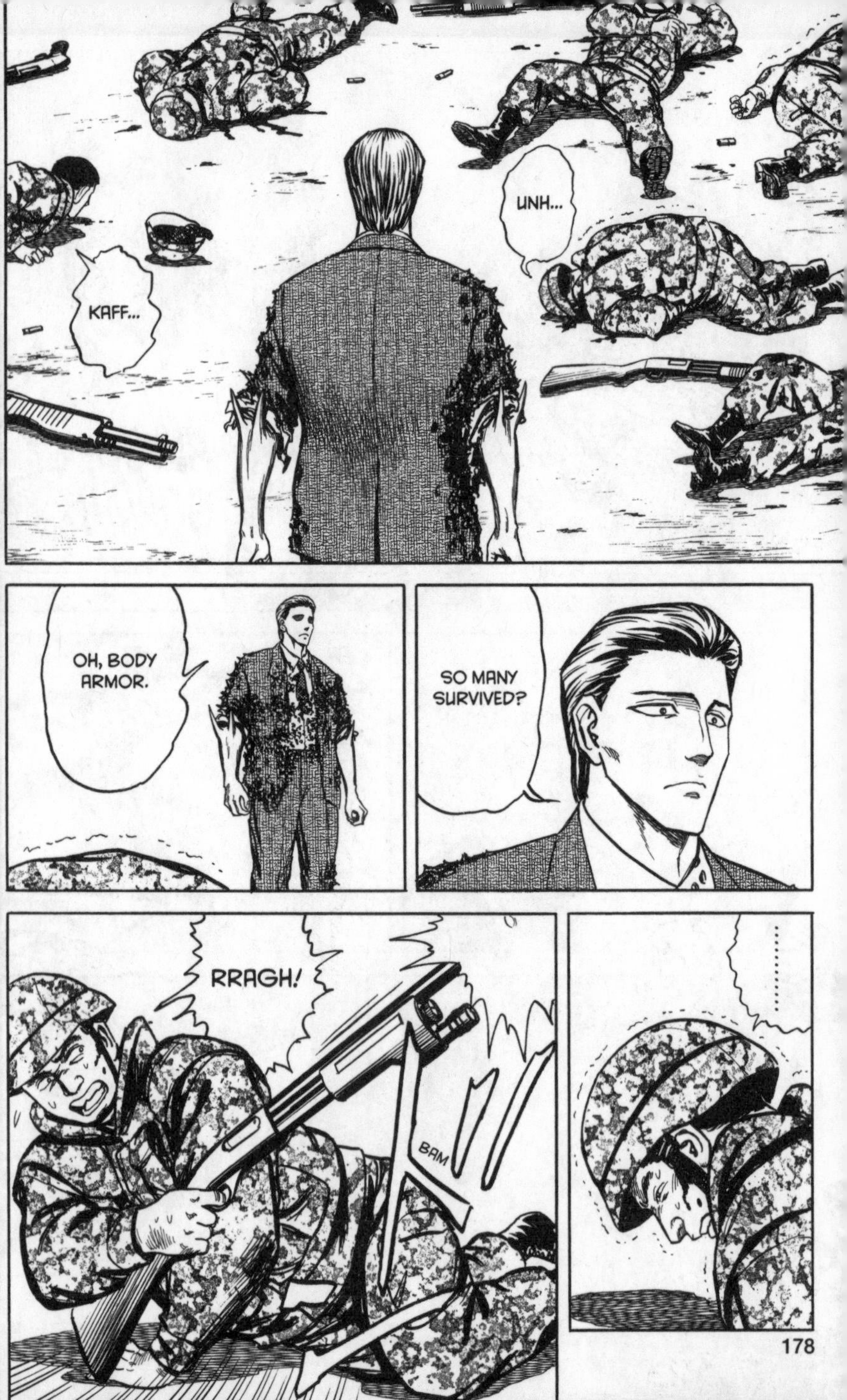
UNH...
KAFF...
SO MANY SURVIVED?
OH, BODY ARMOR.
......
RRAGH!
BAM

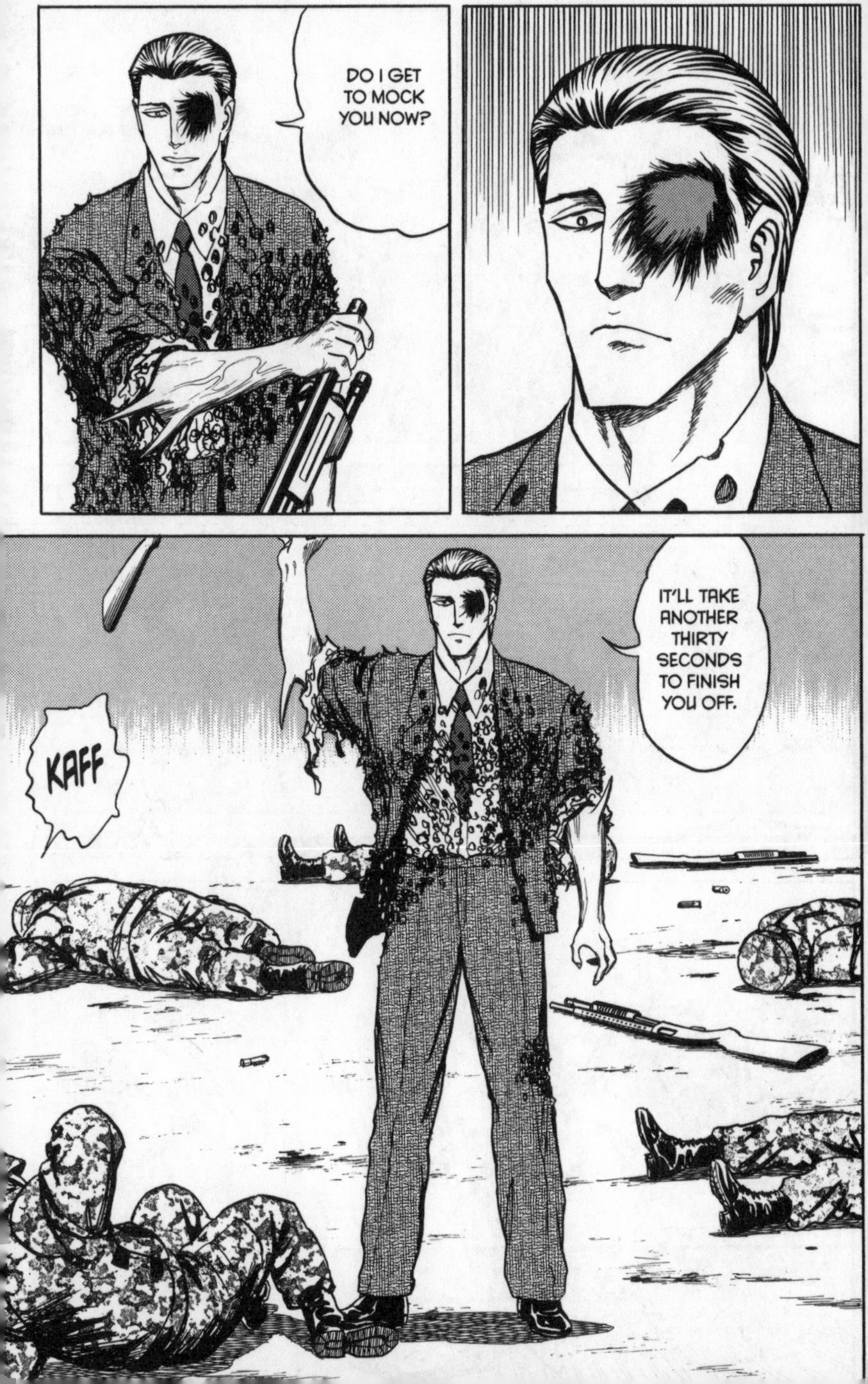
DO I GET TO MOCK YOU NOW?
IT'LL TAKE ANOTHER THIRTY SECONDS TO FINISH YOU OFF.
KAFF

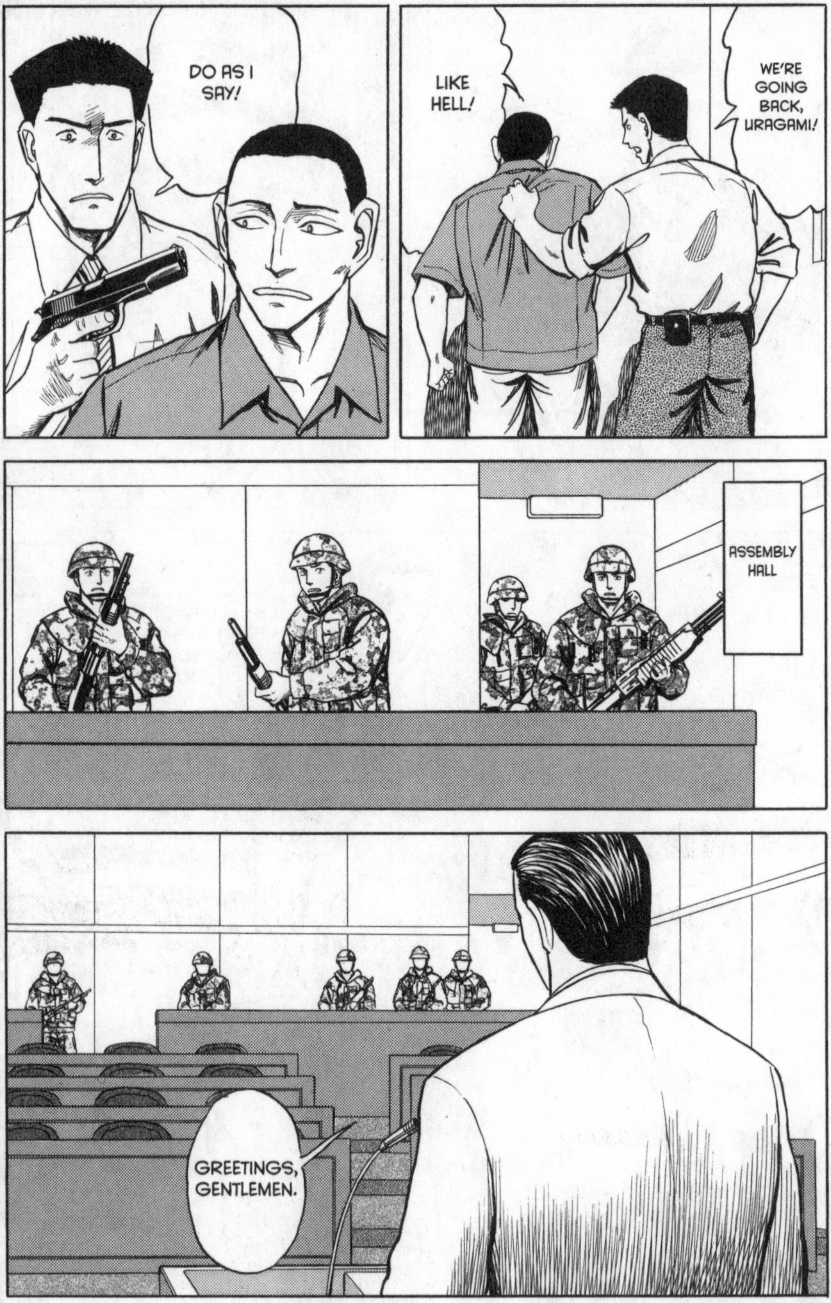
WE'RE GOING BACK, URAGAMI!
LIKE HELL!
DO AS I SAY!
ASSEMBLY HALL
GREETINGS, GENTLEMEN.

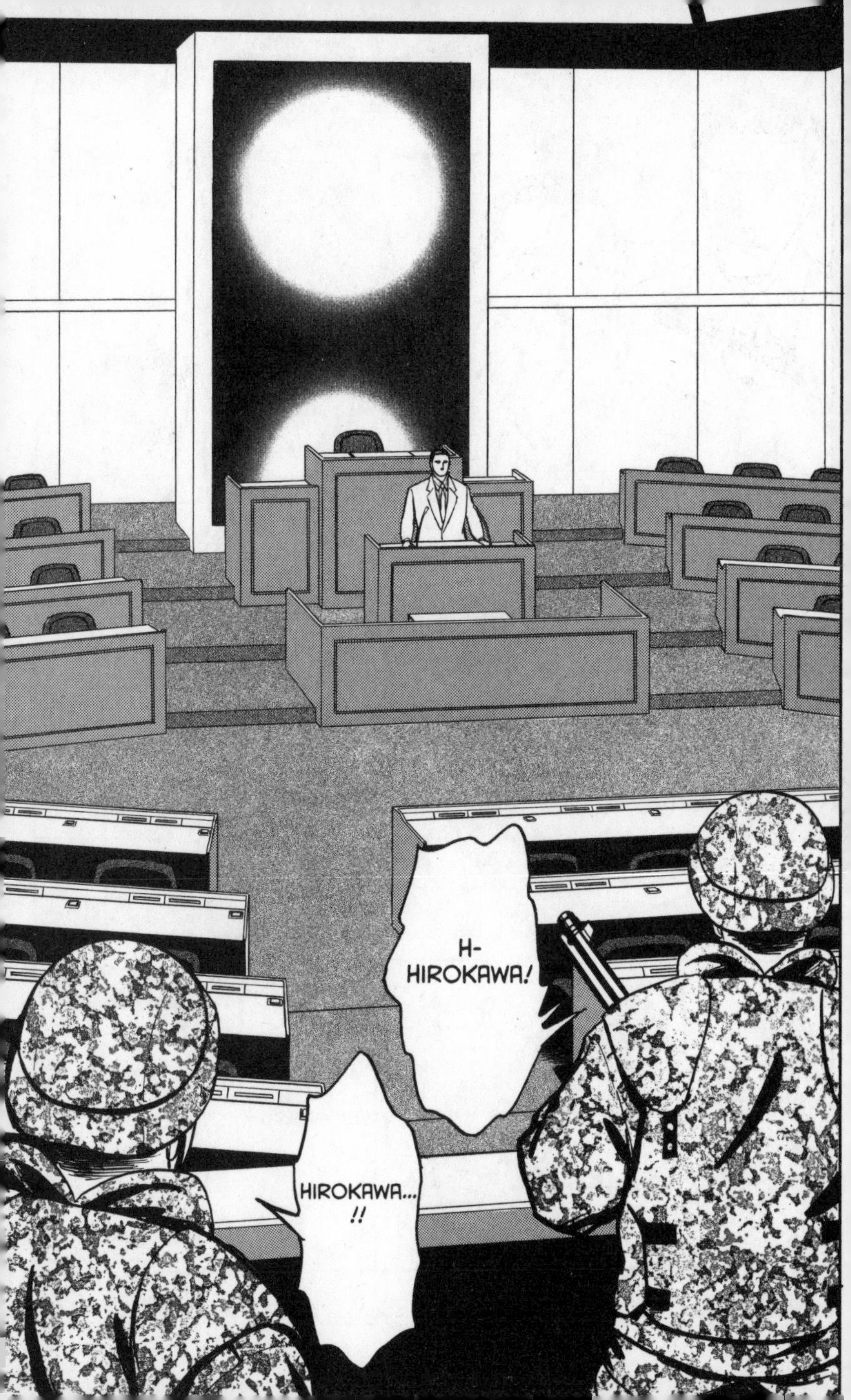
H-HIROKAWA!
HIROKAWA... !!

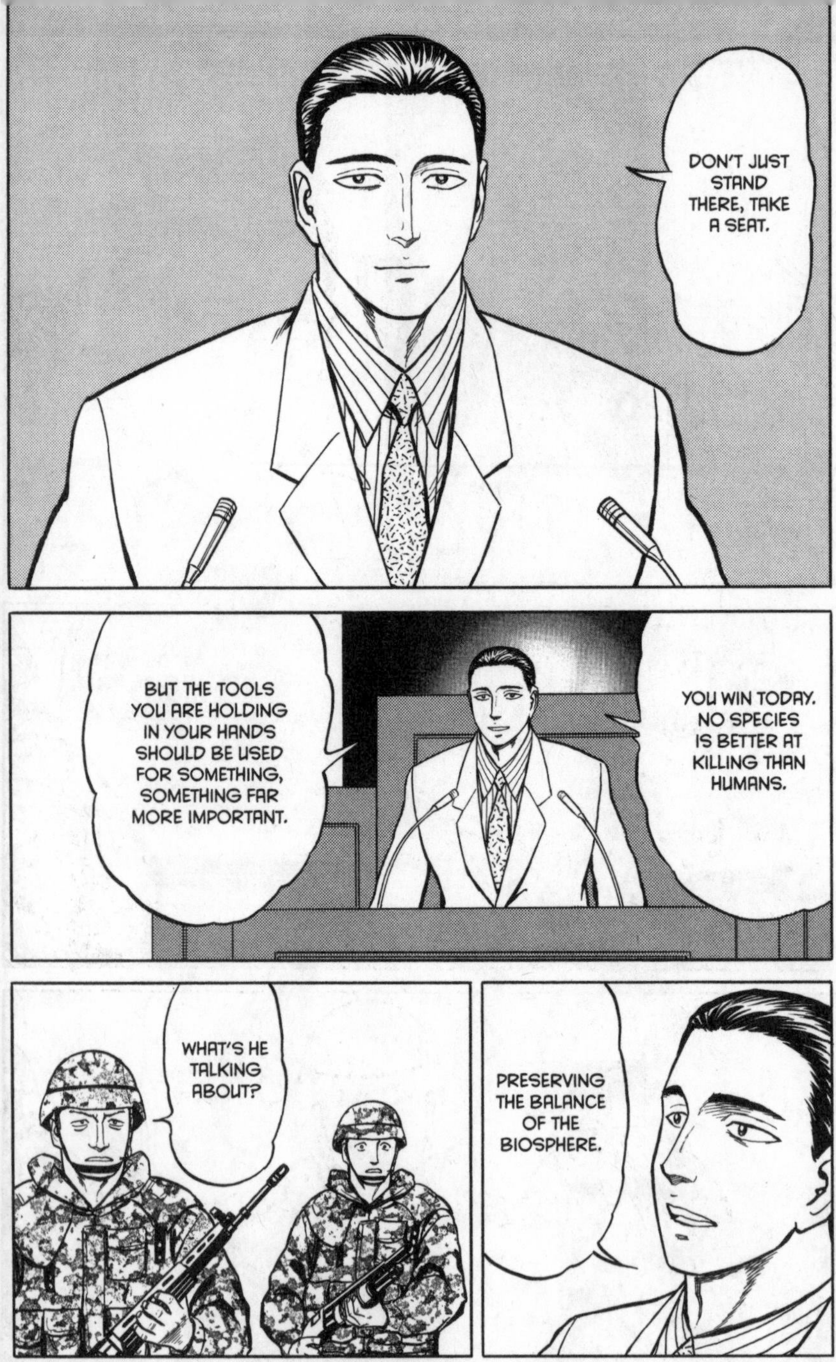
DON'T JUST STAND THERE, TAKE A SEAT.
YOU WIN TODAY. NO SPECIES IS BETTER AT KILLING THAN HUMANS.
BUT THE TOOLS YOU ARE HOLDING IN YOUR HANDS SHOULD BE USED FOR SOMETHING, SOMETHING FAR MORE IMPORTANT.
PRESERVING THE BALANCE OF THE BIOSPHERE.
WHAT'S HE TALKING ABOUT?

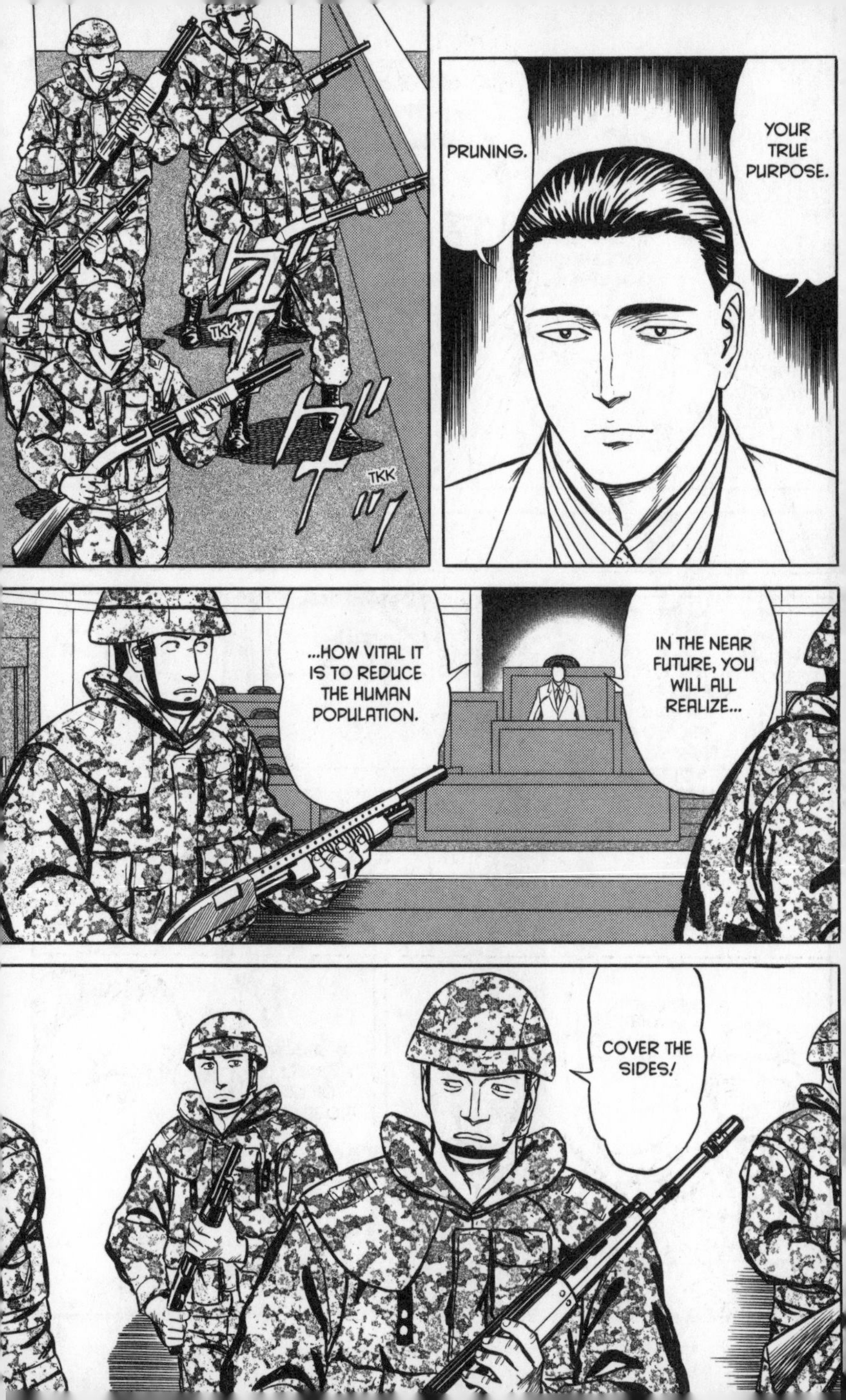
YOUR TRUE PURPOSE.
PRUNING.
TKK
TKK
IN THE NEAR FUTURE, YOU WILL ALL REALIZE...
...HOW VITAL IT IS TO REDUCE THE HUMAN POPULATION.
COVER THE SIDES!

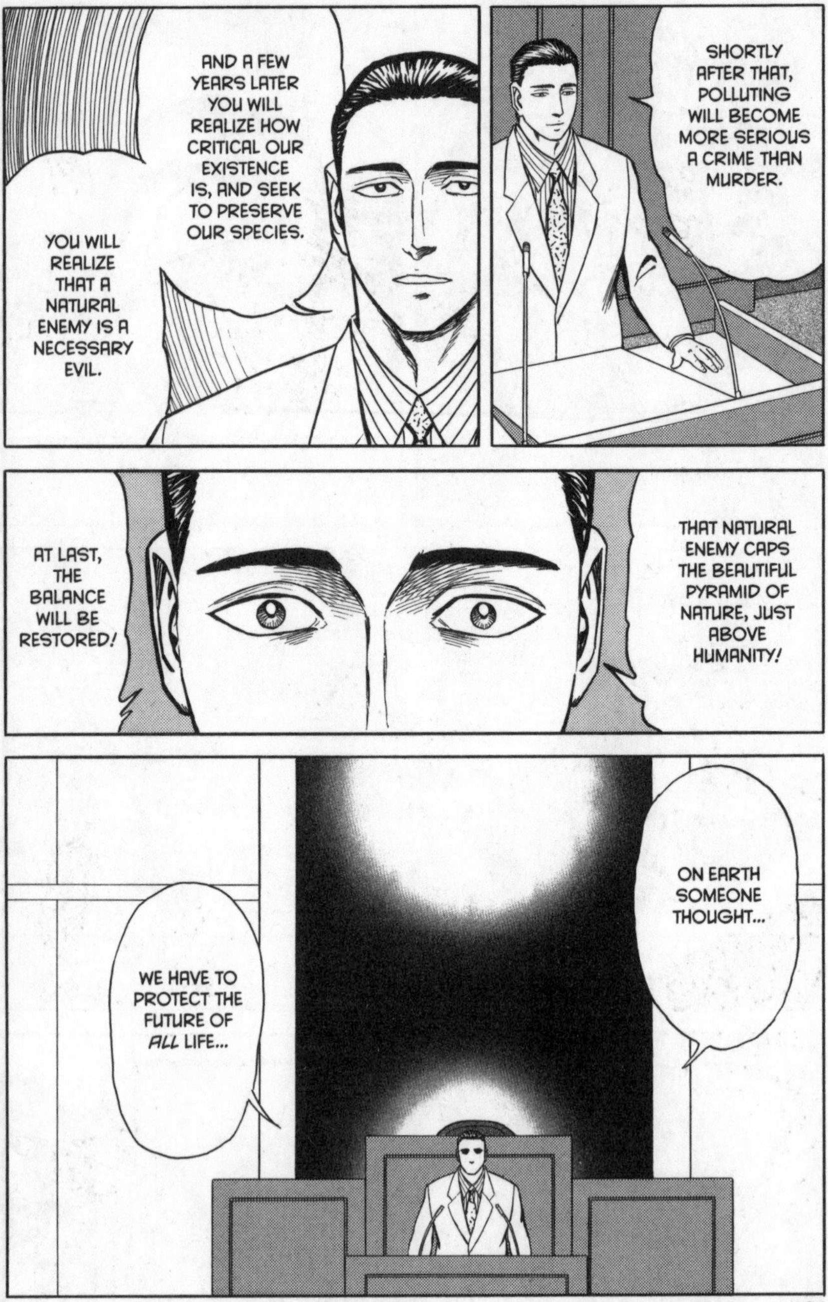
SHORTLY AFTER THAT, POLLUTING WILL BECOME MORE SERIOUS A CRIME THAN MURDER.
AND A FEW YEARS LATER YOU WILL REALIZE HOW CRITICAL OUR EXISTENCE IS, AND SEEK TO PRESERVE OUR SPECIES.
YOU WILL REALIZE THAT A NATURAL ENEMY IS A NECESSARY EVIL.
THAT NATURAL ENEMY CAPS THE BEAUTIFUL PYRAMID OF NATURE, JUST ABOVE HUMANITY!
AT LAST, THE BALANCE WILL BE RESTORED!
ON EARTH SOMEONE THOUGHT...
WE HAVE TO PROTECT THE FUTURE OF *ALL* LIFE...

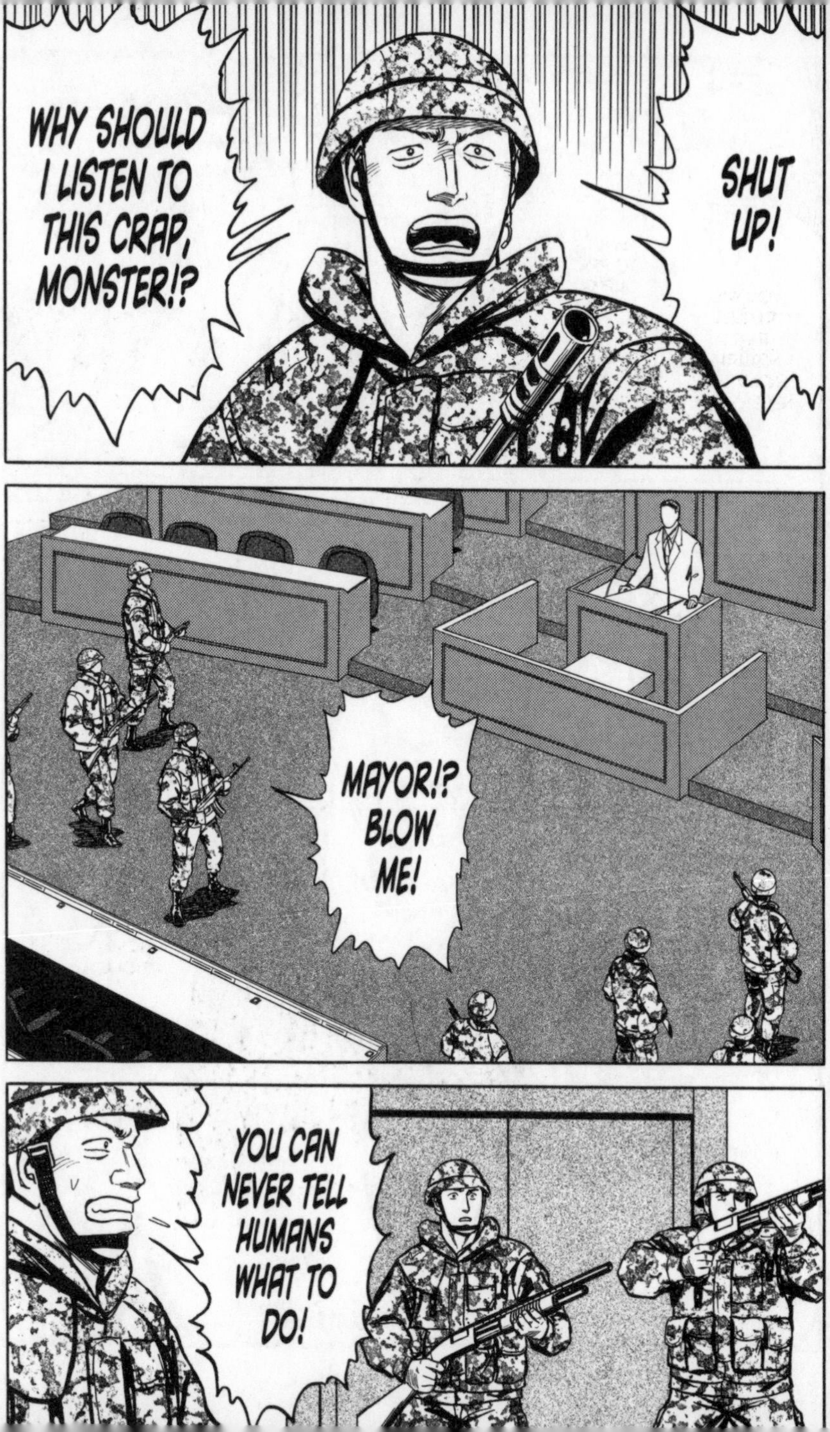
SHUT UP!
WHY SHOULD I LISTEN TO THIS CRAP, MONSTER!?
MAYOR!? BLOW ME!
YOU CAN NEVER TELL HUMANS WHAT TO DO!

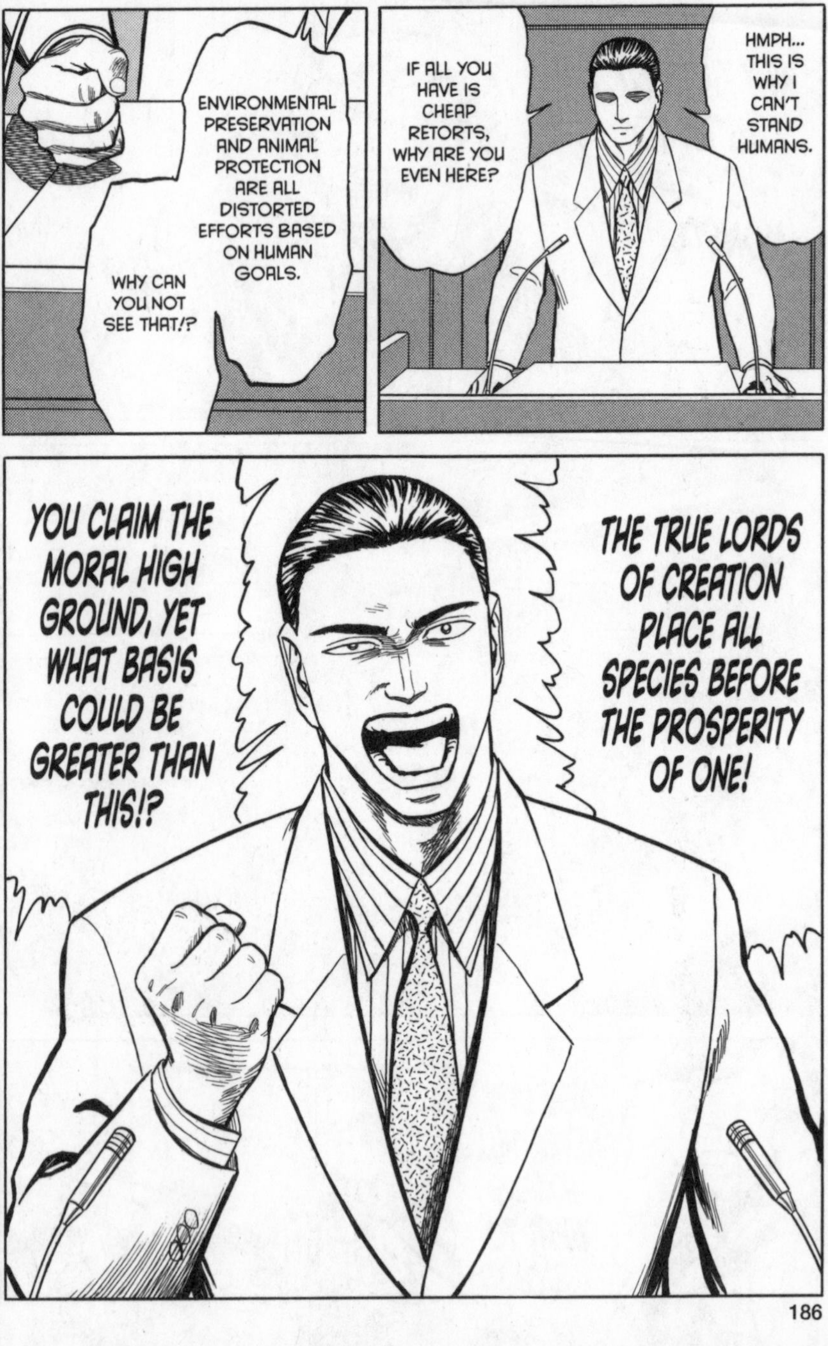
HMPH... THIS IS WHY I CAN'T STAND HUMANS.
IF ALL YOU HAVE IS CHEAP RETORTS, WHY ARE YOU EVEN HERE?
ENVIRONMENTAL PRESERVATION AND ANIMAL PROTECTION ARE ALL DISTORTED EFFORTS BASED ON HUMAN GOALS.
WHY CAN YOU NOT SEE THAT!?
THE TRUE LORDS OF CREATION PLACE ALL SPECIES BEFORE THE PROSPERITY OF ONE!
YOU CLAIM THE MORAL HIGH GROUND, YET WHAT BASIS COULD BE GREATER THAN THIS!?

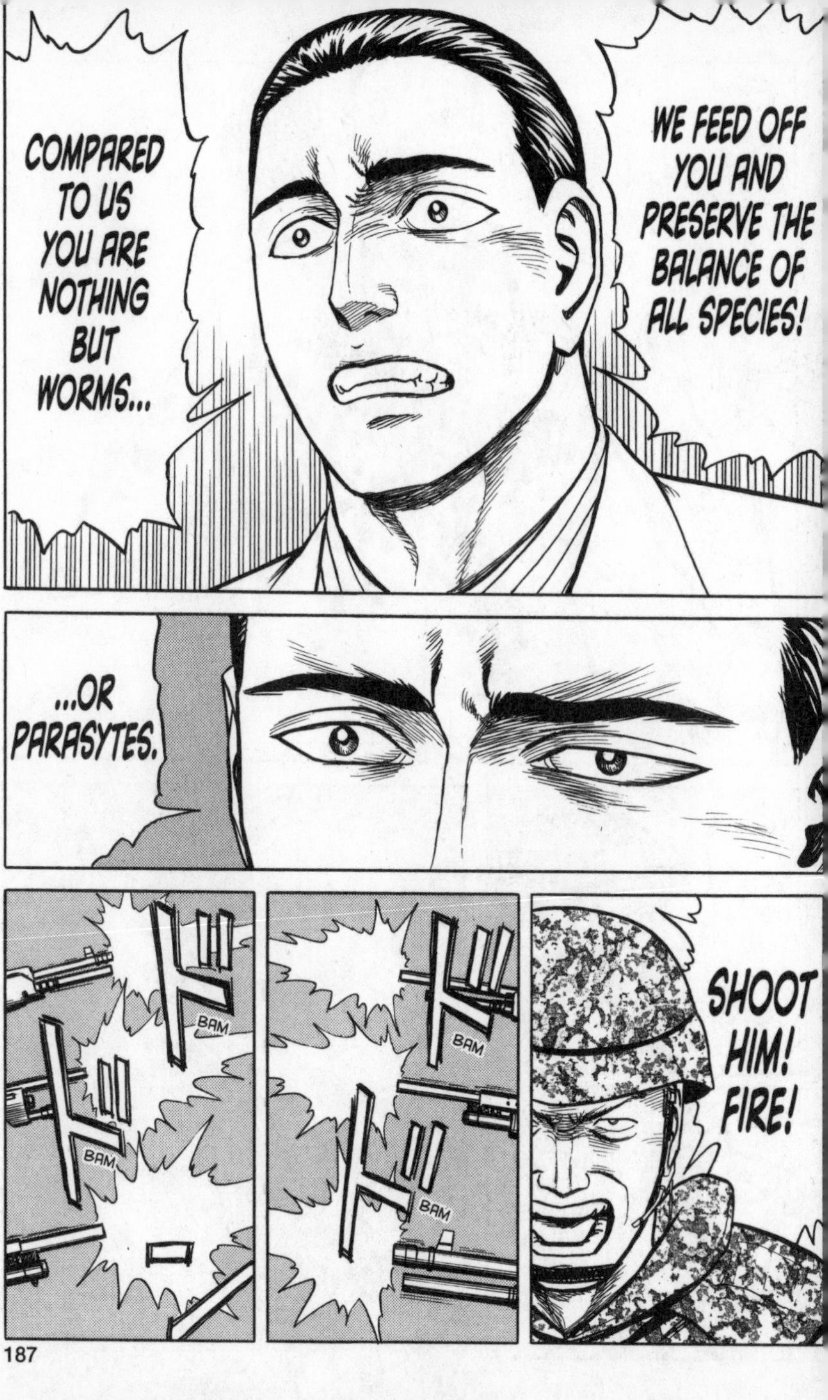
WE FEED OFF YOU AND PRESERVE THE BALANCE OF ALL SPECIES!
COMPARED TO US YOU ARE NOTHING BUT WORMS...
...OR PARASYTES.
SHOOT HIM! FIRE!
BAM
BAM
BAM
BAM

GOT HIM!

WE GOT THE BOSS! WE DID IT!

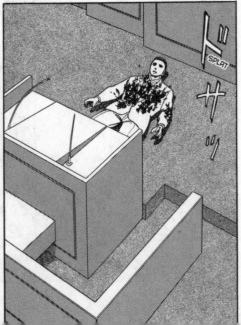

SPLAT

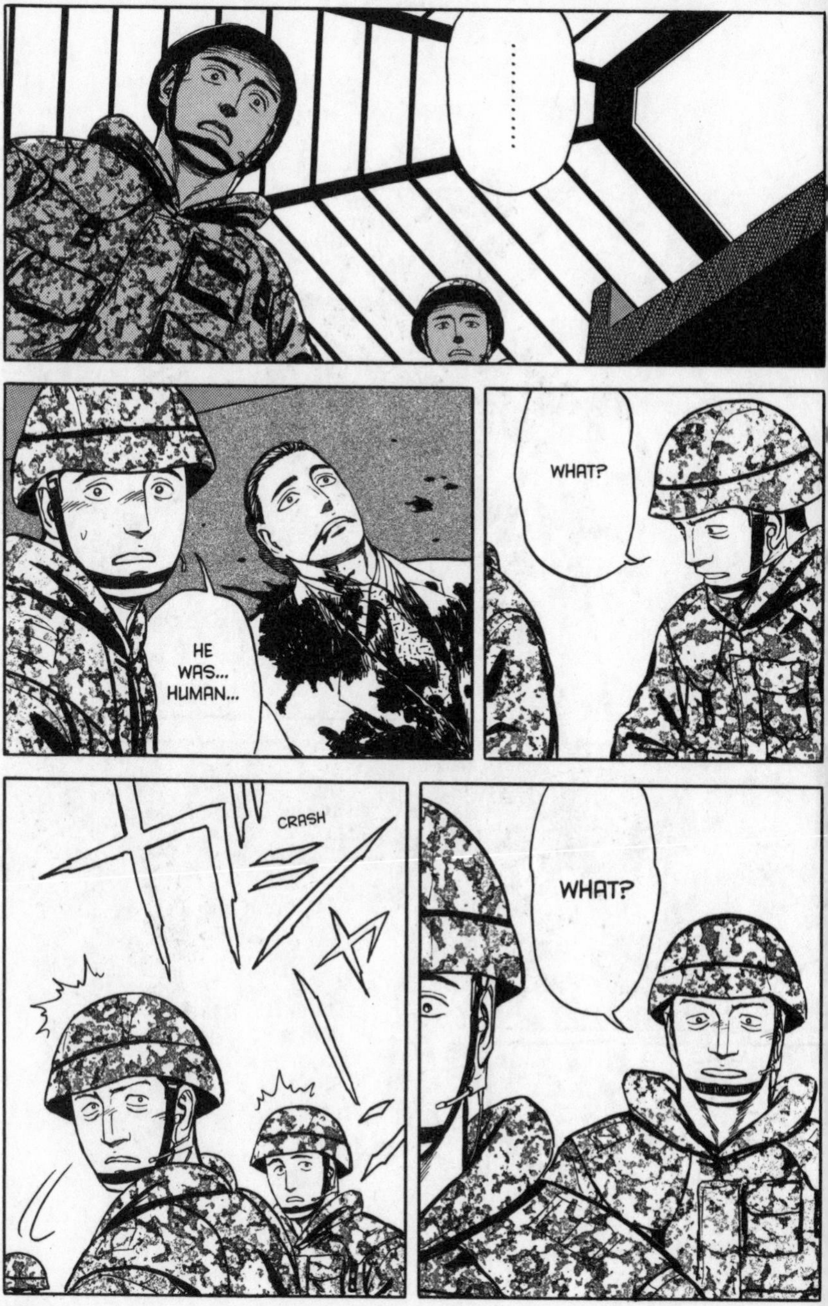
......
WHAT?
HE WAS... HUMAN...
WHAT?
CRASH

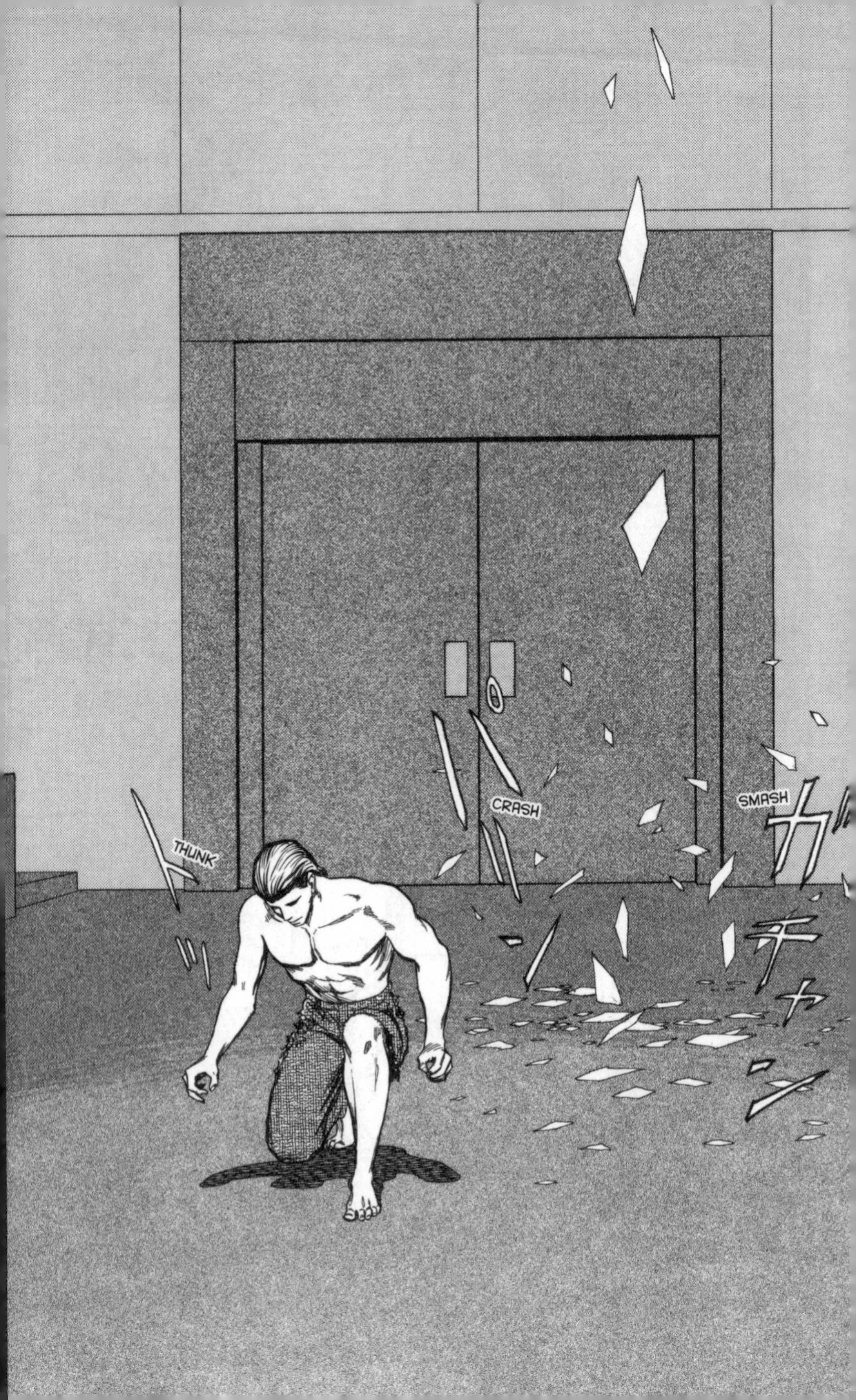
SMASH
CRASH
THUNK

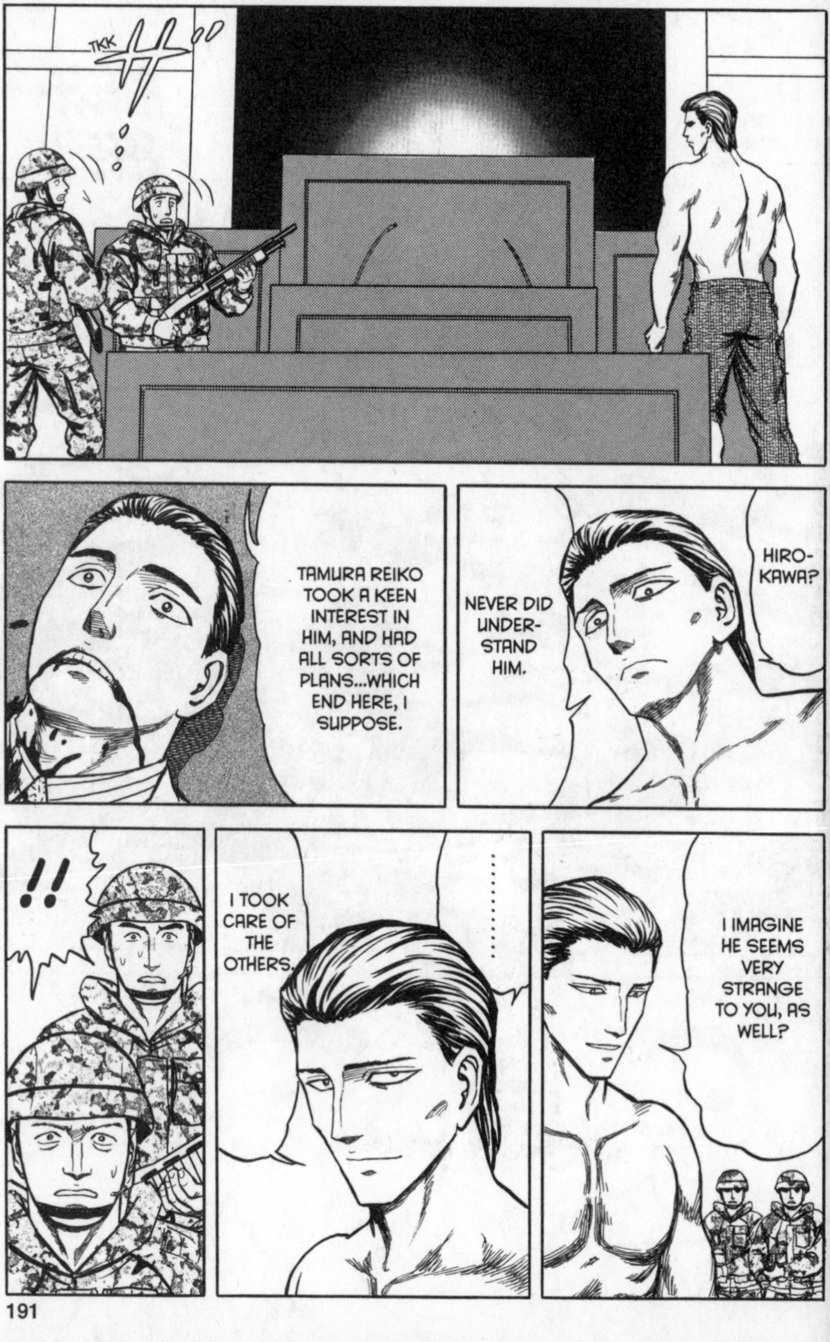
TKK
HIRO-KAWA?
NEVER DID UNDER-STAND HIM.
TAMURA REIKO TOOK A KEEN INTEREST IN HIM, AND HAD ALL SORTS OF PLANS...WHICH END HERE, I SUPPOSE.
I IMAGINE HE SEEMS VERY STRANGE TO YOU, AS WELL?
......
I TOOK CARE OF THE OTHERS.
!!

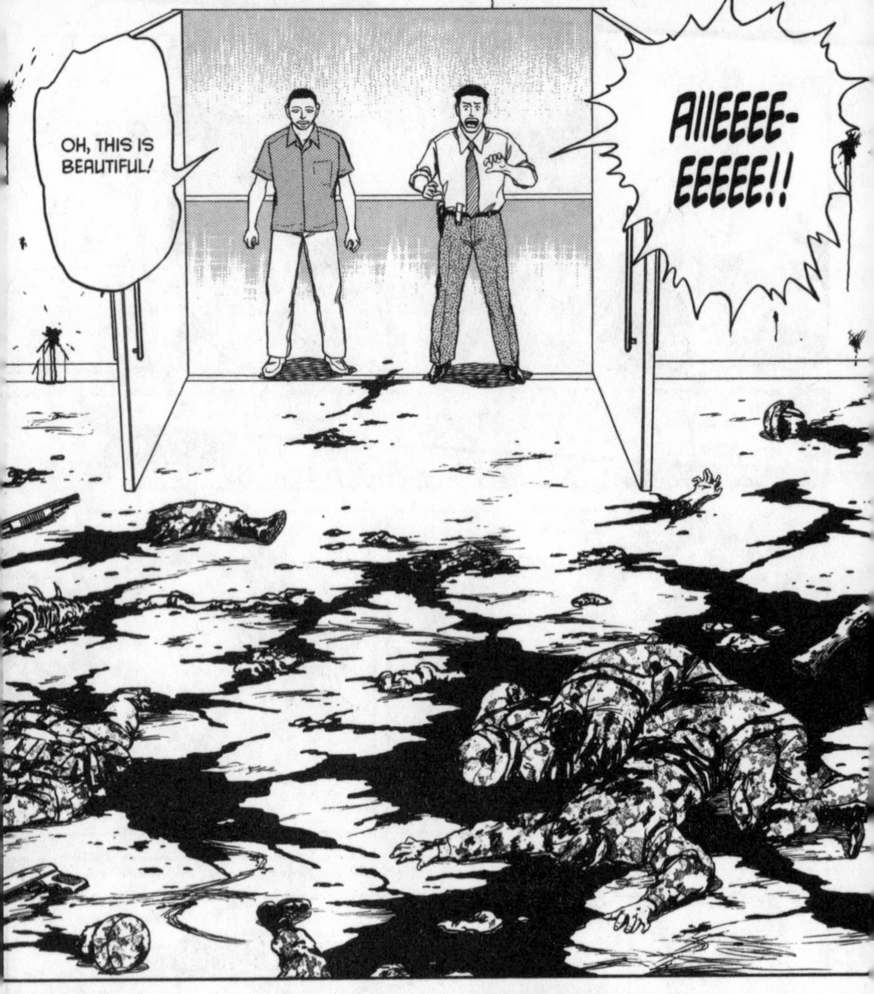
AIIEEEE-EEEEE!!
OH, THIS IS BEAUTIFUL!

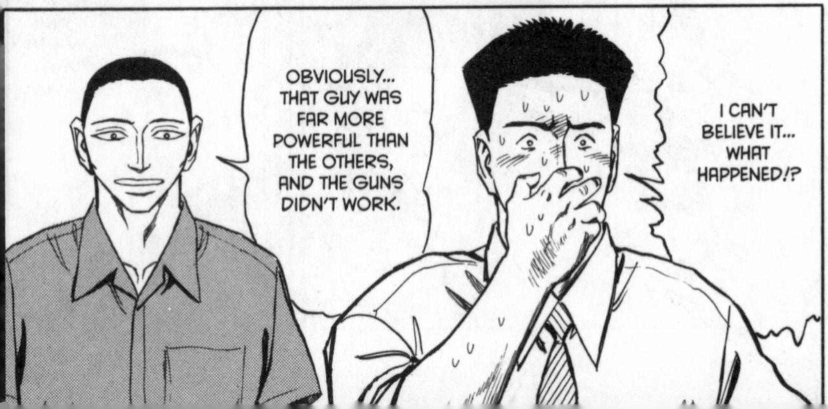
I CAN'T BELIEVE IT... WHAT HAPPENED!?
OBVIOUSLY... THAT GUY WAS FAR MORE POWERFUL THAN THE OTHERS, AND THE GUNS DIDN'T WORK.

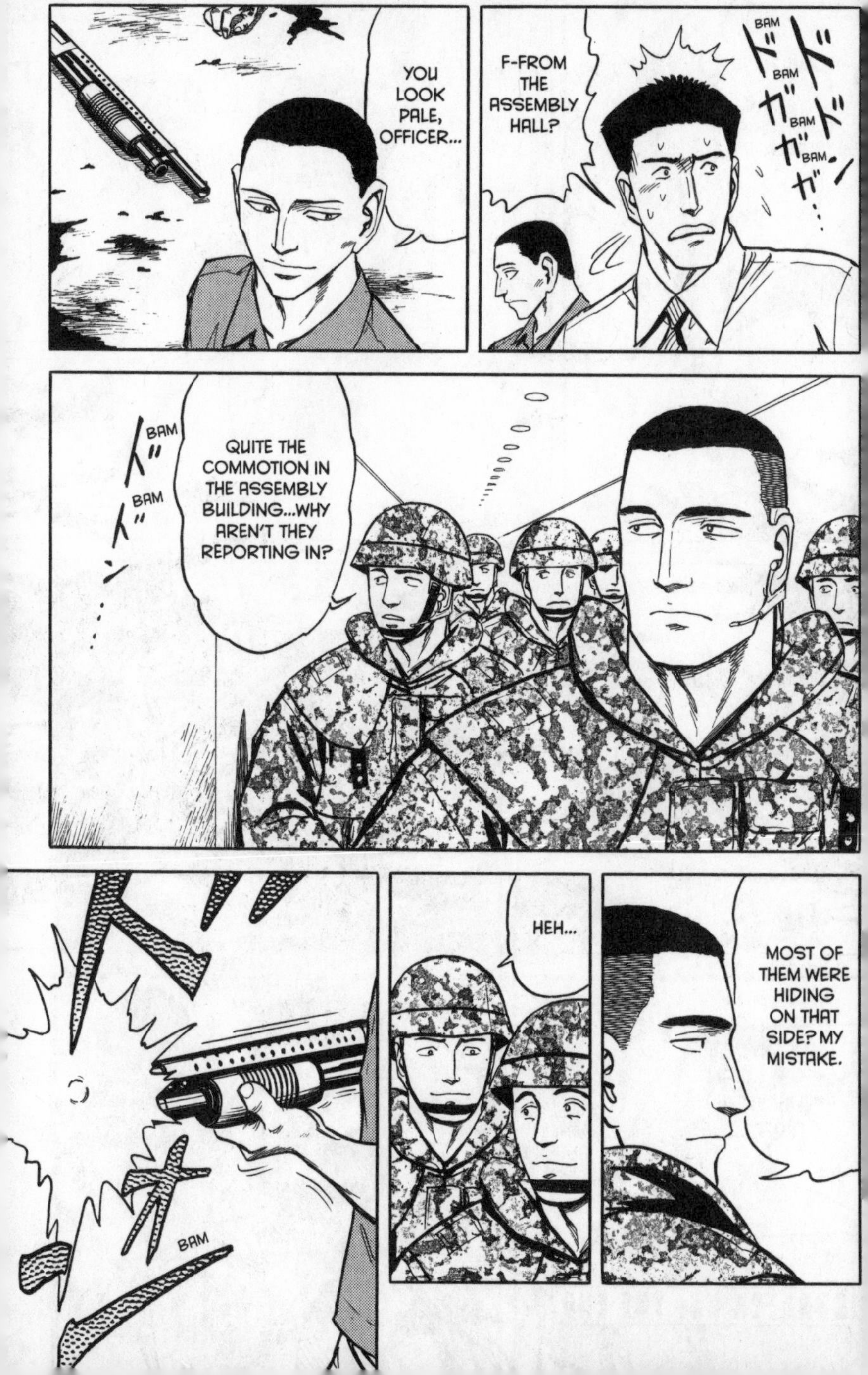
BAM
BAM
BAM
BAM
F-FROM THE ASSEMBLY HALL?
YOU LOOK PALE, OFFICER...
BAM
BAM
QUITE THE COMMOTION IN THE ASSEMBLY BUILDING...WHY AREN'T THEY REPORTING IN?
MOST OF THEM WERE HIDING ON THAT SIDE? MY MISTAKE.
HEH...
BAM

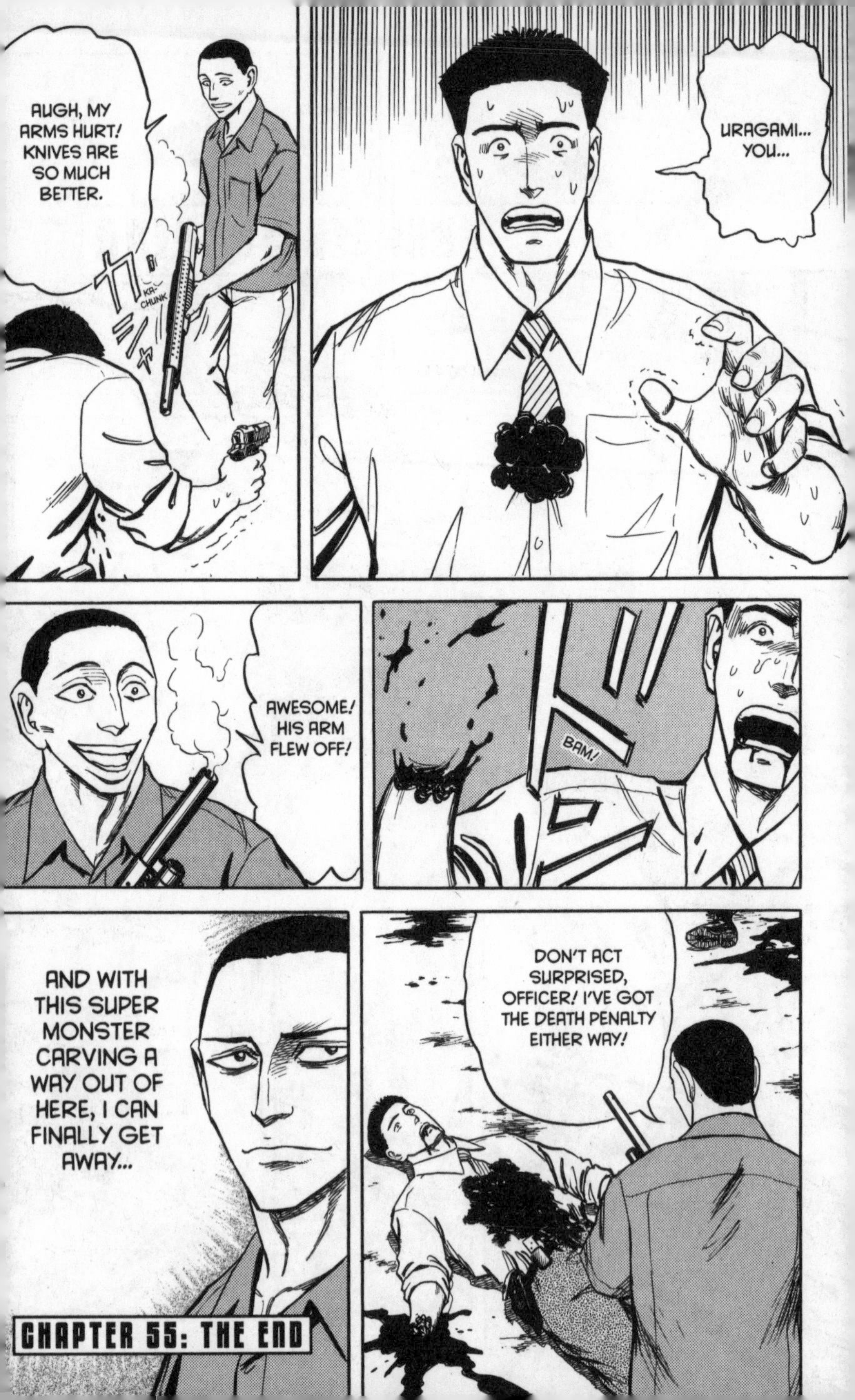
URAGAMI... YOU...
AUGH, MY ARMS HURT! KNIVES ARE SO MUCH BETTER.
KA-CHUNK
BAM!
AWESOME! HIS ARM FLEW OFF!
DON'T ACT SURPRISED, OFFICER! I'VE GOT THE DEATH PENALTY EITHER WAY!
AND WITH THIS SUPER MONSTER CARVING A WAY OUT OF HERE, I CAN FINALLY GET AWAY...
CHAPTER 55: THE END

CHAPTER 56: HEAD

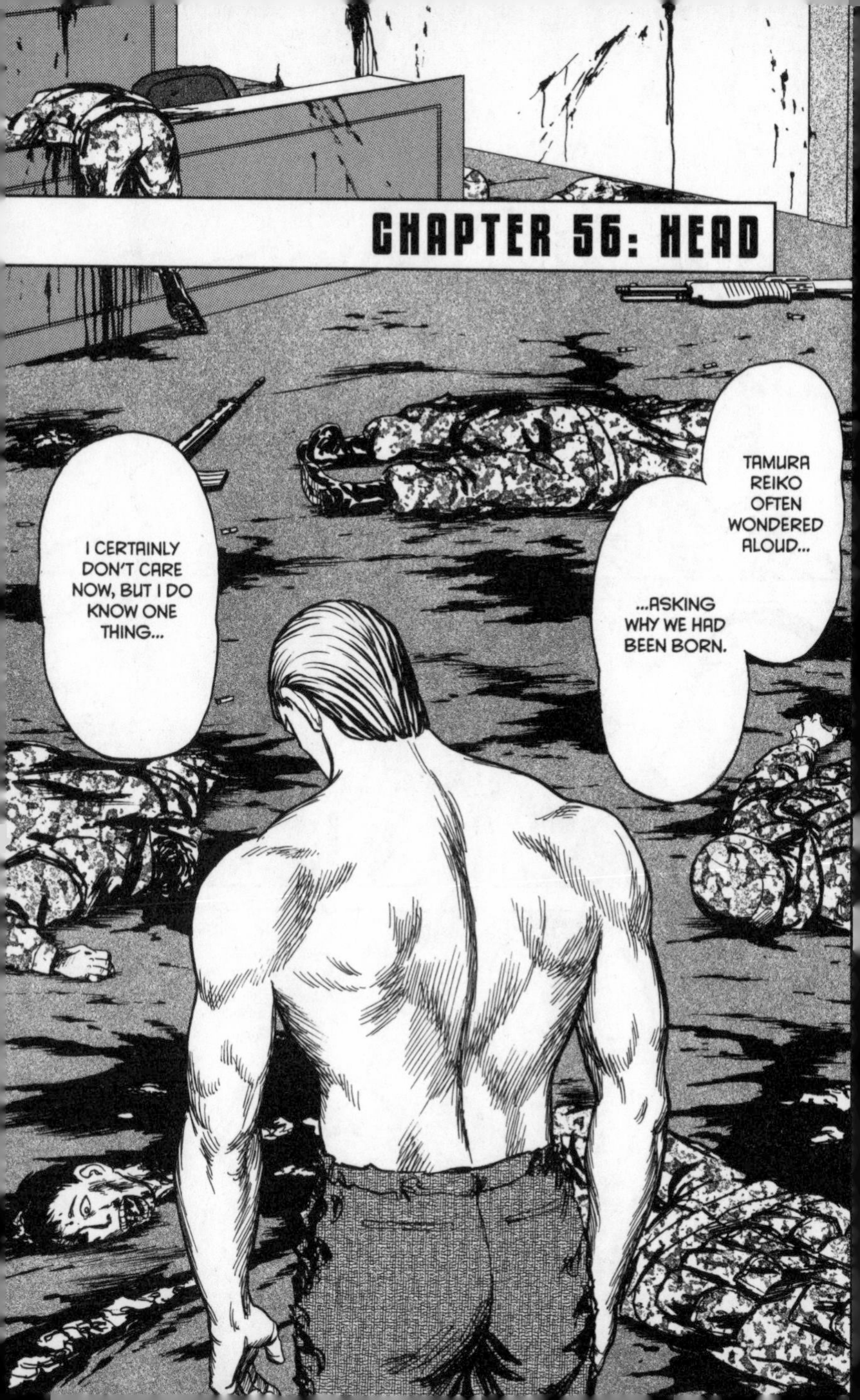
TAMURA REIKO OFTEN WONDERED ALOUD...
...ASKING WHY WE HAD BEEN BORN.
I CERTAINLY DON'T CARE NOW, BUT I DO KNOW ONE THING...

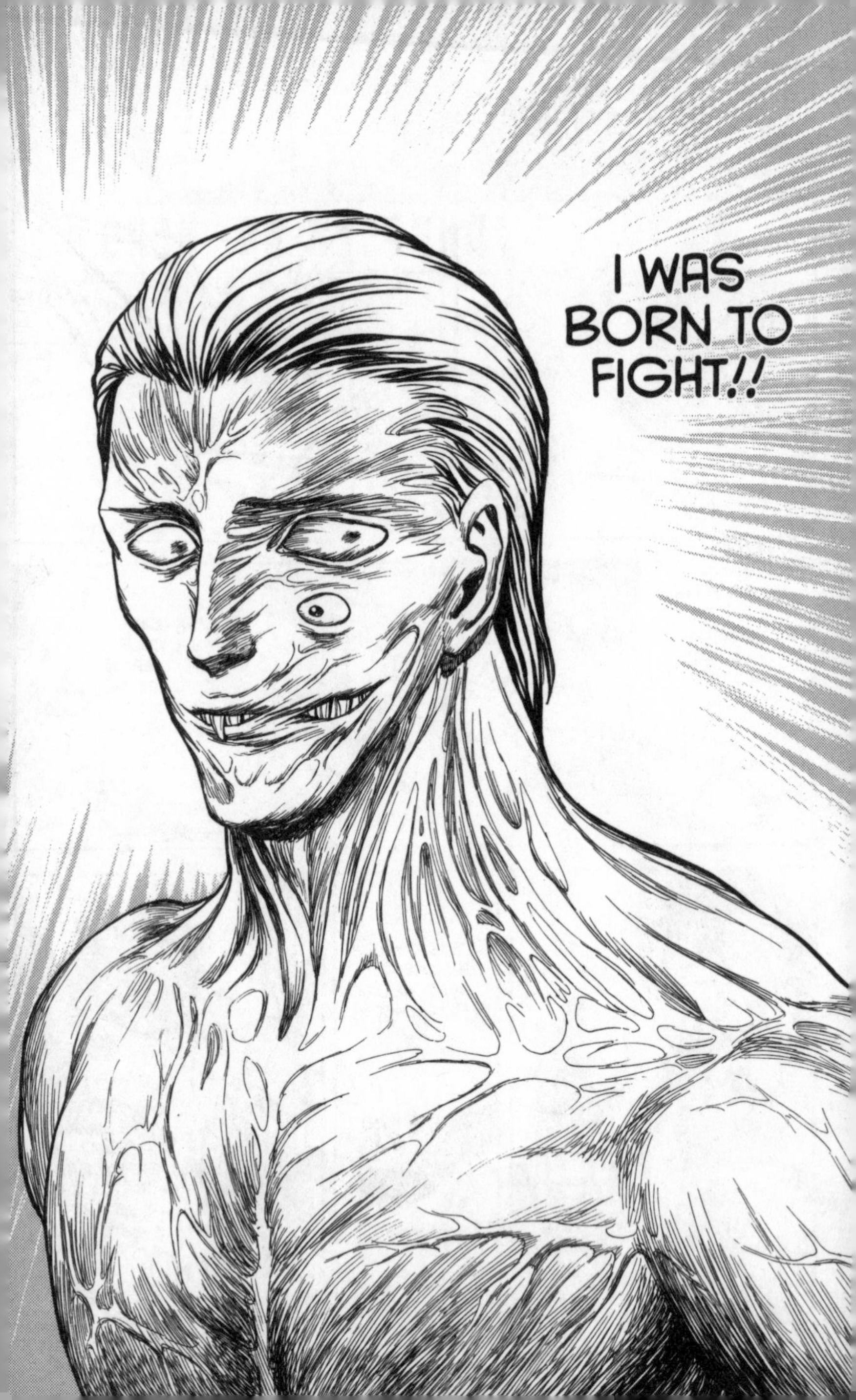
I WAS BORN TO FIGHT!!

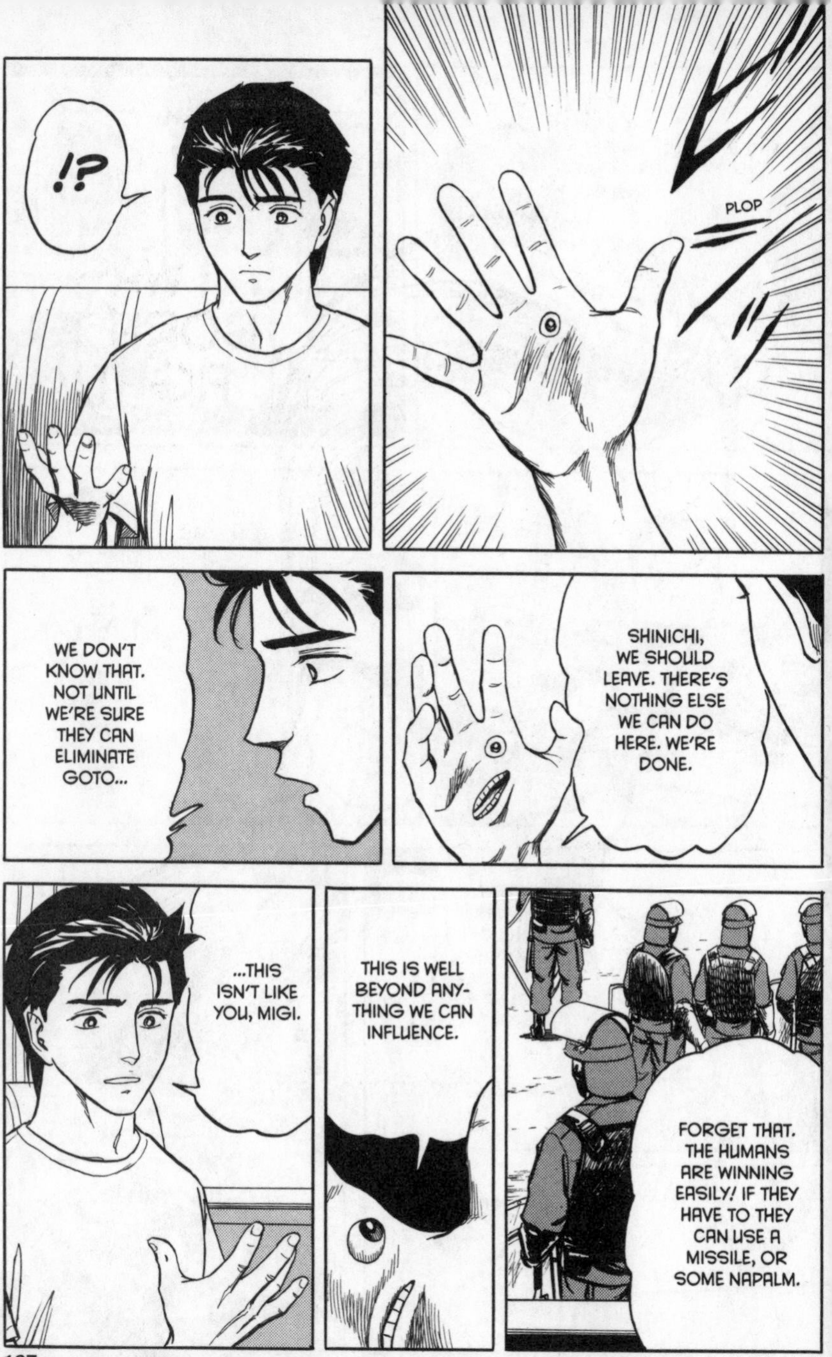
PLOP
!?
SHINICHI, WE SHOULD LEAVE. THERE'S NOTHING ELSE WE CAN DO HERE. WE'RE DONE.
WE DON'T KNOW THAT. NOT UNTIL WE'RE SURE THEY CAN ELIMINATE GOTO...
FORGET THAT. THE HUMANS ARE WINNING EASILY! IF THEY HAVE TO THEY CAN USE A MISSILE, OR SOME NAPALM.
THIS IS WELL BEYOND ANY-THING WE CAN INFLUENCE.
...THIS ISN'T LIKE YOU, MIGI.

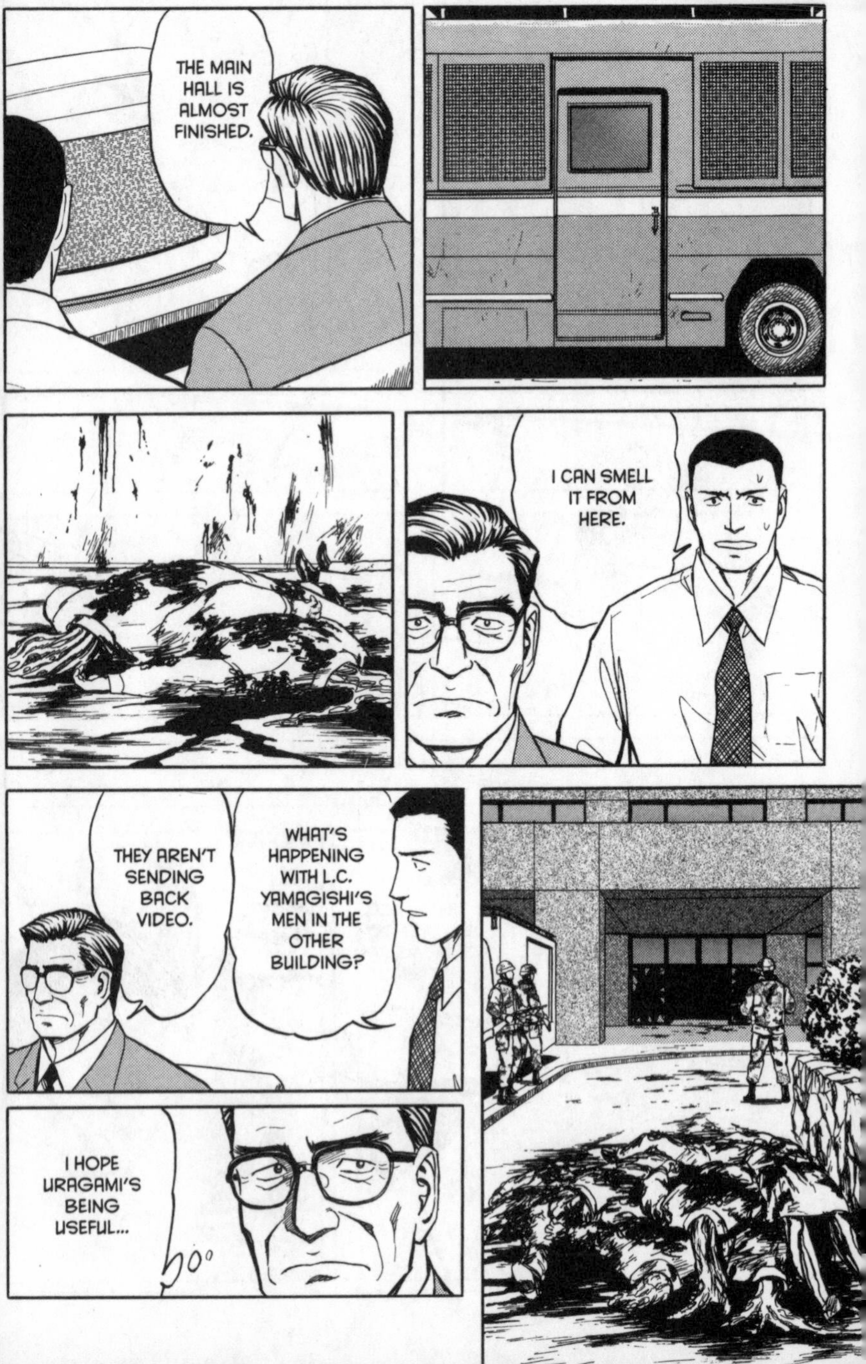
THE MAIN HALL IS ALMOST FINISHED.
I CAN SMELL IT FROM HERE.
WHAT'S HAPPENING WITH L.C. YAMAGISHI'S MEN IN THE OTHER BUILDING?
THEY AREN'T SENDING BACK VIDEO.
I HOPE URAGAMI'S BEING USEFUL...

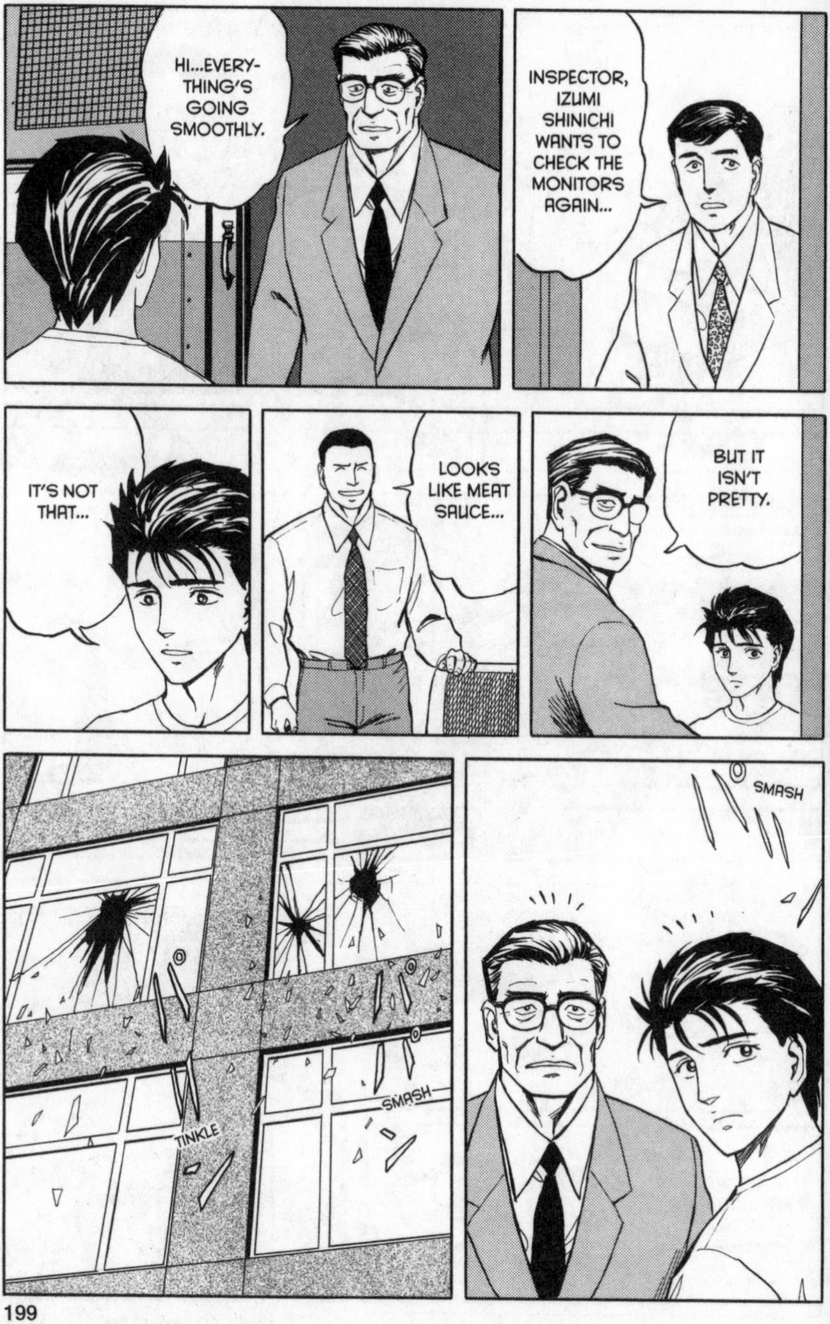
INSPECTOR, IZUMI SHINICHI WANTS TO CHECK THE MONITORS AGAIN...
HI...EVERY-THING'S GOING SMOOTHLY.
BUT IT ISN'T PRETTY.
LOOKS LIKE MEAT SAUCE...
IT'S NOT THAT...
SMASH
SMASH
TINKLE

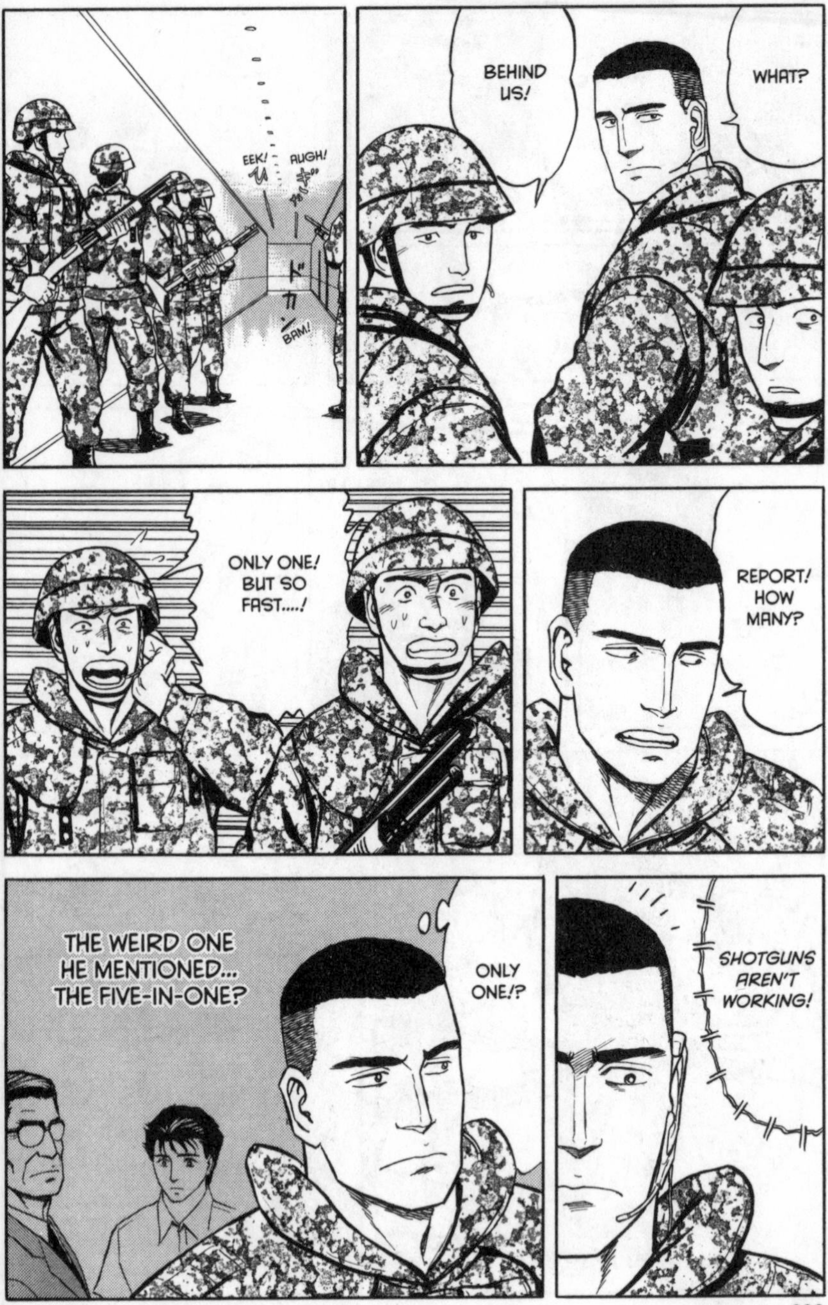
WHAT?
BEHIND US!
AUGH!
EEK!
BAM!
REPORT! HOW MANY?
ONLY ONE! BUT SO FAST.....!
SHOTGUNS AREN'T WORKING!
ONLY ONE!?
THE WEIRD ONE HE MENTIONED... THE FIVE-IN-ONE?

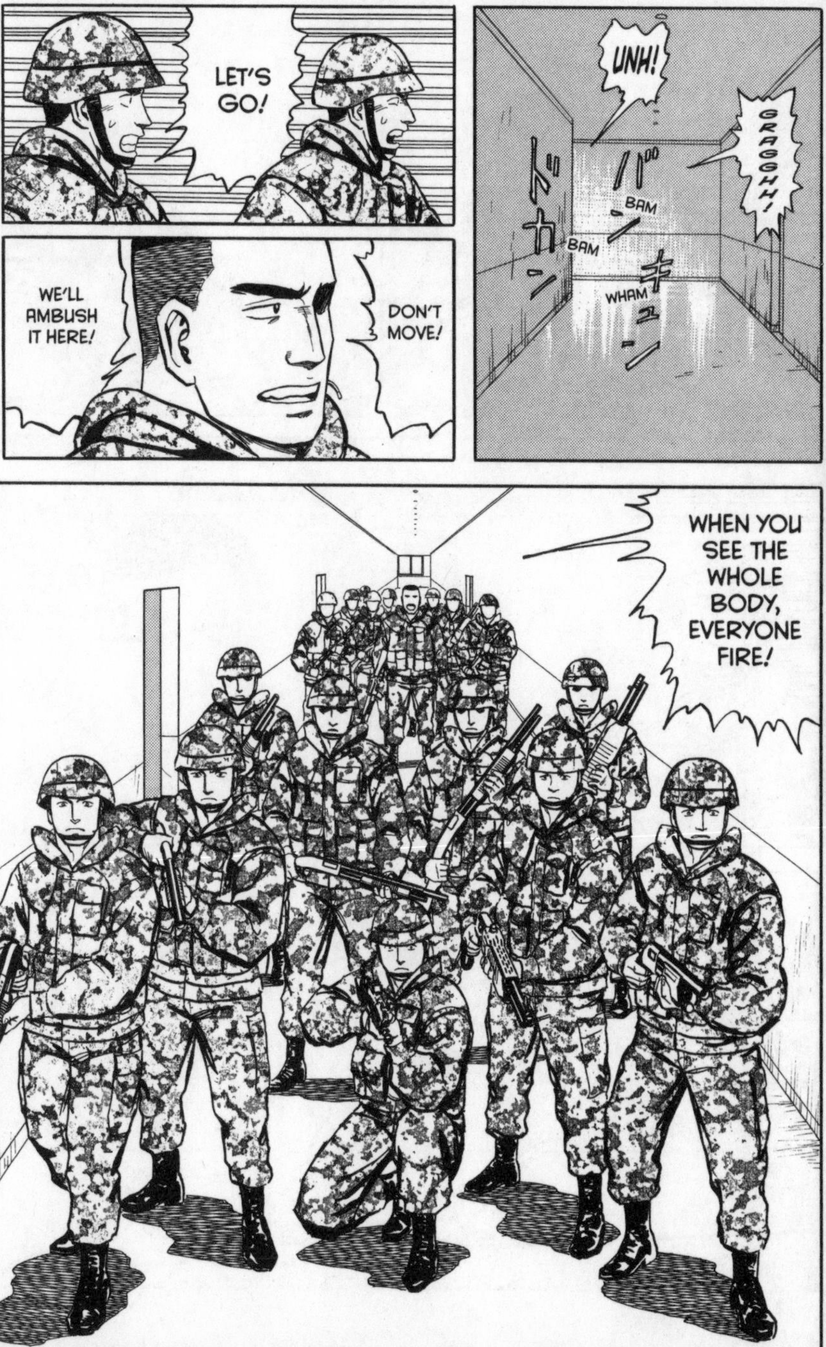
UNH!
GRAGGHH!
BAM
BAM
WHAM
LET'S GO!
DON'T MOVE!
WE'LL AMBUSH IT HERE!
WHEN YOU SEE THE WHOLE BODY, EVERYONE FIRE!

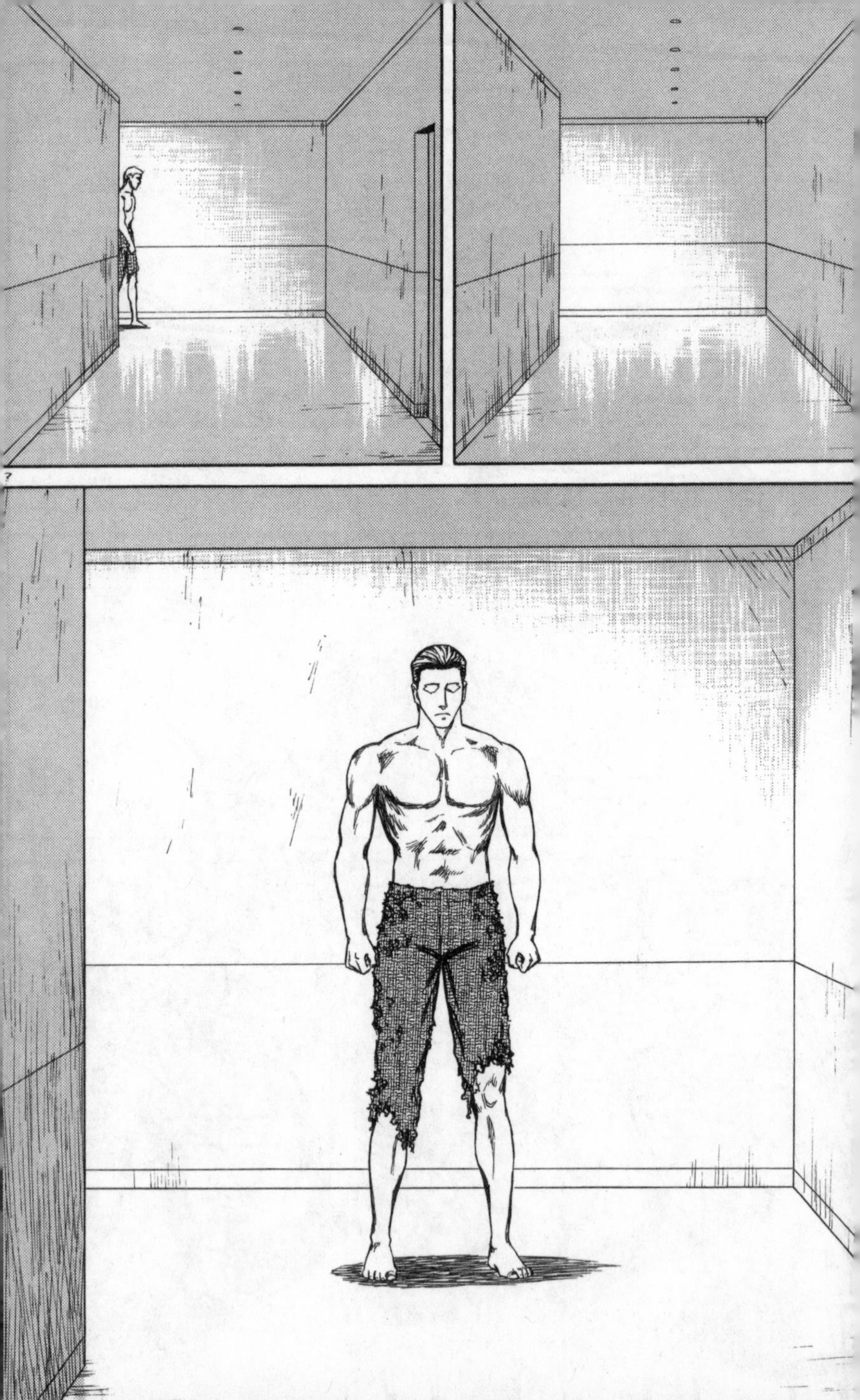

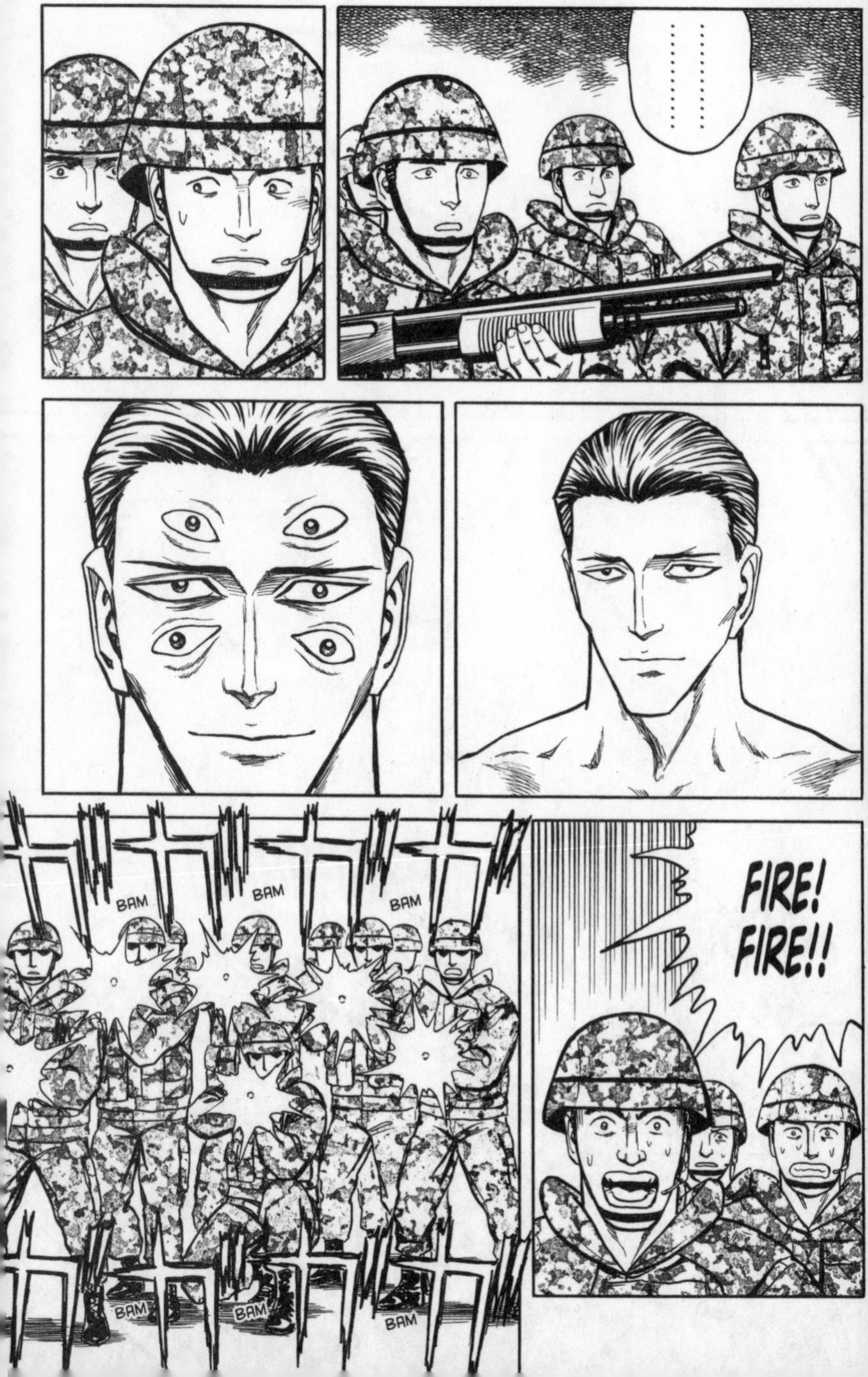
……
FIRE!
FIRE!!
BAM
BAM
BAM
BAM
BAM
BAM

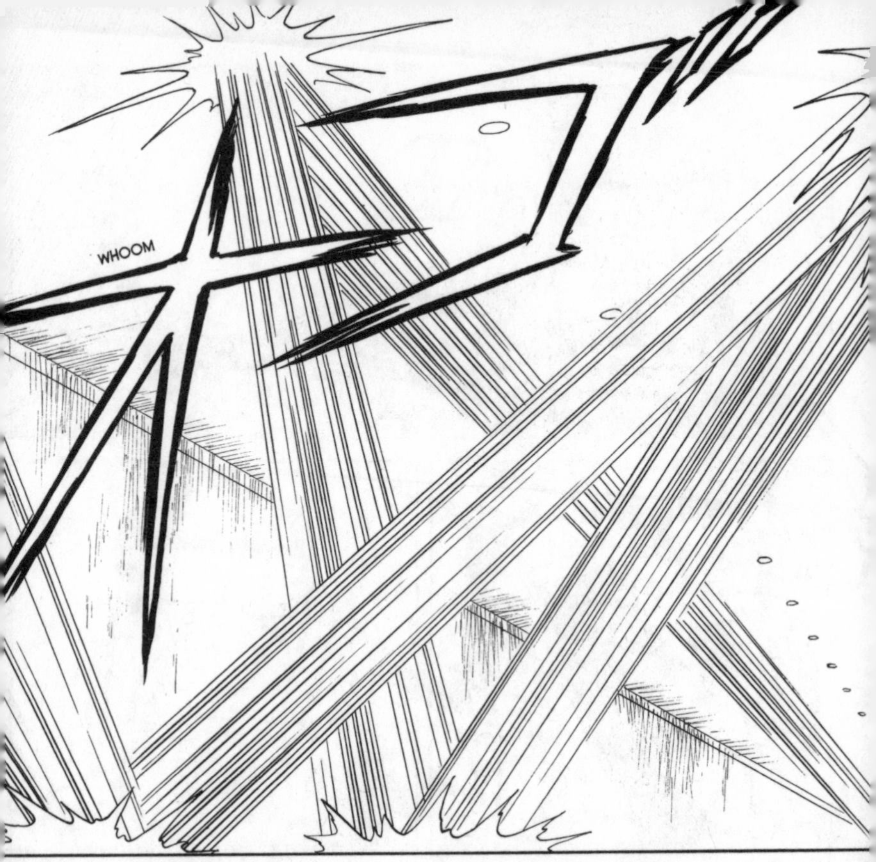
WHOOM
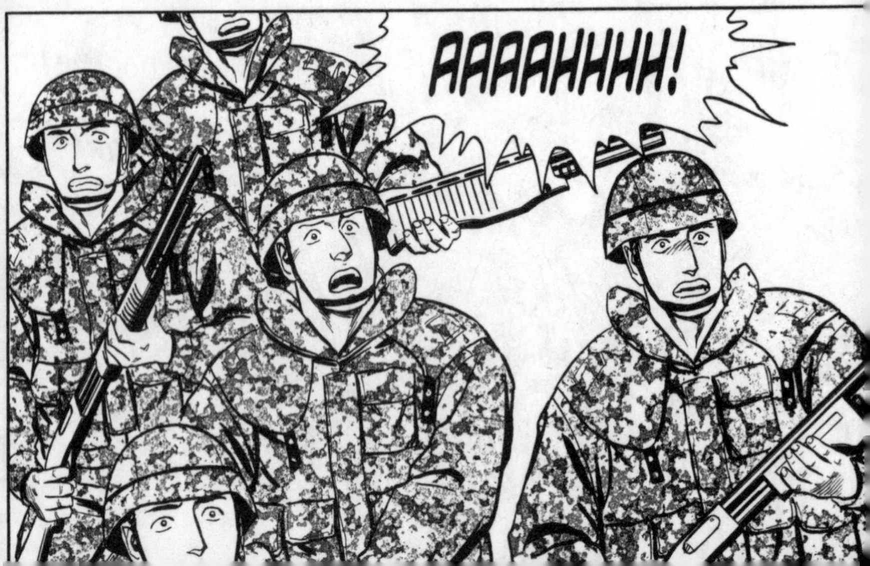
AAAAHHHH!

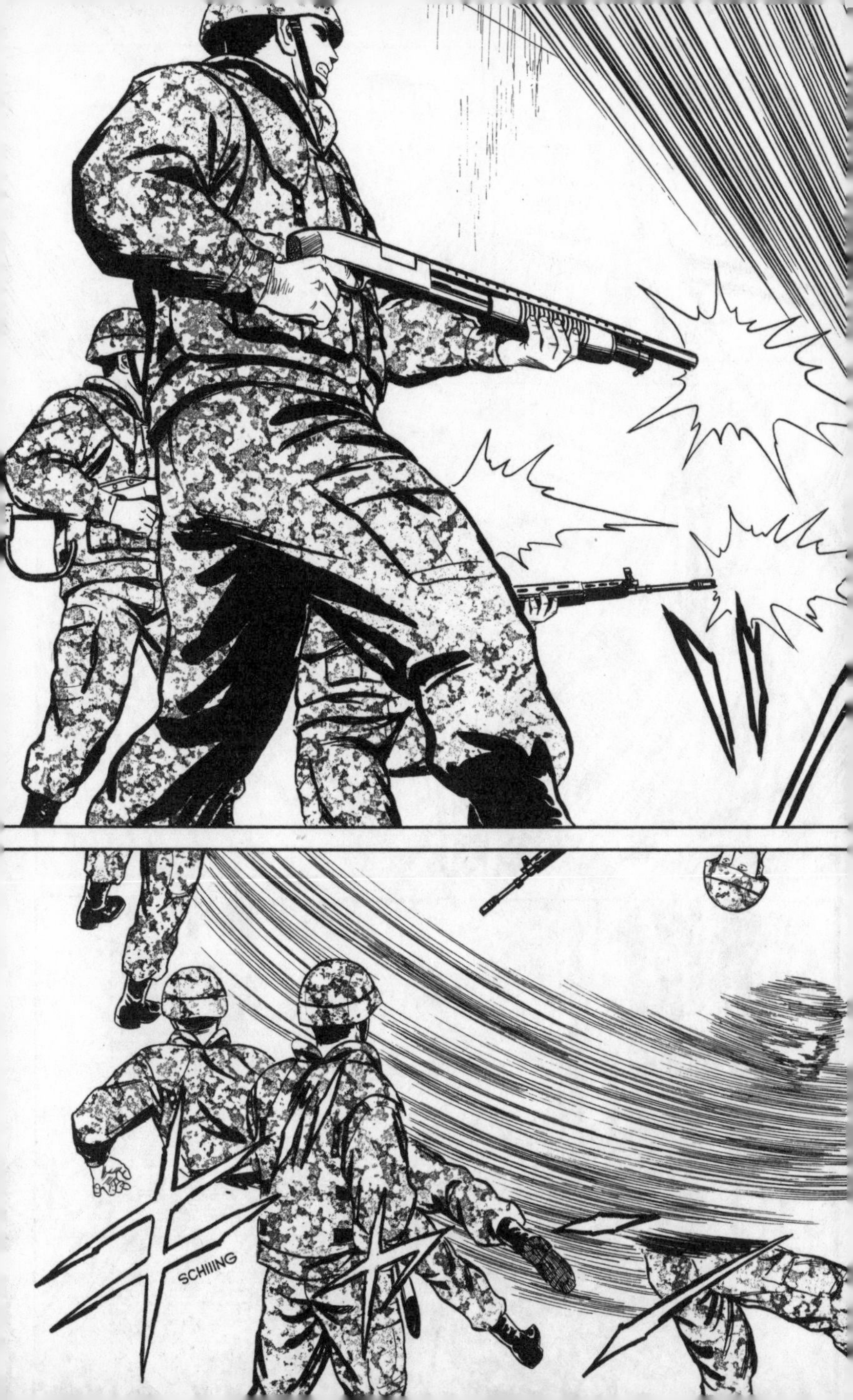
SCHIIING

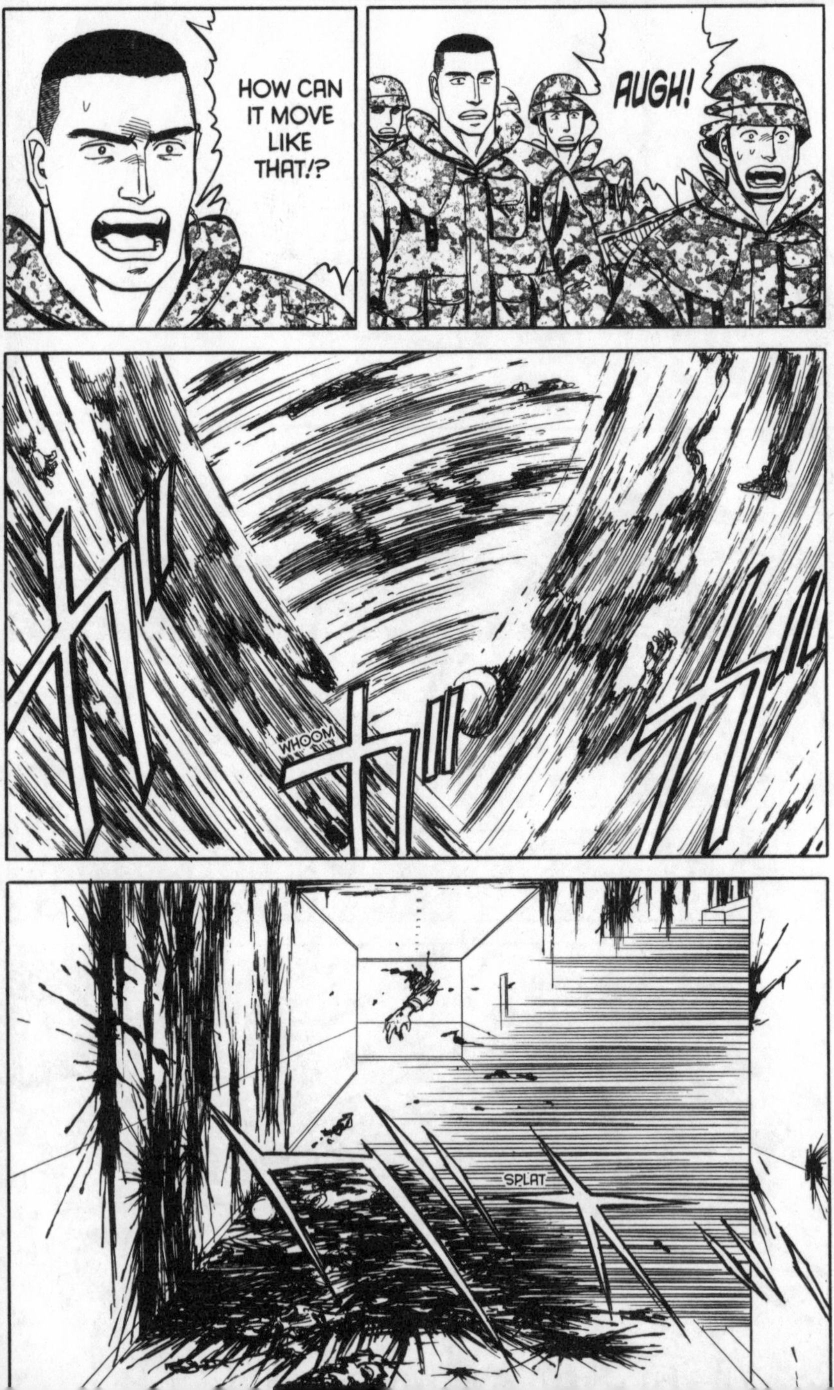
AUGH!
HOW CAN IT MOVE LIKE THAT!?
WHOOM
SPLAT

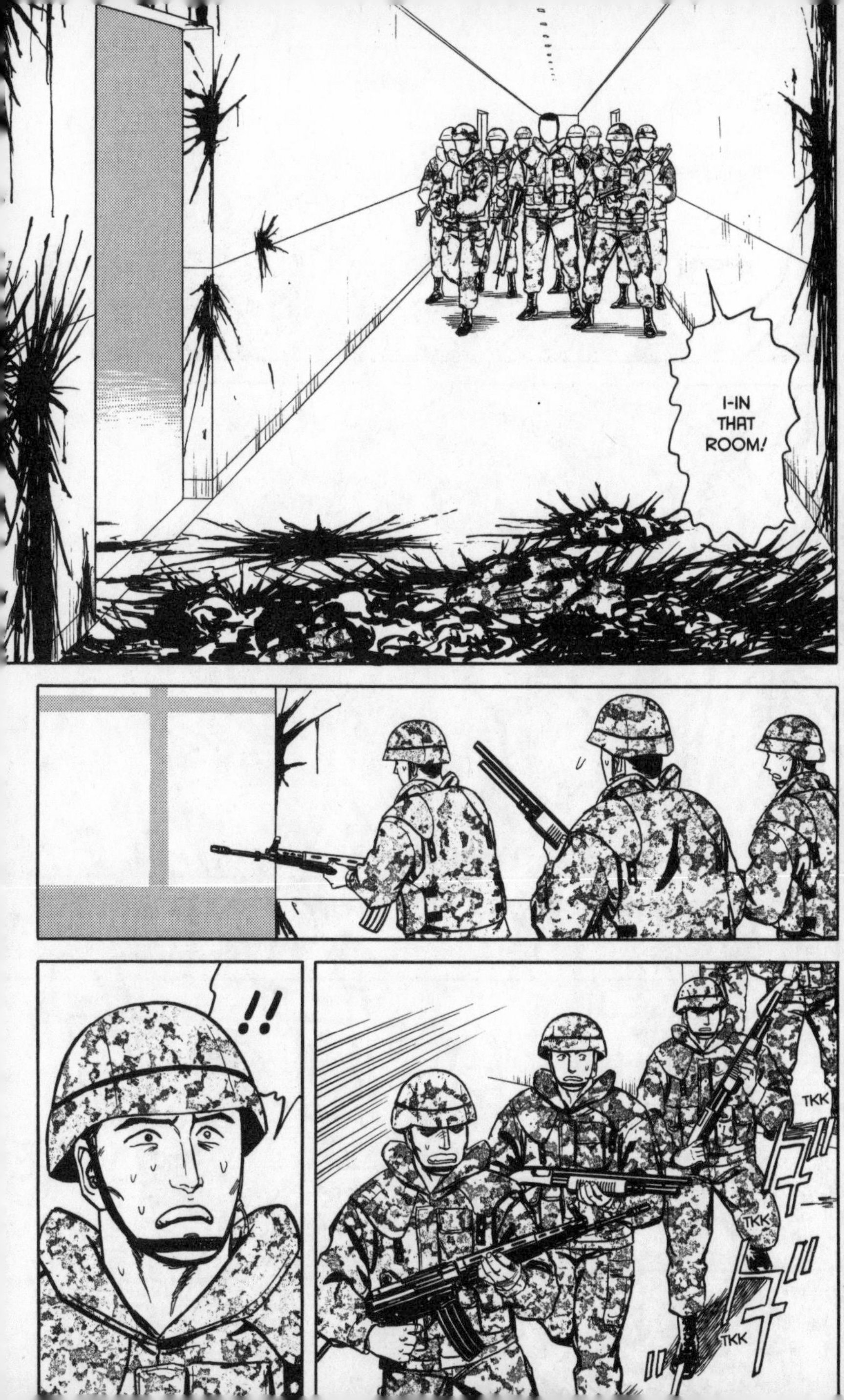
I-IN THAT ROOM!
TKK
TKK
TKK
!!

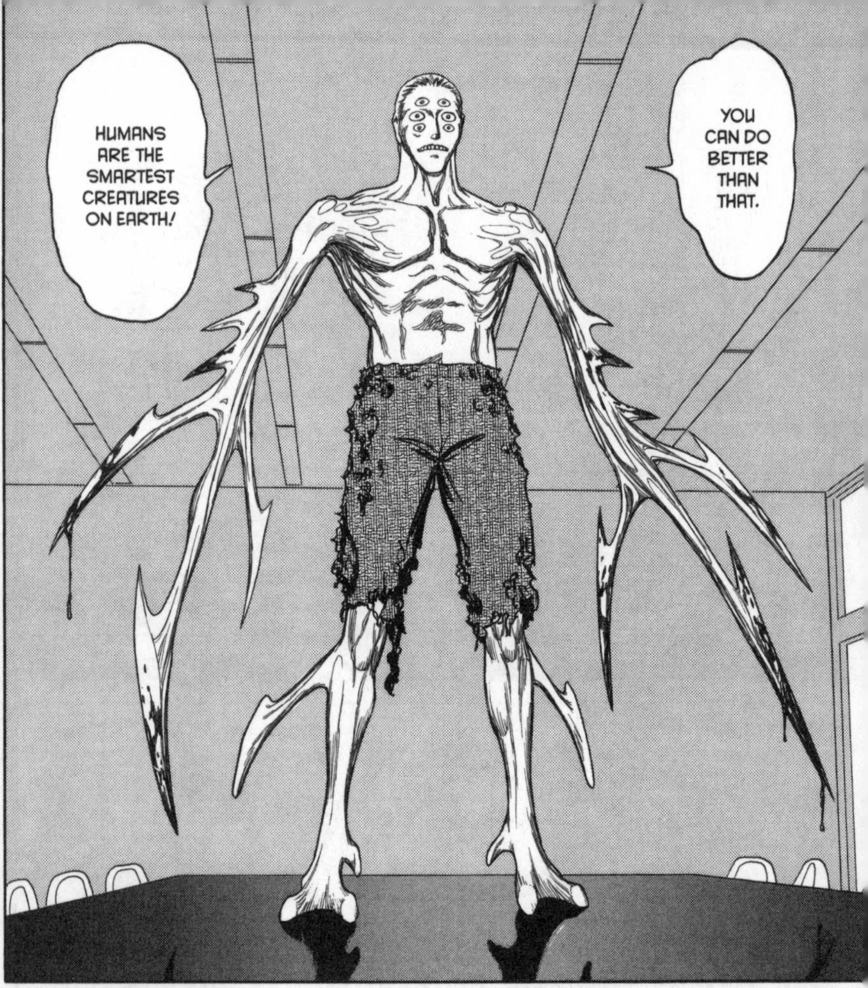
YOU CAN DO BETTER THAN THAT.
HUMANS ARE THE SMARTEST CREATURES ON EARTH!

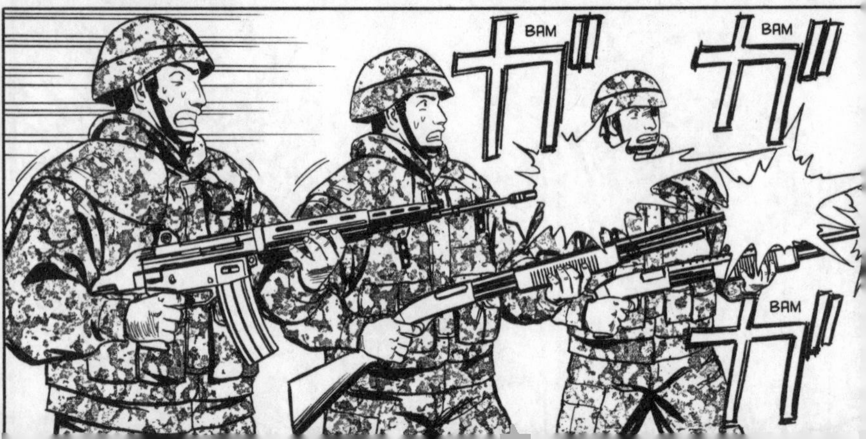
BAM
ガ
BAM
ガ
BAM
ガ

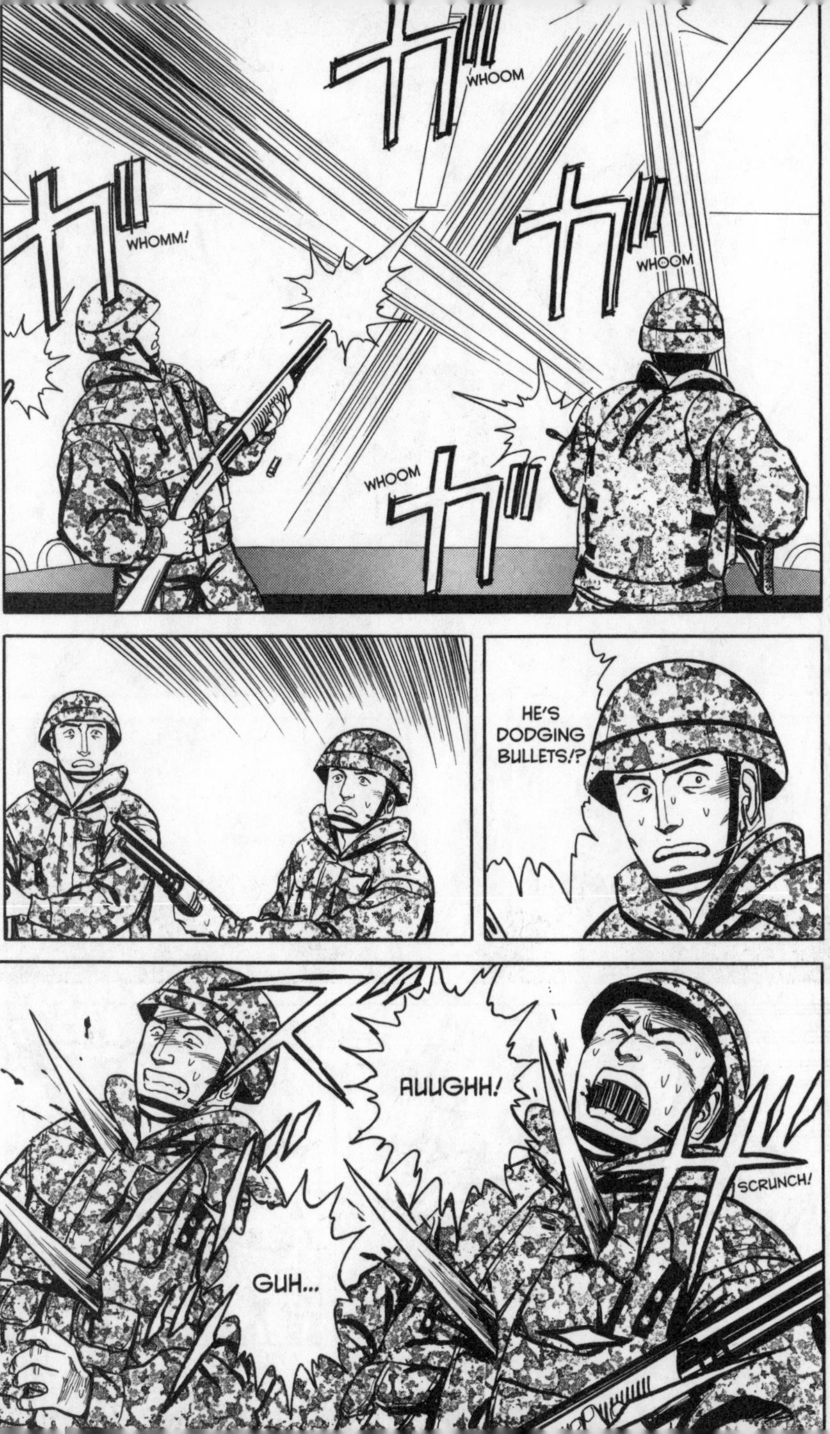
WHOOM
WHOOM
WHOMM!
WHOOM
HE'S DODGING BULLETS!?
AUUGHH!
SCRUNCH!
GUH...

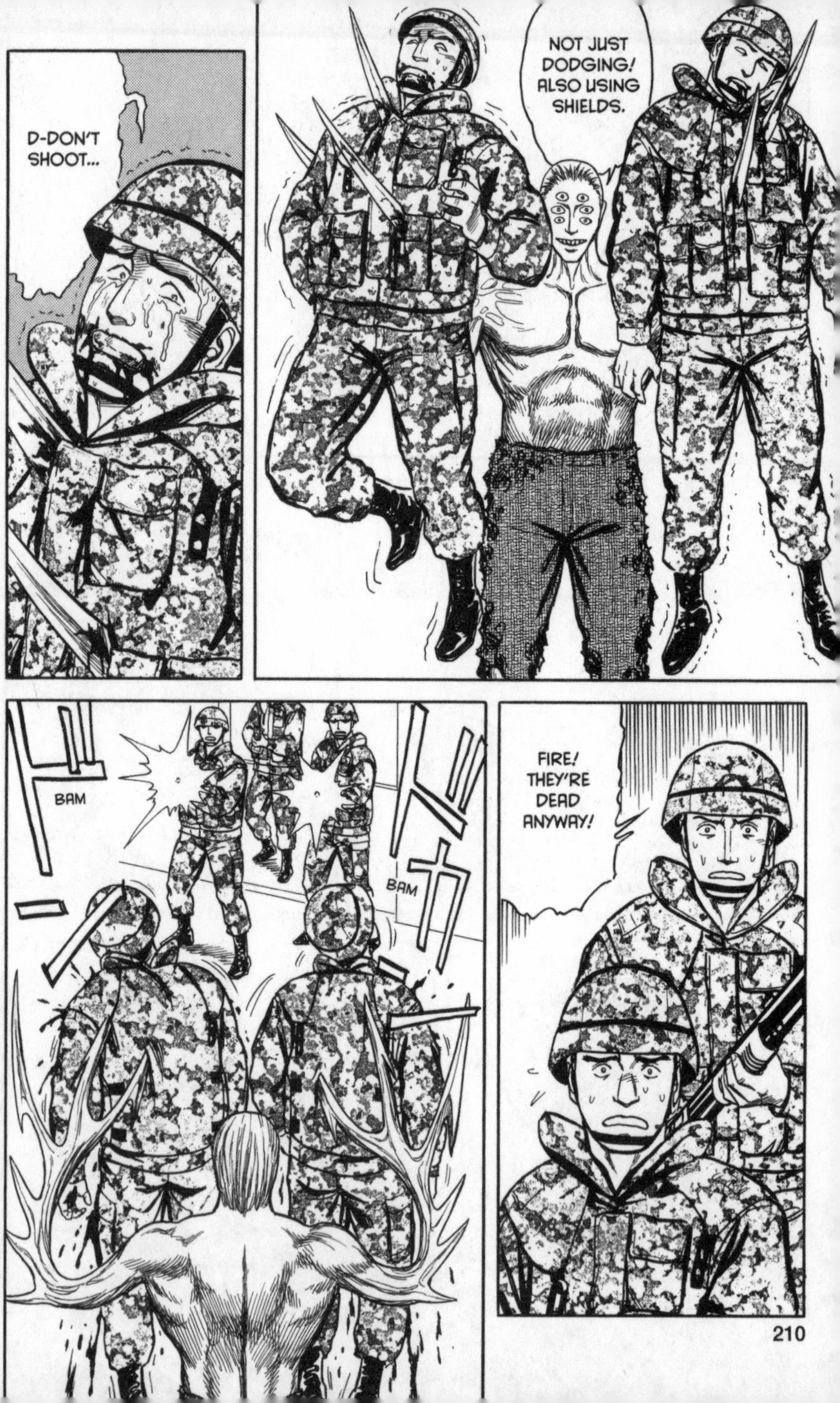
NOT JUST DODGING! ALSO USING SHIELDS.
D-DON'T SHOOT...
FIRE! THEY'RE DEAD ANYWAY!
BAM
BAM

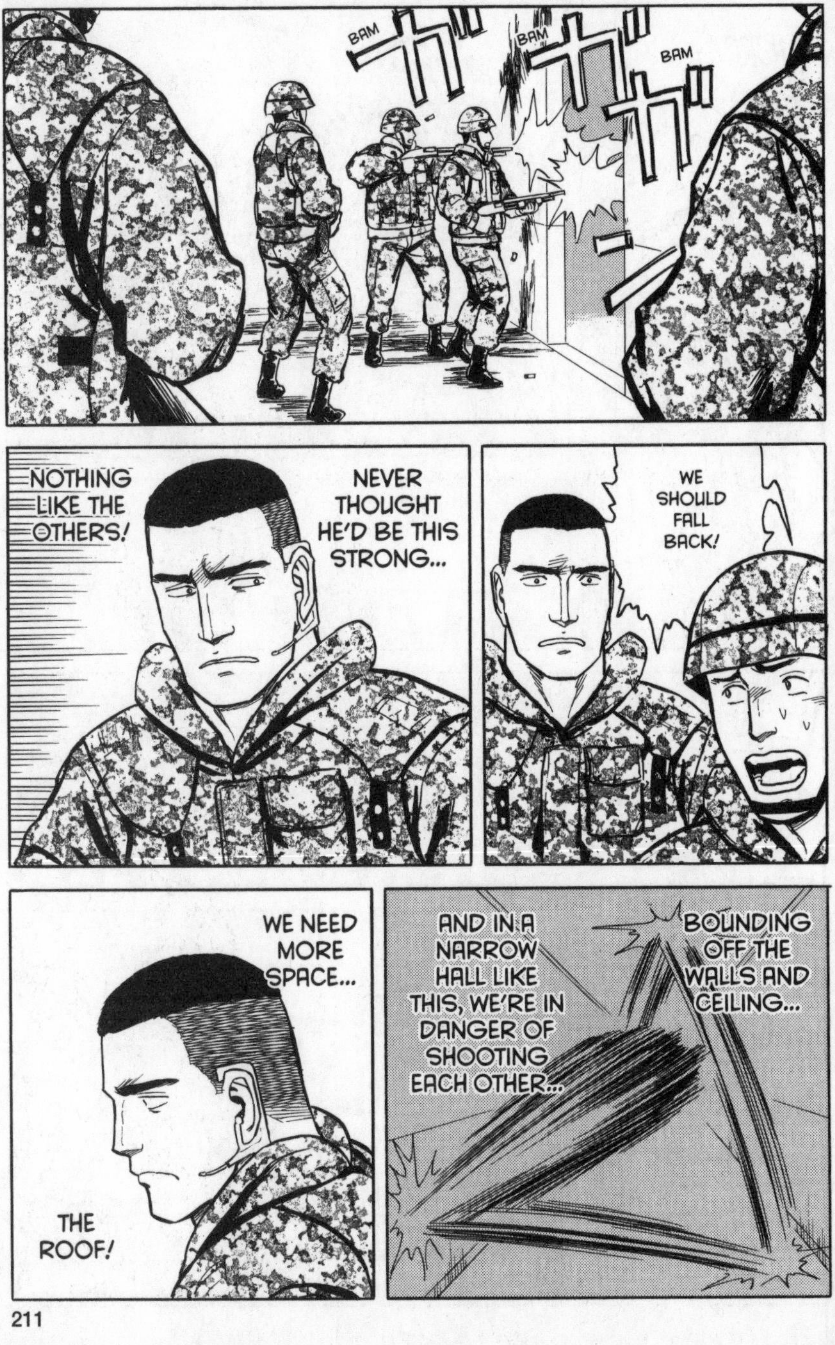
BAM
BAM
BAM
WE SHOULD FALL BACK!
NEVER THOUGHT HE'D BE THIS STRONG...
NOTHING LIKE THE OTHERS!
BOUNDING OFF THE WALLS AND CEILING...
AND IN A NARROW HALL LIKE THIS, WE'RE IN DANGER OF SHOOTING EACH OTHER...
WE NEED MORE SPACE...
THE ROOF!

HURRY!
FALL BACK!

TO THE
ROOF!!

CHACK
チャッ

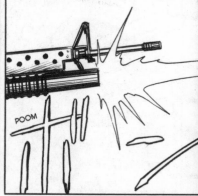

POOM

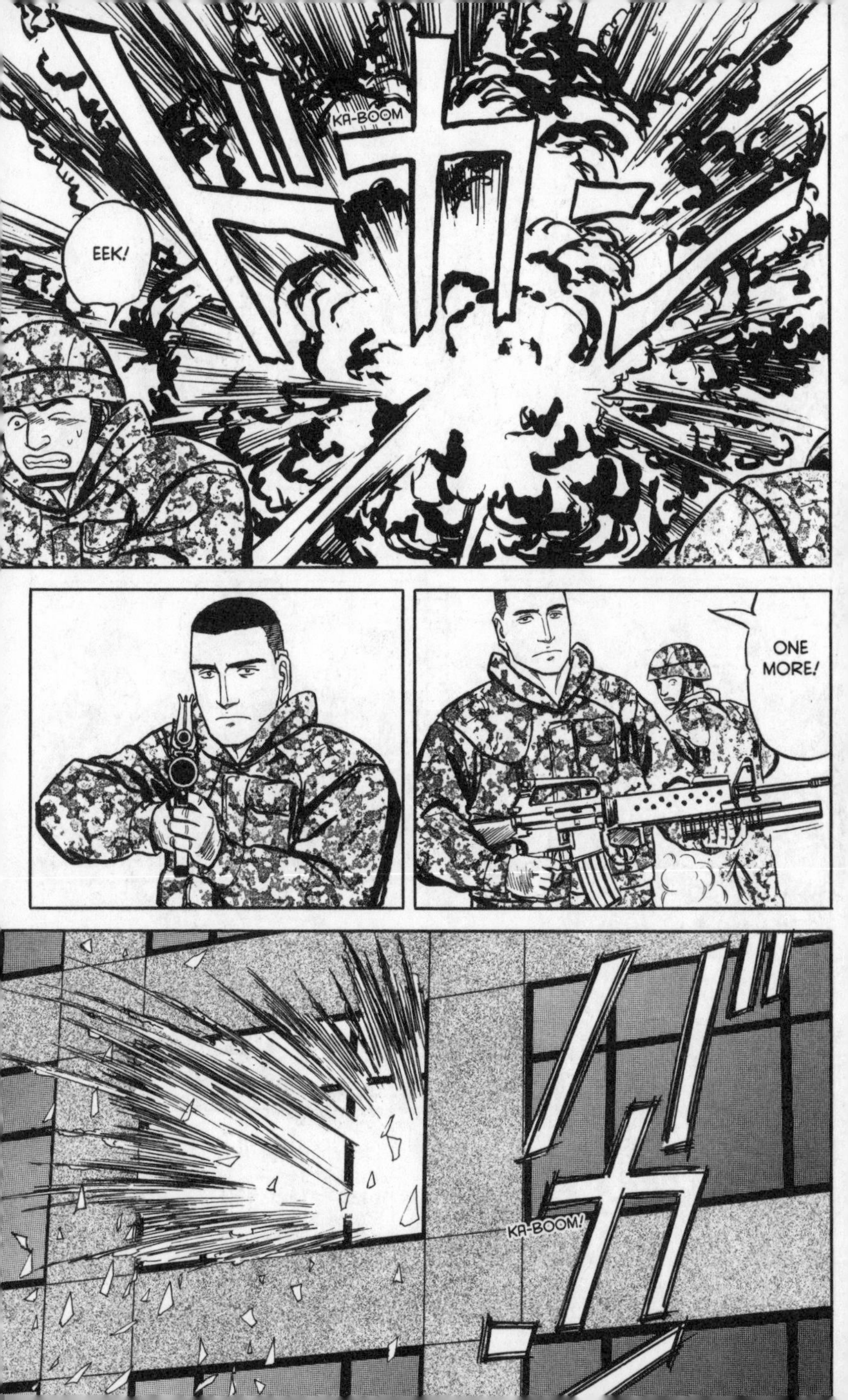
KA-BOOM
EEK!
ONE MORE!
KA-BOOM!

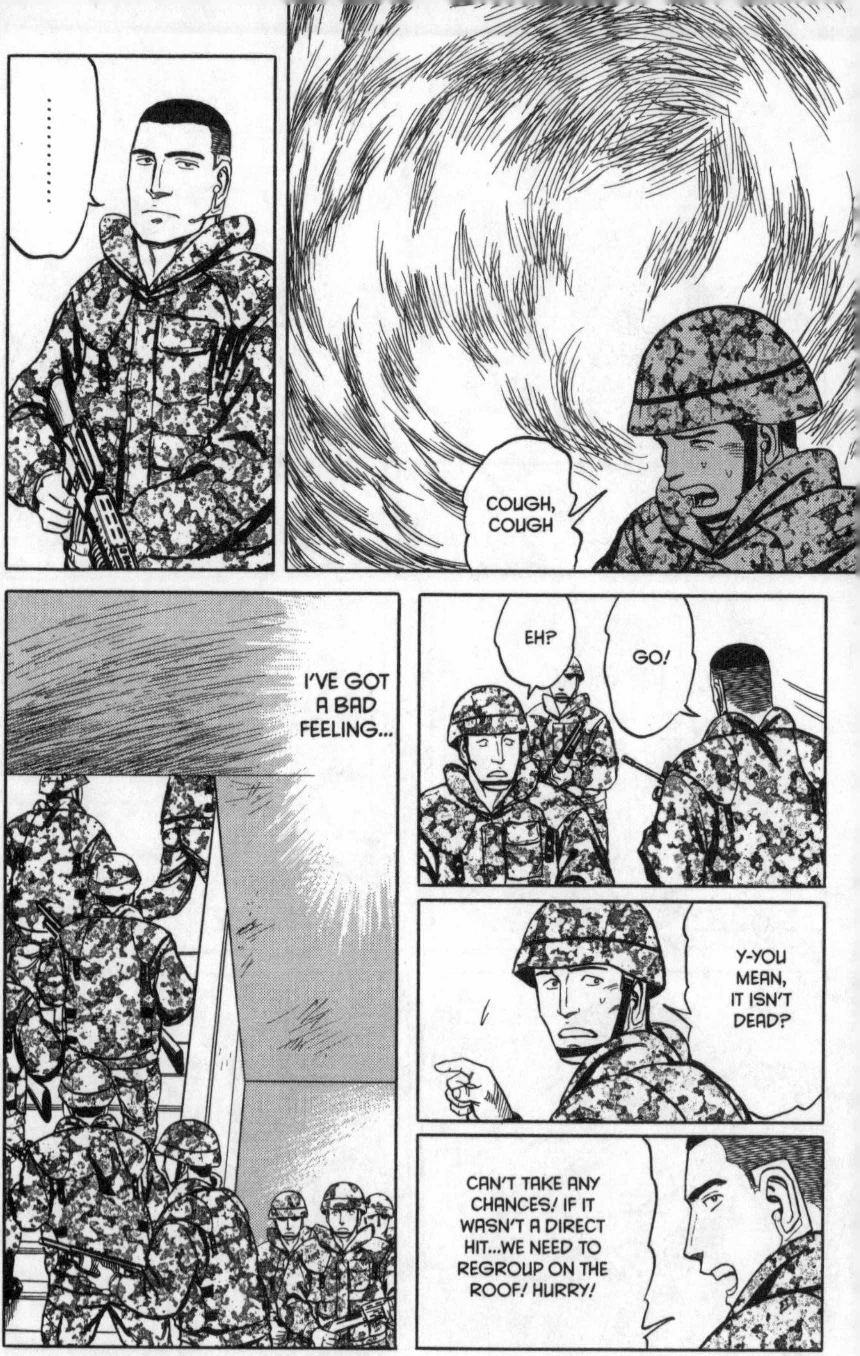

COUGH, COUGH
......
GO!
EH?
Y-YOU MEAN, IT ISN'T DEAD?
CAN'T TAKE ANY CHANCES! IF IT WASN'T A DIRECT HIT...WE NEED TO REGROUP ON THE ROOF! HURRY!
I'VE GOT A BAD FEELING...

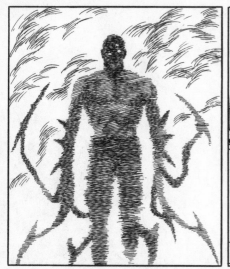

THIS ENEMY IN THIS PLACE...
BAD COMBINATION.

AUGH!
IT'S ALIVE!

HURRY!

THOUGHT
SO...

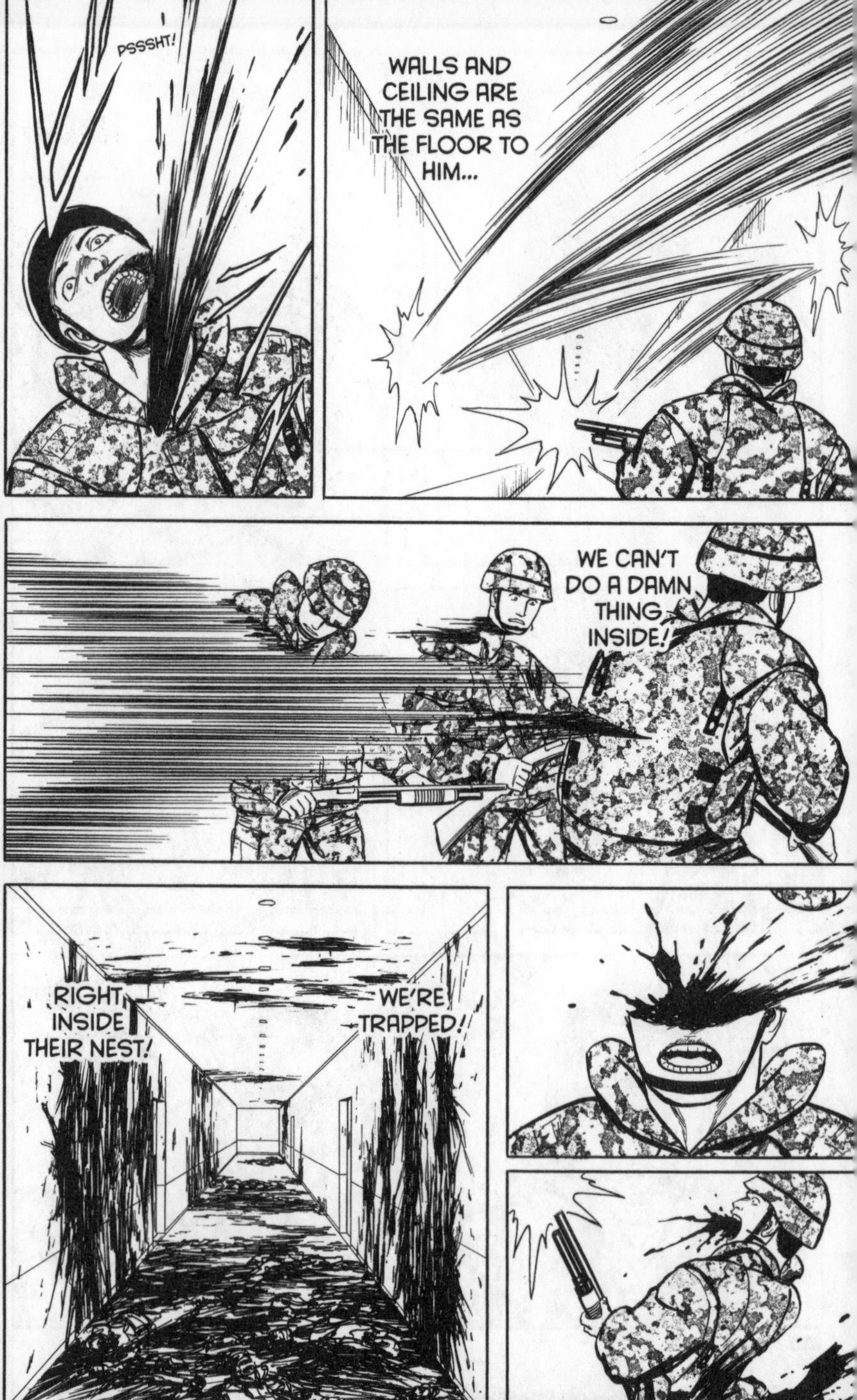
WALLS AND CEILING ARE THE SAME AS THE FLOOR TO HIM...
PSSSHT!
WE CAN'T DO A DAMN THING INSIDE!
WE'RE TRAPPED!
RIGHT INSIDE THEIR NEST!

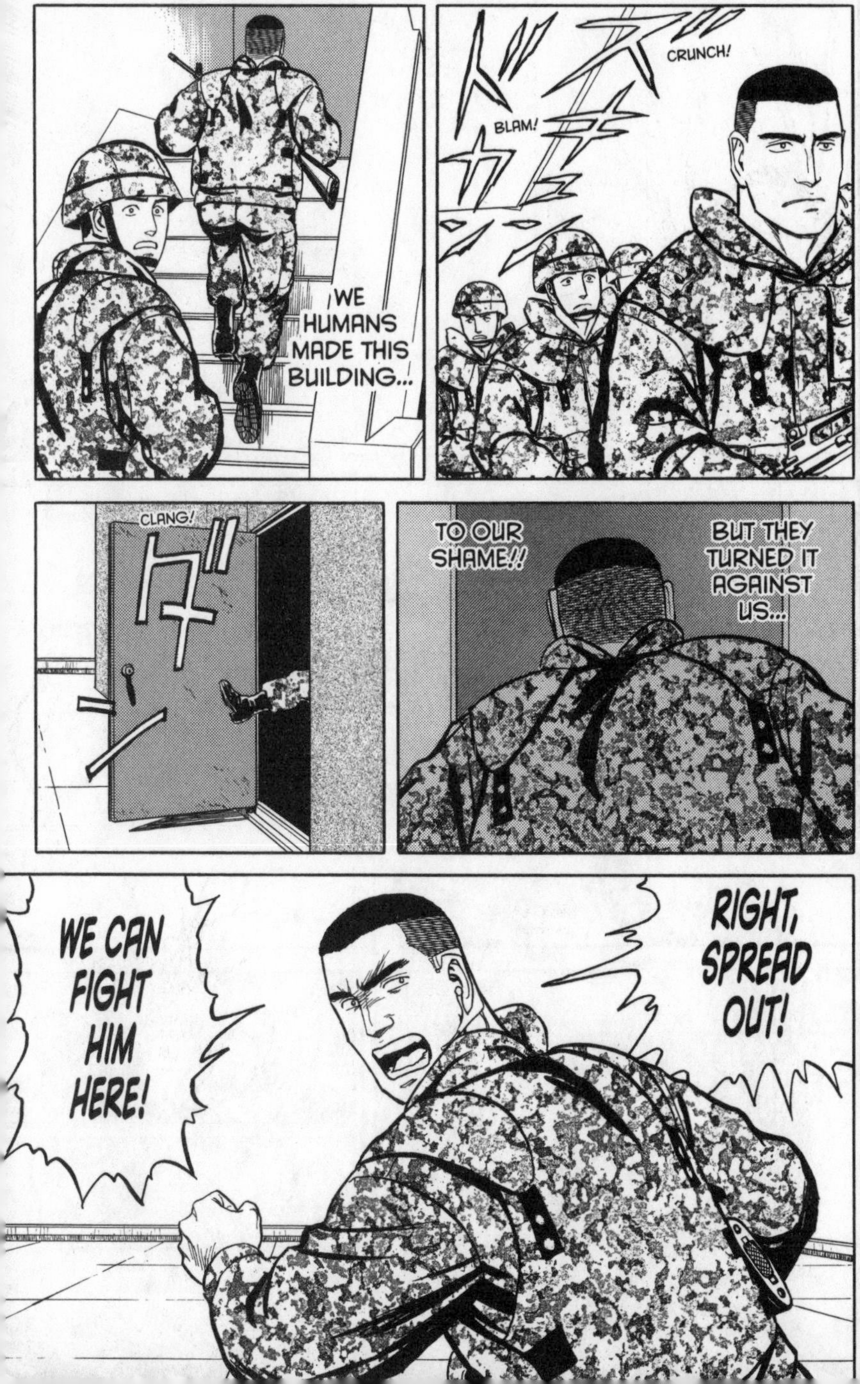
CRUNCH!
BLAM!
WE HUMANS MADE THIS BUILDING...
BUT THEY TURNED IT AGAINST US...
TO OUR SHAME!!
CLANG!
RIGHT, SPREAD OUT!
WE CAN FIGHT HIM HERE!

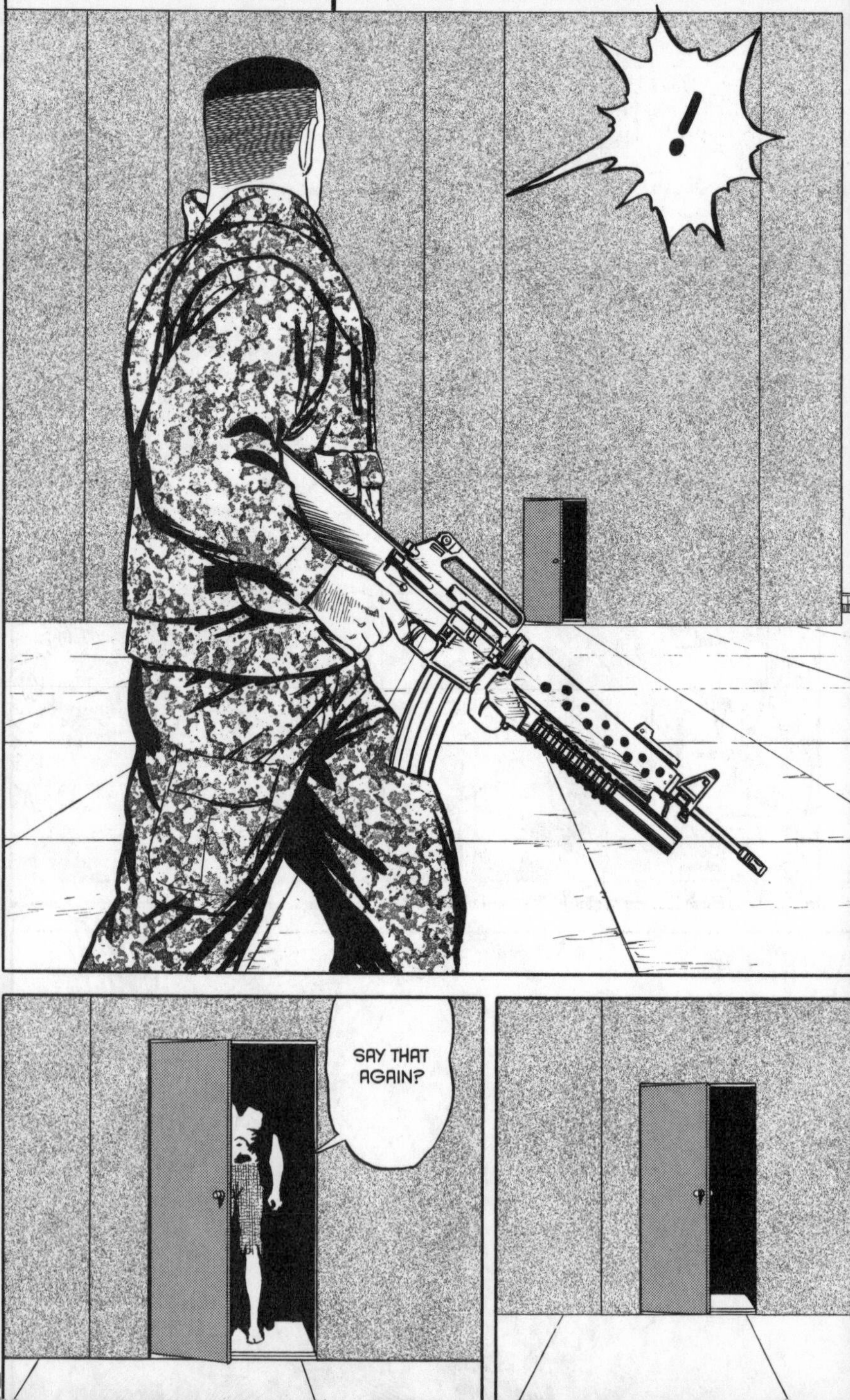
!
SAY THAT AGAIN?

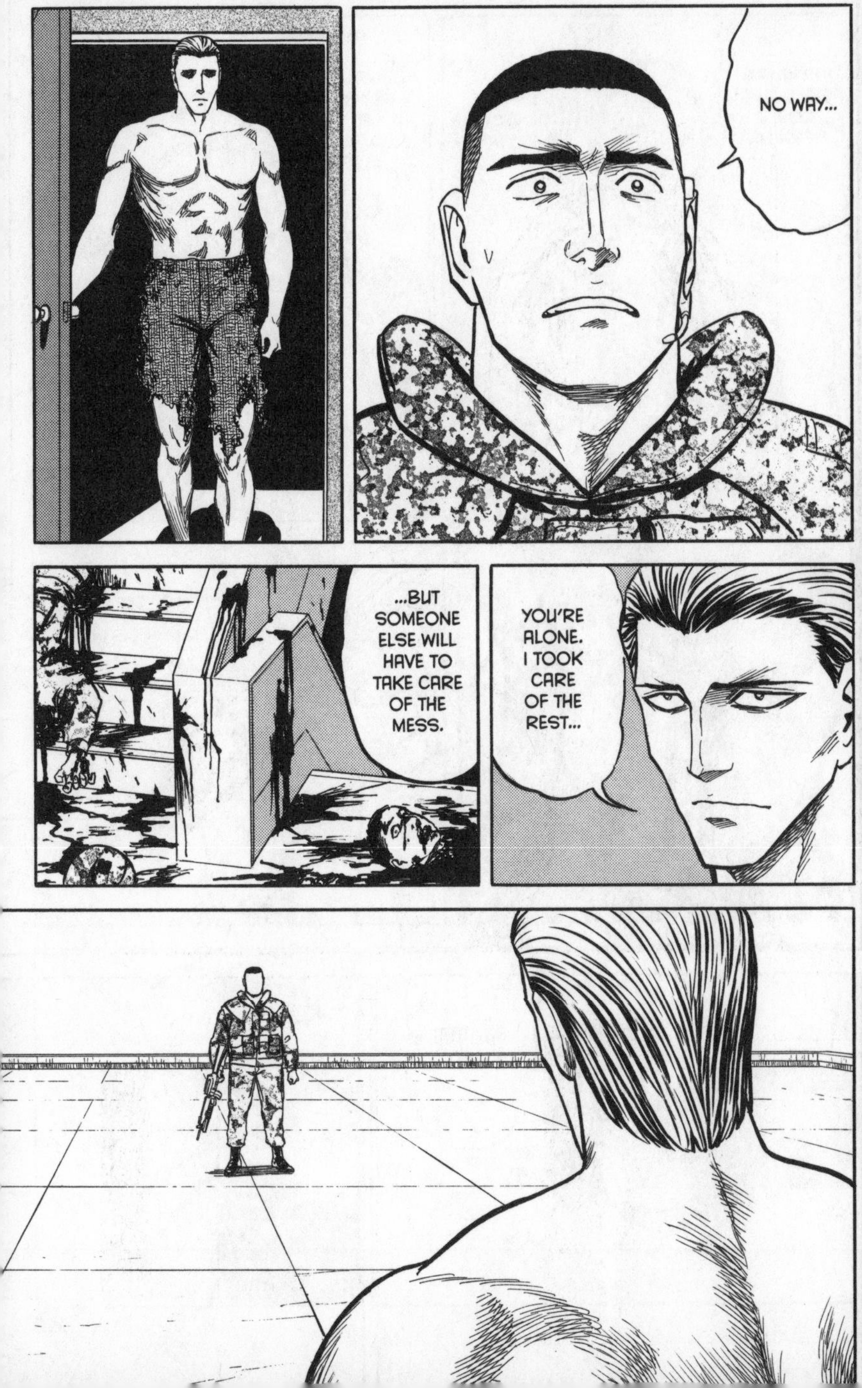
NO WAY...
YOU'RE ALONE. I TOOK CARE OF THE REST...
...BUT SOMEONE ELSE WILL HAVE TO TAKE CARE OF THE MESS.

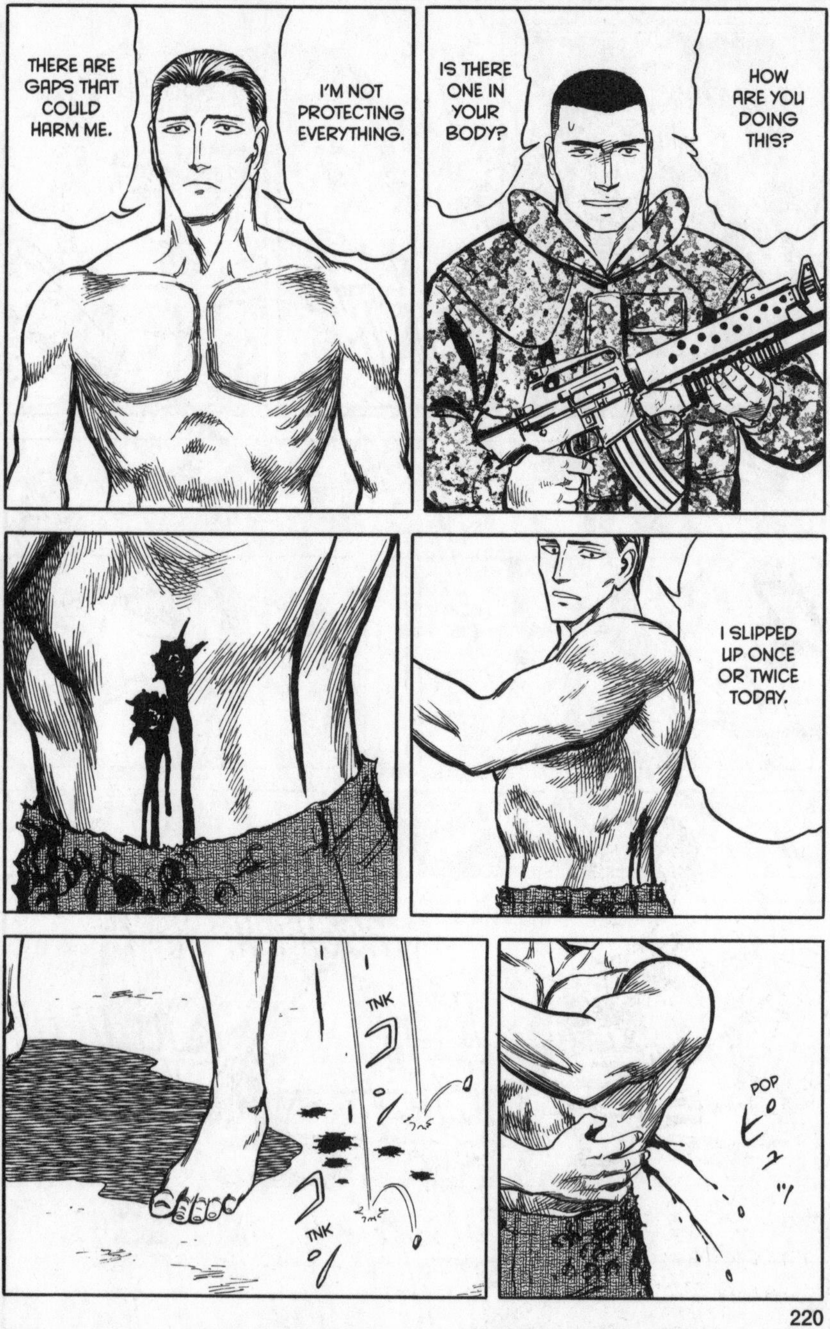
HOW ARE YOU DOING THIS?
IS THERE ONE IN YOUR BODY?
I'M NOT PROTECTING EVERYTHING.
THERE ARE GAPS THAT COULD HARM ME.
I SLIPPED UP ONCE OR TWICE TODAY.
POP
TNK
TNK

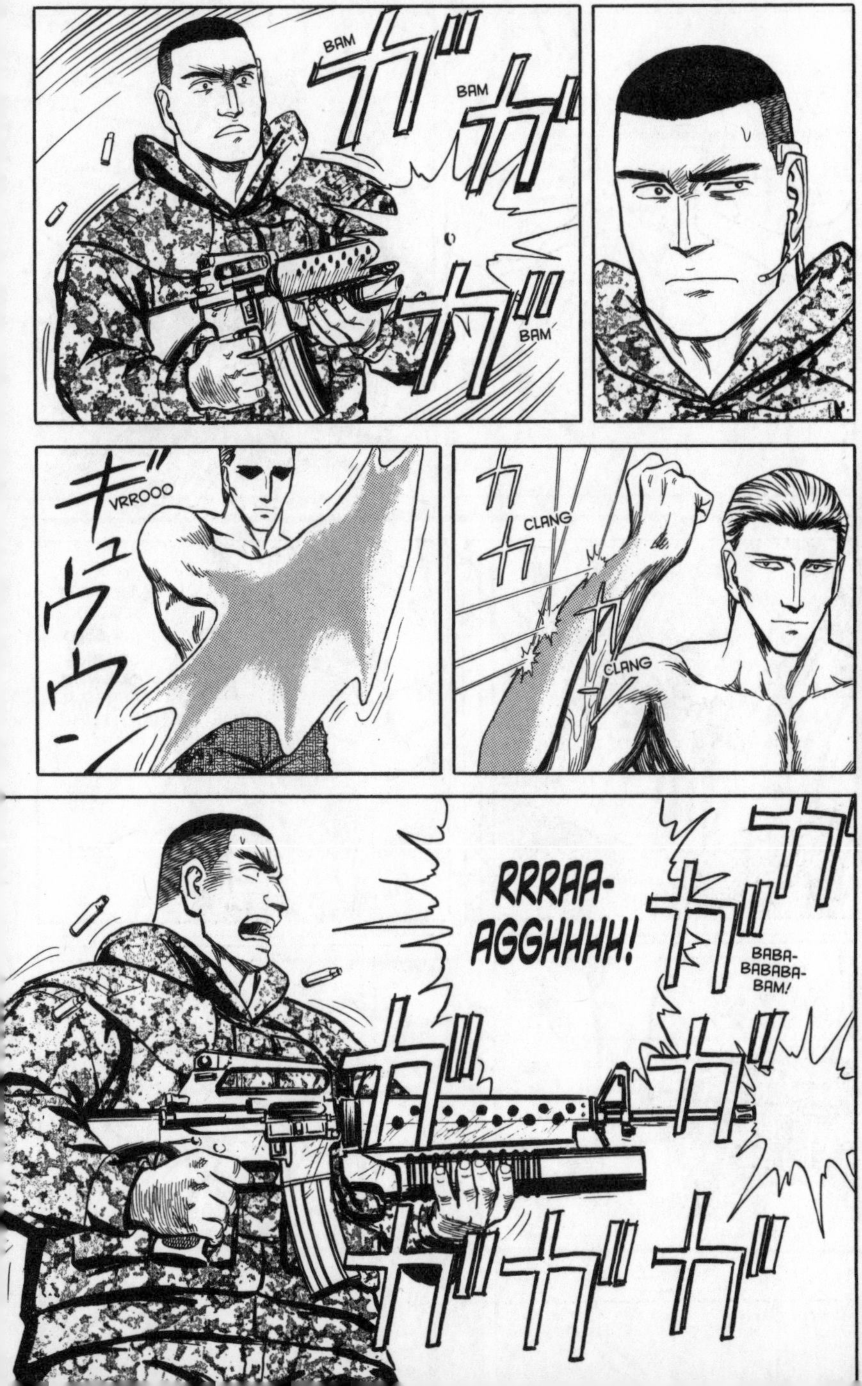
BAM
BAM
BAM
CLANG
CLANG
VRROOO
RRRAA-AGGHHHH!
BABA-BABABA-BAM!

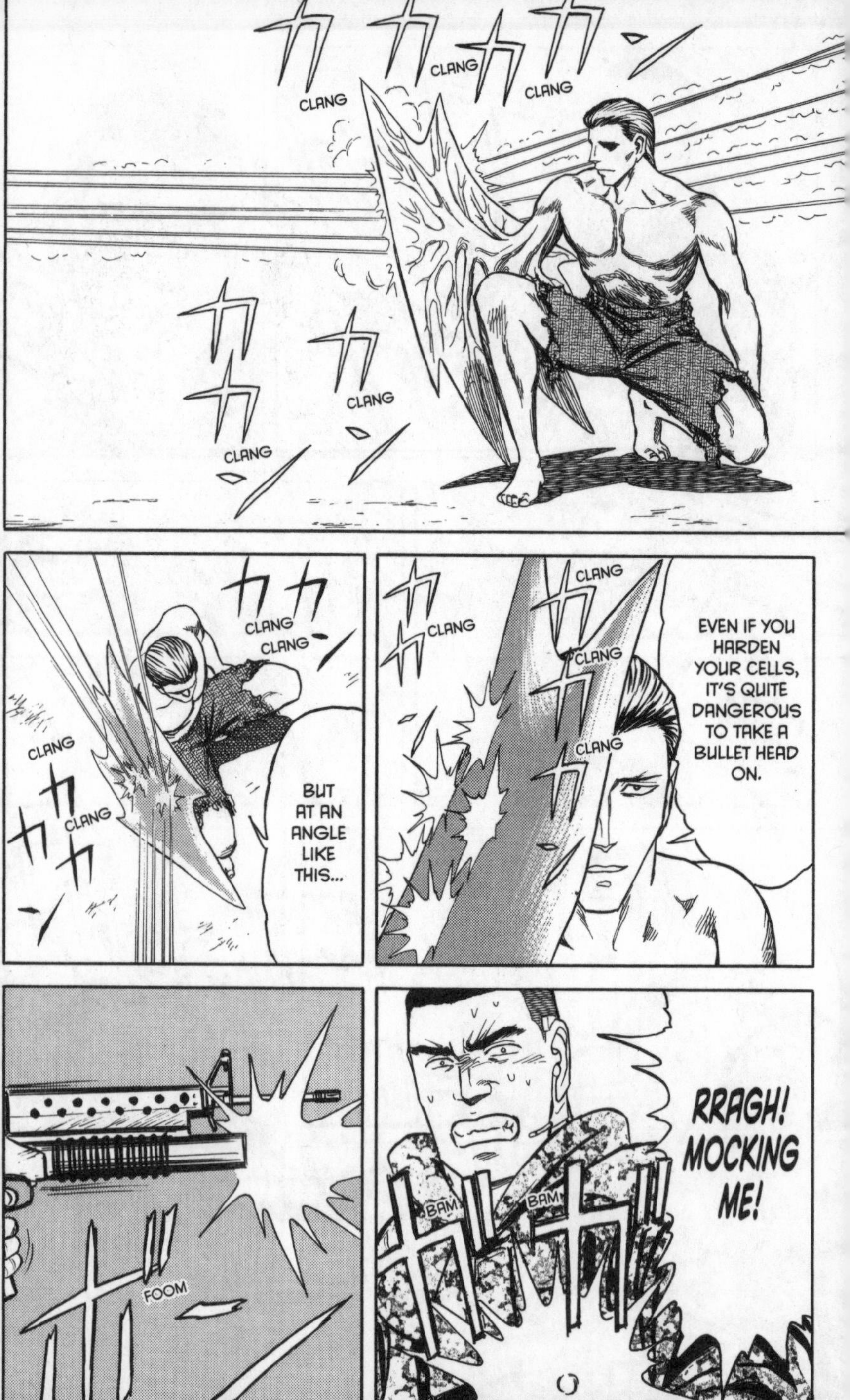
CLANG
CLANG
CLANG
CLANG
CLANG
EVEN IF YOU HARDEN YOUR CELLS, IT'S QUITE DANGEROUS TO TAKE A BULLET HEAD ON.
CLANG
CLANG
CLANG
CLANG
CLANG
CLANG
BUT AT AN ANGLE LIKE THIS...
CLANG
CLANG
RRAGH! MOCKING ME!
BAM
BAM
FOOM

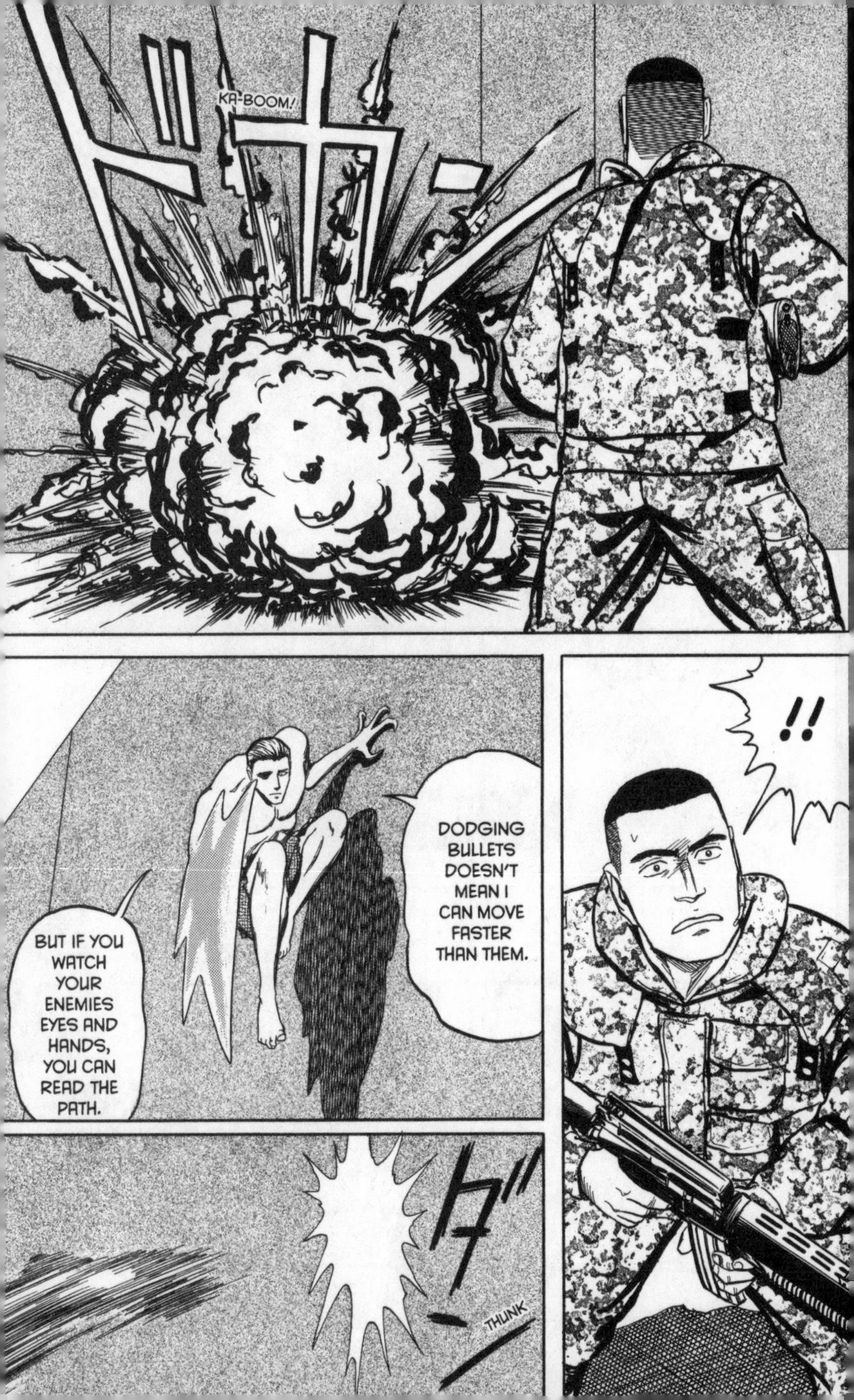
KA-BOOM!
!!
DODGING BULLETS DOESN'T MEAN I CAN MOVE FASTER THAN THEM.
BUT IF YOU WATCH YOUR ENEMIES EYES AND HANDS, YOU CAN READ THE PATH.
THUNK

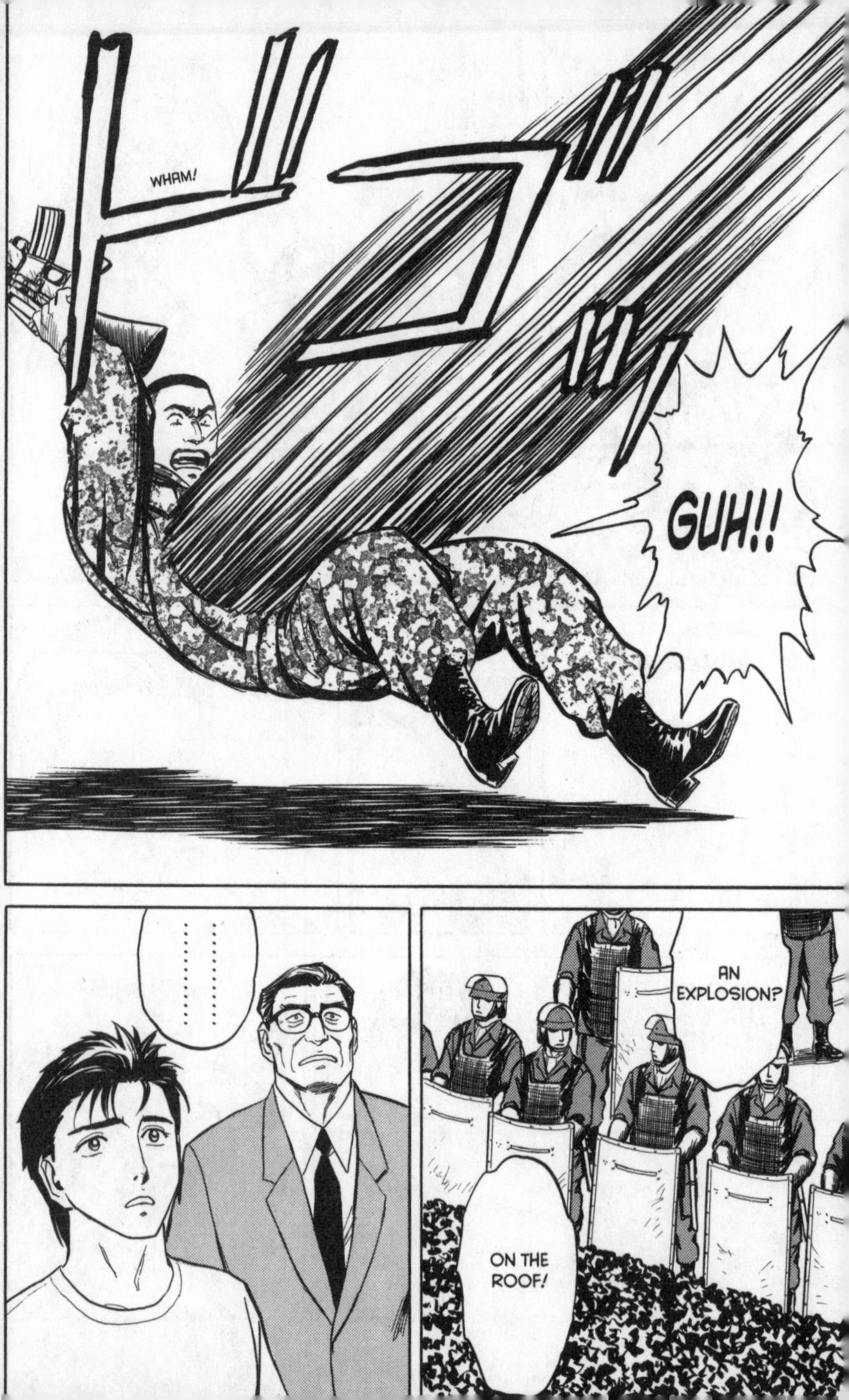
WHAM!
GUH!!
AN EXPLOSION?
ON THE ROOF!
......

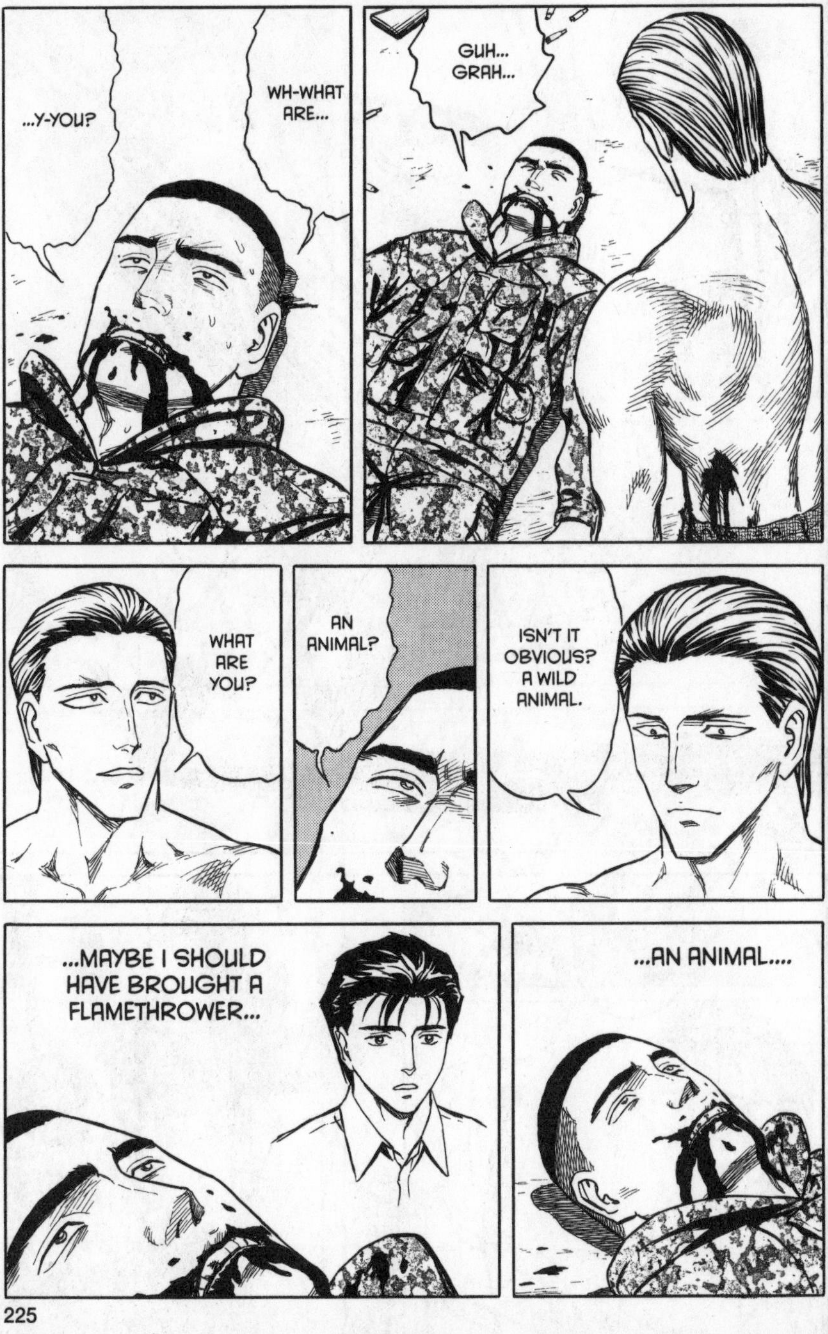
GUH... GRAH...
WH-WHAT ARE...
...Y-YOU?
ISN'T IT OBVIOUS? A WILD ANIMAL.
AN ANIMAL?
WHAT ARE YOU?
...AN ANIMAL....
...MAYBE I SHOULD HAVE BROUGHT A FLAMETHROWER...

...CLEAR!

THAT'S THE LAST OF THEM!

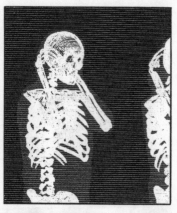

WHAT?

SIGH...

NO RESPONSE FROM L.C. YAMAGISHI!

LOOK OUT!

AH! HEY!!

THEY'RE FINISHED? BUT...

SOME-THING'S FALLING!

226

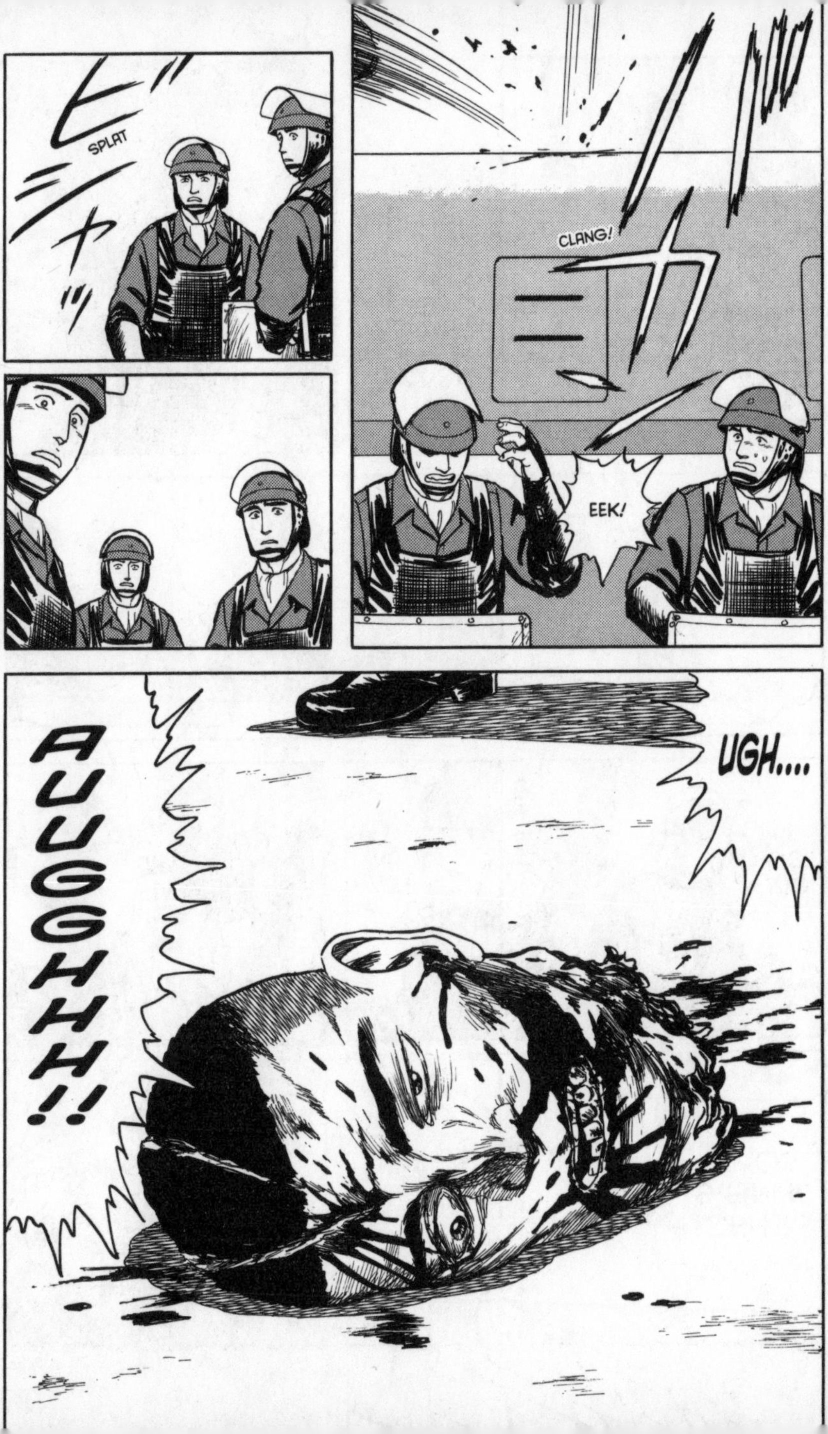
CLANG!
EEK!
SPLAT
UGH....
AUUGGHHH!!

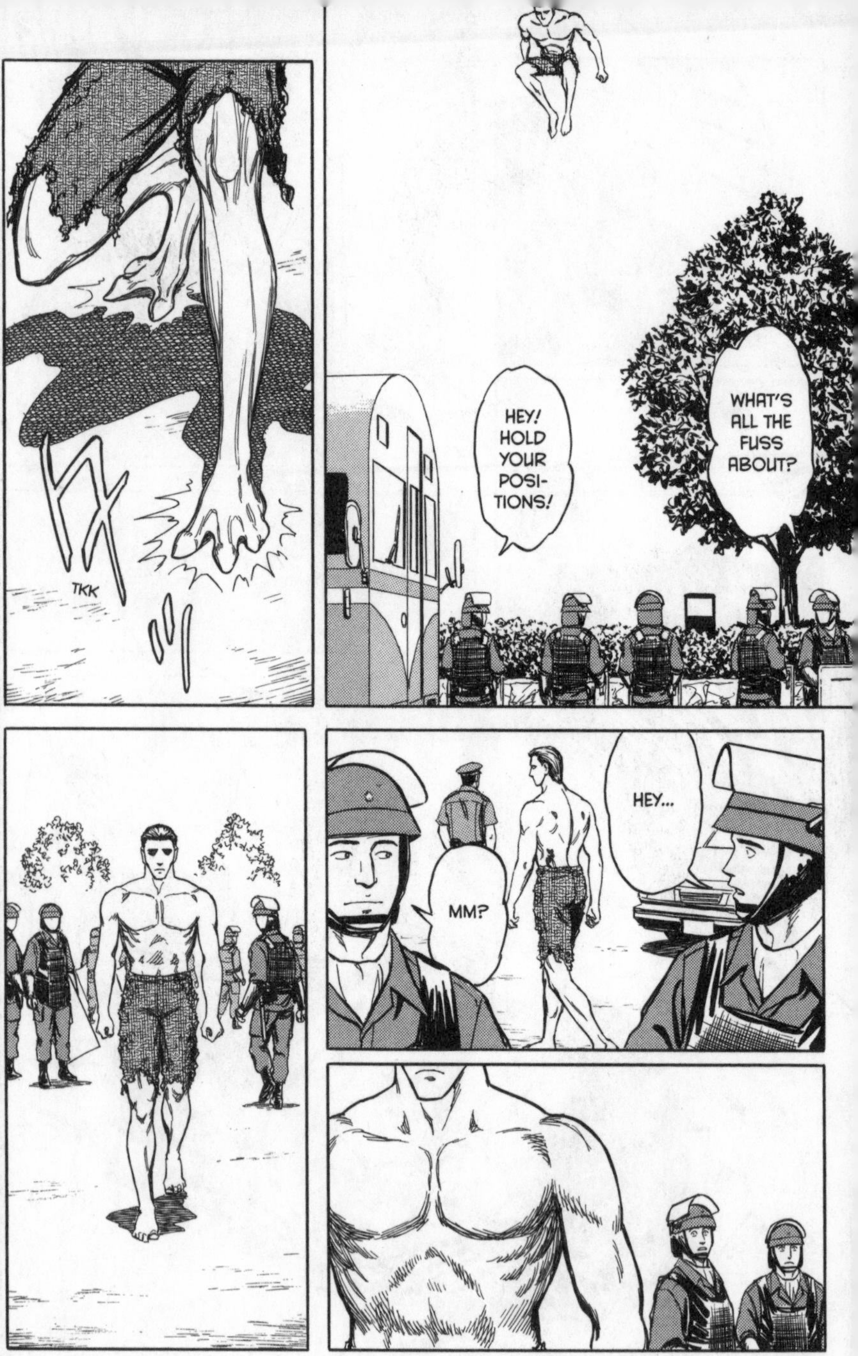
WHAT'S ALL THE FUSS ABOUT?
HEY! HOLD YOUR POSI- TIONS!
TKK
HEY...
MM?

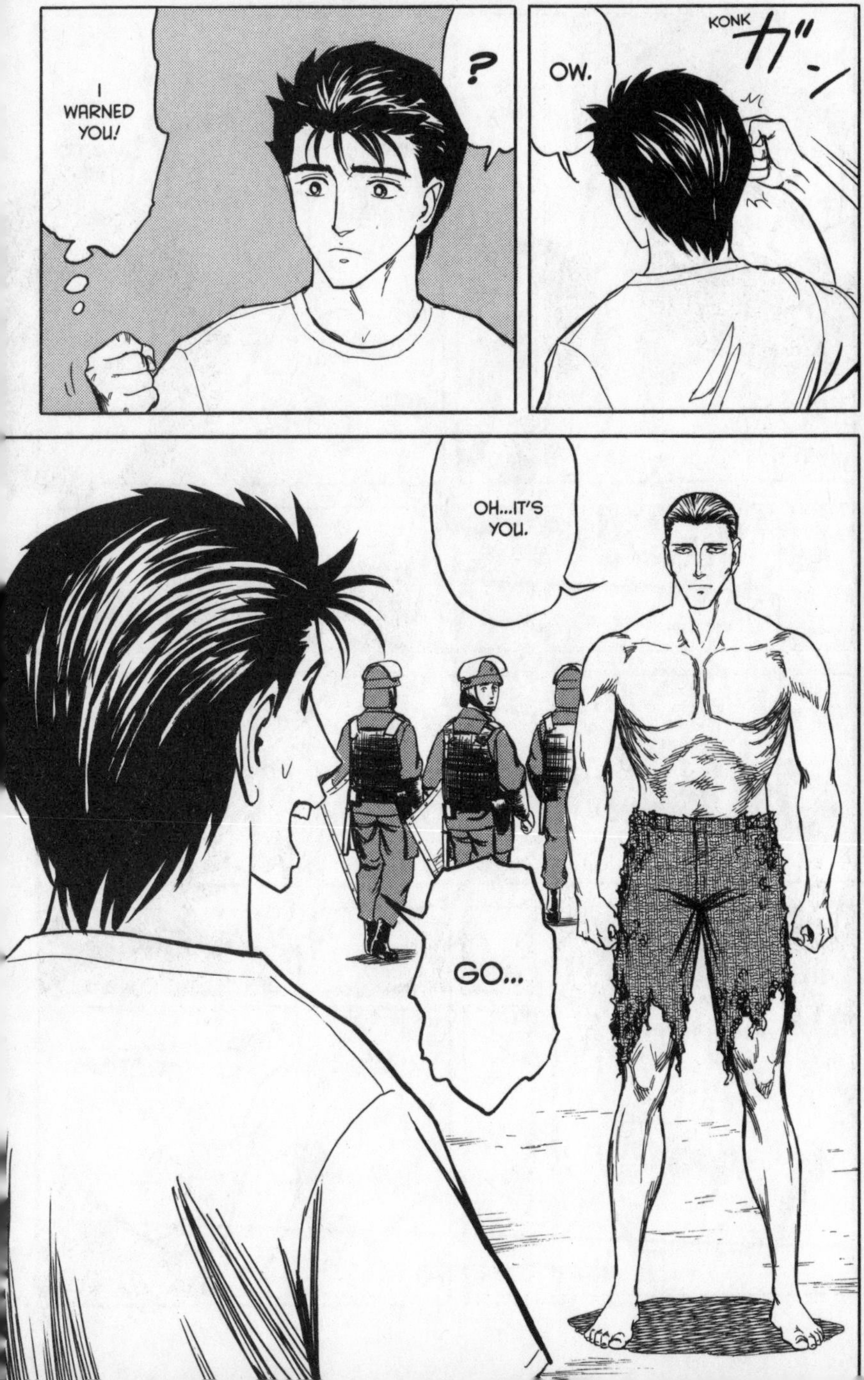
KONK
OW.
?
I WARNED YOU!
OH...IT'S YOU.
GO...

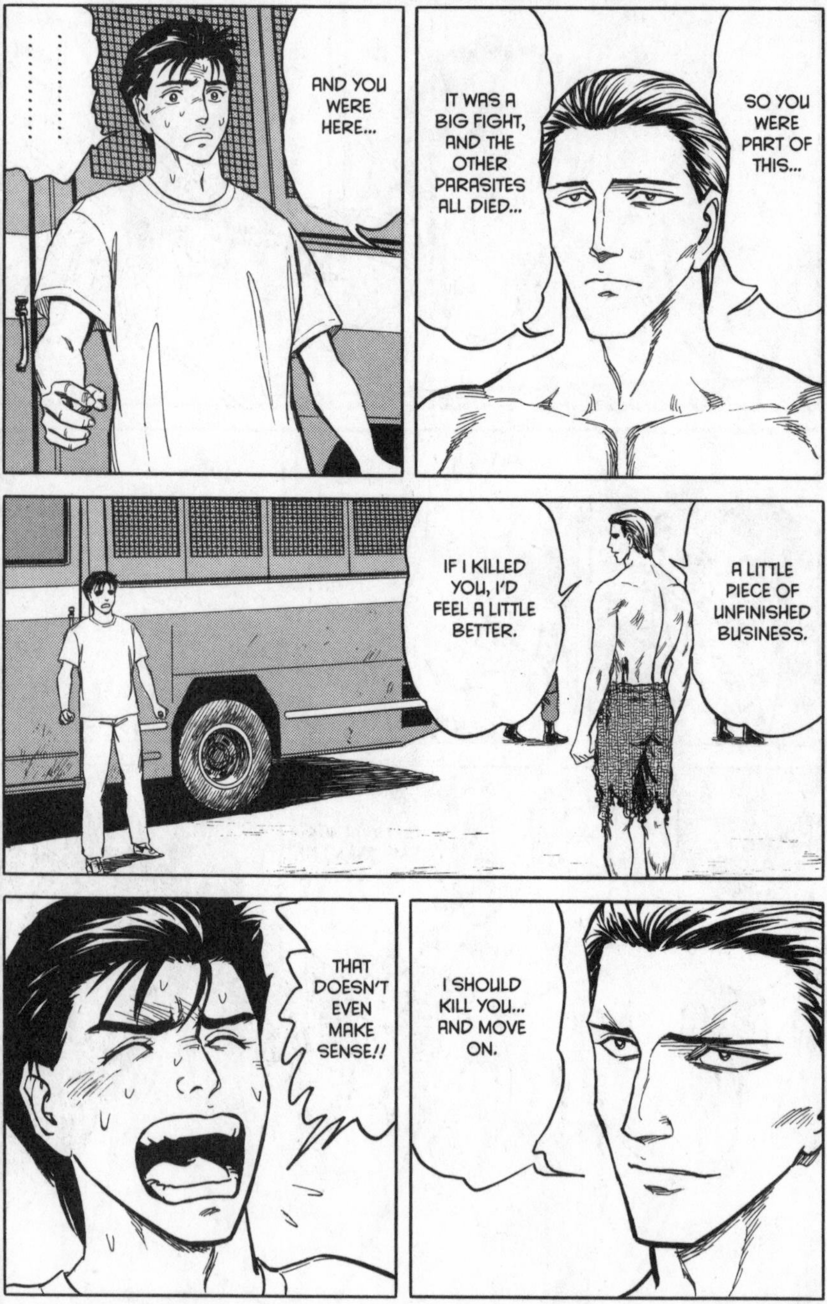
SO YOU WERE PART OF THIS...
IT WAS A BIG FIGHT, AND THE OTHER PARASITES ALL DIED...
AND YOU WERE HERE...
......
A LITTLE PIECE OF UNFINISHED BUSINESS.
IF I KILLED YOU, I'D FEEL A LITTLE BETTER.
I SHOULD KILL YOU... AND MOVE ON.
THAT DOESN'T EVEN MAKE SENSE!!

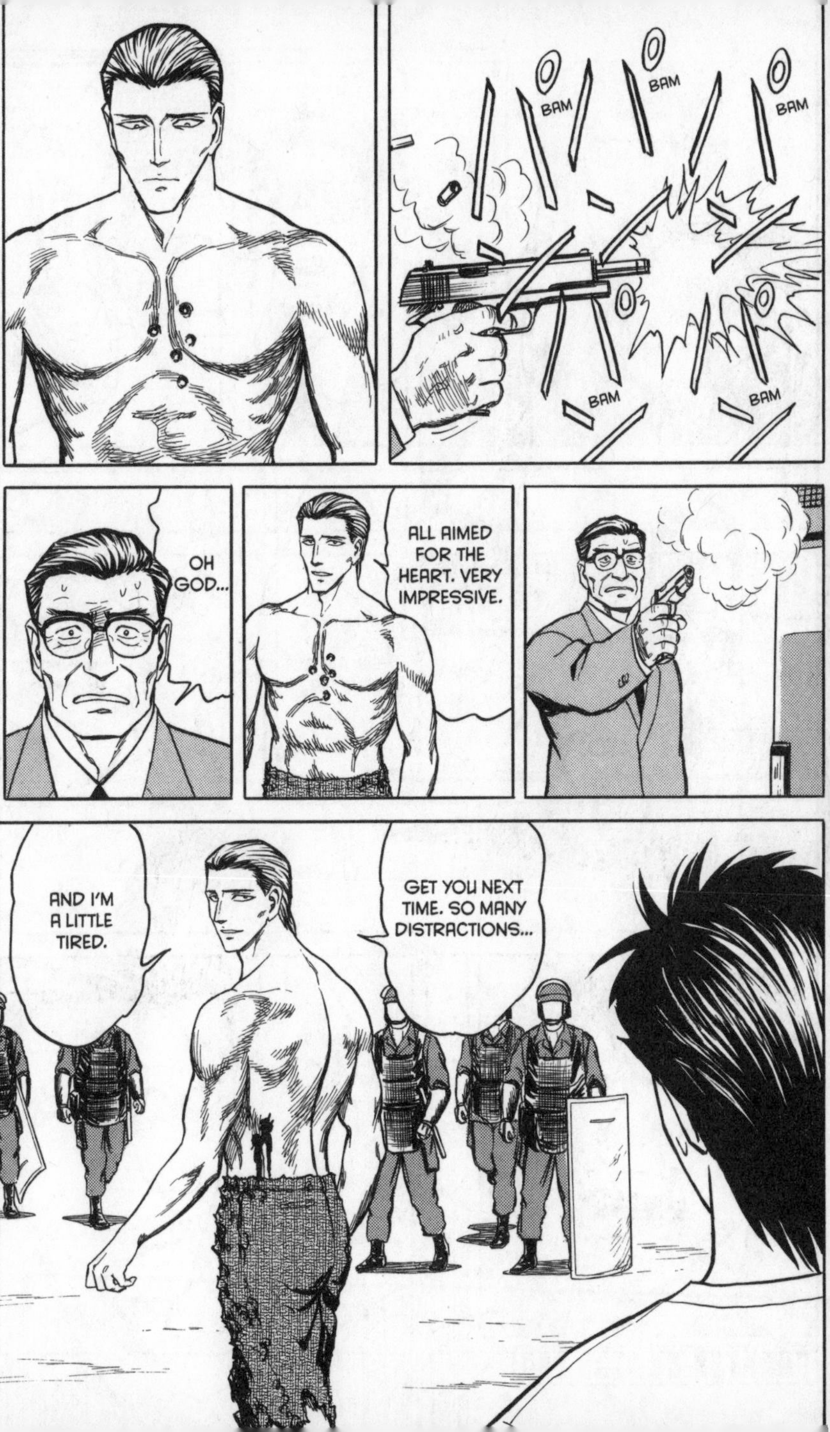
BAM
BAM
BAM
BAM
BAM
ALL AIMED FOR THE HEART. VERY IMPRESSIVE.
OH GOD...
GET YOU NEXT TIME. SO MANY DISTRACTIONS...
AND I'M A LITTLE TIRED.

SHOO...

TKK

I-IZUMI-KUN! WH-WHAT DID HE WANT WITH YOU?

H-HE FLEW...!?

THIS IS BAD. NEXT TIME WE'LL DIE!!

H-HOW COULD I?

I...I DON'T KNOW!

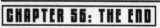

CHAPTER 56: THE END

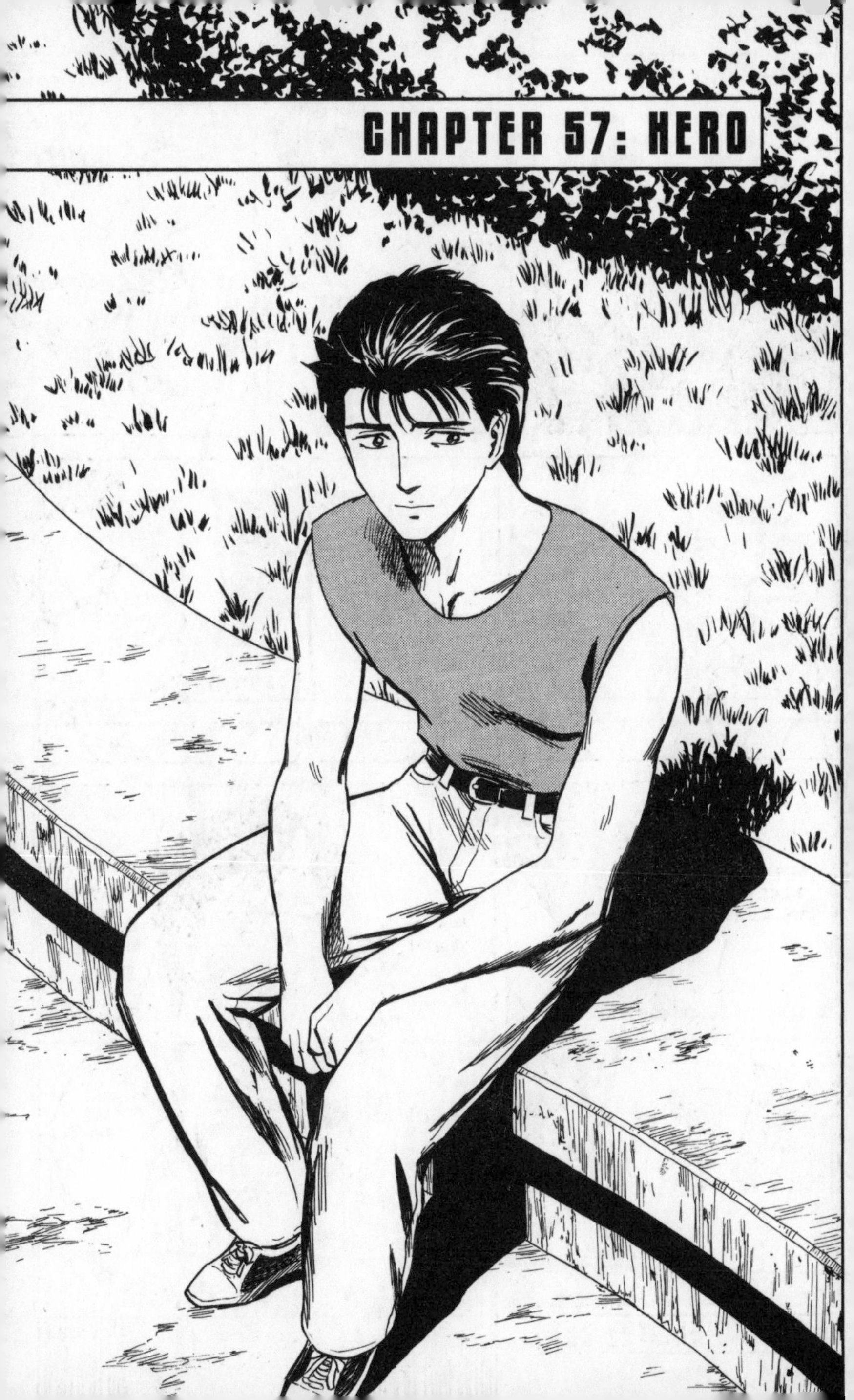
CHAPTER 57: HERO

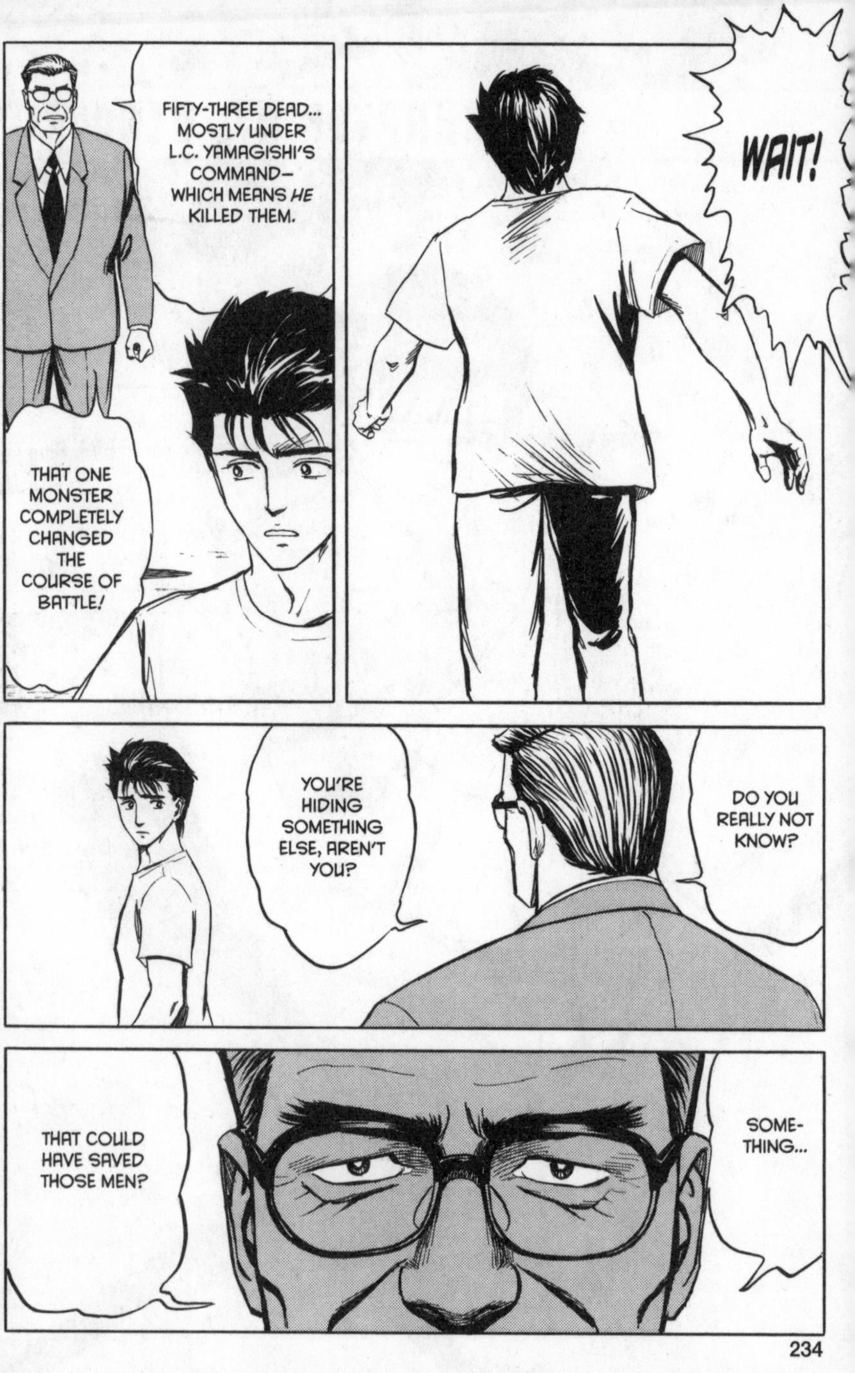
WAIT!
FIFTY-THREE DEAD... MOSTLY UNDER L.C. YAMAGISHI'S COMMAND— WHICH MEANS *HE* KILLED THEM.
THAT ONE MONSTER COMPLETELY CHANGED THE COURSE OF BATTLE!
DO YOU REALLY NOT KNOW?
YOU'RE HIDING SOMETHING ELSE, AREN'T YOU?
SOME-THING...
THAT COULD HAVE SAVED THOSE MEN?

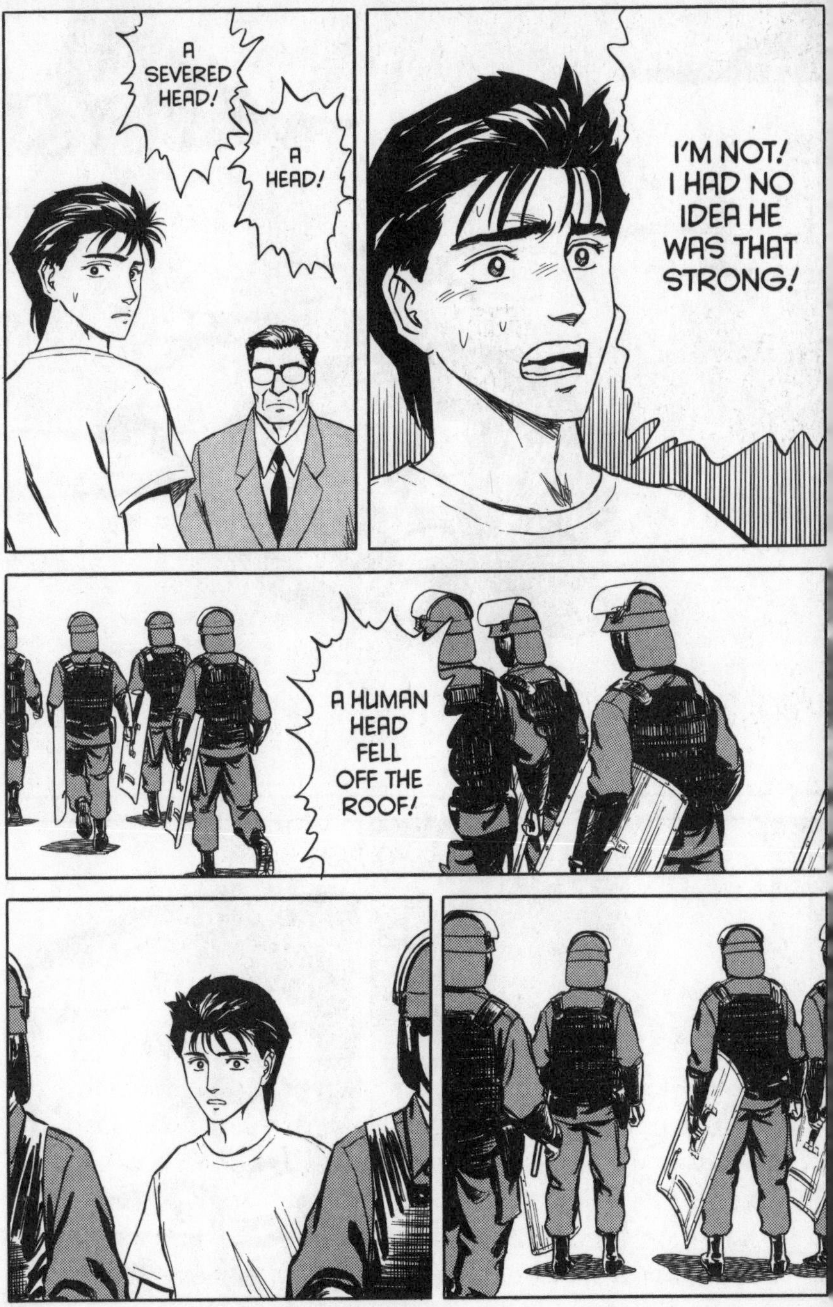
I'M NOT! I HAD NO IDEA HE WAS THAT STRONG!
A HEAD!
A SEVERED HEAD!
A HUMAN HEAD FELL OFF THE ROOF!

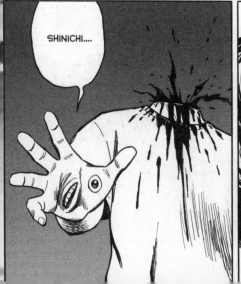

SHINICHI....

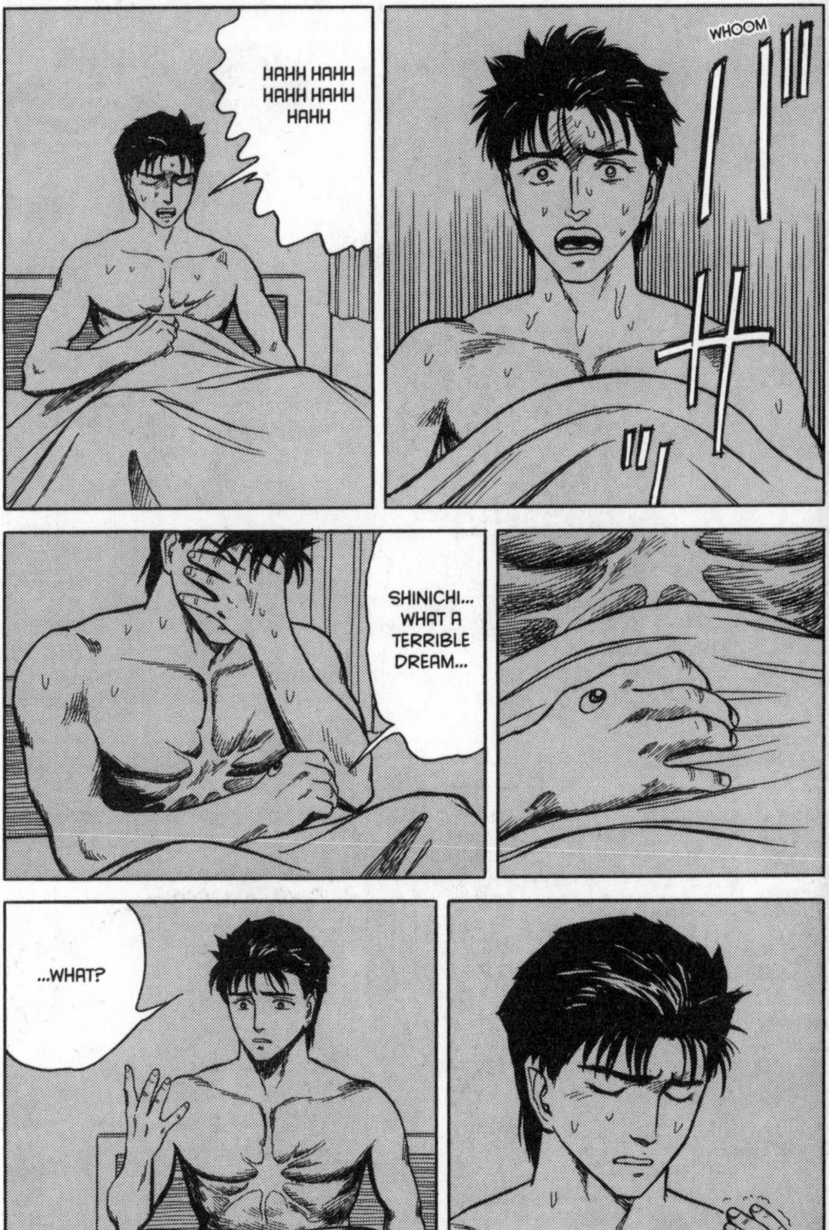
WHOOM
HAHH HAHH HAHH HAHH HAHH
SHINICHI... WHAT A TERRIBLE DREAM...
...WHAT?

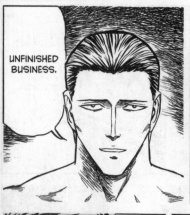

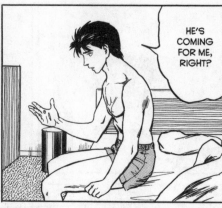

HE'S COMING FOR ME, RIGHT?
UNFINISHED BUSINESS.
I CAN FEEL IT.
ANY DAY NOW.
I SHOULD KILL YOU...AND MOVE ON.
SO WE'RE DEAD?
DON'T GIVE UP SO EASILY.
IF WE GET SOME HELP... UDA...?
NO!! WE CAN'T GET HIM MIXED UP IN THIS.

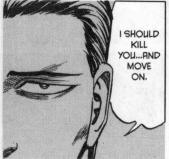

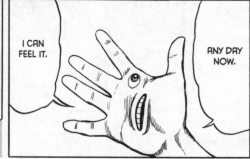

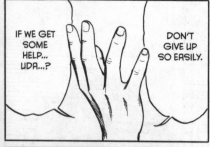

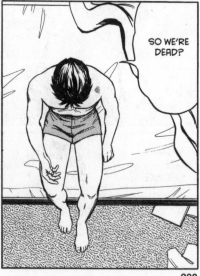

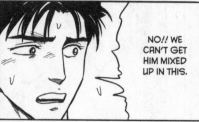

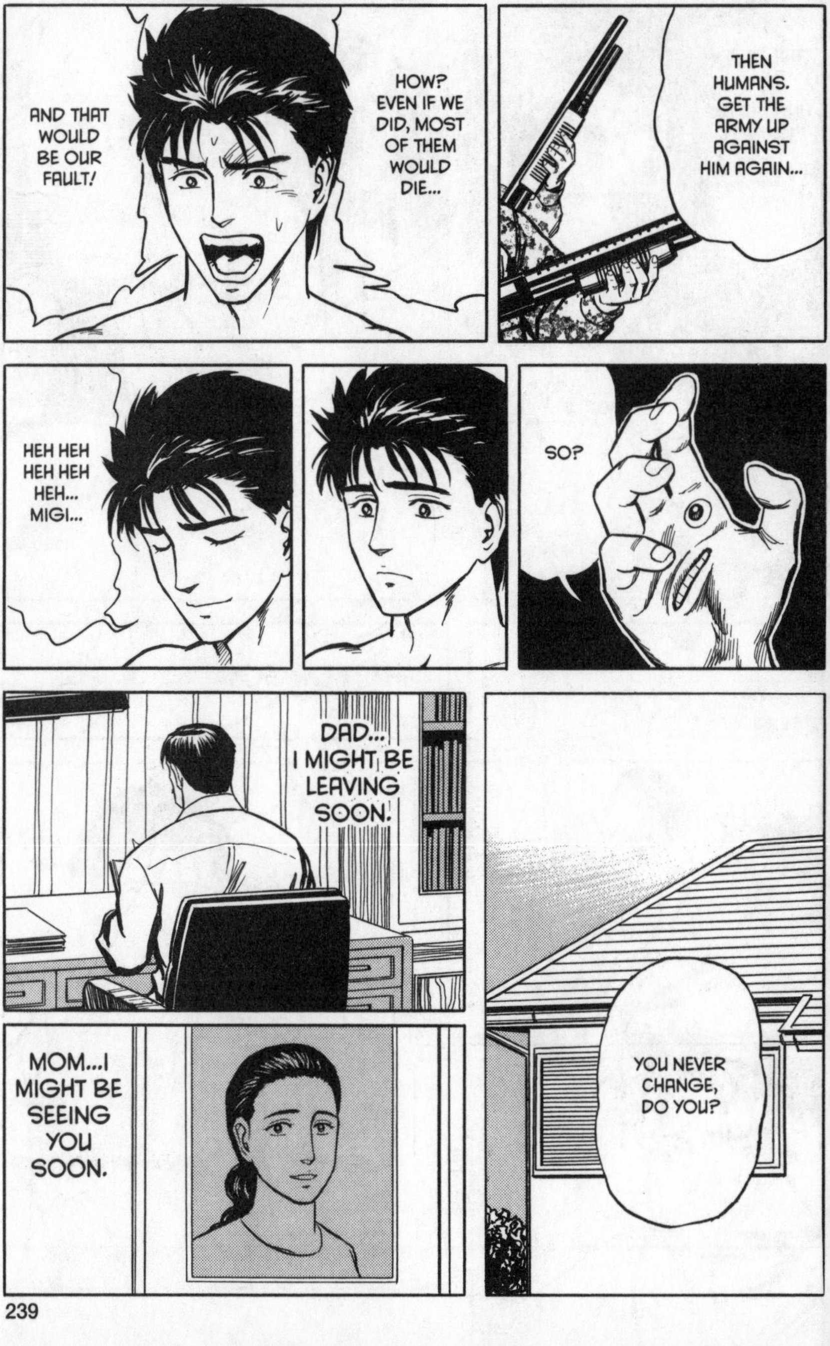
THEN HUMANS. GET THE ARMY UP AGAINST HIM AGAIN...
HOW? EVEN IF WE DID, MOST OF THEM WOULD DIE...
AND THAT WOULD BE OUR FAULT!
SO?
HEH HEH HEH HEH HEH... MIGI...
YOU NEVER CHANGE, DO YOU?
DAD... I MIGHT BE LEAVING SOON.
MOM...I MIGHT BE SEEING YOU SOON.

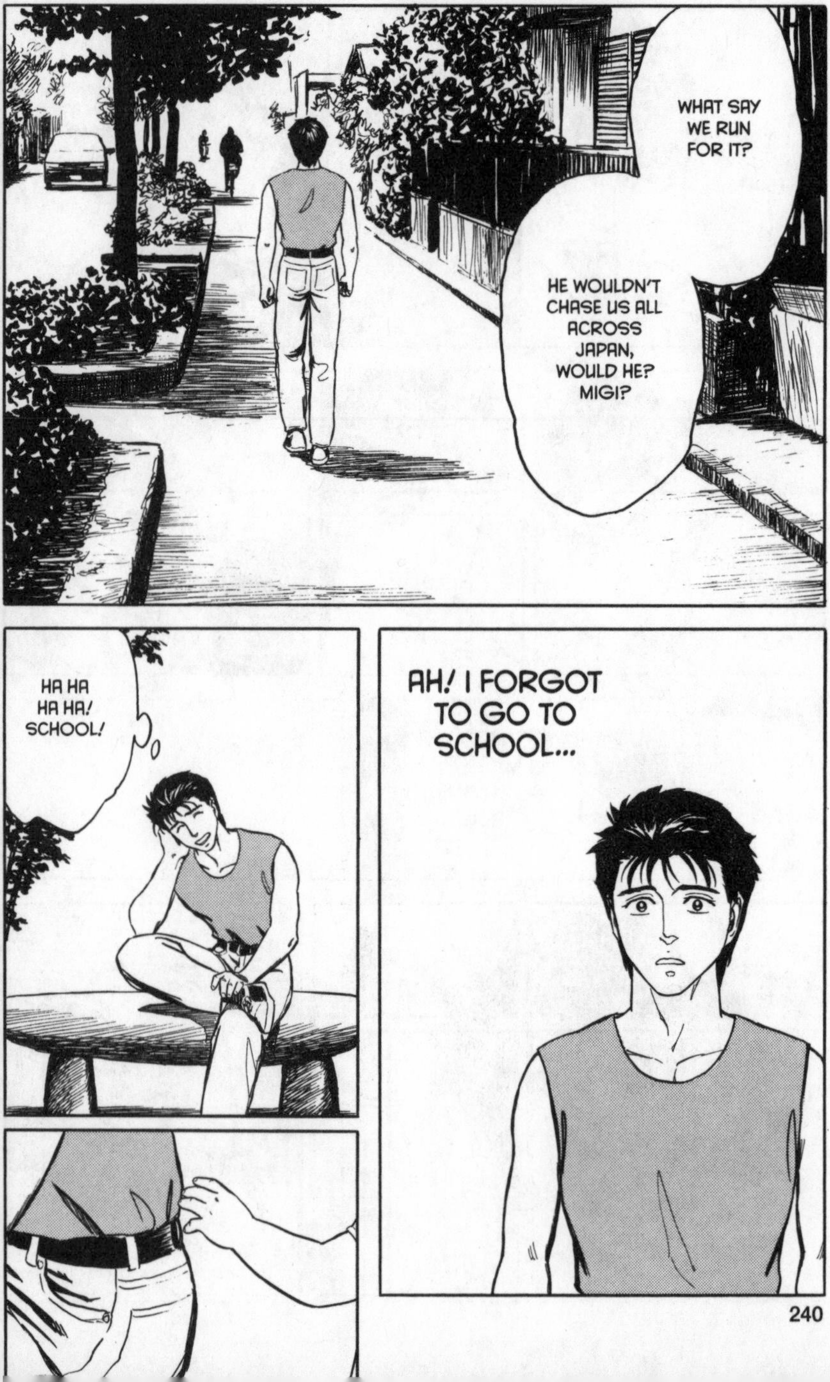
WHAT SAY WE RUN FOR IT?
HE WOULDN'T CHASE US ALL ACROSS JAPAN, WOULD HE? MIGI?
AH! I FORGOT TO GO TO SCHOOL...
HA HA HA HA! SCHOOL!

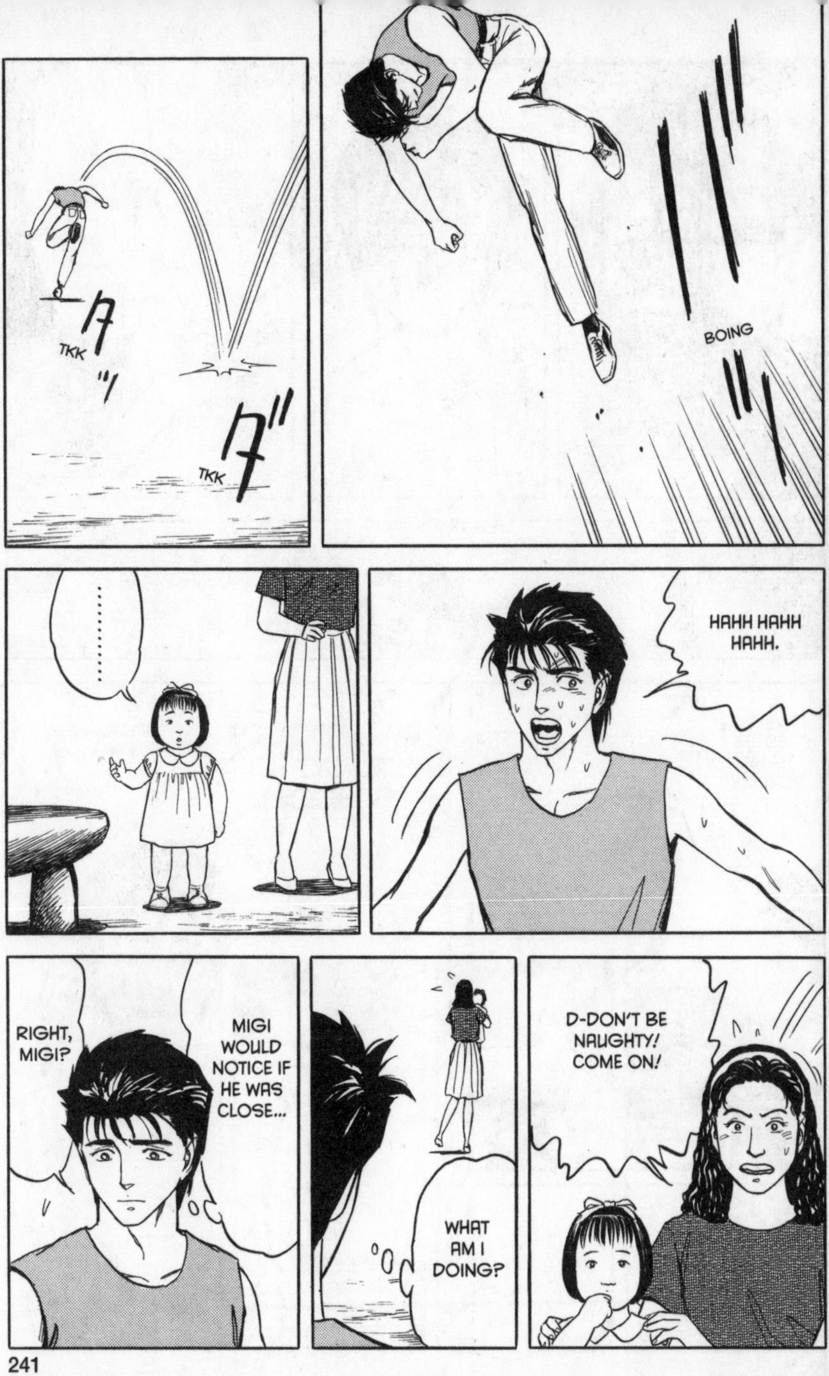
BOING
TKK
TKK
HAHH HAHH HAHH.
....
D-DON'T BE NAUGHTY! COME ON!
WHAT AM I DOING?
MIGI WOULD NOTICE IF HE WAS CLOSE...
RIGHT, MIGI?

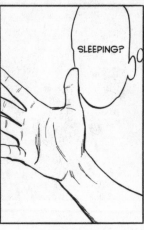

SLEEPING?

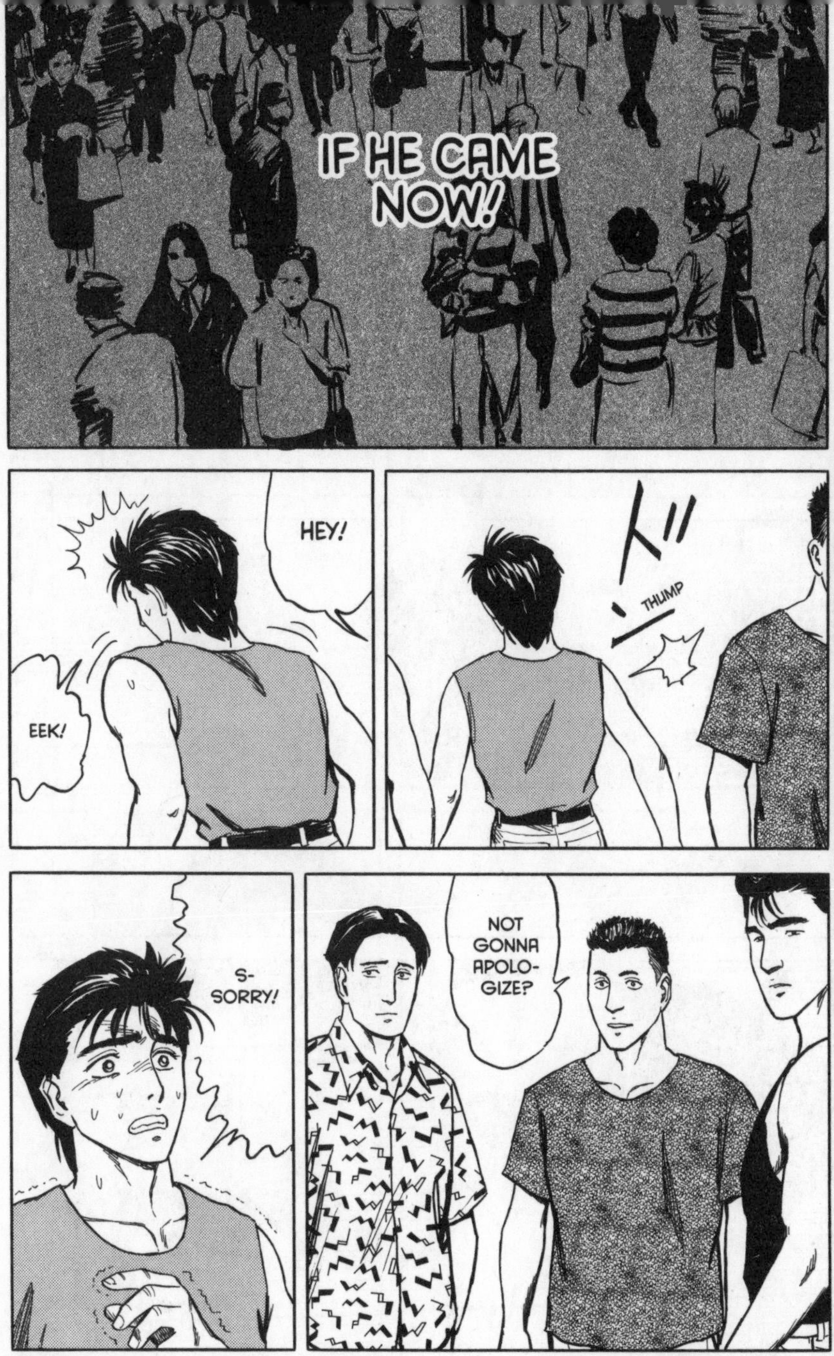
IF HE CAME NOW!
ドッ
THUMP
HEY!
EEK!
NOT GONNA APOLOGIZE?
S- SORRY!

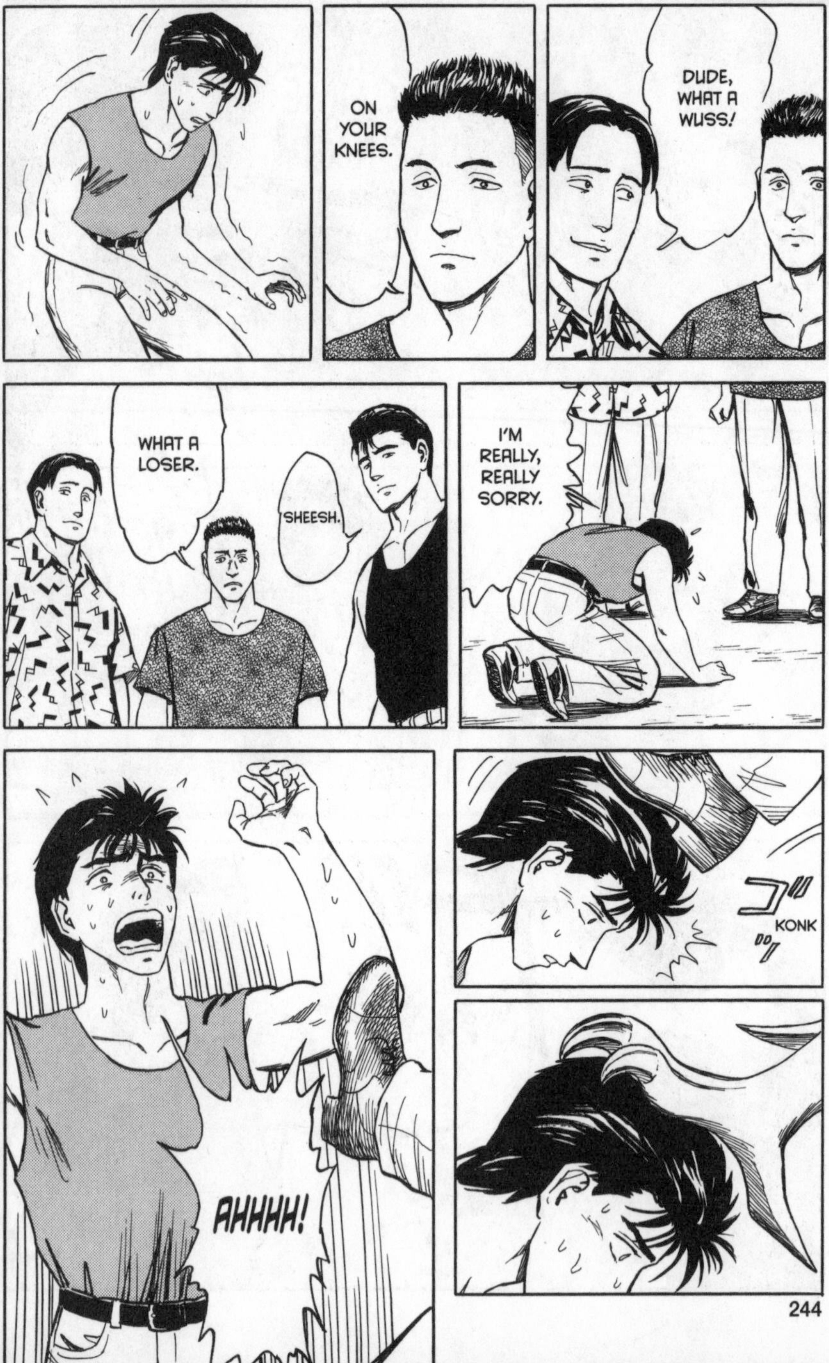
DUDE, WHAT A WUSS!
ON YOUR KNEES.
I'M REALLY, REALLY SORRY.
SHEESH.
WHAT A LOSER.
ゴッ
KONK
AHHHH!

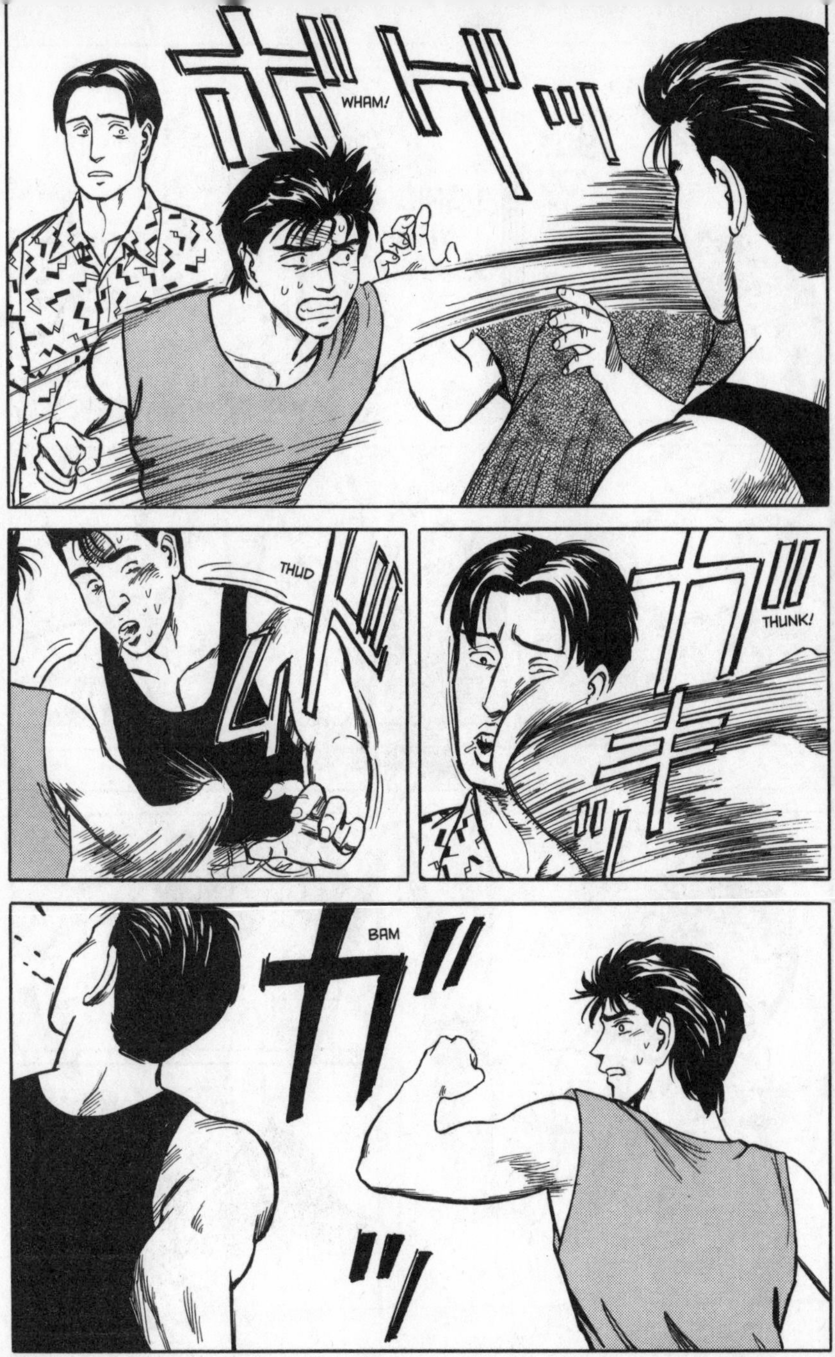
ボドッ
WHAM!
ガキッ
THUNK!
ドム
THUD
ガッ
BAM

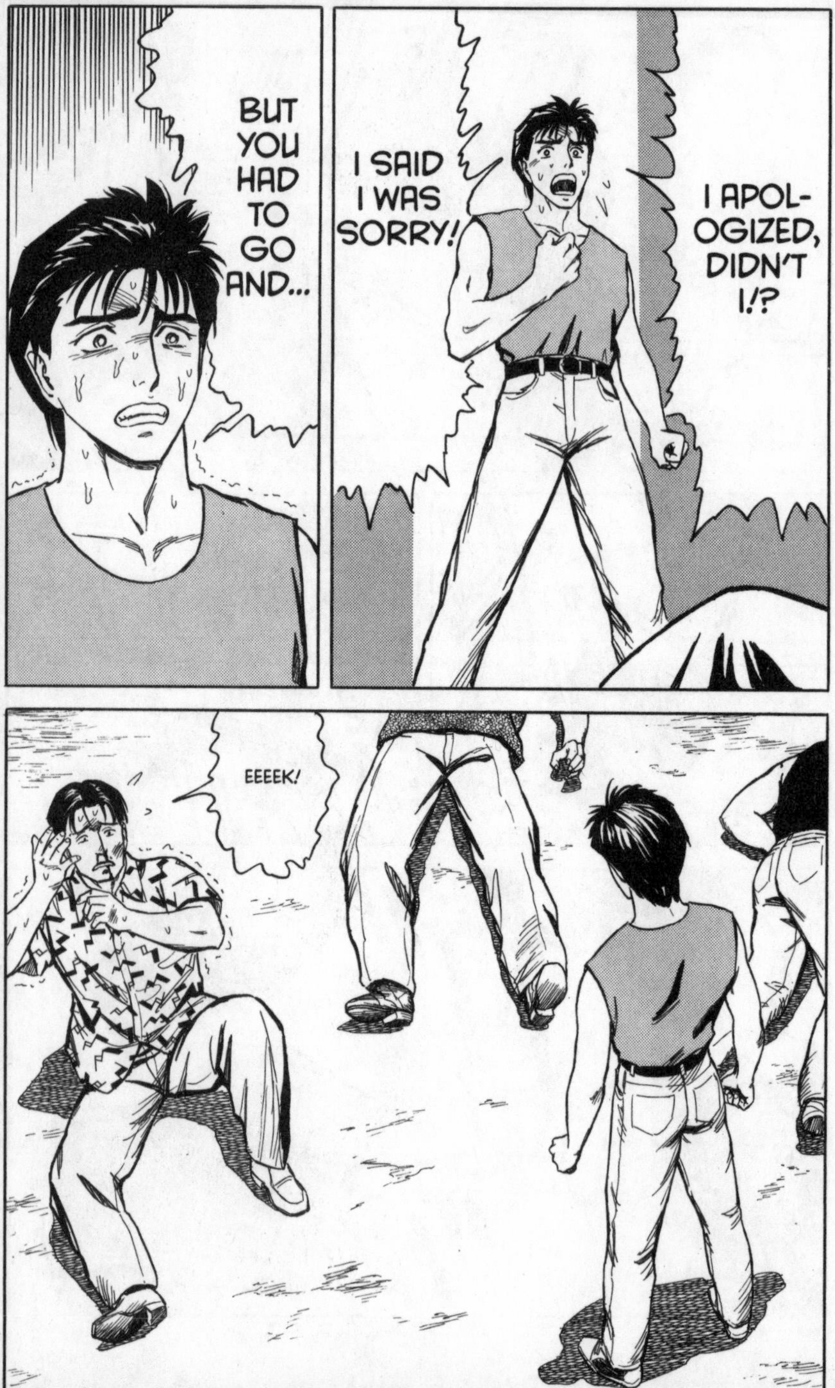
I APOLOGIZED, DIDN'T I!?
I SAID I WAS SORRY!
BUT YOU HAD TO GO AND...
EEEEK!

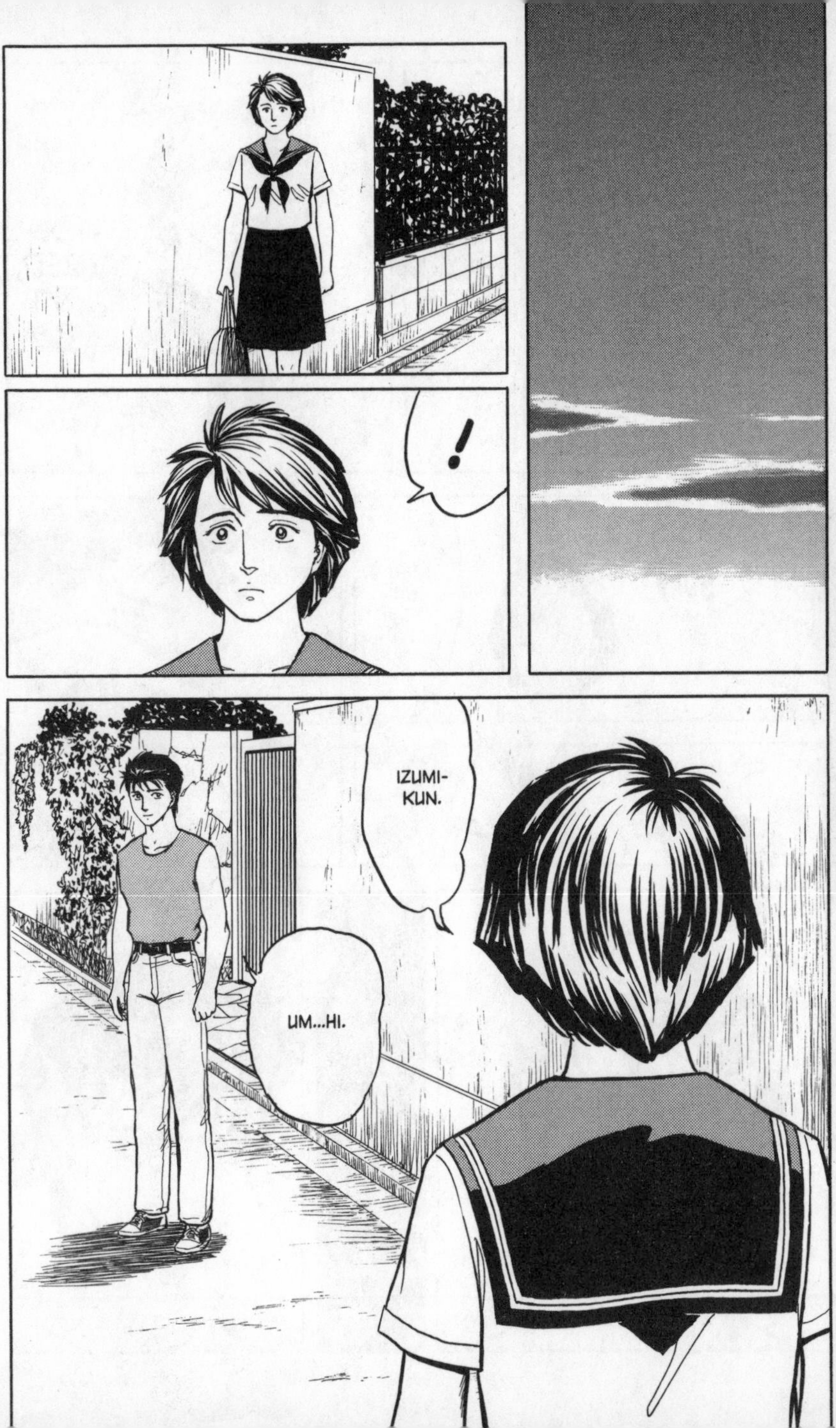
!
IZUMI-KUN.
UM...HI.

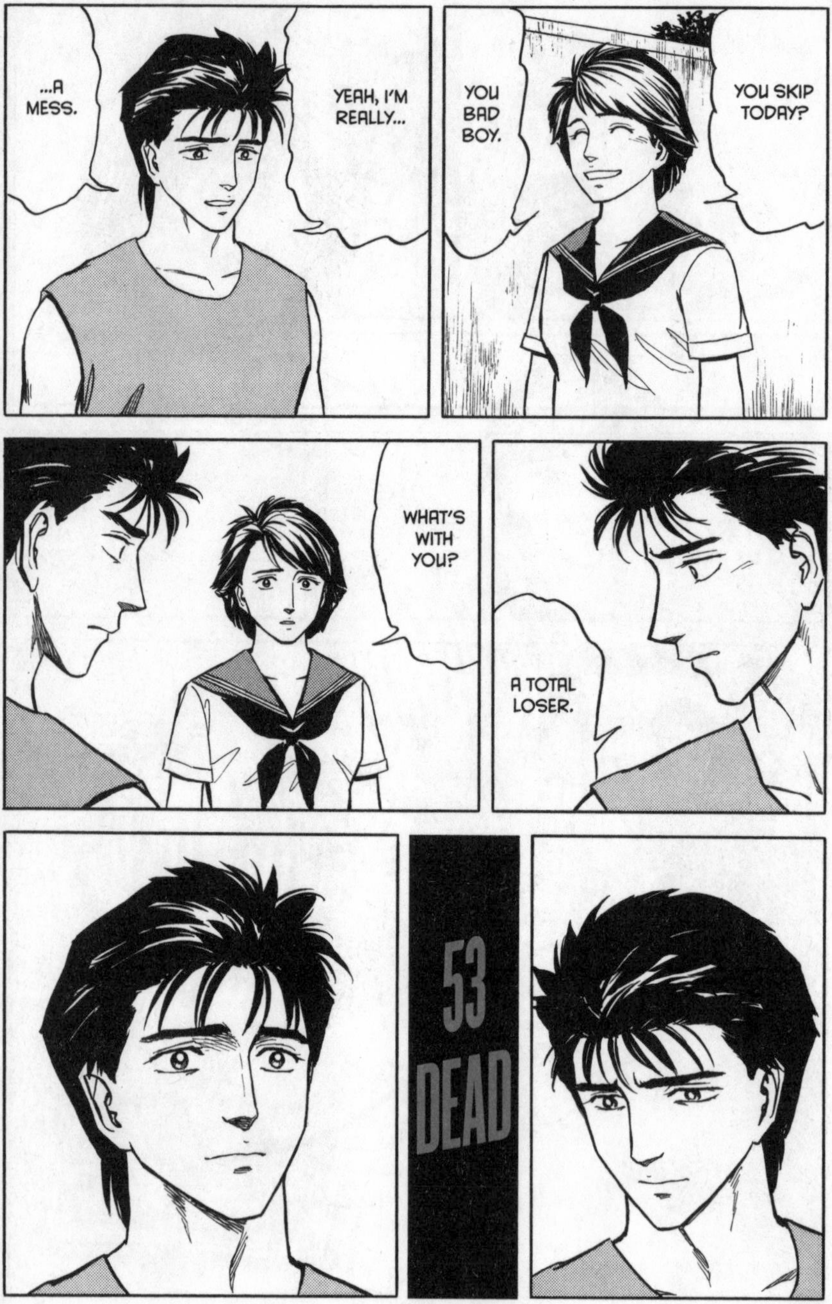
YOU SKIP TODAY?
YOU BAD BOY.
YEAH, I'M REALLY...
...A MESS.
A TOTAL LOSER.
WHAT'S WITH YOU?
53 DEAD

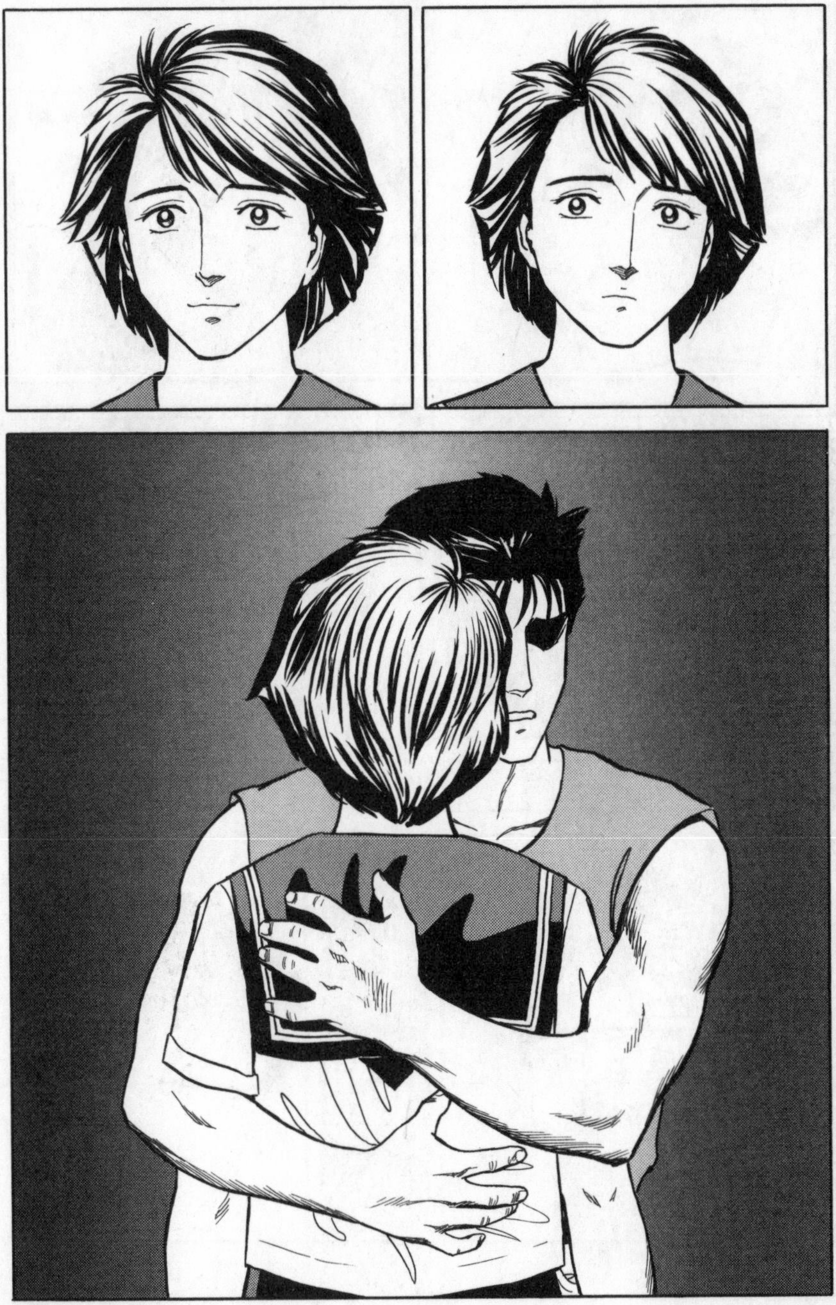

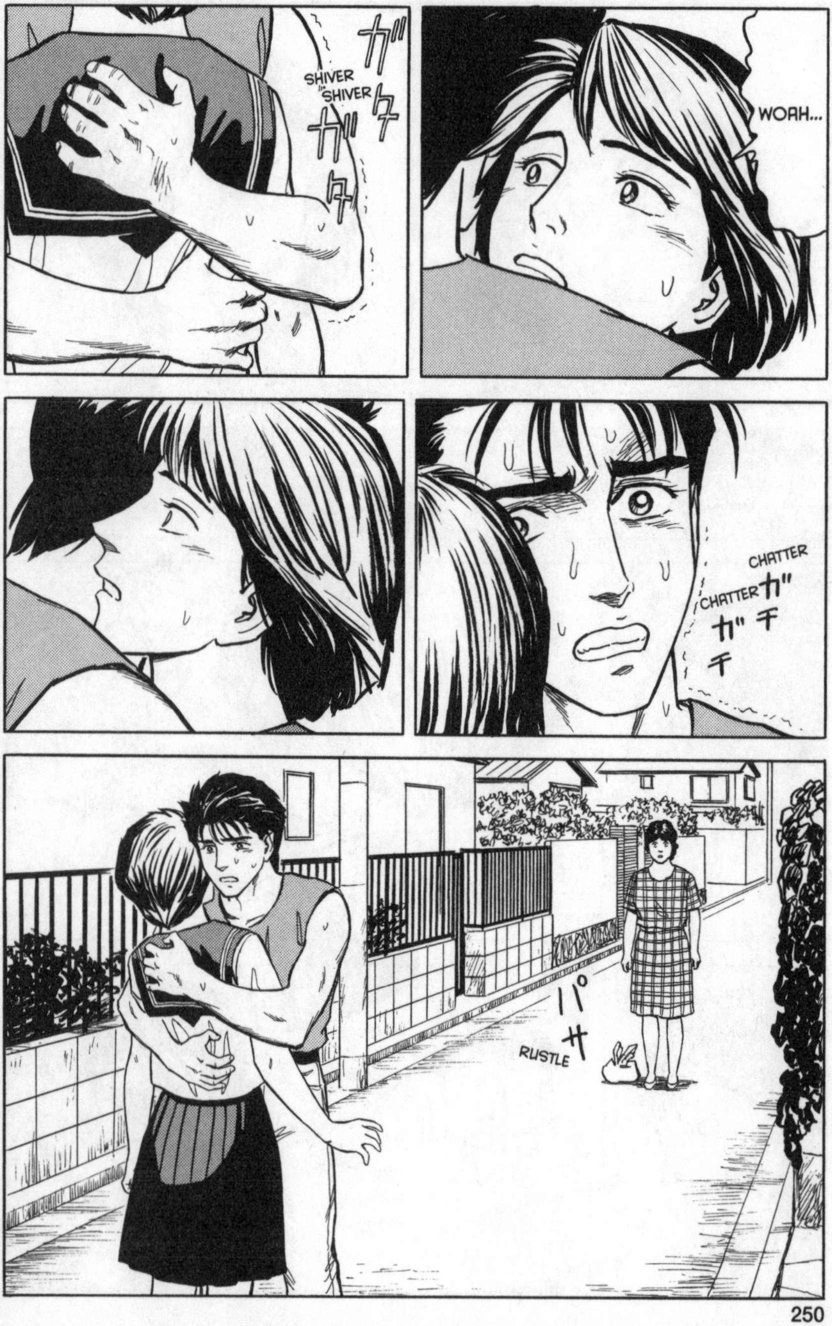
WOAH...
SHIVER SHIVER
ガタガタ
CHATTER CHATTER
ガチガチ
RUSTLE
パサ

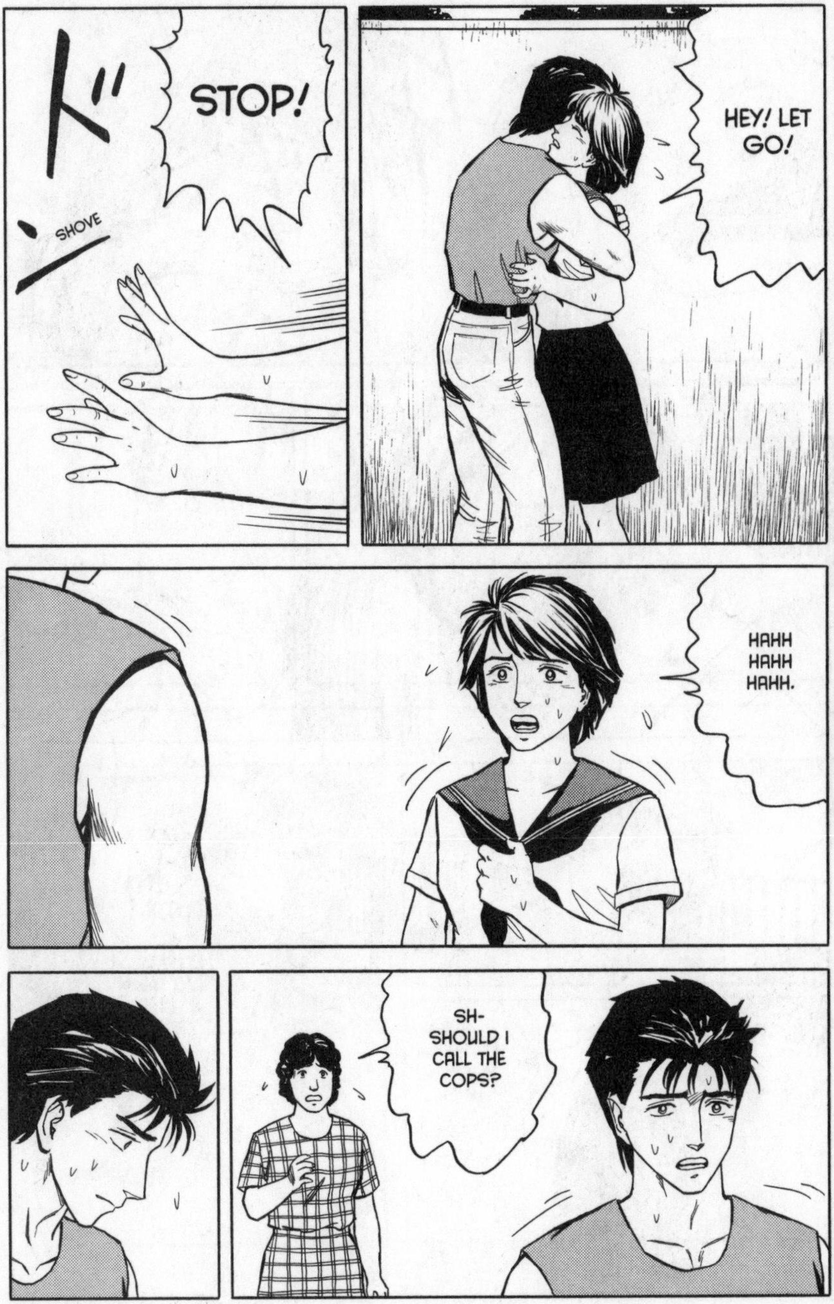
HEY! LET GO!
ド
STOP!
SHOVE
HAHH HAHH HAHH.
SH- SHOULD I CALL THE COPS?

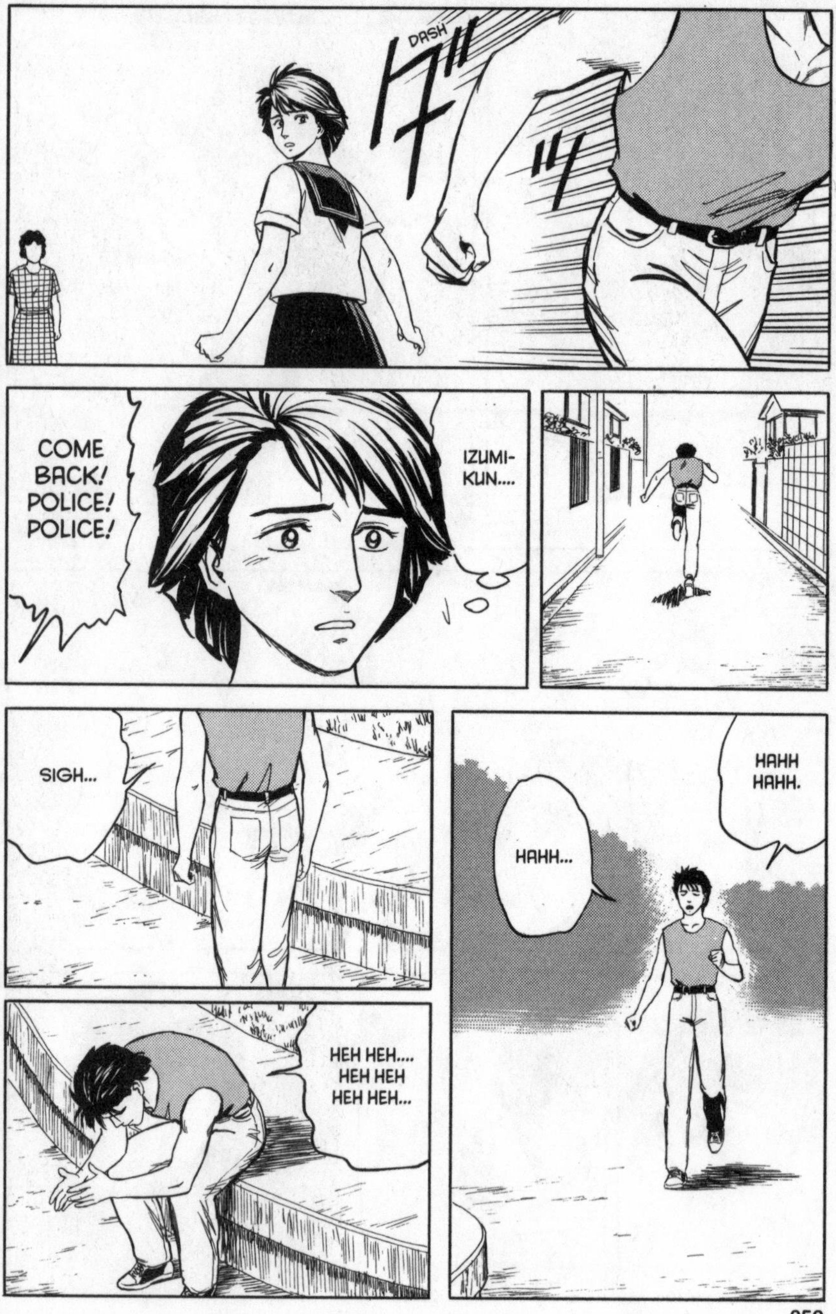
DASH
IZUMI-KUN....
COME BACK! POLICE! POLICE!
HAHH HAHH.
HAHH...
SIGH...
HEH HEH.... HEH HEH HEH HEH...

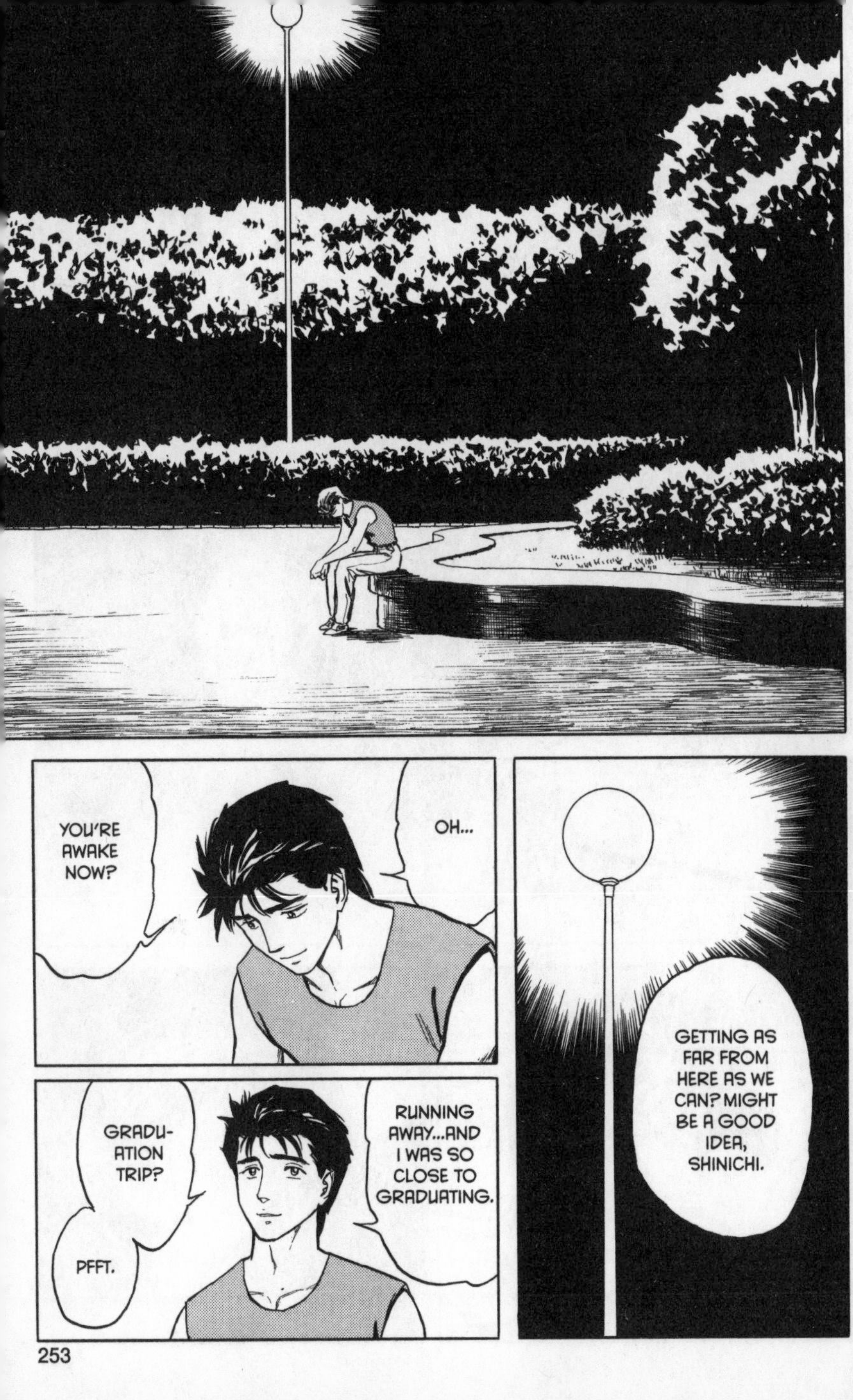
GETTING AS FAR FROM HERE AS WE CAN? MIGHT BE A GOOD IDEA, SHINICHI.
OH...
YOU'RE AWAKE NOW?
RUNNING AWAY...AND I WAS SO CLOSE TO GRADUATING.
GRADU-ATION TRIP?
PFFT.

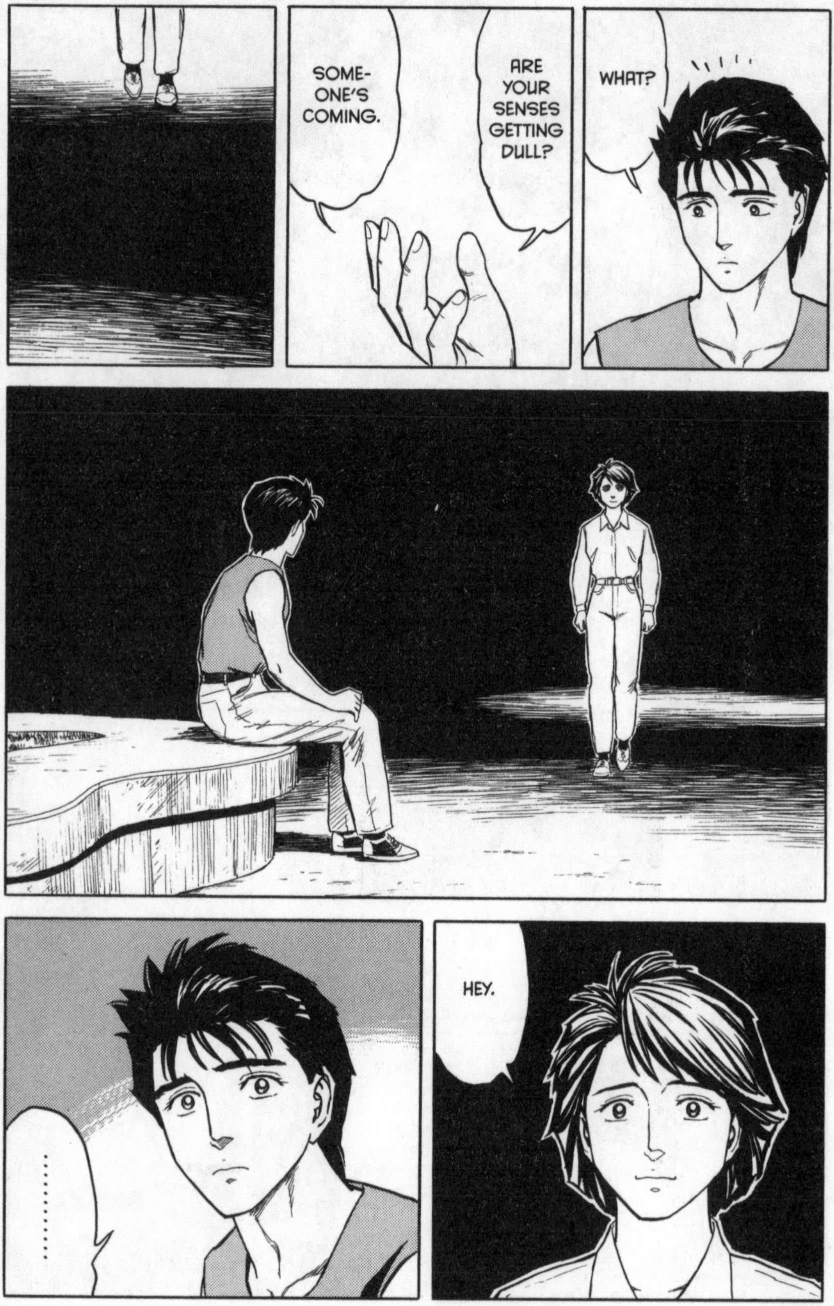
WHAT?
ARE YOUR SENSES GETTING DULL?
SOME-ONE'S COMING.
HEY.
....

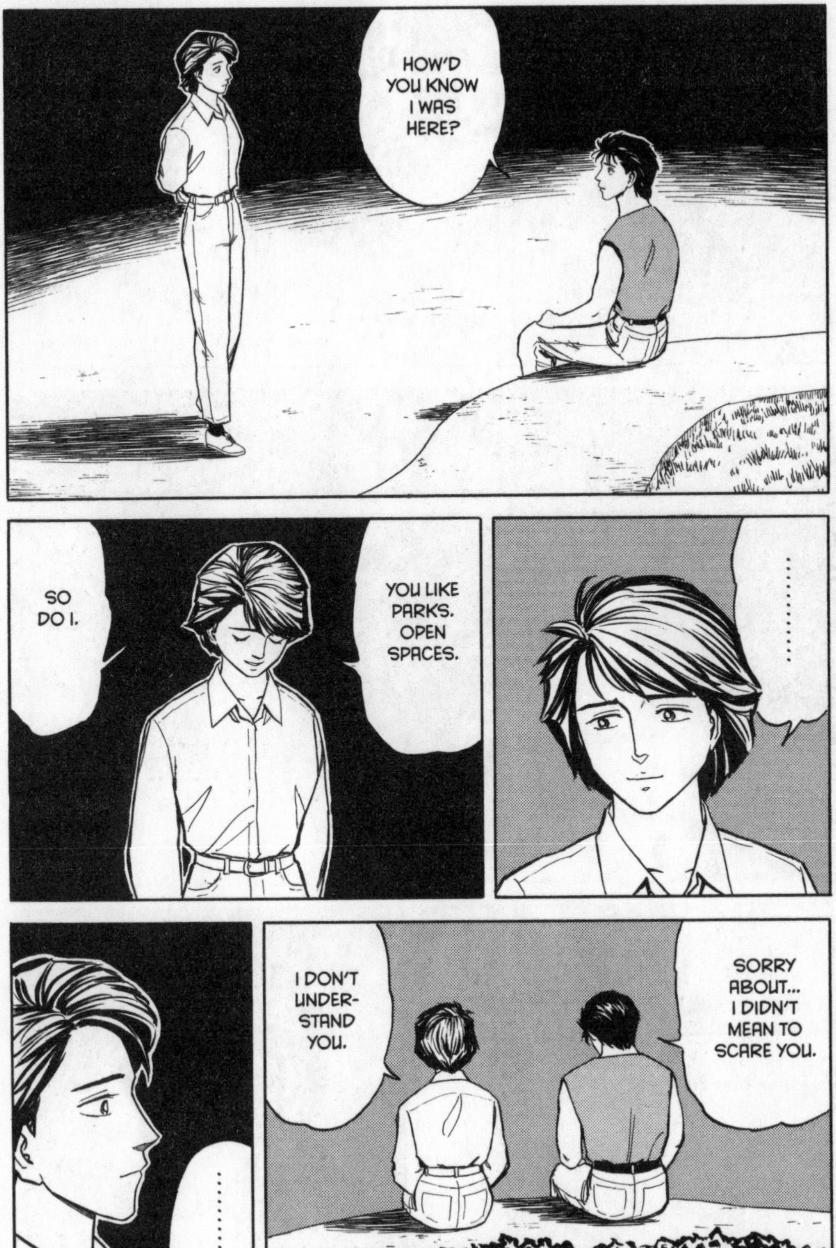
HOW'D YOU KNOW I WAS HERE?
......
YOU LIKE PARKS. OPEN SPACES.
SO DO I.
SORRY ABOUT... I DIDN'T MEAN TO SCARE YOU.
I DON'T UNDER-STAND YOU.
......

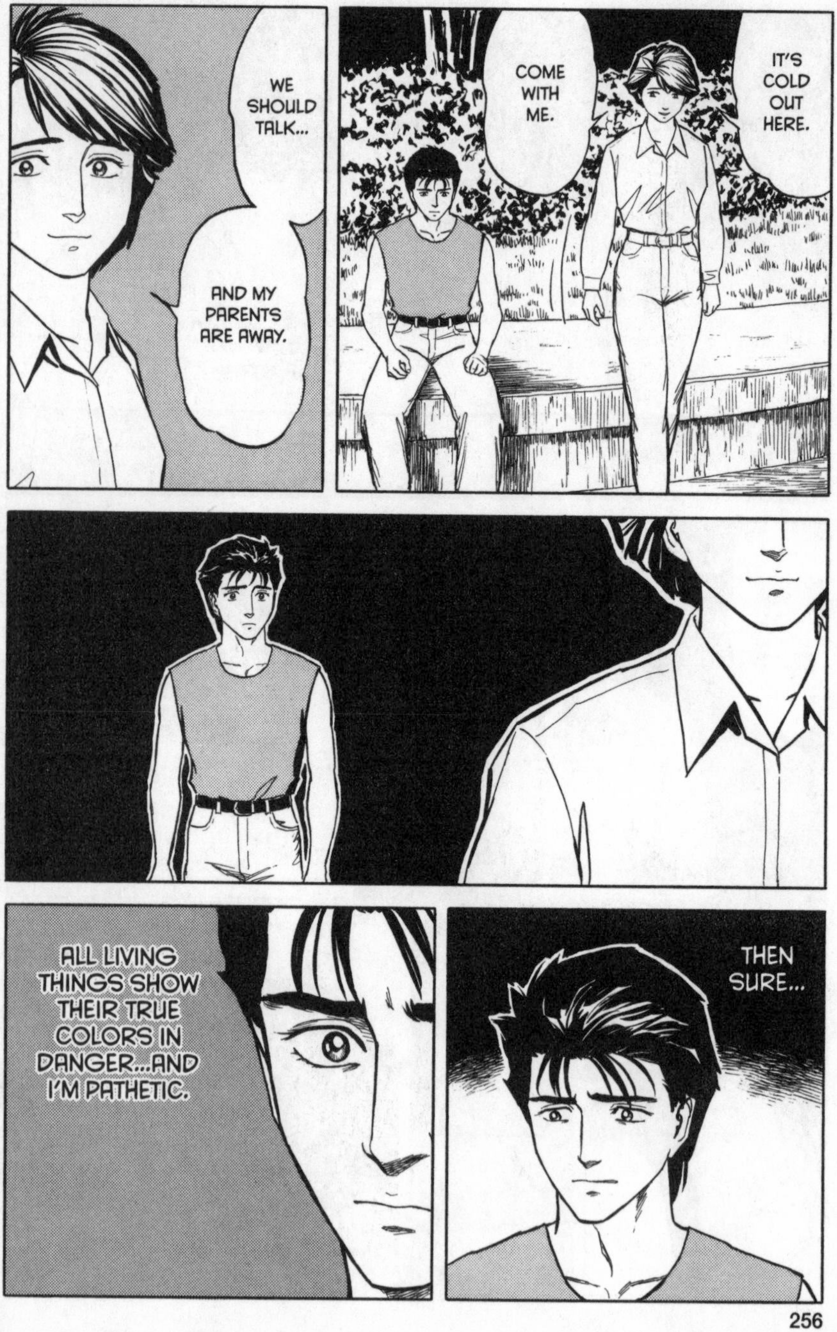
IT'S COLD OUT HERE.
COME WITH ME.
WE SHOULD TALK...
AND MY PARENTS ARE AWAY.
THEN SURE...
ALL LIVING THINGS SHOW THEIR TRUE COLORS IN DANGER...AND I'M PATHETIC.

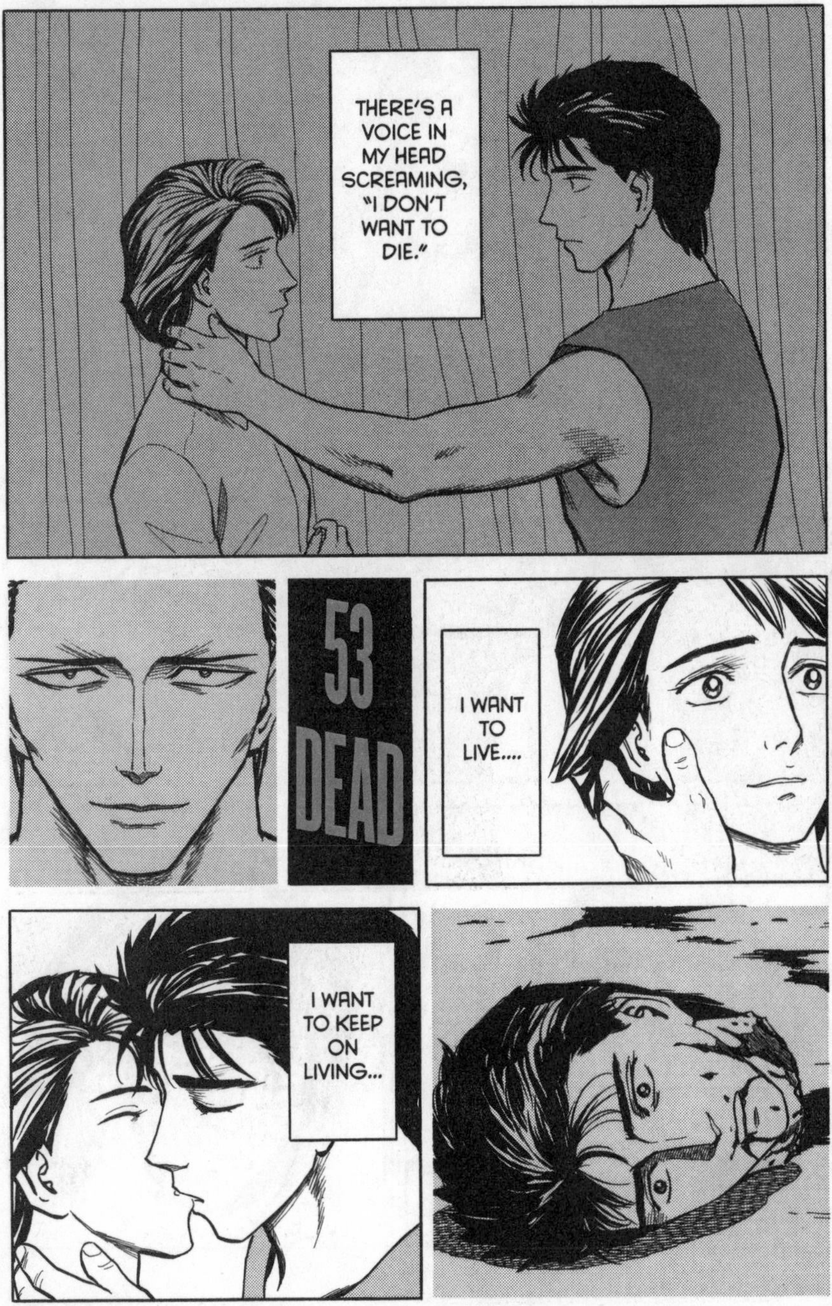
THERE'S A VOICE IN MY HEAD SCREAMING, "I DON'T WANT TO DIE."
I WANT TO LIVE....
53 DEAD
I WANT TO KEEP ON LIVING...

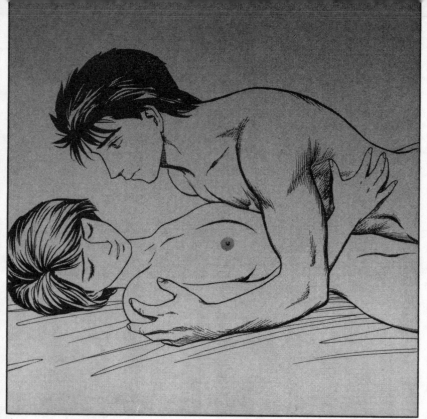

SATOMI...

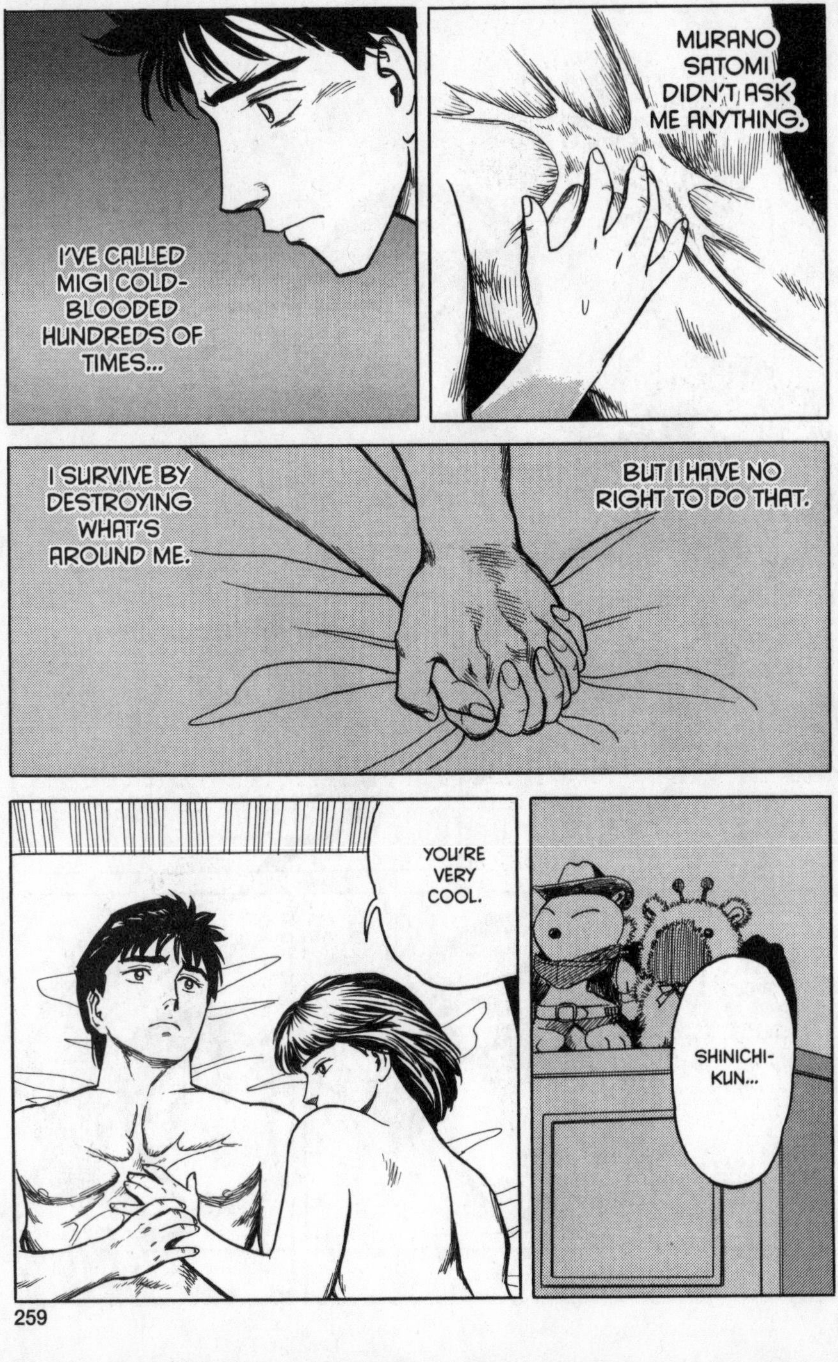
MURANO SATOMI DIDN'T ASK ME ANYTHING.
I'VE CALLED MIGI COLD-BLOODED HUNDREDS OF TIMES...
BUT I HAVE NO RIGHT TO DO THAT.
I SURVIVE BY DESTROYING WHAT'S AROUND ME.
SHINICHI-KUN...
YOU'RE VERY COOL.

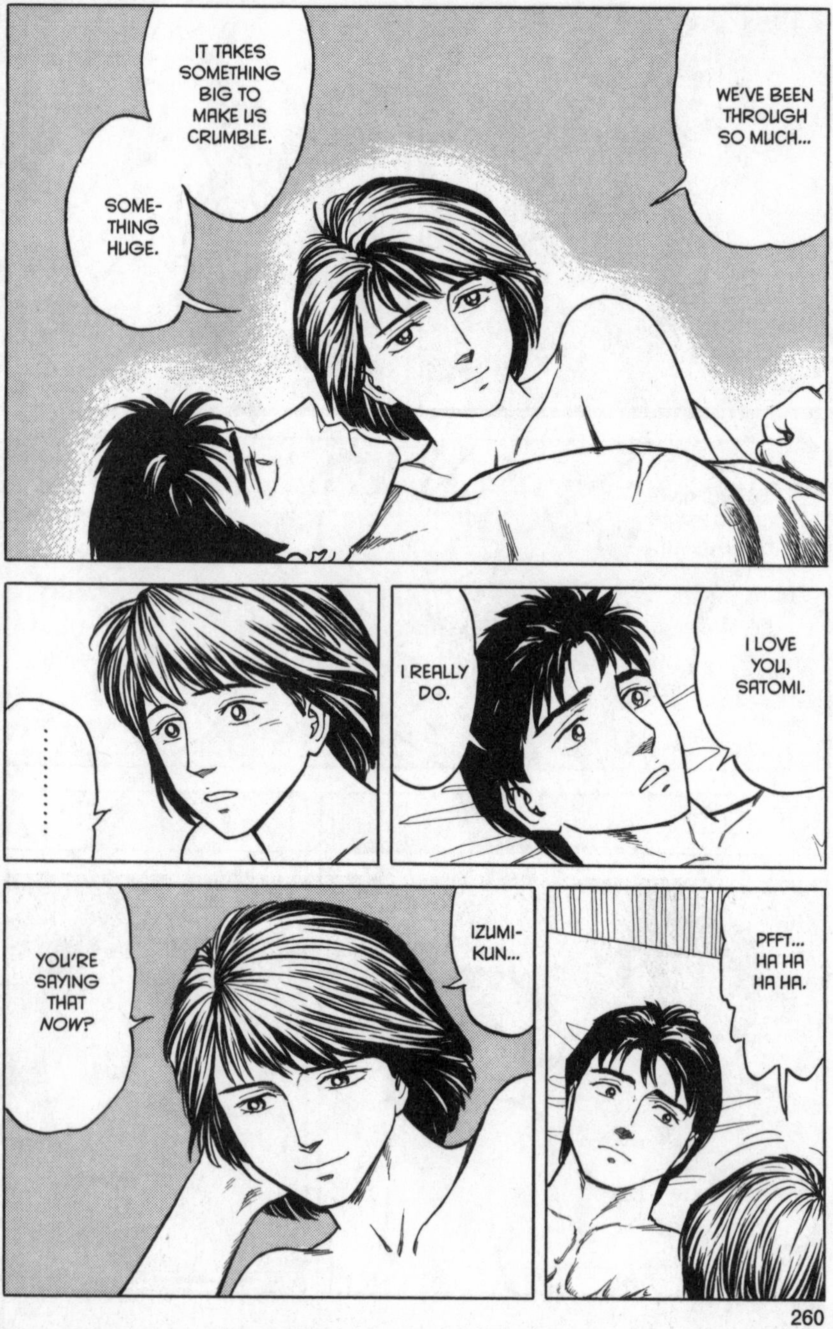
WE'VE BEEN THROUGH SO MUCH...
IT TAKES SOMETHING BIG TO MAKE US CRUMBLE.
SOME-THING HUGE.
I LOVE YOU, SATOMI.
I REALLY DO.
......
PFFT... HA HA HA HA.
IZUMI-KUN...
YOU'RE SAYING THAT *NOW*?

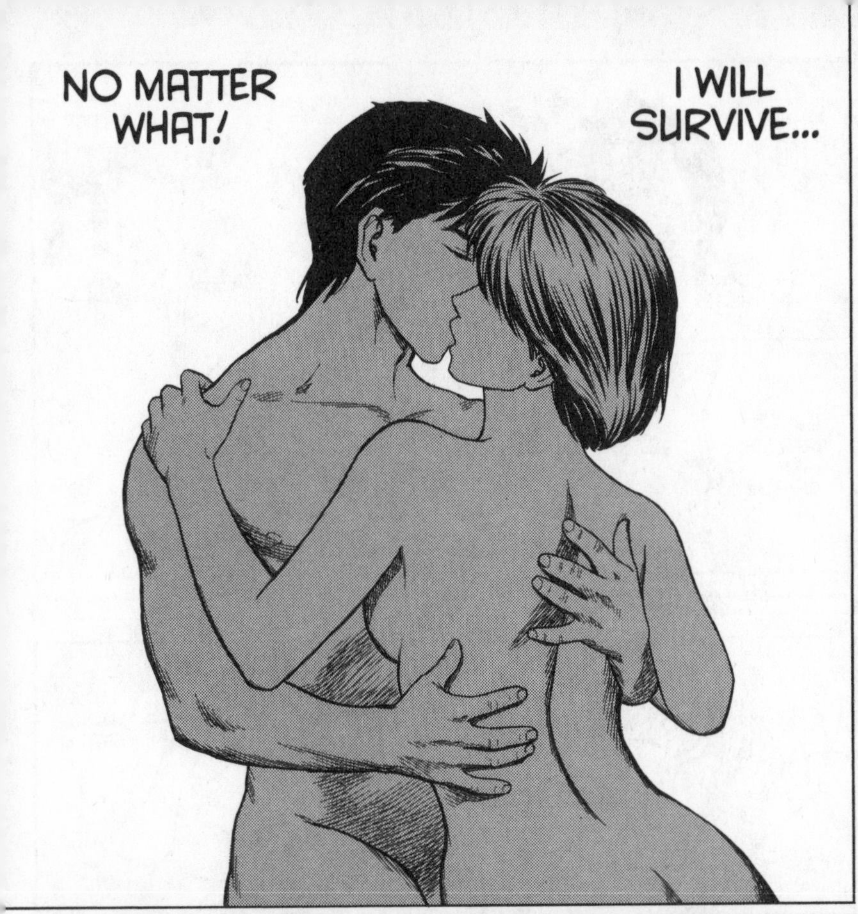
I WILL SURVIVE...
NO MATTER WHAT!
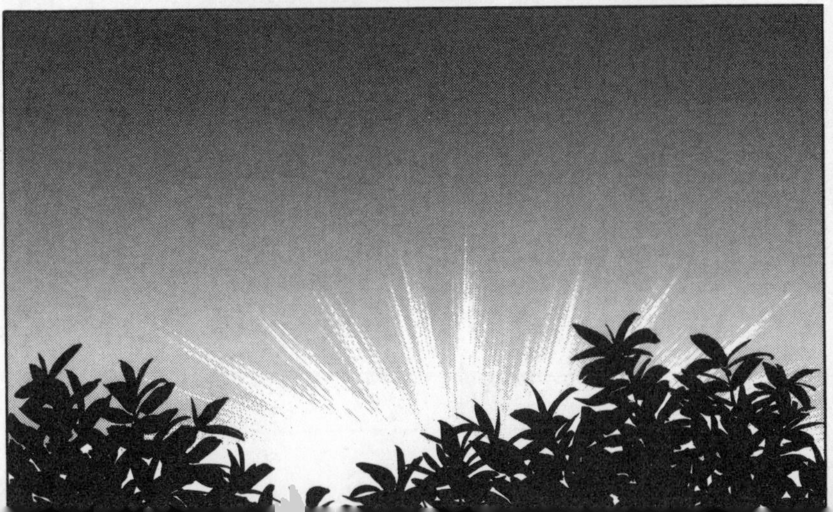

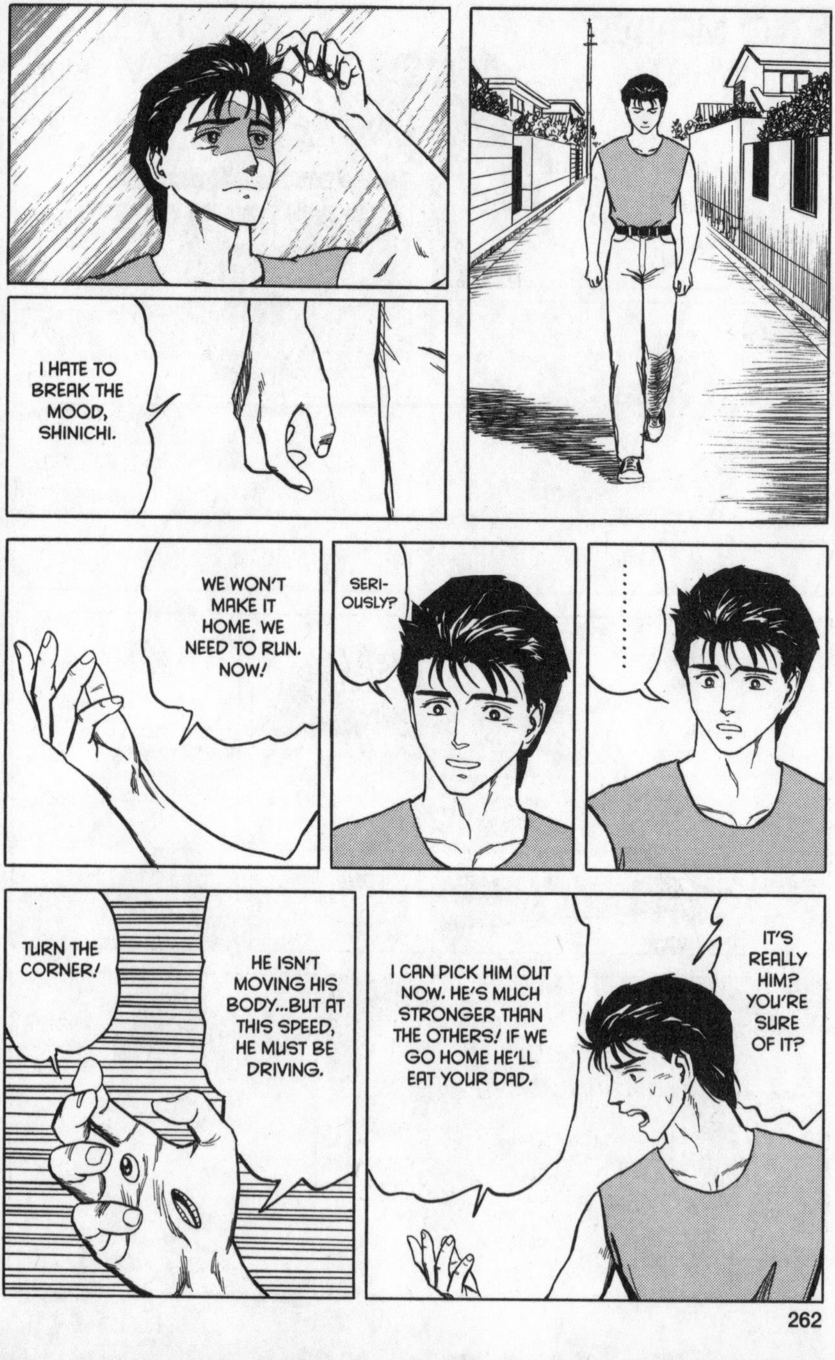
I HATE TO BREAK THE MOOD, SHINICHI.
......
SERI-OUSLY?
WE WON'T MAKE IT HOME. WE NEED TO RUN. NOW!
IT'S REALLY HIM? YOU'RE SURE OF IT?
I CAN PICK HIM OUT NOW. HE'S MUCH STRONGER THAN THE OTHERS! IF WE GO HOME HE'LL EAT YOUR DAD.
HE ISN'T MOVING HIS BODY...BUT AT THIS SPEED, HE MUST BE DRIVING.
TURN THE CORNER!

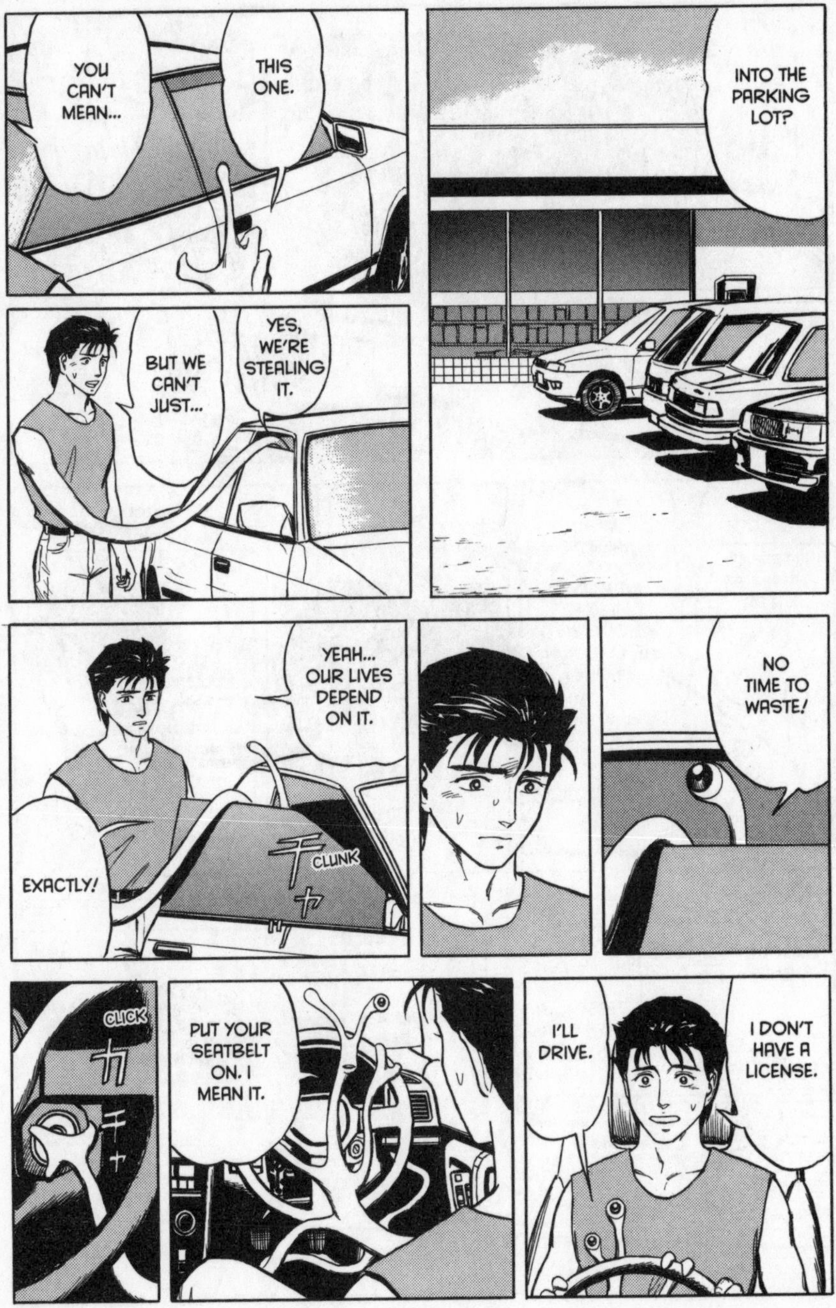
INTO THE PARKING LOT?
THIS ONE.
YOU CAN'T MEAN...
YES, WE'RE STEALING IT.
BUT WE CAN'T JUST...
NO TIME TO WASTE!
YEAH... OUR LIVES DEPEND ON IT.
CLUNK
EXACTLY!
I DON'T HAVE A LICENSE.
I'LL DRIVE.
PUT YOUR SEATBELT ON. I MEAN IT.
CLICK

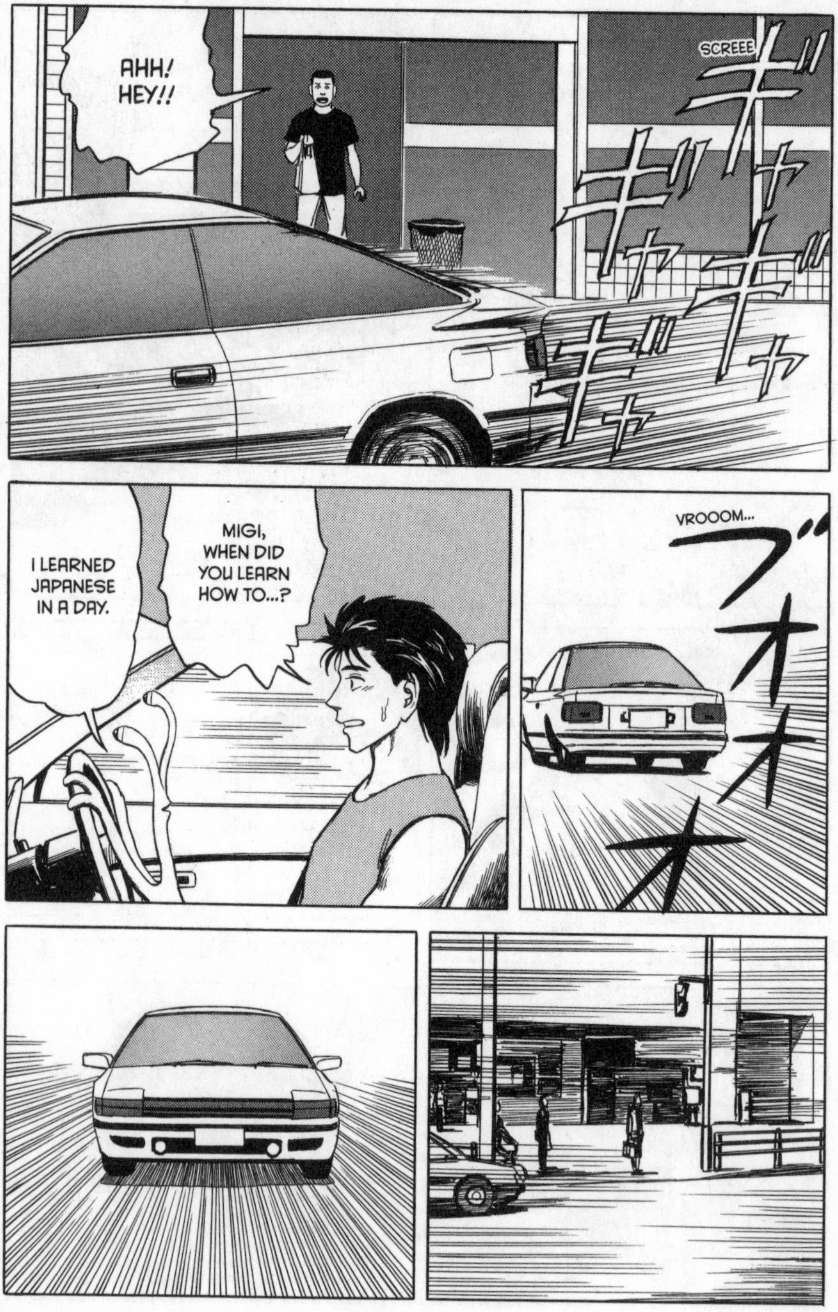
SCREEE
AHH! HEY!!
VROOOM...
MIGI, WHEN DID YOU LEARN HOW TO...?
I LEARNED JAPANESE IN A DAY.

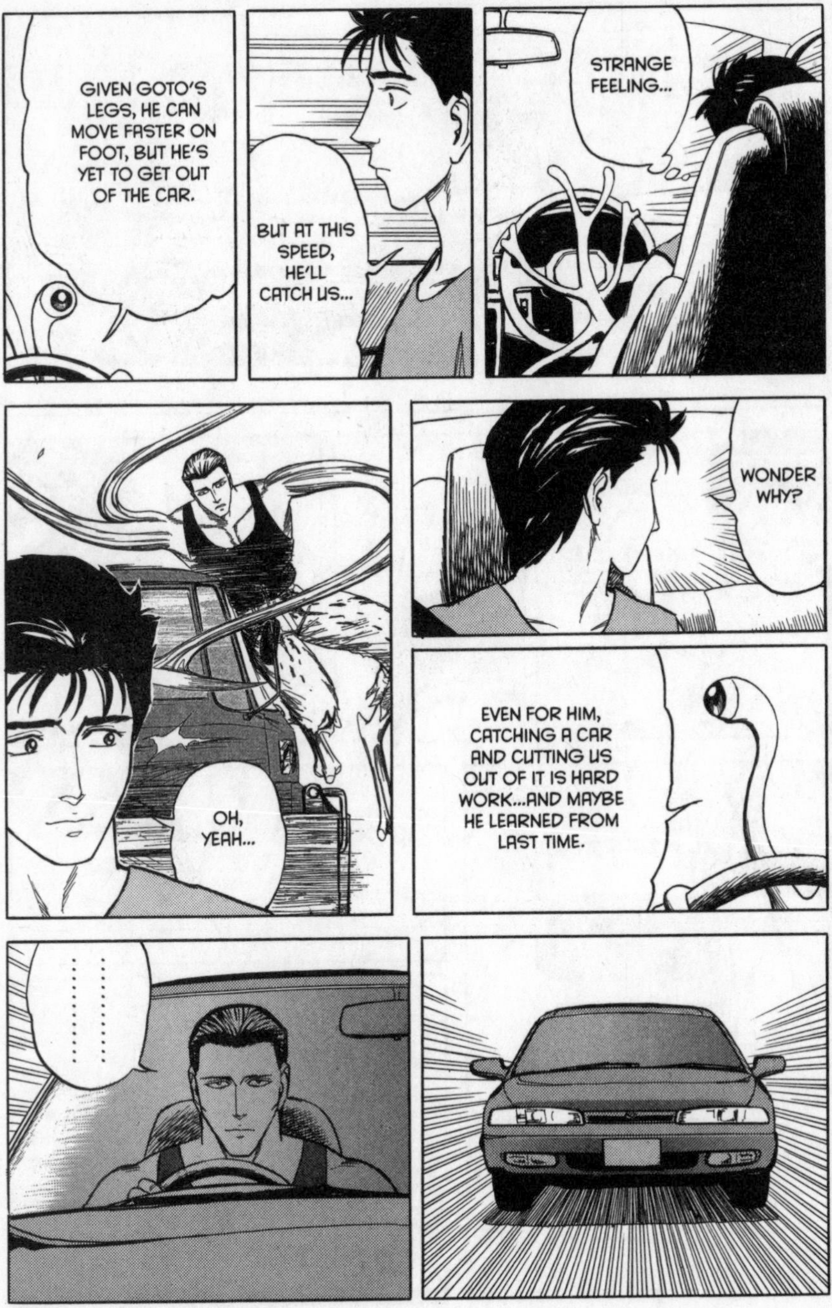
STRANGE FEELING...
BUT AT THIS SPEED, HE'LL CATCH US...
GIVEN GOTO'S LEGS, HE CAN MOVE FASTER ON FOOT, BUT HE'S YET TO GET OUT OF THE CAR.
WONDER WHY?
EVEN FOR HIM, CATCHING A CAR AND CUTTING US OUT OF IT IS HARD WORK...AND MAYBE HE LEARNED FROM LAST TIME.
OH, YEAH...
......

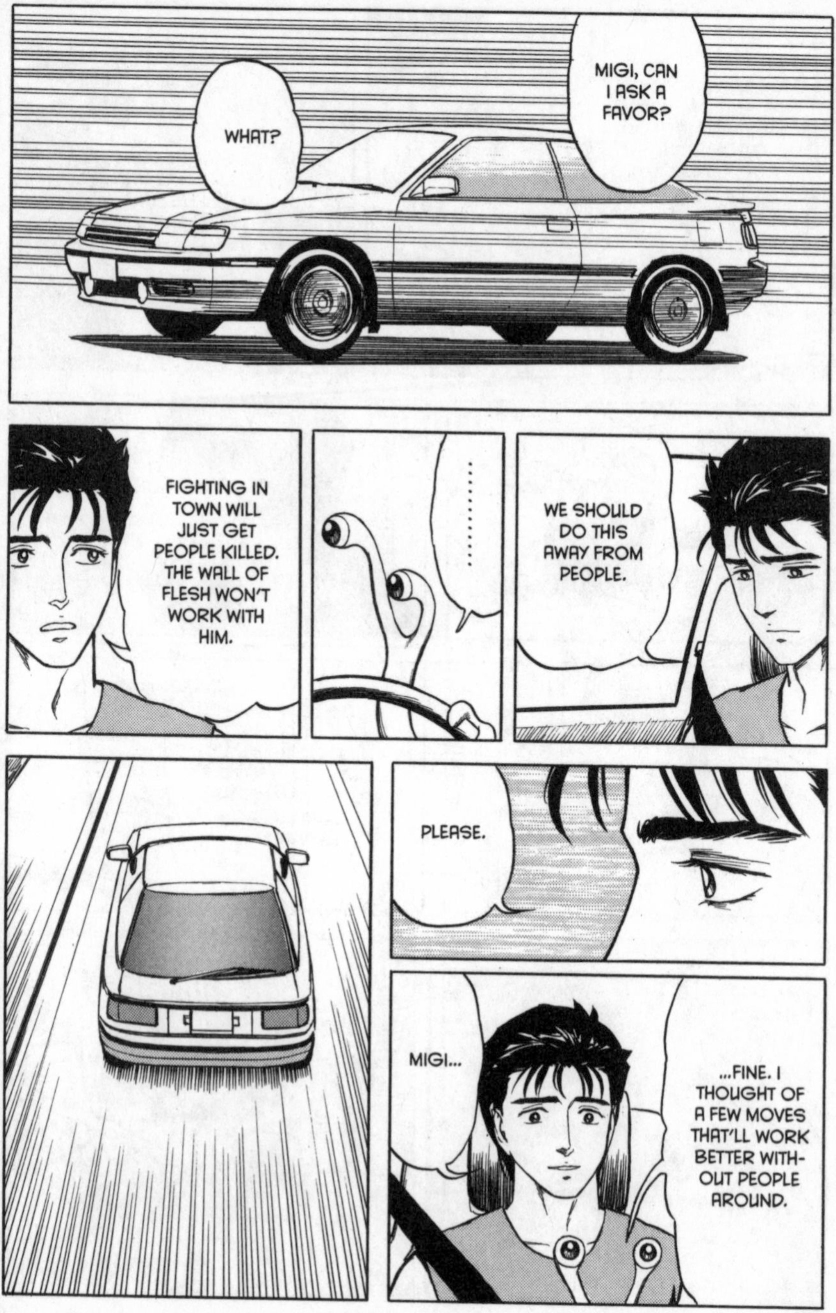
MIGI, CAN I ASK A FAVOR?
WHAT?
WE SHOULD DO THIS AWAY FROM PEOPLE.
......
FIGHTING IN TOWN WILL JUST GET PEOPLE KILLED. THE WALL OF FLESH WON'T WORK WITH HIM.
PLEASE.
MIGI...
...FINE. I THOUGHT OF A FEW MOVES THAT'LL WORK BETTER WITH-OUT PEOPLE AROUND.

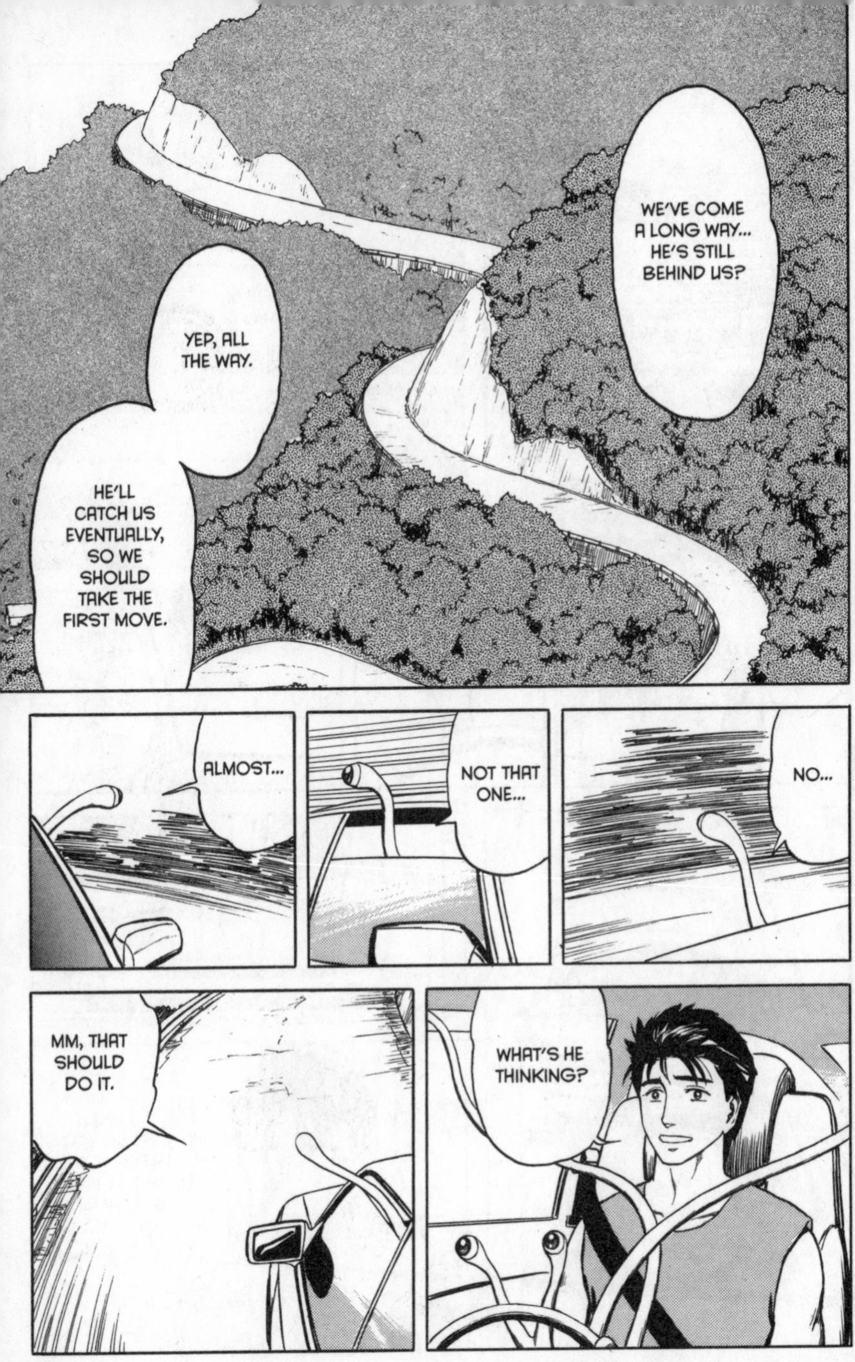
WE'VE COME A LONG WAY... HE'S STILL BEHIND US?
YEP, ALL THE WAY.
HE'LL CATCH US EVENTUALLY, SO WE SHOULD TAKE THE FIRST MOVE.
NO...
NOT THAT ONE...
ALMOST...
WHAT'S HE THINKING?
MM, THAT SHOULD DO IT.

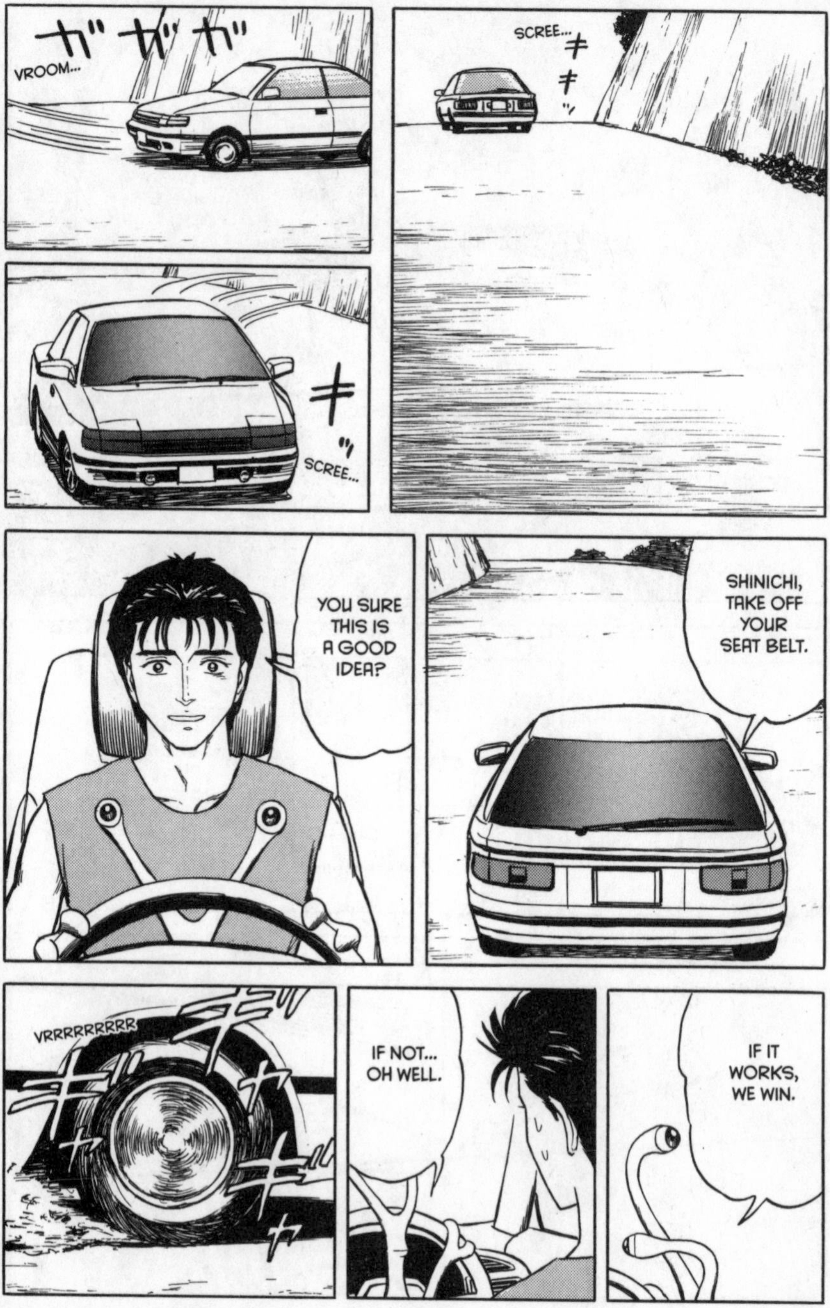
SCREE...
キキッ
VROOM...
ガガガ
キッ
SCREE...
SHINICHI, TAKE OFF YOUR SEAT BELT.
YOU SURE THIS IS A GOOD IDEA?
IF IT WORKS, WE WIN.
IF NOT... OH WELL.
VRRRRRRRRR

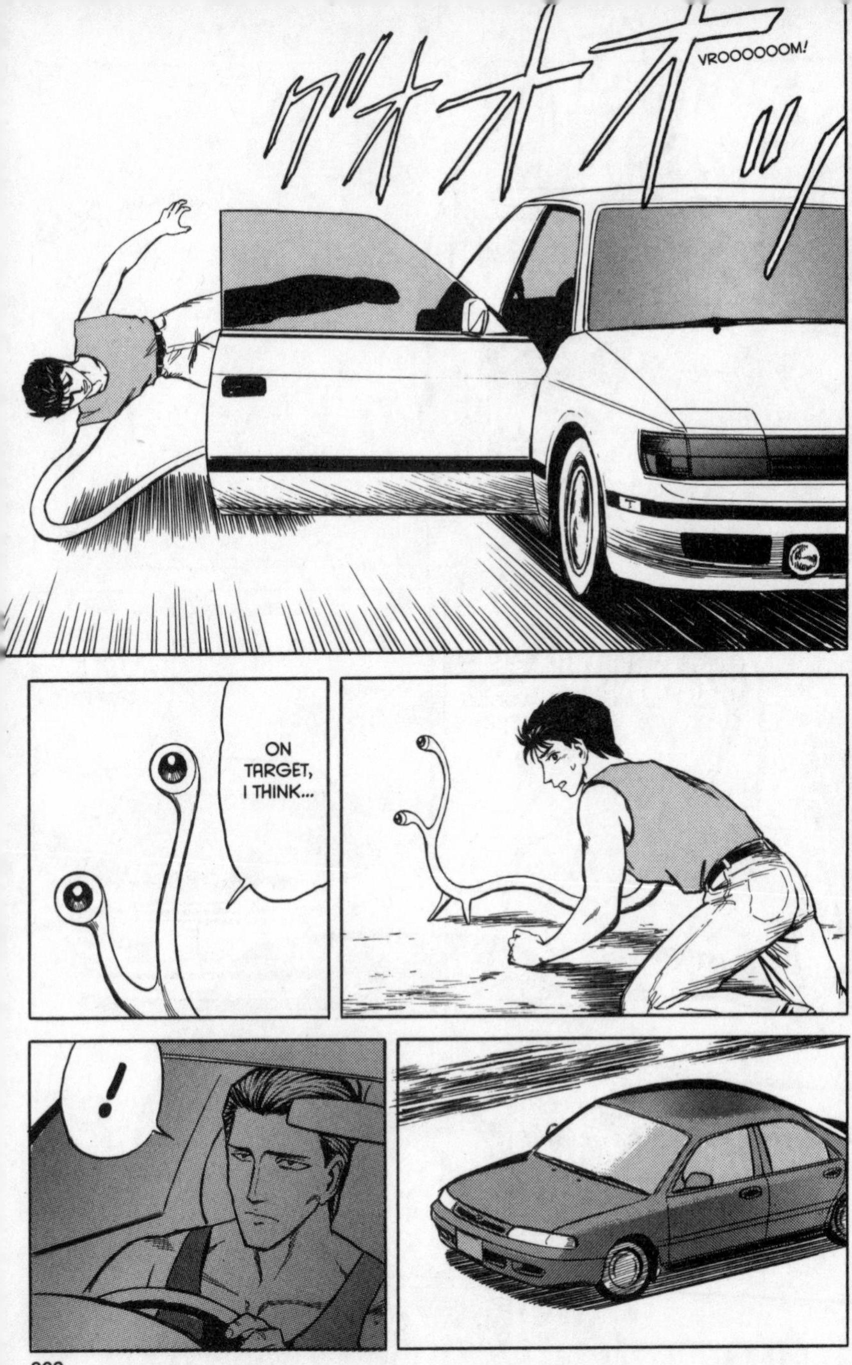
グオオオッ
VROOOOOOM!
ON TARGET, I THINK...
!

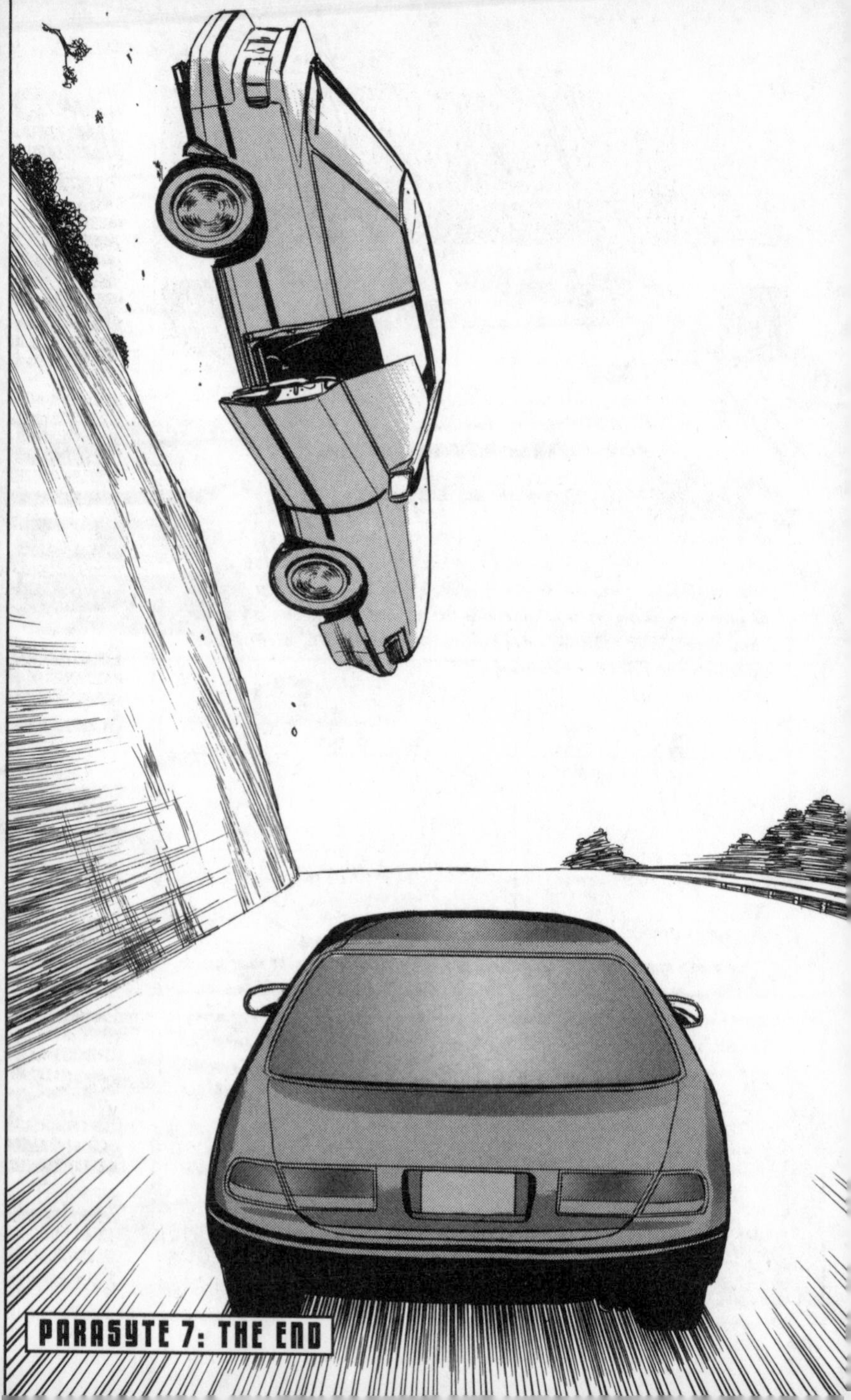
PARASYTE 7: THE END

THE READERS ASK, THE AUTHOR ANSWERS

From the Monthly Afternoon Readers' page...

PARASYTE 7

vol. 14

"The characters in *Parasyte* are so realistic they all look like people I've seen before. This makes me even more curious what they're going to do next. One of the fake psychics looked just like me!"
(Gunma Prefecture, Dodoria, 19, Student)

"I didn't realize this until I introduced Uragami, but extremely evil characters (or extremely good ones)—and extreme characters—are very hard to draw. Probably because they don't feel realistic. Lots of writers claim you just have to create characters with strong personalities and let them do what they want, but making characters with realistic, strong personalities is another challenge."
(Hitoshi Iwaaki)

(From *Afternoon*, December 1993)

"Is it impossible for humans to acknowledge life-forms other than themselves?"
(Hyoga Prefecture - You-chan)

"It wasn't really a conscious plan on my part to depict mankind as the bad guys, but quite a lot of people find the parasites' actions a lot less horrific than those of the humans. This volume, for example; I was only trying to make everyone act naturally, the soldiers like soldiers, the average citizens like normal people, but it ended up like this. Personally, I don't spend a lot of time deploring my own species..."
(Hitoshi Iwaaki)

(From *Afternoon*, April 1994)

THE READERS ASK, THE AUTHOR ANSWERS

From the Monthly Afternoon Readers' page...

PARASYTE 7 vol. 15

"Goto told Hirokawa he could escape the building easily. What kind of power does he have? I'm looking forward to finding out!"
(Gunma Prefecutre, Nazo wo Toke, 16, Student)

"When Hirokawa ended up dying rather easily, without escaping, some people may have been rather taken aback. But I don't think it's accurate to say Hirokawa was powerless. Given his supreme confidence in his own moral superiority, in a sense he was actually harder to deal with than Uragami. It might be that Hirokawa did not die, but will soon be born..."
(Hitoshi Iwaaki)

(From *Afternoon*, May 1994)

"I think Goto is starting to develop human emotions in a very different fashion from Tamura Reiko."
(Kanagawa Prefecture, Kana Fan, 20)

"Goto's recent actions can hardly be described as unconscious or instinctive. Migi and Tamura Reiko's actions could hardly be described as purely mechanical or practical either. But I think something about them fundamentally prevents them from getting along with humans. I have no idea how many species on Earth are capable of coexisting happily with human beings, but how would humans react to a creature they don't understand, which is not friendly at all? This is one of this story's themes."
(Hitoshi Iwaaki)

(From *Afternoon*, July 1994)

Japanese is a tricky language for most Westerners, and translation is often more an art than a science. For your edification and reading pleasure, here are notes on some of the places where we could have gone in a different direction or where a Japanese cultural reference is used.

Parasytes, page 187

The original rhetorical device has Hirokawa referring to humans as parasites, or *kiseichuu*, and then correcting the last kanji from "insect" to "beast," forming the title of this chapter and the series as a whole. For that reason, I've used the unconventional "y" spelling, even though I've consistently spelled the word with an "i" while referring to the parasites themselves. In Japanese, neither word is used to refer to the monsters. Instead, they're called *parasaito* in katakana. The suggestion here is that the Parasyte in the title is, in fact, humanity. Or at least, that's my take on it. I hope the translation reflects that!

SHINICHI... WHAT A TERRIBLE DREAM...

Bad dreams, page 237

The way Migi phrases this in the original Japanese suggests he had the same dream, but English doesn't seem to make that as clear.

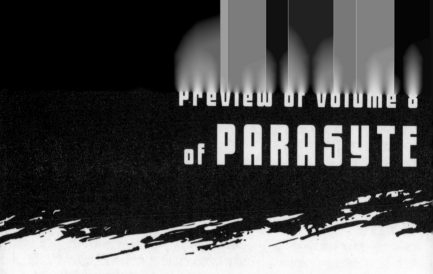

Preview of Volume 8

of PARASYTE

We're pleased to present you with a preview from volume 8.
This volume is available in English, but for now you'll have to make do with Japanese!

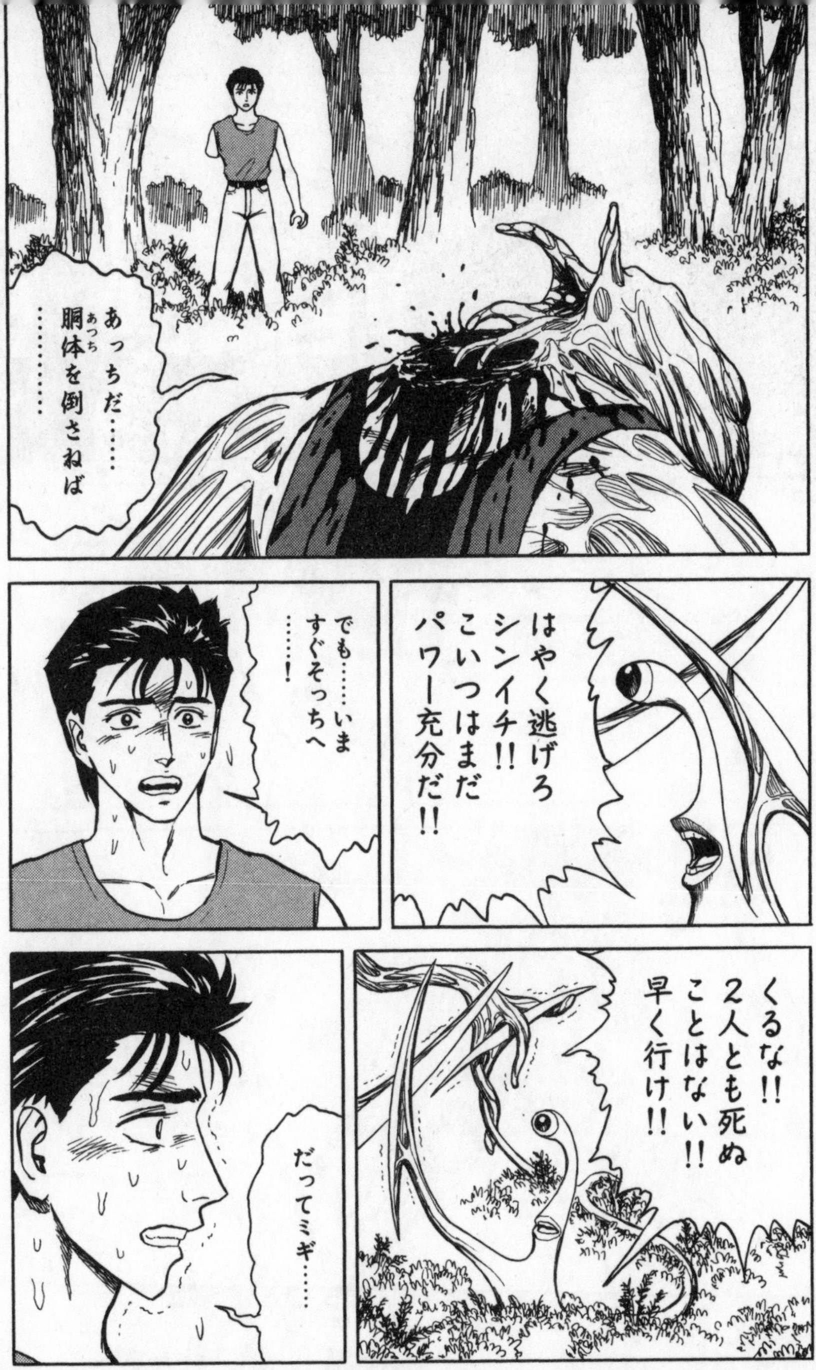
あっちだ……
胴体を倒さねば
……
はやく逃げろ
シンイチ!!
こいつはまだ
パワー充分だ!!
でも……いま
すぐそっちへ
……!
くるな!!
2人とも死ぬ
ことはない!!
早く行け!!
だってミギ……

ぐあっ!!

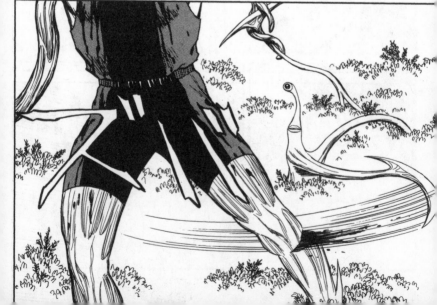

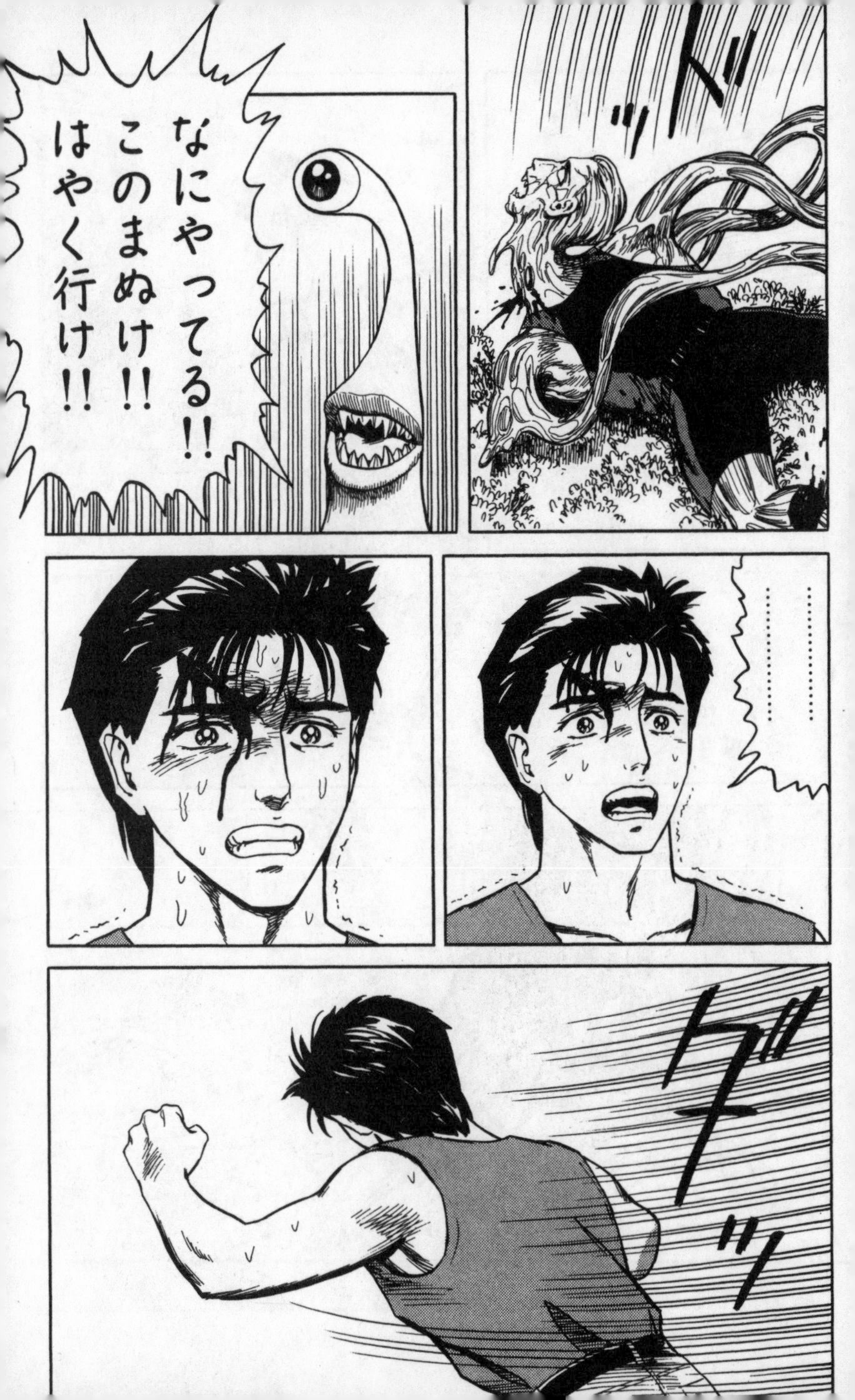
ドッ
なにやってる!!
このまぬけ!!
はやく行け!!
……
ダッ

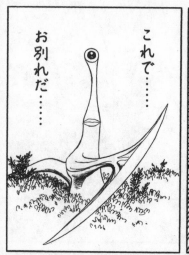

これで……
お別れだ……

さようなら
シンイチ……

シンイチ……

いちばんはじめに
きみに出会って
……
きみの……
脳を奪わなくて
よかったよ……

おかげで友だちとして
……
いろいろな
楽しい……
思い出を……